Possibilities and Complexities of Decolonising Higher Education

The chapters in this book highlight the possibilities and complexities of putting decolonial theory to work in higher education in Northern and Southern contexts across the globe. This book looks at decolonial work as praxis involving transformation at a range of levels from theoretical development, national policy, institutional policy and culture, academic discipline, programme, course, classroom, student and the self. Our authors argue that praxis in their contexts includes working at institutional level to undo the historical power of 'coloniality' in universities in the metropoles, introducing Indigenous knowledges into curricula and undoing the effects of 'coloniality' in embodiment, temporality and whiteness. We, as editors, argue for the need for transformation of the self as well as structures, and highlight qualities such as reflexivity on our own entanglements with coloniality, and why they occur, in this undoing. The approach offered in this book emphasises the connection between significant personal change as a pre-condition and an epistemological process to connect critical decolonial theory and our teaching practice. The book was originally published as a special issue of the journal *Teaching in Higher Education*.

Aneta Hayes is Senior Lecturer in Education at Keele University, UK and an Executive Editor for *Teaching in Higher Education*. Her research interests include critical studies of internationalisation (including decolonisation), teaching excellence and global education developments, including glocalised perspectives.

Kathy Luckett is Emeritus Professor in the Centre for Higher Education Development at the University of Cape Town and Executive Editor for Teaching in Higher Education. Her research interests include the sociology of knowledge and curriculum studies in the Humanities, focusing on Africana, decolonial and postcolonial studies; and access, equity and multilingualism in higher education.

Greg William Misiaszek is Associate Professor at Beijing Normal University's (BNU) Faculty of Education and Associate Director of the Paulo Freire Institute, UCLA. His work focuses on critical, Freirean environmental pedagogies (e.g., ecopedagogy) through theories of globalizations, citizenships, decoloniality, race, gender, Southern/Indigenous issues, linguistics and postdigitalism, among other critical lenses.

Possibilities and Complexities of Decolonising Higher Education

Critical Perspectives on Praxis

Edited by
Aneta Hayes, Kathy Luckett and
Greg William Misiaszek

LONDON AND NEW YORK

First published 2023
by Routledge
4 Park Square, Milton Park, Abingdon, Oxon OX14 4RN

and by Routledge
605 Third Avenue, New York, NY 10158

Routledge is an imprint of the Taylor & Francis Group, an informa business

Chapters 1, 2, 5–9 and 11–16 © 2023 Taylor & Francis
Chapter 3 © 2021 Farzana Shain, Ümit Kemal Yıldız, Veronica Poku and Bulent Gokay. Originally published as Open Access.
Chapter 4 © 2021 Sharanya Menon, Crystal Green, Irène Charbonneau, Elina Lehtomäki and Boby Mafi. Originally published as Open Access.
Chapter 10 © 2021 Jillian Seniuk Cicek, Alan Steele, Sarah Gauthier, Afua Adobea Mante, Pamela Wolf, Mary Robinson and Stephen Mattucci. Originally published as Open Access.

With the exception of Chapters 3, 4 and 10, no part of this book may be reprinted or reproduced or utilised in any form or by any electronic, mechanical, or other means, now known or hereafter invented, including photocopying and recording, or in any information storage or retrieval system, without permission in writing from the publishers. For details on the rights for Chapters 3, 4 and 10, please see the chapters' Open Access footnotes.

Trademark notice: Product or corporate names may be trademarks or registered trademarks, and are used only for identification and explanation without intent to infringe.

British Library Cataloguing in Publication Data
A catalogue record for this book is available from the British Library

ISBN13: 978-1-032-44762-9 (hbk)
ISBN13: 978-1-032-44765-0 (pbk)
ISBN13: 978-1-003-37382-7 (ebk)

DOI: 10.4324/9781003373827

Typeset in Minion Pro
by Newgen Publishing UK

Publisher's Note
The publisher accepts responsibility for any inconsistencies that may have arisen during the conversion of this book from journal articles to book chapters, namely the inclusion of journal terminology.

Disclaimer
Every effort has been made to contact copyright holders for their permission to reprint material in this book. The publishers would be grateful to hear from any copyright holder who is not here acknowledged and will undertake to rectify any errors or omissions in future editions of this book.

Contents

Citation Information		vii
Notes on Contributors		x

1 Introduction   1
Kathy Luckett, Aneta Hayes and Greg William Misiaszek

2 Struggling for the anti-racist university: learning from an institution-wide
response to curriculum decolonisation   16
*Richard Hall, Lucy Ansley, Paris Connolly, Sumeya Loonat, Kaushika Patel
and Ben Whitham*

3 From silence to 'strategic advancement': institutional responses to
'decolonising' in higher education in England   34
Farzana Shain, Ümit Kemal Yıldız, Veronica Poku and Bulent Gokay

4 Approaching global education development with a decolonial lens: teachers'
reflections   51
*Sharanya Menon, Crystal Green, Irène Charbonneau, Elina Lehtomäki
and Boby Mafi*

5 Refusal as affective and pedagogical practice in higher education
decolonization: a modest proposal   67
Michalinos Zembylas

6 Understanding the challenges entailed in decolonising a Higher Education
institution: an organisational case study of a research-intensive South
African university   83
Anwar Shaik and Peter Kahn

7 'Pillars of the colonial institution are like a knowledge prison': the
significance of decolonizing knowledge and pedagogical practice for Pacific
early career academics in higher education   100
*Marcia Leenen-Young, Sereana Naepi, Patrick Saulmatino Thomsen,
David Taufui Mikato Faʻavae, Moeata Keil and Jacoba Matapo*

CONTENTS

8 Epistemic decolonisation in reconstituting higher education pedagogy in South Africa: the student perspective 116
Shireen Motala, Yusuf Sayed and Tarryn de Kock

9 Disrupting curricula and pedagogies in Latin American universities: six criteria for decolonising the university 133
Carolina Guzmán Valenzuela

10 Indigenizing Engineering education in Canada: critically considered 152
Jillian Seniuk Cicek, Alan Steele, Sarah Gauthier, Afua Adobea Mante, Pamela Wolf, Mary Robinson and Stephen Mattucci

11 Holding space for an Aboriginal approach towards Curriculum Reconciliation in an Australian university 174
Jade Kennedy, Alisa Percy, Lisa Thomas, Catherine Moyle and Janine Delahunty

12 A *Calle* decolonial hack: Afro-Latin theorizing of Philadelphia's spaces of learning and resistance 191
Amalia Dache, Jasmine Blue, Devaun Bovell, Deja Miguest, Sydney Osifeso and Fabiola Tucux

13 Distilling pedagogies of critical water studies 212
Sheeva Sabati, Linnea Beckett, Kira Cragun-Rehders, Alyssa Najera, Katerina Hise and Anna Geiger

14 Decolonising while white: confronting race in a South African classroom 227
Sally Matthews

15 Navigating student resistance towards decolonizing curriculum and pedagogy (DCP): a temporal proposal 236
Kirsten T. Edwards and Riyad A. Shahjahan

16 Four 'moments' of intercultural encountering 244
Meike Wernicke

Index 255

Citation Information

The chapters in this book were originally published in the journal *Teaching in Higher Education*, volume 26, issue 7–8 (2021). When citing this material, please use the original page numbering for each article, as follows:

Chapter 1

Possibilities and complexities of decolonising higher education: critical perspectives on praxis
Aneta Hayes, Kathy Luckett and Greg Misiaszek
Teaching in Higher Education, volume 26, issue 7–8 (2021), pp. 887–901

Chapter 2

Struggling for the anti-racist university: learning from an institution-wide response to curriculum decolonisation
Richard Hall, Lucy Ansley, Paris Connolly, Sumeya Loonat, Kaushika Patel and Ben Whitham
Teaching in Higher Education, volume 26, issue 7–8 (2021), pp. 902–919

Chapter 3

From silence to 'strategic advancement': institutional responses to 'decolonising' in higher education in England
Farzana Shain, Ümit Kemal Yıldız, Veronica Poku and Bulent Gokay
Teaching in Higher Education, volume 26, issue 7–8 (2021), pp. 920–936

Chapter 4

Approaching global education development with a decolonial lens: teachers' reflections
Sharanya Menon, Crystal Green, Irène Charbonneau, Elina Lehtomäki and Boby Mafi
Teaching in Higher Education, volume 26, issue 7–8 (2021), pp. 937–952

Chapter 5

Refusal as affective and pedagogical practice in higher education decolonization: a modest proposal
Michalinos Zembylas
Teaching in Higher Education, volume 26, issue 7–8 (2021), pp. 953–968

Chapter 6

Understanding the challenges entailed in decolonising a Higher Education institution: an organisational case study of a research-intensive South African university
Anwar Shaik and Peter Kahn
Teaching in Higher Education, volume 26, issue 7–8 (2021), pp. 969–985

Chapter 7

'Pillars of the colonial institution are like a knowledge prison': the significance of decolonizing knowledge and pedagogical practice for Pacific early career academics in higher education
Marcia Leenen-Young, Sereana Naepi, Patrick Saulmatino Thomsen, David Taufui Mikato Fa'avae, Moeata Keil and Jacoba Matapo
Teaching in Higher Education, volume 26, issue 7–8 (2021), pp. 986–1001

Chapter 8

Epistemic decolonisation in reconstituting higher education pedagogy in South Africa: the student perspective
Shireen Motala, Yusuf Sayed and Tarryn de Kock
Teaching in Higher Education, volume 26, issue 7–8 (2021), pp. 1002–1018

Chapter 9

Disrupting curricula and pedagogies in Latin American universities: six criteria for decolonising the university
Carolina Guzmán Valenzuela
Teaching in Higher Education, volume 26, issue 7–8 (2021), pp. 1019–1037

Chapter 10

Indigenizing Engineering education in Canada: critically considered
Jillian Seniuk Cicek, Alan Steele, Sarah Gauthier, Afua Adobea Mante, Pamela Wolf, Mary Robinson and Stephen Mattucci
Teaching in Higher Education, volume 26, issue 7–8 (2021), pp. 1038–1059

Chapter 11

Holding space for an Aboriginal approach towards Curriculum Reconciliation in an Australian university
Jade Kennedy, Alisa Percy, Lisa Thomas, Catherine Moyle and Janine Delahunty
Teaching in Higher Education, volume 26, issue 7–8 (2021), pp. 1060–1076

Chapter 12

A Calle decolonial hack: Afro-Latin theorizing of Philadelphia's spaces of learning and resistance
Amalia Dache, Jasmine Blue, Devaun Bovell, Deja Miguest, Sydney Osifeso and Fabiola Tucux
Teaching in Higher Education, volume 26, issue 7–8 (2021), pp. 1077–1097

Chapter 13

Distilling pedagogies of critical water studies
Sheeva Sabati, Linnea Beckett, Kira Cragun-Rehders, Alyssa Najera, Katerina Hise and Anna Geiger
Teaching in Higher Education, volume 26, issue 7–8 (2021), pp. 1098–1112

Chapter 14

Decolonising while white: confronting race in a South African classroom
Sally Matthews
Teaching in Higher Education, volume 26, issue 7–8 (2021), pp. 1113–1121

Chapter 15

Navigating student resistance towards decolonizing curriculum and pedagogy (DCP): a temporal proposal
Kirsten T. Edwards and Riyad A. Shahjahan
Teaching in Higher Education, volume 26, issue 7–8 (2021), pp. 1122–1129

Chapter 16

Four 'moments' of intercultural encountering
Meike Wernicke
Teaching in Higher Education, volume 26, issue 7–8 (2021), pp. 1130–1140

For any permission-related enquiries please visit:
www.tandfonline.com/page/help/permissions

Notes on Contributors

Lucy Ansley, School of Applied Social Sciences, De Montfort University, Leicester, UK.

Linnea Beckett, (H)ACER: The Apprenticeship in Community-Engaged Research and Colleges 9 and 10, University of California, Santa Cruz, CA, USA.

Jasmine Blue, School of Social Policy & Practice, University of Pennsylvania, Philadelphia, PA, USA.

Devaun Bovell, Graduate School of Education, University of Pennsylvania, Philadelphia, PA, USA.

Irène Charbonneau, Faculty of Education and Psychology, University of Oulu, Oulu, Finland; Faculty of Education, Stockholm University, Stockholm, Sweden.

Paris Connolly, School of Applied Social Sciences, De Montfort University, Leicester, UK.

Kira Cragun-Rehders, (H)ACER: The Apprenticeship in Community-Engaged Research, University of California, Santa Cruz, CA, USA.

Amalia Dache, Graduate School of Education, University of Pennsylvania, Philadelphia, PA, USA.

Tarryn de Kock, University of Sussex, Human Sciences Research Council, Pretoria, South Africa.

Janine Delahunty, Learning, Teaching and Curriculum, University of Wollongong, Wollongong, Australia.

Kirsten T. Edwards, Educational Leadership & Policy Studies, University of Oklahoma, Norman, OK, USA.

David Taufui Mikato Fa'avae, Te Kura Toi Tangata (School of Education), University of Waikato, Hamilton, New Zealand.

Sarah Gauthier, Department of Civil, Geological and Environmental Engineering, University of Saskatchewan, Saskatoon, Canada.

Anna Geiger, (H)ACER: The Apprenticeship in Community-Engaged Research, University of California, Santa Cruz, CA, USA.

Bulent Gokay, School of Social, Political and Global Studies, Keele University, Keele, UK.

Crystal Green, Faculty of Education, University of California, Los Angeles, CA, USA.

NOTES ON CONTRIBUTORS

Carolina Guzmán Valenzuela, Faculty of Education and Humanities, Universidad de Tarapacá, Arica, Chile.

Richard Hall, Education Division, Faculty of Health and Life Sciences, De Montfort University, Leicester, UK.

Aneta Hayes, School of Social, Political and Global Studies, Keele University, Newcastle-under-Lyme, United Kingdom.

Katerina Hise, (H)ACER: The Apprenticeship in Community-Engaged Research, University of California, Santa Cruz, CA, USA.

Peter Kahn, Centre for Higher Education Studies, University of Liverpool, Liverpool, UK.

Moeata Keil, School of Social Sciences, University of Auckland, Auckland, New Zealand.

Jade Kennedy, Learning, Teaching and Curriculum, University of Wollongong, Wollongong, Australia.

Marcia Leenen-Young, Te Wānanga o Waipapa, University of Auckland, Auckland, New Zealand.

Elina Lehtomäki, Faculty of Education and Psychology, University of Oulu, Oulu, Finland.

Sumeya Loonat, Faculty of Business and Law, De Montfort University, Leicester, UK.

Kathy Luckett, Centre for Higher Education Development, University of Cape Town, Cape Town, South Africa.

Boby Mafi, Faculty of Education and Psychology, University of Oulu, Oulu, Finland.

Afua Adobea Mante, Department of Soil Science, University of Manitoba, Winnipeg, Canada.

Jacoba Matapo, School of Critical Studies in Education, University of Auckland, Auckland, New Zealand.

Sally Matthews, Department of Political and International Studies, Rhodes University, Grahamstown, South Africa.

Stephen Mattucci, Lassonde Education Innovation Studio, York University, Toronto, Canada.

Sharanya Menon, Faculty of Education and Psychology, University of Oulu, Oulu, Finland.

Deja Miguest, College of Arts & Sciences, University of Pennsylvania, Philadelphia, PA, USA.

Greg William Misiaszek, Faculty of Education, Normal University, Beijing, China.

Shireen Motala, Faculty of Education, University of Johannesburg, Johannesburg, South Africa.

Catherine Moyle, Learning, Teaching and Curriculum, University of Wollongong, Wollongong, Australia.

Sereana Naepi, School of Social Sciences, University of Auckland, Auckland, New Zealand.

Alyssa Najera, (H)ACER: The Apprenticeship in Community-Engaged Research, University of California, Santa Cruz, CA, USA.

Sydney Osifeso, Graduate School of Education, University of Pennsylvania, Philadelphia, PA, USA.

Kaushika Patel, Faculty of Health and Life Sciences, De Montfort University, Leicester, UK.

Alisa Percy, Institute for Interactive Media and Learning, University of Technology Sydney, Sydney, Australia.

Veronica Poku, Department of Education Studies, Goldsmiths – University of London, London, UK.

Mary Robinson, Engineering Undergraduate Office, University of Waterloo, Waterloo, Canada.

Sheeva Sabati, College of Education, California State University, Sacramento, Sacramento, CA, USA.

Yusuf Sayed, Centre for International Teacher Education (CITE), Cape Peninsula University of Technology (CPUT), Capetown South Africa.

Jillian Seniuk Cicek, Centre for Engineering Professional Practice and Engineering Education, University of Manitoba, Winnipeg, Canada.

Farzana Shain, Department of Education Studies, Goldsmiths – University of London, London, UK.

Riyad A. Shahjahan, Educational Administration, Michigan State University, East Lansing, MI, USA.

Anwar Shaik, Grassroots Community College, Cape Town, South Africa.

Alan Steele, Department of Electronics, Carleton University, Ottawa, Canada.

Lisa Thomas, Learning, Teaching and Curriculum, University of Wollongong, Wollongong, Australia.

Patrick Saulmatino Thomsen, Te Wānanga o Waipapa, University of Auckland, Auckland, New Zealand.

Fabiola Tucux, Graduate School of Education, University of Pennsylvania, Philadelphia, PA, USA.

Meike Wernicke, Department of Language & Literacy Education, University of British Columbia, Vancouver, BC, Canada.

Ben Whitham, Department of Politics, People and Place, De Montfort University, Leicester, UK.

Pamela Wolf, Department of Civil Engineering, University of British Columbia, Vancouver, Canada.

Ümit Kemal Yıldız, Institute of Education, University of Manchester, Manchester, UK.

Michalinos Zembylas, Program of Educational Studies, Open University of Cyprus, Latsia, Cyprus; Chair for Critical Studies in Higher Education Transformation, Nelson Mandela University, Port Elizabeth, South Africa.

Introduction

Kathy Luckett , Aneta Hayes and Greg William Misiaszek

Introduction

In our original call for a Special Issue in *Teaching in Higher Education* on the above title, we claimed that, despite high levels of interest in the 'decolonial turn', 'little has been written in higher education journals on how and to what extent the supremacy of Western modernity is *actually* being challenged in knowledge production in different disciplines, curricula, pedagogic, cultural and linguistic practices *on the ground* in university policy and practice'. We were proved wrong – for we were overwhelmed by well over a hundred responses to our call – hence the need for a bumper-sized special issue that discusses the possibilities and complexities of practical efforts to decolonise higher education.

We are excited to be curating this rich collection of papers that includes approaches, research, narratives and voices that historically have not featured much in publications devoted to higher education based in the global North such as this one. We attribute this opening up of scholarship beyond the constraints of Eurocentric/ Northern control not only to the take-up of decolonial theory, conceptualised and popularised by Latin American scholars since the 1980s, but also to the urgency around the decolonisation project created by student protests and grass-roots activist groups in higher education during the past decade. Furthermore, as Mbembe (2021) points out, there has been more generally a 'redrawing of the global intellectual map' so that 'the world can now be studied from everywhere and anywhere' (Mbembe 2021, 21).

Indeed, it was Southern decolonial theorists, and from Latin America in particular, who stretched the concept of decolonisation to apply it to epistemology and knowledge production beyond its original meaning of political and cultural emancipation from colonial domination. The decolonial theory now involves contesting the hegemony, legacy and limitations of Eurocentric epistemologies, Northern control of knowledge production, the 'coloniality' of the cultures, languages and disciplines of institutions of higher education and interrogating whose interests are served by this knowledge and its practices (Mignolo and Escobar 2010). When referring to 'coloniality' in this editorial, we adopt prominent theorist of decoloniality, Maldonado-Torres's definition which conceptualises coloniality as:

> long-standing patterns of power that emerged as a result of colonialism, but that define culture, labor, intersubjective relations, and knowledge production well beyond the strict

limit of colonial administrations. Thus, coloniality survives colonialism. It is maintained alive in books, in the criteria for academic performance, in cultural patterns, in common sense, in the self-image of peoples, in aspirations of self, and many other aspects of our modern experience. In a way, as modern subjects we breathe coloniality all the time and everyday. (Maldonado-Torres 2007, 243)

It was black South African student protests against institutional cultures of settler whiteness in 2015 that triggered contemporary interest in a renewed wave of decolonial scholarship in both global Northern and Southern universities. Contemporary movements (these include *RhodesMustFall, FeesMustFall, Decolonising the Mind, Why is my Curriculum White?, Liberate my Degree, We are the university* the *Critical Internationalisation Network* and a range of decolonising collectives, networks and groups based in specific institutions) have critiqued institutional cultures, curricula and pedagogic practices – at the peripheries and at the centres – for perpetuating coloniality in ways that misrecognise their identities, leading to exclusion and perennial 'attainment gaps'. We suggest that what defines the current decolonial turn in higher education from previous student revolts such as that of 1968 (which brought together anti-war, anti-capitalist, anti-imperialist, black power and feminist movements), is that this time the movements are led by students and academics from subaltern social groups who draw on theories from the South and its diaspora. These theories include Latin American decolonial theory, critical race theory and the Black radical tradition more broadly. Indeed, as showcased in this Special Issue (SI), the decolonial critique is not only opening up previously protected spaces that hitherto privileged Eurocentric knowledge in universities in the metropoles and the peripheries, but in settler societies where historically colonisers practised epistemicide. The SI shows how Indigenous knowledge are being introduced into curricula and legitimated for academic study. In 'Theory from the South', Comaroff and Comaroff (2012) argued almost a decade ago, that it is from the South that critical social theory and practice will develop to address the as yet unresolved social challenges of the twenty-first century. The production of theory from the South (as opposed to the generation of data for Northern researchers) is also emphasised by Connell (2007, 2013), noting that Southern theory is not a fixed set of propositions but rather a challenge to develop new decolonising projects with globally expanded resources.

Indeed, this issue's articles are witness to this challenge and the fact that the socio-cultural, political and epistemic change processes involved in the 'decolonial turn' in higher education are anything but straight forward or uncontested. Working for a plural society – a pluriverse of cosmologies, epistemologies, ontologies, axiologies, cultures, languages, norms and practices – is challenging and hitherto a burden carried only by subaltern and dominated groups. Indeed, Andreotti et al. (2015) describe the pedagogical challenges involved in exposing 'the darker side of modernity' as 'formidable, given the interdependence of the various violent social relations that constitute modernity's shadow' (2015, 25). Mignolo, a founding scholar of the contemporary decolonial turn has stated that 'decoloniality' is 'neither a field of study, nor a discipline, but a way of being in the world, interrogating the structures of knowledge and of knowing that have thrown us' (Mignolo and Walsh 2018, 381). As witnessed in this issue, such an open-ended definition of 'decoloniality', especially in the context of higher education *praxis* – that is, aligning theory, values and practice, (Freire 1996) – invites a heterogeneity of conceptual, strategic and practical approaches to taking up the decolonial project. This is confirmed by experts in the 'field'- '[d]ecolonising involves a multitude of definitions, interpretations, aims and strategies' (Bhambra, Gebrial, and Nişancıoğlu 2018, 2); the concept itself has 'multiple meanings' and diverse and contested investments (Sium, Desai, and Ritskes 2012); there 'exist a number of paradoxes, disagreements, and diverse visions for decolonial futures and possible means of arriving at these different futures' (Stein and Andreotti 2016, 479). The complexity of decolonial work is well captured by Achille Mbembe, in his concept of 'planetary entanglement'[1],

> This is a deeply heterogeneous world of flows, fractures and frictions, accidents and collisions. (…) The paradoxes of mobility and closure, of entanglement and separation, of continuities and discontinuities between the inside and the outside, the local and the global, or of temporariness and permanence pose new challenges to critical thought and intellectual inquiry. (Mbembe 2021, 20–21)

Further, as this issue demonstrates, there is a range of dimensions, social geographies and loci of enunciation from where decolonising work can occur – for example, as argued in the paper by Guzmán Valenzuela (2021) the Latin American intercultural universities work at six levels: the economic, political, cultural, epistemological, relational and ecological. As we will see, this issue's authors are working from different institutional roles and contexts and with a variety of units of analysis. They thus approach decolonial work on different dimensions such as theoretical development, national policy, institutional policy and culture, an academic discipline, programme, course, classroom, their students and the self. We return to the question of reflexivity and self-transformation below.

One widely accepted and broad definition of curriculum is Cornbleth's curriculum as contextualised social practice; the analysis of which requires interrogating both socio-historical structure and concrete experience (Cornbleth 1990). If we accept this definition, then decolonial work on curriculum and pedagogic practice demands turning our internal concerns for change into real-world projects and practices in particular historical, institutional and classroom contexts (Archer 2000). As we will see, this requires high levels of 'reflexive literacy' in order to read the ways in which the institutional spaces in which we work are structured by history, power, culture and identity (by coloniality) and to 'feel' our way into the possibilities offered by particular situational logics and contexts. As well as formal knowledge about the historical and discursive formation of knowledge and contexts, a critical, situated reading draws on tacit, embodied, phenomenological and experiential knowing and also demands ethical judgments about what is possible and what must be resisted (Clegg 2005).

Below we provide brief summaries of the research on curriculum and pedagogic practice in this SI. The articles highlight the challenges posed by the diverse contexts in which decolonial activists and practitioners are working. In our summaries, we point to high levels of reflexivity evident in the practices discussed by the authors. We hope readers will appreciate the creativity of the practices described in this issue, as the authors illustrate how decolonial theory might be put to work in a range of different and complex situations.

We divide our discussion of the authors' contexts and approaches into the themes 'Universities in the Metropoles', 'Dealing with embodiment, temporality and place-based effects of whiteness' and 'The Introduction of Indigenous Knowledge into the Curriculum'. Under these themes, we highlight how the authors read their contexts critically and exhibit forms of reflexivity as they think and write about the possibilities and constraints of their (and others) contextually embedded practices. Many of the papers describe the need for transformation of subjectivities as well as structures, mentioning affective qualities such as vulnerability, honesty, and the need for building respectful relationships. Many of the papers highlight dialogic reflexivity that requires vulnerability and offering dignity to others when grappling with individual and collective structural complicity in colonial violence. In these ways, the authors in this SI illustrate realisations of anti-colonial dispositions which can involve countering cultures of whiteness or holding uncomfortable and vulnerable spaces as a means of facilitating anti-racist/decolonial pedagogy. They also demonstrate how decolonising movements are shaped in each locale by conditions facing racialised groups in the contemporary moment. Developing such anti-colonial dispositions is viewed as important by the authors in this issue, because present debates around decolonisation of higher education are often too narrowly framed in terms of epistemology and structures of knowledge production. The authors' contributions are summarised below according to our rough typology of the different contexts in which they practise.

Universities in the metropoles

These authors, writing from hegemonic roles and contexts, highlight the imperative of critically examining our assumptions about everyday practices in higher education. They also point out the limitations and resistances to decolonial work in these spaces.

Hall, Ansley, Connolly, Loonat, Patel and Whitham (2021) and Shain, Yildiz, Poku, and Gokay (2021) have written in this issue about working reflexively within dominant paradigms and spaces in ways that challenge the reproduction of universal, eurocentric and hegemonic narratives, power relations, opportunistic career advancements and social hierarchies. Hall et al (2021) argue that reflexivity in decolonising work involves an ongoing critique of the idea of the University, its structures, cultures and practices. The focus of their argument is on 'diversifying structures, cultures and practices; decentering dominant knowledge production; devaluing hierarchies and revaluing relationality; disinvesting from power structures; diminishing predominant voices and magnifying those made silent' (p. 907). They argue that those working in hegemonic spaces who attempt to undo eurocentrism and cultures of whiteness have to contend with 'willful ignorance', 'practices of inertia' and 'structures of dissipation' (pp. 909–912). Hall et al (2021) advocate interrogating 'the impact of monocultural approaches' and situating work with senior management 'against their material and historical Eurocentrism', for example interrogating 'low-risk approaches to problem-solving; (how) traditional, discipline-based structures of academic institutions work towards denial, rest upon historical, methodological essentialism, reinforced by ideas of objectivity and the metrics of attainment, continuation and progression, and the data sets of demographics' (p. 911).

This HE context, as relatedly shown by Shain et al (2021), writing about the UK context, throws up a range of institutional responses to the decolonial challenge that include 'strategic rejection', 'reluctant acceptance' and 'strategic advancement' (p. 929) as 'many universities have made claims to decolonisation of the curriculum through strategic and often opportunistic advancements' (...) because decolonising work has (...) become strategically important (...). As universities compete for more students, they also must demonstrate their commitment to university-wide change and to eliminating racialised inequalities' (p. 924). Shain et al (2021) argue that to tackle this 'interest convergence', there is 'a need for grass-roots networks to maintain independence from university structures and processes to counter institutional co-option, incorporation and the dilution of the radical message of decolonising' (p. 922).

The radical message of decolonisation and its grass-roots networks necessitate, as argued by Menon, Green, Charbonneau, Lehtomäki and Mafi (2021), reflecting on our underlying assumptions about teaching and learning processes (decoloniality in interaction and practices) and its learning outcomes (students' experiences and achievements). Menon et al (2021) argue that there is an instability in knowing the limitations of the university as a colonial space while still engaging in decolonial practice and building a career within academia on the premise of deconstructing the institution. This begs the question, 'can the university, and courses offered through the university, truly be a space for engaging in decolonial work?' (p. 945) Their argument is that 'decoloniality is not meant to supplant the dogma of the Western episteme within higher education with another, singular and totalising decolonial episteme, but rather to *de-center* the West and affirm the re-emergences, re-existences and liberation of people dominated by the global westernising project' (p. 939).

Zembylas (2021) argues that this can be achieved by the refusal of the colonial university. In his contribution, Zembylas theorises the affective contours of refusal, a pedagogic practice that produces political effects and desires which challenge normative manifestations of power and control. Unusually, he looks at universities as sites of estrangements and intimacies – that is, potentially affective sites of struggle against coloniality. Zembylas's argument is that through refusal, we challenge normalised coercive violence and that only by identifying our complicity in reproducing harmful promises and colonial effects, can we establish new solidarities, commitments, and possibilities for decolonisation. 'Pedagogies of refusal' may therefore compel, for instance, the students to think about white complicity in colonial trauma; a topic discussed in several papers in this issue.

Dealing with embodiment, temporality and place-based effects of whiteness

This group of articles work specifically with the challenges to dismantling whiteness and the paradox of doing so from within university contexts where coloniality is perpetuated.

Shaik and Kahn (2021) deal with the question of colonial trauma and whiteness in their analysis of a case study of a research-intensive South African university, where the call for decolonisation emerged amidst student protests on campus. Their analysis found that the normalisers of colonial structures cannot be relied on to deliver 'real decolonisation' but instead continued to act in defence of both their privilege and colonised structures. Shaik and Kahn (2021) analyse this to be a consequence of collective 'fractured reflexivity' that causes 'intellectual and cultural solipsism' (p. 971), defined as an inability to 'make sense' of ideas and experiences that lie beyond the imaginary of one's own group (in this case white South Africans). They argue that this accounts for 'the perpetuation of an exclusionary cultural and intellectual environment as a result of a constriction in their (whites') reflexivity' (p. 980). Social and cultural solipsism was found to play a causal role in constricting both the personal and the collective reflexivity of those shaping the university's academic environment in this settler society.

The paper by Matthews (2021) further deconstructs the role of whiteness in creating colonial oppression as she writes self-reflexively about her own hesitation in decolonising her teaching. Matthews (2021) argues that *'identity* matters when talking about decoloniality – whites need to think carefully about the effects of their whiteness on decolonial scholarship' (p. 1113). Whiteness is a reminder of the long history of white dominance in educational spaces in South Africa and of the fact that whites are still very much over-represented as academics, authors and educational authorities'. She talks about *embodiment* and how the bodies in which we dwell affect how others respond to us and interpret what we say. Matthews (2021, 1113) writes:

> There is a danger that writing on the topic of decolonisation may do more to help alleviate the guilt of white academics and to ensure their continued prominence in academia than it does to meaningfully contribute to decolonial struggles.

Edwards and Shahjahan (2021) approach the topic of whiteness from a slightly different perspective; for them it is not so much a matter of embodiment, but rather a temporal one. Edwards and Shahjahan (2021) argue that a temporal lens is useful because 'since decolonizing is deeply contextual, historical, and political, educators attempting to decolonize education must recognize both the shifts in content and temporal orientation needed to influence student learning.' (pp. 1127–1128) Thus, 'engaging decolonized accounts of time via class dialogue about white violence throughout history and its nonlinear, recursive presence across time, disrupts how they (students) perceive the world and themselves.' (p. 1125) In their paper, Edwards and Shahjahan present a 'Temporal Proposal' for shifting students' temporal orientations as a means of decolonising curriculum and pedagogy which challenge students' orientations to the past, their allocations of time in the present and their orientations to the future and their desires for 'ideal future selves' are tied to the global labour market.

Another way of dealing with whiteness is described by Wernicke (2021) through the lens of language education in Canada. Wernicke understands language as always political and inextricably connected to identity, culture, and knowledge, 'where we see intercultural understanding not only in terms of cultural but also epistemological difference'. (p. 1138) The paper engages directly with Canada's colonial history by framing a language course within the local context of reconciliation, which, the paper argues, gets students to move away from assuming a stable cultural identity. The course promotes *interculturalidad* – that is, Indigenous peoples' role in furthering intercultural understanding and emphasises multilingualism, decolonisation and epistemic diversity. Through language, Wernicke (2021) gets students to reflect on their relationship to the land they are on and how to 'see' themselves in the curricula, something that most find difficult. Understanding language as a matter of recognition and validation, as well as epistemic access, marks a 'social practice-based perspective of language, performance of identity, and a situated process of meaning-making that requires decentering from pre-existing assumptions and practices'. (p. 1133) The author aims to get students 'to enter the world with another', 'to learn from and not about the Other' and potentially arrive at transformed understandings. She emphasises the importance of listening – deep, responsible, and ethical listening.

Indeed, it is often argued, it is a lack of deep, responsible and ethical listening that poses a barrier for Indigenous academics working in universities in settler societies. This is highlighted in the contribution by Leenen-Young, Naepi, Thomsen, Fa'avae,

Keil and Matapo (2021), six PECA (Pacific Early Career Academics) writing in the context of New Zealand. In their contribution, the authors reflect on how the lack of relational dialogue with their knowledge, perpetuated by 'standard didactic western pedagogical practices', made them reflect on their own ontological and epistemological spaces. The authors use written *talanoa* (relational narrative inquiry or dialogue, a methodology centred on creating and building relationships) to share their reflections on their *praxis* and deep sense of tension when attempting to redefine the educational space in their lecture theatres by prioritising their Pacific knowledge as valid and significant ways of knowing. Their *talanoa* demonstrates the challenges posed by 'the unspoken hierarchies of knowledge baked into the system' and of 'making known the inertia that can allow for continued colonial domination'. (p. 989)

Motala, Sayed and de Kock (2021) also draw on dismantling whiteness and the unspoken hierarchies of knowledge, in their contribution, which they see as posing challenges to Indigenous students in settler societies. In working with black South African students in Education, who hold diverse views on meanings of decolonisation, Motala et al (2021) argue for the importance of 'making visible the fine line between a form of radicalism that pushes for the disruption and dismantling of archaic practices, institutions and modes of knowing, and radicalism that descends into Afrophobia, essentialism and primordialism'. (p. 1009)

Their paper looks at processes of pedagogic change and pedagogic encounters, from the perspective of students, as a way of understanding what decolonisation might mean in practice and how it may be realised (…) and how the curriculum is experienced and transacted. Motala et al's (2021) findings show that students' understandings of decolonisation are partial, incomplete, contradictory, and contested. The views of the students range from, on the one hand those perceiving decolonisation of the curricula as opening up the possibilities of radical ways of knowing, but also, for many, it resonated most with how the pedagogic act is transacted and less with which canons of knowledge are affirmed or subjugated. In this perspective, decolonising the curriculum is about reconstituting the sociality of the pedagogic encounter in various ways, including seeing the students as active partners in the learning act together with the lecturer and, in so doing, (re)affirming what experiences and knowledge students bring to the pedagogic encounter. A third student perspective was evident in their data, captured in this student's remark:

> Decolonization for some might mean having food and water and a place to stay while I'm studying, whereas for others, it might be what exactly is in the curriculum. (p. 1008)

This is a poignant reminder that the struggle for epistemic decolonisation is integrally related to struggles against poverty and structural inequality.

In summing up this section, we draw together some of the limitations and tensions in pedagogic encounters to decolonise that have been raised by the authors. Their reflections recognise the paradox of the modern university whose decolonial ambitions cannot be fully realised because of its historical colonial roots, structural factors as well as coloniality within. Thus, as argued by Menon et al (2021) in this issue, to fully embrace the decolonial option 'would be to begin otherwise, by deconstructing the axes of race and capitalism which undergird the colonial matrix of power'. (p. 949) Menon et al (2021) ask: Is 'delinking' (from coloniality) really possible for institutions with colonial foundations? Can modern universities really serve as spaces for 'beyond reform' decolonization? Also in this issue, Leenen-Young et al (2021) lament the constraints that the colonial foundation of their university imposes on their agency and projects where 'only personal acts of decolonization' are possible. They name the university a 'knowledge prison', and emphasise how they 'are almost limited to personal acts of decolonization while the wider structural and foundational coloniality of the institution remains intact'. (p. 997) Hall et al (2021, citing Johnson 2020, 89) argue in their contribution that decolonising should seek to reveal the subtle, everyday – and often unconsciously produced – racist cultures that texture the 'white background of academia' and 'perpetuate normative whiteness'. This is why Matthews (2021) asks 'Can white people play a *genuine* role in decolonising university curricula?' (p. 1114) Her answer, 'Whites should try to do so, but not assume their ability to do so or their right to participate in decolonial projects – their position is *unavoidably* ambivalent'. (p. 1116) Matthews (2021) continues to argue that 'whites are so eager to be 'part of the solution' that they do not stop for long enough to reflect on the ways in which they might be part of the problem'. There is nonetheless literature which argues that white academics can push back against their own (white) embodiment and the effects it has on their work (see for example, the Special Issue in 'Whiteness and Education' – 'White scholars working against whiteness'). These academics do so by making whiteness visible, through critique, in their personal lives, as well as their teaching and research, in their social, epistemic and community relations with Indigenous, minoritised and racialised partners. 'They choose to trouble whiteness and racism in their lives, classrooms and scholarship in order to better comprehend whiteness and to deconstruct it' (Locke 2017, 1).

Given such limitations and tensions, *we* therefore ask, what are the implications of the paradox of the modern university and whiteness for decolonial *praxis*? It seems that authentic *praxis* in this context may mean, as put by Menon et al (2021) in this issue, to 'continue to struggle, reflect and learn from our entanglements with coloniality and the intricate and contradictory nature of how we understand and interpret decoloniality as part of the university structure'. (p. 948) This may mean that we use pedagogic methods that prompt reflexivity (in ourselves and our students) around our discomforts, binaries and oppressions that may arise because we have not worked sufficiently with how we (intentionally or not) produce and perpetuate coloniality. Below we summarise examples provided by authors of how they attempted to deal with these discomforts and oppressions through the introduction of Indigenous Knowledge into the curriculum and by emphasising experiential and situated learning, place and positionality, and importantly for our analysis, affect, attitude and self-critique.

The introduction of indigenous knowledge into the curriculum

Several authors in this issue focused on the extent to which a curriculum recognises Indigenous voices and authors and those from the Global South as epistemic equals. Many of the papers written in settler contexts, particularly those where colonised communities historically suffered epistemicide, equate decolonisation with the recovery and introduction of Indigenous Knowledge into the higher education curriculum.

Guzmán-Valenzuela (2021), Seniuk Cicek, Steele, Gauthier, Mante, Wolf, Robinson and Mattucci (2021) and Kennedy, Percy, Thomas, Moyle and Delahunty (2021) provide analyses of Indigenous Knowledge recovery in the curriculum. Guzmán-Valenzuela (2021) analyses the literature on curriculum and pedagogies of intercultural indigenous education in Latin American universities (legal constitutions in both Mexico and Ecuador legally recognise Indigenous people and their right to access and study a degree in a university that includes Indigenous Knowledge or practices). The curricular practices and pedagogies examined in the paper are considered by Guzmán-Valenzuela (2021) as 'critical border' educational projects because they have been produced from the borders (peripheral contexts and institutions in peripheral regions in Latin America) and they promote a socialisation of power by empowering Indigenous communities to break the coloniality of power at universities. Guzmán-Valenzuela (2021) however concludes that such decolonial projects are not immune from challenges such as budgetary restrictions, accreditation demands and a lack of legal or educational recognition.

In another meta-analysis in this issue, Seniuk Cicek et al (2021) evaluate self-reported contributions from 25 engineering programmes and four engineering organisations on the work being done to bring Indigenous peoples, knowledge, and perspectives into the dominant structures of engineering education in Canada. The authors advocate an Indigenous approach to knowledge termed 'two-eyed seeing' which, they argue, works to deconstruct the colonial lens and facilitates the practice of 'culturally safe' engineering as well as 'cultural humility'. 'Two-eyed seeing' is defined in the paper as learning to see from one eye with the strengths of Indigenous Knowledge and ways of knowing, and from the other eye with the strengths of Western knowledge and ways of knowing … and learning to use both these eyes together, for the benefit of all'. (p. 1043) The approach is seen to be helpful in deconstructing the colonial lens and understanding marginalised perspectives. Seniuk Cicek et al (2021) ask discipline-specific questions, such as 'What do we let go and what do we bring in to advance decolonization of engineering education?' and how to reconcile the two ways of knowing – the 'positivistic mindset' of engineering and the more constructivist mindsets of Indigenous ways of knowing?

In the contribution by Kennedy et al (2021), the Australian *Indigenous Strategy* (2017–2020), which has been developed to provide a sector-wide approach to 'closing the gap' between Indigenous and non-Indigenous Australians, is critiqued. By way of contrast, Kennedy et al (2021) make a case for 'substantive reconciliation' – a respectful and reciprocal approach to curriculum reconciliation with Aboriginal Knowledge that are situated in the Country. The paper reports on understanding *Jindaola*, a program led by a local Aboriginal Knowledge holder within one Australian university, which engages academic and professional staff in an 'Aboriginal way' towards curriculum reconciliation. The programme brings together Aboriginal local knowledge holders, Elders from the local Aboriginal community and academics. The *Jindaola* program focuses on actively and subversively using the space and resources of the neo-colonial university to create conditions for developing new subjectivities and a reconciliation of knowledge in Australia.

Other contributors across the SI also emphasise local ways and places in settler societies as a means of critically introducing Indigenous Knowledge into the curriculum. In the contribution by Dache, Blue, Bovell, Miguest, Osifeso and Tucux (2021), we read about a place-based research methodology that uses a 'Postcolonial Geographic Epistemology' to map dominated populations and spaces of resistance in Philadelphia's communities of colour. The methodology described in the paper is called *Calle* (street) and it enables students to learn resistant local histories, and about how space is reclaimed through spirituality and creative expression. The data reported in the paper shows that students are engaged sensorially and cognitively and experience how history can be told in different ways that allow for a (re)contextualisation of the academic work used in teaching. The methodology is described by Dache et al (2021) as paving the way for visibility of the Afro-Latinx population within higher education and urban communities, focusing on a working-class Afro-Latinx form of capital that emerges from residing in urban areas that are sites for resistance and domination. Such places offer 'informal and non-traditional methods of learning from Philadelphia's residents and neighbourhoods and of resisting whiteness embedded in normative pedagogical practices of universities.' (p. 1093)

The final paper that we summarise here, by Sabati, Beckett, Cragun-Rehders, Najera, Hise and Geiger (2021), has been written collectively by academics and students, reporting on a course 'Water Justice: Global Insights for a Critical Resource'. It critically interrogates California's model of intensive water extraction and contemporary policy initiatives in California that aim to manage severely depleted groundwater aquifers through data collection and monitoring. Similarly, to the paper by Dache et al (2021) above, Sabati et al (2021) report on 'a place-based anti-colonial research collaboration, which centres students as knowledge producers, as collaborators and researchers, and unsettles their understanding of Western research as a universal paradigm. This 'unsettling' happens through training students in the politics of knowledge production and the ethics of community-engagement. They are trained to think like critical ethnographers, as they study grassroots approaches to groundwater governance. Such training, according to the authors, complicates Western science as universal knowledge because students work through their own conditioning as Western scientific thinkers. The methodology prompts students to reflect on how their understanding of their experiences, places, and the histories of place, have been socially constructed through their own schooling or the assumptions they acquired over time. The focus is on the authors' own positionality, as educators, as learners and as collaborators on the groundwater sustainability project, and as people distinctly situated in relation to questions of water justice, and how this inflects their own process of analysis.

The collection of papers under this final theme also points to frustrations, failures and setbacks, suggesting that much work remains to decentre the Northern epistemes that have been institutionalised and universalised through the modern university system, the modern disciplines and the five hegemonic (ex-colonial) European languages (Grosfoguel 2013, 74). We have a long way to go before previously colonised peoples (who are still subjected to coloniality) can reclaim their intellectual sovereignty and before the 'pluriverse' is ready to celebrate and benefit from Southern theory and wisdom[2]. In realising a pluriverse of knowledge, we believe that one of the most taxing challenges that remain, especially for those working with Indigenous Knowledge, is working on the internal relations of knowledge systems. To date, most work on the 'decolonial turn' in higher education has focussed on historical and social injustice and the need to disrupt external political and social relations to knowledge. This means the focus has been on how the socio-historical contexts of the production of knowledge, its ownership and control and the 'positionality' of its knowers commits epistemic violence on those historically colonised and still excluded from knowledge production, and the institutionalised power and authority it confers. If we care about epistemic and social justice, the importance of undoing 'coloniality' cannot be emphasised enough.

However, working for justice and working for truth, although entangled in practice, are analytically not the same. All knowledge systems have forms of legitimation and validation

– based on both external power relations and internal criteria and norms. This means that meta-reflexive decolonial work should also attend to the internal relations of knowledge systems (Morreira et al. 2021). In this regard, we encourage those who can access Indigenous Knowledge, cultures and languages to follow through and take up the hard intellectual work required to bring these rich and overlooked resources into the public domain to surface their internal relations and norms. What are other ways of making knowledge claims? How can they be validated, are they teachable and learnable, by whom and in what contexts? These are essential and complex questions. Working towards these goals entails engaging reflexively with the internal relations of knowledge systems – working with Indigenous concepts, definitions, meanings, the apprehension and formation of objects and subjects of knowledge, translations and methodologies. This is so that they might enrich intellectual conversations and the pluriverse's stock of knowledge – and on their own terms. The less reflexive alternative is to romanticise or mystify 'other' ways of knowing so that they remain closed, exclusive and secretive – which could become just another way of using social power to set up new hierarchies of knowers.

Decolonial praxis and reflexivity

We hope that the summaries showcased above capture efforts by higher education academics and practitioners to move from the 'ought' of decolonial theory to the 'is' of curriculum and pedagogic practice, that is, to engage with the complexity of *praxis*. The 'problem' of the enactment and embodiment of *praxis*, that is, making the connection between intellectual questions and abstractions (that theorise oppression, for example) and finding the resources, services and capabilities to address them, is not new to educationists and there have been many attempts to resolve this – for example, through the well-worn concept of the 'reflexive practitioner' (Schön 1983; Loughran 1996). Paulo Freire (1996), the father of critical pedagogy, had this to say about *praxis*: that its complexities would only be resolved through 'true commitment to the people, involving the transformation of the reality by which they are oppressed' (*Ibid*. 126). There are three dimensions to transformative *praxis*: theory, values and practice, which means that 'discovery cannot be purely intellectual but must involve action; nor can it be limited to mere activism but must include serious reflection: only then will it be a praxis' (*Ibid*. 133). Freire's understanding of praxis has been elaborated by Gadotti, one of Freire's students and founder of the Freire Institute in São Paulo:

> All pedagogy refers to practice and intends to be put into practice.(...) To act pedagogically is to put theory into practice *par excellence*. It is to discover and elaborate instruments of social action. In doing so, one becomes aware of the essential unity between theory and practice. Pedagogy, as the theory of education, cannot abstract itself from the intended practice. Pedagogy is, above all, a theory of praxis. (Gadotti 1996, 7)

Thus, following the authors in this SI, we argue that decolonial *praxis* entails a movement from theory to social action. This is not only intellectual and cognitive work, but also means working on relationships, affect, values, norms, ontological assumptions – and the self – before *praxis* becomes manifest in transformed pedagogies.

We have shown how the authors in this SI demonstrate reflexivity and creativity in taking up decolonising work in a diversity of contexts and from different *loci* of enunciation. We venture further to suggest that high levels of reflexivity may well be a precondition for carrying out decolonial work effectively, regardless of the context and positionality from which one works. Mbembe (2021) would agree, for when looking back on the failed promises of political decolonisation, which he terms a 'non-event', he describes how the decolonisation project must now become 'an Event' that 'enacts assertion and refoundation', 'a force of self-creation and invention including the need to rehabilitate endogenous forms of knowledge and language' (2021, 53). Further, he describes how the reconstitution of the (colonised) subject involves 'enormous epistemic, psychic and even aesthetic work' for in order to 'heal the wounds inflicted by the certainties of bio-racism and racecraft, it was necessary to know oneself' (2021, 53).

The need for meta-reflexivity is also captured in Andreotti et al's (2015) *Cartography of Decolonization* but from the perspective of the global North, in which they warn that 'if we approach decolonization through Cartesian, self-, logo-, and anthropo- centric forms of agency, we may unintentionally enact precisely the dominance we seek to address'. Andreotti et al. (2015) caution against the temptation to settle for 'fixed teleologies, normativity, consensus and innocence', causing a 'foreclosure of the complexities and complicities' (27); suggesting instead that the pedagogical challenge we face includes the incoherence (and frustration) of the juxtaposed, incommensurable contexts we in which we teach and live (35). They explain that their concept of 'hospicing' modernity, 'demands a critique that is self-implicated rather than heroic, vanguardist or 'innocent'; it entails 'seeing oneself in modernity's limits – that which is dying' (28). In a similar vein, Sharon et al. (2020) emphasise the difficult work of self-transformation and attending to affect and attitude when undertaking decolonialising work. They warn against 'arrogance, self-righteousness, dogmatism, and perfectionism' and encourage attributes such as humility, stamina and self-reflexivity. In working for cognitive, affective and relational justice, they advocate 'a pedagogical commitment to invite deepened engagement with the complexities and contradictions' of the work, asserting that this requires no less than 'existential surrender' (Stein et al 2020, 57–63).

There is some resonance between Andreotti et al's (2015) and Stein et al's (2020) descriptions of what it takes to work with 'modernity's shadow' and Archer's (2012) theorisation of the 'reflexive imperative' required by later modernity; particularly her concept of 'meta-reflexivity', a mode of 'internal deliberation' exhibited by those who are 'aliens to normative conventionalism' and profoundly disenchanted with and committed to reshaping the social order. Archer argues that the practice of 'meta-reflexivity' is critical for effective action for social and cultural change in a society dominated by a logic of competition driven by institutional hegemony of market and state (2012, 206–207). Importantly for our purposes, she adds that if a concern is to become realised as a project in practice, it must include internal self-critique.[3]

To sum up, we return to our understanding of decolonial *praxis*. The reproduction of coloniality in higher education, as argued by many authors in this SI, is perpetuated by a lack of reflexivity among higher education managers, academics and teachers of their own epistemological situatedness. This tends towards monologue as opposed to 'liberating dialogue' (Freire 1996) or what our authors refer to as essentialism, co-option and states of inertia. While Freire proposes that dialogue will differ across contexts and positionalities, a decolonial *praxis* for higher education can be conceptualised broadly as an approach that emphasises the connection between significant personal change and concrete teaching strategies, resources and practices. De Sousa Santos proposes that this should not be underpinned by merely a 'self-contained intellectual exercise', needing continuous interrogation to counter epistemological absences which reinforce 'the separation of the scientist vis-á-vis his or her object of research, including his or her own past sociological knowledge' (Santos 2018, 28). It needs to be *carried out* in light of the context of the struggle that 'provides noncognitive dimensions that condition the ways in which absent social groups and knowledge become present' (*Ibid*, 27). Only then will we be more critically self-reflexive and develop a capacity for epistemological and ontological pluralism. The link between *praxis* and reflexivity reflect Freire's original work and is again captured by the authors in this SI, who, like Freire, de Sousa Santos and Archer, see reflection (including self-critique) and action as imperative in any transformative (here decolonial) work, and therefore as constituting authentic *praxis*.

Notes

1. Mbembe (2021) uses 'planetary' rather than 'global(ly)' to emphasise that in the Age of the Anthropocene we are 'entangled' with our environment, the planet as well as with each other.
2. Southern theory and wisdom are much needed to balance and correct the way knowledge has been put to use in the global North, to serve narrow materialist interests with dire consequences for the planet and the poor.
3. We should point out in the context of this SI, that typical of her location and generation, and despite her analytical and methodological rigour, Archer's corpus fails to acknowledge the colonial constitution of modernity and tends to universalize from the European experience.

Disclosure statement

No potential conflict of interest was reported by the author(s).

ORCID

Kathy Luckett ⓘ http://orcid.org/0000-0002-3544-4221

References

Andreotti, Vanessa, et al. 2015. "Mapping Interpretations of Decolonization in the Context of Higher Education." *Decolonization: Indigeneity, Education & Society* 4 (1): 20–40.

Archer, M. 2000. *Being Human. The Problem of Agency*. Cambridge: Cambridge University Press.

Archer, M. 2012. *The Reflexive Imperative in Late Modernity*. Cambridge: Cambridge University Press.

Bhambra, G. K., D. Gebrial, and K. Nişancıoğlu. 2018. *Decolonising the University*. London: Pluto Press.

Cicek, J. S., A. Steele, S. Gauthier, A. A. Mante, P. Wolf, M. Robinson, and S. Mattucci. 2021. "Indigenizing Engineering Education in Canada: Critically Considered." *Teaching in Higher Education* 26 (7–8): 1038–1059.

Clegg, S. 2005. "Theorising the Mundane: The Significance of Agency." *Studies in the International Sociology of Education* 15 (2): 149–164.

Comaroff, J., and J. Comaroff. 2012. *Theory from the South: or, How Euro-America is Evolving Toward Africa*. New York: Paradigm.

Connell, R. 2007. *Southern Theory: The Global Dynamics of Knowledge in Social Science*. Sydney: Allen & Unwin.

Connell, R. 2013. "Using Southern Theory: Decolonizing Social Thought in Theory, Research and Application." *Planning Theory* 13 (2): 210–223. https://doi.org/10.1177/1473095213499216.

Cornbleth, C. 1990. *Curriculum in Context*. Ann Arbor, MI: University of Michigan.

Dache, A., J. Blue, D. Bovell, D. Miguest, S. Osifeso, and F. Tucux. 2021. "A Calle Decolonial Hack: Afro-Latin Theorizing of Philadelphia's Spaces of Learning and Resistance." *Teaching in Higher Education* 26 (7–8): 1077–1097.

Edwards, K. T., and R. A. Shahjahan. 2021. "Navigating Student Resistance Towards Decolonizing Curriculum and Pedagogy (DCP): A Temporal Proposal." *Teaching in Higher Education* 26 (7–8): 1122–1129.

Freire, P. 1996. *Pedagogy of the Oppressed*. UK: Penguin Classics.

Gadotti, M. 1996. *Pedagogy of Praxis: A Dialectical Philosophy of Education*. New York, NY: SUNY Press.

Grosfoguel, R. 2013. "The Structure of Knowledge in Westernized Universities: Epistemic Racism/Sexism and the Four Genocides of the Long 16th Century." *Human Architecture: Journal of the Sociology of Self-Knowledge* 11 (1): 73–90.

Hall, R., L. Ansley, P. Connolly, S. Loonat, K. Patel, and B. Whitham. 2021. "Struggling for the Anti-Racist University: Learning from an Institution-Wide Response to Curriculum Decolonisation." *Teaching in Higher Education* 26 (7–8): 902–919.

Hayes, A., K. Luckett, and G. Misiaszek. 2021. "Possibilities and Complexities of Decolonising Higher Education: Critical Perspectives on Praxis." *Teaching in Higher Education* 26 (7–8): 887–900.

Kennedy, J., A. Percy, L. Thomas, C. Moyle, and J. Delahunty. 2021. "Holding Space for an Aboriginal Approach Towards Curriculum Reconciliation in an Australian University." *Teaching in Higher Education* 26 (7–8): 1060–1076.

Leenen-Young, M., S. Naepi, P. S. Thomsen, D. T. M. Fa'avae, M. Keil, and J. Matapo. 2021. "'Pillars of the Colonial Institution are Like a Knowledge Prison': The Significance of Decolonizing Knowledge and Pedagogical Practice for Pacific Early Career Academics in Higher Education." *Teaching in Higher Education* 26 (7–8): 986–1001.

Locke, L. A. 2017. "Editorial." *Whiteness and Education* 2 (1): 1–3. DOI: 10.1080/23793406.2017.1361792.

Loughran, J. J. 1996. *Developing Reflective Practice: Learning about Teaching and Learning through Modelling*. London: Falmer Press.

Maldonado-Torres, N. 2007. "On the Coloniality of Being: Contributions to the Development of a Concept." *Cultural Studies* 21 (2-3): 240–270.

Matthews, S. 2021. "Decolonising While White: Confronting Race in a South African Classroom." *Teaching in Higher Education* 26 (7–8): 1113–1121.

Mbembe, A. 2021. *Out of the Dark Night*. New York: Columbia University Press. https://doi.org/10.7312/mbem16028-003.

Menon, S., C. Green, I. Charbonneau, E. Lehtomäki, and B. Mafi. 2021. "Approaching Global Education Development with a Decolonial Lens: Teachers' Reflections." *Teaching in Higher Education* 26 (7–8): 937–952.

Motala, S., Y. Sayed, and T. de Kock. 2021. "Epistemic Decolonisation in Reconstituting Higher Education Pedagogy in South Africa: The Student Perspective." *Teaching in Higher Education* 26 (7–8): 1002–1018.

Mignolo, W., and A. Escobar. 2010. *Globalization and the Decolonial Option*. Abingdon: Routledge.

Mignolo, Walter D., and Catherine E. Walsh. 2018. *On Decoloniality: Concepts, Analytics, Praxis*. Durham: Duke University Press.

Morreira, S., K. Luckett, S. Kumalo, and M. Ramgotra. 2021. "Introduction: Decolonising Curricula and Pedagogy in Higher Education." In *Decolonising Curricula and Pedagogy in Higher Education Bringing Decolonial Theory into Contact with Teaching Practice*, edited by S. Morreira, K. Luckett, S. Kumalo, and M. Ramgotra. Abingdon: Routledge.

Sabati, S., L. Beckett, K. Cragun-Rehders, A. Najera, K. Hise, and A. Geiger. 2021. "Distilling Pedagogies of Critical Water Studies." *Teaching in Higher Education* 26 (7–8): 1098–1112.

Santos, B. d. S. 2018. *The End of the Cognitive Empire: The Coming of Age of Epistemologies of the South*. Durham: Duke University Press.

Schön, D. 1983. *The Reflective Practitioner*. London: Temple Smith.

Shaik, A., and P. Kahn. 2021. "Understanding the Challenges Entailed in Decolonising a Higher Education Institution: An Organisational Case Study of a Research-Intensive South African University." *Teaching in Higher Education* 26 (7–8): 969–985.

Shain, F., Ü. K. Yıldız, V. Poku, and B. Gokay. 2021. "From Silence to 'Strategic Advancement': Institutional Responses to 'Decolonising' in Higher Education in England." *Teaching in Higher Education* 26 (7–8): 920–936.

Sium, A., C. Desai, and E. Ritskes. 2012. "Towards the 'tangible unknown': Decolonization and the Indigenous future." *Decolonization: Indigeneity, Education & Society* 1 (1): 1–13.

Stein, S., et al. 2020. "Gesturing Towards Decolonial Futures: Reflections on Our Learnings Thus Far." *Nordic Journal of Comparative and International Education (NJCIE)* 4 (1): 43–65.

Stein, S., and V. O. de Andreotti. 2016. "Decolonization and Higher Education." In *Encyclopedia of Educational Philosophy and Theory*, edited by M. Peters. Singapore: Springer. doi: 10.1007/978-981-287-532-7_479-1.

Valenzuela, C. G. 2021. "Disrupting Curricula and Pedagogies in Latin American Universities: Six Criteria for Decolonising the University." *Teaching in Higher Education* 26 (7–8): 1019–1037.

Wernicke, M. 2021. "Four 'Moments' of Intercultural Encountering." *Teaching in Higher Education* 26 (7–8): 1130–1140.

Zembylas, M. 2021. "Refusal as Affective and Pedagogical Practice in Higher Education Decolonization: A Modest Proposal." *Teaching in Higher Education* 26 (7–8): 953–968.

Struggling for the anti-racist university: learning from an institution-wide response to curriculum decolonisation

Richard Hall [ID], Lucy Ansley, Paris Connolly, Sumeya Loonat, Kaushika Patel and Ben Whitham [ID]

ABSTRACT
Increasingly, institutions are amplifying work on race equality, in order to engage with movements for Black lives and decolonising. This brings universities into relations with individual and communal issues of whiteness, white fragility and privilege, double and false consciousness, and behavioural code switching. Inside formal structures, built upon cultures and practices that have historical and material legitimacy, engaging with such issues is challenging. The tendency is to engage in formal accreditation, managed through engagement with established methodologies, risk management practices and data reporting. However, this article argues that the dominant articulation of the institution, which has its own inertia, which reinforces whiteness and dissipates radical energy, needs to be re-addressed in projects of decolonising. This situates the communal work of the institution against the development of authentic relationships as a movement of dignity.

Introduction: an intersecting critique

Decolonising the University has a long and rich history, which is explicitly connected to post- and anti-colonialism, making visible subaltern or subordinate identities, Black[1] power and indigeneity, and critical race or anti-racist studies (see, for instance, Andreotti et al. 2015; Bhambra, Gebrial, and Nisancioglu 2018; Gabriel and Tate 2017; Heleta 2016; Pimblott 2019; Tuhiwai Smith, Tuck, and Yang 2018). This work overflows into more recent critiques of education, including critical university studies and the abolition of the University, as well as staff–student protests like Black Lives Matter and Rhodes Must Fall (Meyerhoff 2019). These movements argue for a new conception of the University, grounded in dignity and life, and challenge dominant ideological positions that privilege particular voices.

Collectively, these analyses and struggles push beyond reimagining the curriculum and modes of assessment. They challenge educators, students and professional services' staff to interrogate the distinct-but-interconnected processes of colonisation and racialisation in their own practices and lives. The project of decolonising is both a critique of institutions and a critique of knowledge, and it questions the following.

- The role of the University in reproducing cultures and structures of privilege and power.
- The creation of relationships of inclusion and exclusion between staff and students, institutions and stakeholders, and institutions and society.
- The dominance of white, male views of reality (ontology) and ways of producing knowledge about the world (epistemology).
- The hegemonic (dominant and manufactured) position of knowledge generated in the global North in addressing crises.
- The value of alternative histories and conceptions of a meaningful education and life.
- The relationship between, first, economic value and value-for-money, and second, humane values and human flourishing.

A key point raised in movements of decolonising is a shared questioning of human positionality in relation to these issues, in order to venture beyond them. Here, French, Sanchez, and Ullom (2020) argue for 'composting' as a metaphor that centres humanity and feelings, stories, histories, relationships, cultures and lands, and enables positions to be recycled or reimagined through a deep engagement with truth-telling. Yet this focus on place and land has been negatively critiqued by Garba and Sorentino (2020) in their analysis of Tuck and Yang's (2012) seminal *decolonization is not a metaphor*. Garba and Sorentino (2020, np) push questions of the symbolism and material reality of a range of Black, anti-Black, Indigenous and settler-colonial positions, in particular in relation to 'slavery's role in rendering the emerging conceptions of God, globality, humanity, politics, history, and economy coherent for the purposes of capitalism and conquest.'

These are very difficult critiques with which universities must grapple. Is it possible for their senior management teams, staff, students, partner organisations and stakeholders, alongside their funders, governors and regulators, to acknowledge the historical and ongoing effects of: exploitative institutional practices and strategies; silencing of certain bodies, identities, cultures and knowledges; and, imposing claims about the universality of the epistemological and ontological certainties of the global North? Such questioning seeks to open new pathways for knowing, doing and being in the world, which are currently obscured by existing hierarchical and disciplinary separations between individuals and disciplines, reinforced through managerialism and performance management.

The slow rate of institutional change has run up against an increasingly dynamic, horizontal movement erupting at the level of society. The global Black Lives Matter struggle impacts universities through its educational projects, and student-led movements, such as UCL's 'Why is my curriculum white?' and the University of Cape Town's #RhodesMustFall campaigns, challenge dominant, institutional positions. In response, and as an extension of their equality, diversity and inclusion (EDI) agendas, many Universities have set up core groups to focus on the process of decolonising or to explore how to capitalise upon formal accreditation routes like the Race Equality Charter (REC). Other institutional challenges have been tabled, for instance: the attainment gap between individuals and groups who have been labelled Black, Asian and Minority Ethnic (BAME) and white, home students (Advance HE 2019); and, the gap in understanding *both* the experiences of international students and their place in strategic EDI objectives (Tannock 2018), *and* the attainment gap between international and home students (Equality Challenge Unit (ECU) 2015).

Such initiatives tend to amplify a disconnection between grassroots, identity-based struggles and formal, regulated institutions. As Ahmed (2012) notes, institutional work is notoriously hierarchical, and tends to make judgements about who might be included based upon idealised notions of who is deserving, and collapses equality into ideas of meritocracy governed by equality of opportunity. Ahmed (2004, np) highlights what she calls the 'politics of admissions,' whereby the institution simply admitting to bad practice is seen to define the appropriate horizon for the anti-racist University. Instead, she argues that such admissions need to be 'taken up,' which Moosavi (2020) also highlights through his descriptions of how some universities have jumped on the *decolonial bandwagon* without understanding or addressing the risks of the work becoming tokenistic.

The work of decolonising, or building a culture of decoloniality, carries *both* a symbolic idea *and* a lived reality of the University that is *neither* unitary, universal, and/or linear, *nor* Eurocentric in its assumptions. The focus upon Eurocentrism is important in revealing the perceived superiority implicit in the structures, cultures and practices of global North institutions. As a result, it reproduces marginalisation through domination revealed in the power of particular epistemologies, ontologies and voices. This reinforces modes of coloniality that are historical and material (Santos 2017), and questions the assumed power of the status quo as an ongoing unfolding of decolonial practices as a method for challenging the University.

In part, this is why specific discourses are taking on a more politicised flavour in the global North, including: mental health support and stigma for Black students and students of colour (Kam, Mendoza, and Masuda 2018); the lack of promotion for Black women within HE (Rollock 2019); the rise of reported, racist hate crimes on campuses (Kayali and Walters 2021); linguistic racism (Dobinson and Mercieca 2020); the differential impacts of Covid-19 (Harper 2020); and, the negative experiences of institutional procedures for communities made marginal (Glasener, Martell, and Posselt 2019). It also underpins the work of some Australian institutions in indigenising the curriculum (Walter and Guerzoni 2020), and in work on the impact of HE on Indigenous people across Latin America and Mexico (University of Bath 2020).

This article emerges from the convergence of these analyses of the lived experiences of the University and the limits of institutional possibility for developing emancipatory cultures and practices, inside national HE systems that themselves need to respond to political and economic directives. It takes as its starting point a discussion of one United Kingdom (UK)-based, institution-wide experiment, Decolonising DMU (De Montfort University). Decolonising DMU is an ongoing critique of the idea of the University, and its structures, cultures and practices, which looks to build the anti-racist University through a dialogue grounded in dignity. It recognises that this is a process of engaging in difficult, painful and genuinely risky conversations, in order for meaningful change to unfold.

In articulating the horizon of possibility for such work, this article will describe and analyse struggles in relation to: first, how the Decolonising DMU approach is situated against *both* decolonial and indigenous critiques of the University, *and*, the project's emergent relationship to the institution; second, the impacts of dominant cultures which reinforce whiteness; third, how established structures dissipate radical energy and militate against change; and fourth, institutional practices that have high inertia. The article will close by discussing the implications of these material realities for change, in order to question how decolonisation affects the idea and practices of the University.

Decolonising DMU: a critique of the University

Decolonising DMU (2021a) was initiated in November 2019 as the next step in building the anti-racist University, predicated upon structures, cultures and practices of equality. It moved beyond DMU's attainment-focused, Freedom to Achieve intervention (Ansley 2018), which was part of a collaborative, two-year, Higher Education Funding Council for England, and then Office for Students' *Catalyst* project, led by Kingston University (McDuff et al. 2020). Whilst the significant difference in the percentage of Black/of colour students awarded a good honours degree is a sector-wide issue, Decolonising DMU situated longitudinal outcomes for students upon their short-and medium-term engagement with the institution as a whole.

Moving beyond the attainment gap is central to addressing the reductionist position of individual deficits that can be overcome through personal resilience and tenacity to engage with a system that delivers a methodologically framed student experience (Arday, Belluigi, and Thomas 2020; Hall 2020). In so doing, it built explicitly upon the outcomes of Freedom to Achieve, which had worked with 40 programmes across the institution, and sought to stitch this into other EDI work, including on the REC (Advance HE n.d.).

These outcomes highlighted that attainment for Black and of colour students is structured by factors that are immanent to each other, and that emerge inside and outside the classroom.[2] During 2018–2019, surveys with students ($n = 233$), staff ($n = 44$), and participation in co-creation events with students and staff ($n = 142$) generated six themes (Ansley 2018; Ansley and Hall 2019).

- The importance of trusting and authentic relationships on campus.
- A feeling of not belonging leading to exclusion.
- Developing approaches to teaching and learning with which students can connect.
- The creation of safe and pluralistic communities on campus.
- Developing cultures that enable personal development.
- Supporting diverse needs in relation to employability and post-University life.

Within these themes there were differences for groups of international students, and also for some home students. For example, students of Pakistani, Caribbean and 'Other White' heritage were most likely to feel unrepresented within their learning experience. There were also differences across each of the institution's four faculties, including in terms of changes to staff practices in the classroom, which tended to focus upon in-class teaching, revisions to assignment styles, changes to curriculum content or changes to personal tutoring.

Reshaping this project beyond the attainment gap reveals the power dynamics in an institution-driven, rather than student-instigated, decolonising initiative. The class positionality and concomitant social, cultural, and economic capital configuration of students impacts modes of political activism within universities. The complex, demographic backgrounds of DMU's students affects their ability to make demands for decolonising. Consequently, the decolonising initiative at DMU was taken by the institution itself, including activist scholars. At its core it is striving to develop a more co-created, student-led approach that is governed by the University's EDI Strategy, and its Executive Board. In this, the operational team includes professional services' staff, academics and students working as champions on particular, cross-institutional themes. Yet, it is important to acknowledge that a 'top-down' or corporate institutional dynamic is *both* a limitation on the work of decentring power, *and* also sharpens the project's ambitions to devalue hierarchies and magnify the diversity of voices.

The first year of Decolonising DMU developed priorities around: institutional structures, cultures and practices (effectively aligned with the REC, and including work on University policies); staff development (including developing communities of practice and a toolkit); student engagement (including partnership-working with the student union); Library and Learning Services (including decolonising collections and reading lists, and staff development); and research (including enriching the research environment). Here, the institution was forced to consider the relationships between factors that enable/disable students from seeing themselves, their identities, images, histories and stories reflected in it.

These priorities were developed in a subsequent survey with students ($n = 35$) and staff ($n = 66$) in Spring 2020. The numbers engaging were significantly hit by the Covid-19 pandemic, and this flags the potential for the day-to-day realities of epidemiological uncertainty and crisis to reproduce institutional inertia. As individuals struggle to survive, live, work and study, engagement with cultural change becomes more difficult. However, issues arising from the surveys reflected some of those that had erupted through the Black Lives Matter movement, including: a concrete focus upon equality; explicit working to tackle discrimination, including in disciplinary processes; representation inside and outside the classroom; and, developing conversations around harassment and discrimination. Whilst staff highlighted 10 separate factors underpinning educational inequality, including biases, deficit thinking and denial, it should also be noted that limited numbers of students ($n = 2$) and staff ($n = 2$) did not agree with the aims of the project.

Other institutions have also begun to work on institutional projects, pivoting around the REC and responses to the Equalities and Human Rights Commission (EHRC) report (2019) on *Tackling Racial Harassment: Universities Challenged* (see, for example, the University of Liverpool 2020). However, Decolonising DMU attempts to generate an active critique of the institution. Its working definition (2021b, np) explicitly 'recognises that racial inequality in Britain originates from colonialism. In seeking to decolonise, we are creating an anti-racist University which allows all to succeed.' Further, the project (Decolonising DMU 2021b) recognises 'that racial inequality has been built over centuries on the dominant western and northern hemispheres and patriarchal interpretations of value and merit.'

These are a deeply challenging set of statements, which connect the project to a set of risks relating to culture, business case, relationships and accountability, including making visible racist incidents; the power of whiteness, white privilege and white fragility; a lack of institutional, emotional resilience; denial of the relationship between privilege and coloniality; placing the burden of responsibility for change on Black/of colour students and staff; reputational challenges, including failing or essentialising the needs of Black/of colour students and staff; and developing institutional courage, mutuality and faith. These issues are situated theoretically in a position paper (Decolonising DMU 2021b, np), which 'seeks to establish *both* a symbolic idea *and* a lived reality of the University that is *neither* unitary, universal, and/or linear, *nor* Eurocentric in its assumptions. It questions the assumed power of the status quo.'

Through the position paper (Decolonising DMU 2021b), the project situates itself as 'a movement of dignity' that engages with the 'complex denials, exclusions and violences, which have been enmeshed with the idea of the University in the global North.' The project centres dialogues around coloniality as a process and the potential for revealing the dignity of difference. It does this by creating spaces and capacities with which to name, learn about and critically discuss basic problems of privilege, inequality, division, exclusion, othering, exploitation, alienation, and institutional and structural oppression. Engaging with these processes is crucial in addressing the ongoing relations of colonial injustice that continue to structure, permeate and pervade our lives today (Maldonado-Torres 2017; Stein and de Andreotti 2016).

Whilst there is much work going on in institutions around the histories and lived experiences of victimisation, harassment and depression, in particular in relation to race, gender, sexuality and disability, there is a fourfold risk: first, those who benefited from privilege are too fragile or immersed in denial to engage; second, those whose lived experience is of racism feel that those experiences are being co-opted and sanitised, or that they are not authentically heard; third, those whose teaching, research and scholarship have been developed in relation to inclusion and social justice do not feel fully engaged or involved; and fourth, the institution perceives too high a reputational, governance or management risk, in particular in relation to culture wars (Curran, Gaber, and Petley 2019).

Decolonising DMU focuses on a complex, whole-institution discussion about the tools, practices and visions for a University that addresses these risks authentically and dialogically, in order to help shape meaningful futures for its staff, students and communities. Here, the focus is upon: diversifying structures, cultures and practices; decentring dominant knowledge production; devaluing hierarchies and revaluing relationality; disinvesting from power structures; and, diminishing predominant voices and magnifying those made silent. Our starting point is the *cultures* within which *whiteness* operates.

Cultures of whiteness

The *cultures* of UK higher education constitute one of the most significant obstacles to its decolonisation. Neoliberal cultures of self-entrepreneurship and individualised competition among staff and students, racist cultures that prioritise white forms of institutional knowledge and behaviour, and sexist or misogynist cultures of patriarchal academic performativity and domination, all militate against meaningful decolonial change (Nyamnjoh 2019). Decades of widening participation policies in UK HE demonstrate that it is entirely possible quantitatively to improve BAME representation among students and staff, without seriously undermining cultures of whiteness. As hooks (1994, 5) notes, efforts at challenging racism in HE can simply 'reinscribe old patterns' of institutional whiteness. She asks how we 'educate young, privileged, predominantly white students to divest of white supremacy' (hooks 1994, 5).

That the dominant, cultural structure of majority-white, global North societies like the UK can be understood and theorised as *white supremacist capitalist patriarchy* (Ahmed 2017; hooks 1982, 2000), confronts that hegemonic culture. Most staff and students in UK HE are socialised into hegemonic cultures, which are reproduced through well-documented power dynamics. Its staff, and especially those who tend to be white and male, and who represent prestige and privilege, *both* energise this dominant culture *and* are the most empowered to change it. For hooks (1994, 6), to decolonise must not simply mean allowing white staff (or students) the space to critically reflect on their pedagogical practices, or it risks keeping in place 'existing structures of domination.' HE culture must be transformed to the extent that Black/of colour students and staff experience it as a positive space, where they might co-produce with others, rather than banking privileged knowledge.

Banking is reproduced by a culture of whiteness that denies alternative narratives and histories, which systemically reproduces *microaggressions*. These may be considered 'the chief vehicle for proracist behaviors' in institutions, and consist of statements, representations, and interactions that are both 'subtle' and 'often automatic, and non-verbal' (Pierce et al. 1977, 65). Linguistic microaggressions are a cornerstone of such behaviours. Statements that focus on the quality of written and spoken English, in particular in relation to the questioning of an individual's home and culture, are well-documented (Sue et al. 2007). Some HEIs have attempted to target these microsocial practices as an intervention in cultures of whiteness, for instance, in enabling 'race equality champions' to challenge microaggressions (University of Sheffield 2020).

Denigrating stereotypes reinforce a message of being *othered*, with the racialised body marked as a trespasser and rendered out of place (Puwar 2004; Johnson and Joseph-Salisbury 2018). This might be a function of intentional or unintentional microaggressions, and some institutions have acknowledged the negative impacts of these, including: 'Loss of self-esteem, feelings of exhaustion, damage to the ability to thrive in an environment, mistrust of peers, staff and the institution, decreases participation and ability to study and students dropping out' (University of Edinburgh 2020, np). Feelings of exhaustion have been analysed as racial battle fatigue, which negatively impacts the mental health of Black/of colour staff and students at the intersection of 'the physiological, psychological, and behavioral strain exacted on racially marginalized and stigmatized groups' (Smith 2008, 617). Whilst this strain is witnessed in the numbers of Black students seeking specific mental health support, University counsellors are not always trained or equipped with the skills to support staff and students with such experiences (Leading Routes 2020).

Decolonising DMU is working explicitly to shine a light on these cultures of whiteness, which reproduce a sense that some bodies are in-deficit because they do not measure-up. Institutionally, it is focused upon the linguistic practices, interpretations and uses of its policy framework. Its communities of practice explore existing tropes around: white, working-class boys; anti-white racism; and, the assumption that evidence of student performance is objective truth. Its emerging analyses of the institutional research environment, encourages a richer conversation around voice, privilege and prestige in research. In its library workstream, workshops are focused upon real examples of linguistic microaggressions faced by students and staff. Partnership work with the students union is predicated upon being unapologetic in confronting harassment.

The intention is to build cultures through which recognition of privilege and belonging are explicitly acknowledged. This reflects on Johnson and Joseph-Salisbury's (2018) question: *Are you supposed to be in here?* They argue that 'our goal is not to find a way to belong here. We aim to find a way to thrive here' (Johnson and Joseph-Salisbury 2018, 156). This is a challenge to cultures of whiteness, reinforced through microaggressions. Here, Decolonising DMU seeks to reveal the subtle, everyday, and often unconsciously produced, racist cultures that texture the 'white background of academia' and 'perpetuate normative whiteness' (Johnson 2020, 89). In this, it has become clear that the University must recognise that institutional racism and cultural whiteness are not only enacted at the level of 'feelings' resulting from microsocial, intersubjective experiences, but also through meso- and macro-level, organised social *structures of dissipation*.

Structures of dissipation

In England, discussions about racial inequality in HE crystallise annually around the release of data identifying degree outcomes. Historically, these consistently evidence the attainment/awarding gap between white and Black/of colour students. Explanations for this have tended to collapse around a binary of: first, a student deficit model, which risks naturalising performance around demographic characteristics; and second, analyses of the negative impacts of a Eurocentric epistemology. However, both University and student representatives argue that any 'gap does not exist in isolation within higher education, but is part of the wider structural nature of racial inequality in the UK' (UUK and NUS 2019, 10).

Crucially, the UUK and NUS report (UUK and NUS 2019) outlined how historical reviews demonstrate the extent to which racial inequality is structured and reproduced. These include criminal justice, education and employment, as noted in *The McPherson Report* (1999), *The Race Disparity Audit* (2016), *The Lammy Review* (2017), and *Race in the Workplace: The McGregor-Smith Review* (2017). In response, campaigns for widening participation encouraged enrolment of Black/of colour students, which increased by just under 16 per cent over a 5-year period from 2013. Yet, this drew attention to the reality that racial disparities affect the student life-cycle, from application and enrolment to continuation, attainment and progression. Moreover, connections were made to issues of promotion and development for Black/of colour staff.

The UK HE sector has slowly begun to recognise the interconnected ethical, moral and business cases for action, with a particular focus upon structures, cultures and practices for staff and student recruitment and representation. At the level of the sector, this catalysed the launch of the REC, the publication of the EHRC *Tackling Racial*

Harassment: Universities Challenged report (2019) and the subsequent UUK *Tackling Racial Harassment in Higher Education* report (2020).

However, for specific communities, such reports merely signalled an ongoing willingness to talk about inequality, without acting. One result has been a deep questioning of the institutional structures that continue to reproduce alienating conditions of learning, teaching and research. For instance, campaigns like *Rhodes Must Fall, Why is my Curriculum White?*, and *why isn't my professor Black?* centre the structural positioning of colonial legacies within *both* the sector *and* actual institutions. The inability of institutions to develop structural responses beyond broadening reading lists and library collections, or seeking REC recognition, catalysed a more radical set of demands around decolonising. These connect to a rich movement of Indigenous and anti-racist praxis, which 'are advocating for a university that is not oblivious to its being implicated in the colonial difference that configures today's local and global realities' (Icaza and Rolando 2018, 108).

This challenges the structural inertia of the University, in particular when it is faced by fluid movements that can act quickly in response to local and global events. This challenges the ethical position of institutions, whose business cases tend to depend upon low-risk approaches to problem-solving in relation to particular kinds of performance. For instance, in the aftermath of the killing of George Floyd in the United States, Black Lives Matter protests and demands brought the reality of racial disparities in the act of living into sharp relief with the structures of universities that are also implicated in a range of inequalities. In the UK, this was compounded by the impact of the Covid-19 pandemic, which again drew attention to differential impacts across groups (Blundell et al. 2020), including in research funding (Inge 2020).

Whilst protests brought many universities to the position of publicly stating their stand against racism and for anti-racism, they also demonstrated how institutional attempts to mitigate the negative impacts of such social shocks, were affected by: the limits of what message could be communicated; the speed of communication; and, the potential energy for change latent within institutional structures. Whilst the Decolonising DMU project launched 6 months earlier, the renewed, societal energy of the Black Lives Matter movement shone a light upon the ways in which institutional structures tend to dissipate such potential, whilst at the same time highlighting the relevance and importance of its work inside those structures, including the classroom.

Gebrial (2018, 25) outlines how critique of the relationship between knowledge, subject methodologies and hierarchies, and the reproduction of institutional structures, might usefully begin from the classroom, where we question exclusion through 'existing power structures.' In projects like Decolonising DMU this leads to uncomfortable, institutional questioning or denial of the connection between what knowledge is to be excluded and the perpetuation of structural inequalities. It is important to recognise how the traditional, discipline-based structures of academic institutions work towards denial, in part because they rest upon historical, methodological essentialism, reinforced by ideas of objectivity.

The Decolonising DMU team acknowledges modes of denial and attempts to act as a mirror for how the plural and hegemonic structures of the University dissipate radical energy through inertia. As Gebrial (2018, 29) articulates, 'at its heart, decolonisation is about recognising the roots of contemporary racism in the multiple material, political, social and cultural processes of colonialism and proceeding from this point; this involves the laborious work of structural change at all levels.' Here, the project also interrogates managerial and disciplinary structures and hierarchies, which reproduce particular epistemologies and ontologies in research, community engagement, student support, quality assurance, academic offences, and so on (see, for instance, Arday, Belluigi, and Thomas 2020; Glasener, Martell, and Posselt 2019).

It is important to note the important relationship between individual and communal agency and formal/informal structures, in a movement of institutional change. The core of this is how ways of knowing, knowledge and evidence are used to reproduce institutional structures that can tend to dissolve or co-opt elements to maintain its dominant forms. For Ahmed (2012) these structures act as walls, through which some bodies can pass, and which deny the lived experiences of others. Again, this tends to dissipate the potential for the renewal of institutions in ways that enliven the learning, teaching, professional services and research experiences of specific communities. The bureaucratic forms of the institution generate efficiency in the delivery of services by normalising the student and staff experience in ways that work against some individuals and groups. This is revealed in: the accessibility of student services, often separated in central units; the homogeneous, technological structuring of the curriculum and learning support; and, the governmental organisation of centralised disciplinary structures.

Issues of (dis)connection with institutional structures were revealed in the initial evaluations from the Freedom to Achieve project and Decolonising DMU. These shone a light upon the potential for certain groups to experience institutional denials of a meaningful, student experience, through a lack of representation in structures, and spaces for authentic activity. This was mirrored by a feeling that institutional structures mapped to particular processes and policies, which reinforced non-belonging and double or false consciousness upon some. Thus, the work of the project on revisiting quality assurance documentation and human resources policies focuses upon 'the need to utilise the resources and position of the institution, while recognising, accounting for and undoing its inherent exclusivity' (Gebrial 2018, 20).

This is a pivotal challenge for projects like Decolonising DMU, precisely because addressing racial inequalities in the classroom, and in the staff–student experience of the institution, has to move beyond the metrics of attainment, continuation and progression, and the data sets of demographics. It pushes the reimagining of the institution away from ignorance of the impact of monocultural approaches, and situates work with governing bodies, executive boards, faculty executives and teaching teams, against their material and historical Eurocentrism. This is a test for institutions, which pride themselves on their alleged liberalism, and which seek to normalise this through awards like the REC. At issue is how to connect such normalisation with the humanised, person-centred voices and narratives of Black/of colour staff and students, which tends to destabilise dominant forms.

As a result, the Decolonising DMU project has to catalyse institutional faith in the ability to deconstruct REC data, to spotlight and highlight inequalities, and bring these into dialogue with the voices of affected students and staff. The risk is that the legacy of dominant structures denies authentic dialogue, and reproduces a new layer of othering for particular communities. As a result, the integration of disparate forms of energy inside and through the institution, rather than their refusal or dispersal, is a moment of tension for the project. It demands recognition, across all levels of the University and in all functional units, of the levels and types of racial harassment and inequalities. This reveals one final challenge, namely that this work is laborious and time-consuming, precisely because it seeks to challenge long-established legacies and change cultures and practices, whilst staff and students are also having to engage with their everyday work. At a time of pandemic, the time and energy required for this is further stretched, as institutional forms have to respond to heightened uncertainty. This act as a drag on long-term projects that are already incremental, and which tend to be conditioned through *practices of inertia*.

Practices of inertia

The practices of the University have a structuring reality for those who work and study in it, be they learning, teaching, assessing, professional services, administration, knowledge transfer and exchange, research and scholarship, commercialisation or public engagement. Each of these have been described in relation to processes of financialisation, marketisation and commodification (Hall 2018; McGettigan 2015), and through them to forms of managerialism and performance management (Erickson, Hanna, and Walker 2020). In this way, and predicated upon specialisation and ranking, different academic activities can be compared across a global terrain (Morrissey 2015). University practices have been impacted by crises, like austerity and Covid-19, and increasingly operate based upon probabilities and risk, conditioned by modes of performance that can be optimised. This develops practices based upon discourses of impact, excellence, entrepreneurship and value-for-money, which tends to push the blame for imperfections and uncertainties onto those deemed unproductive.

The very practices of the University are grounded in the methods of closed professions and disciplines. This is one reason why the diffusion of pedagogic change projects, like student as producer, become difficult to instantiate within, let alone across, institutions (Neary 2020). The power and privilege of professions and disciplines, noted by the American Economics' Association (2020), Particles for Justice (2020), and in the noise around #shutdownSTEM in response to Black Lives Matter, demonstrate *both* inertia *and* an acknowledgement of the need for anti-harassment and anti-discrimination work that critiques how academic disciplines construct the world. Such constructions tend to reinforce dominant perspectives, and delegitimise alternative possibilities that question the system and its structures.

This focus upon reinforcing existing structures by refining subject-based practices is reflected in the regulatory and governance frameworks for HE sectors, which prioritise value-for-money, earnings potential and human capital. The risk-modelling of uncertainties shapes the data-driven optimisation of performance, alongside the development of new intellectual commodities and services (Birch, Chiappetta, and Artyushina 2020). Here, the University's material history, shaped by the power of the market, reveals a social terrain for the commercialisation of research and knowledge production (Hoofd 2017), alongside its use in securitisation and militarisation (Murphy 2020). This tends to stymy the potential to generate new practices based upon alternative life experiences, histories and identities, unless they have economic value.

Thus, whilst there is appetite for transformational or radical institutional change projects, such as those like Freedom to Achieve, these tend to be constrained within normative operational parameters focused upon finessing established systems. This is one reason why institutions are accused of tokenistic responses to crises, like Black Lives Matter, or the differential impact of Covid-19. Too often universities' responses to anti-racist work are seen to be performances (Ahmed 2012). In this, Ahmed (2009, 45) argues that 'Diversity work becomes about changing perceptions of whiteness rather than changing the whiteness of organizations. Doing well, or a good performance, would then be about being perceived as a diverse organization.'

Here, it is not simply the size and complexity of the University as an organisation, which dissipates radical or transformation re-energy. Rather, the material history of cultures and structures creates its own inertia, as 'the legacy of Eurocentrism' (Bhambra, Gebrial, and Nisancioglu 2018, 239) In Decolonising DMU, staff and student responses connect with these legacies through a focus upon authentic relationships, which develop personal connections and enable self-actualisation. Again, it is important to reflect upon the fact that for some communities, a feeling of underrepresentation in institutional spaces remains a live concern, stripping away the content of institutional EDI practices.

Moreover, this tends to be reinforced through practices that replicate white fragility, in their constant demands for demonstrable proof, truth or evidence before any action can be taken. As a result, continuity tends to trump change in anti-racist work, in spite of structural, differential attainment, employability and earnings outcomes. This is a reminder that in spite of legislative trends, there is much historical and material inertia, predicated upon institutional brands, risk management, performance management, and social and intellectual capital (Bhopal and Pitkin 2020).

As a result, there is a need to confront practices that reinforce: fragility and denial; the co-option or sanitisation of lived experiences; the disengagement of those already undertaking anti-racist work; and, the risk-management of perceived reputational damage. Building the anti-racist University, predicated upon practices of dignity, demand a courageous focus upon authentic learning, teaching, research, public engagement and professional services. This brings us back to the idea that decolonising the idea of the University is a movement of dignity, shaped by equality.

Decolonising the idea and practice of the University

The structures that tend to dissipate radical energy, the cultures that reproduce hegemonic norms of whiteness, and practices that reinforce inertia, point towards deep problems that exist in the delivery of change projects. There can be a tendency to see decolonising as EDI-related work, to be managed by local experts who are expected to do the thinking, develop the project plans, and deliver organisational compliance. Where institutions have a focus upon organisational development, change can be subsumed within project and programme management methodologies, which reduce complex social problems to risk-management. However, such methodologies might offer an opportunity to situate the yearning for change against an established framework that brings it into dialogue with other institutional priorities.

In the face of refusal, denial and inertia, there are additional risks in reducing the human experience of the University to a project or programme that can be institutionally mandated and managed. These connect to the depth of institutional buy-in, and whether responsibility for outcomes and impact remains embedded in the project team or the organisation. Significant issues arise where the institutional status of projects fails to centre groups traditionally made marginal, ignores those with expertise, or threatens those with privilege. Here, one ongoing matter arising for Decolonising DMU is its ability to bring grassroots, horizontal activity into dialogue with structural and strategic governance and regulation.

In this, the language of this work, and opening-out the structures, cultures and practices of the institution around communication is crucial, in relation to the staff–student experience, learning, teaching, professional services, research, and community engagement. There is no purity in terms of language and modes of communication. Rather, a willingness to treat dialogue with dignity and always-emergent, reflects the need for authentic relationships demanded by students through Freedom to Achieve. Yet, having working positions and aims that are *both* open to critical dialogue *and* always provisional, is difficult for organisations that demand evidential certainty, and inside cultures that claim objectivity and inclusivity.

Decolonising DMU is working on this balance between demands for ongoing performance data, and the needs of its communities for authentic, longitudinal dialogue. This raises deep institutional questions around trust and honesty, in relation to reported metrics and the methodologies upon which they are based. This conditions how institutions address issues of microaggressions, double consciousness, racial battle fatigue, and behavioural code switching (Meghji 2019). These issues reflect the embodied and psychological trauma of ongoing, racial inequalities experienced differentially.

It should be noted that for project teams, tackling these concerns is emotionally laborious and dents resilience. Whilst there is limited conflict within the Decolonising DMU team, tensions have existed over the balance between evaluation and the need for action, in particular where painful lived experiences are revealed. Crucially, such revelations offer white, project partners the opportunity to witness these impacts at first-hand, and negotiate what is to be done holistically. For instance, in terms of behavioural code switching, this work can highlight how whiteness and demands for assimilation inside established forms, codes, cultures and practices, is debilitating for some staff and students. This enables allies to work against white fragility and privilege, and to model openness, transparency and confidence, and further develop pluralistic, authentic relationships.

One crucial issue is how institutions use projects of decolonising to move from resistance to resonance. This matters because such projects can tend to be divisive, catalysing: first, cynicism or denial; second, demands to subsume intersectional analyses under class; and third, to claim colourblindness. Might students and staff who hold such positions be engaged in dialogues, as a movement of dignity that develops authentic relationships inside and outside the University? Or, is there a need for a moral economy inside the University, through which such views might be enabled in relation to academic freedom, but from which the institution disengages? In developing a moral economy, projects might usefully focus upon the legitimising notions for communal action, in terms of rights, obligations and customs that reflect 'the wider consensus of the community' (Thompson 1971, 78).

Rather than an institutionally defensive posture, building the anti-racist University demands a communal, qualitative shift, and allyship (Johnson and Joseph-Salisbury 2018). Beyond pledging allegiance, role models must be seen to act, both inside and outside the classroom, student service, library, laboratory, executive board, governing body, and so on. This also relates to community engagement, including: partnership with the University's Societal Impact and Engagement Directorate on its post-pandemic #buildbackbetter project with Leicester City Council; and, work with research centres and institutes on decolonising theory, methodology, and impact. The challenge is to ensure that experiencing the institution as a 'space invader' (Puwar 2004) becomes the exception, rather than the rule for Black/of colour communities. This shapes the value of activities like decolonising the reading list, developing a content analysis of quality assurance documentation, and holding workshops with governors, as obligations to refuse performative or tokenistic approaches.

One final, crucial point is the need for decolonising projects to disaggregate and make plural the staff and student experience at the University. For instance, there are differential outcomes for African students and Pakistani students, compared to Indian and Chinese students. There are complex disparities between home and international students. How do institutions approach these data and the identities, histories and narratives that underpin them, in ways that are sensitive, and with interventions that do not reinforce deficit models and unconscious biases? Is it possible to use an engagement with a disaggregated, differential and authentic set of experiences to challenge the homogeneity of the institution, which is framed around issues of personalisation inside a reductionist student experience?

This demands tangible participation in decolonising, including: partnerships that build communities of practice; the role of student ambassadors and societies; the community engagement of practice-based researchers; difficult conversations about transnational education; explicit connections to education for sustainable development and decarbonising. Rather than focusing upon the separations between different individuals, is it possible to centre decolonising by reproducing structures, cultures and practices around the unity and connection of that difference? The humanity of the institution emerges from the dignity of those differences, and the common characteristic that ties individuals together is that they are all unique. This is the ongoing challenge for our work, which takes decolonising as a humane, critical pedagogic practice at the level of the institution.

Notes

1. Throughout, Black is capitalised to reflect a communal sense of identity with a specific set of political, social, cultural and aesthetic characteristics. This is reinforced by writers of colour and Black writers who stress the importance of self-identification and reclamation. In this way, Black mirrors the capitalisation of, for instance, *Asian*, *South Asian* and *Indigenous*. We do not capitalise white precisely because this risks legitimising the white privilege that our work seeks to abolish. Moreover, whilst whiteness operates as a terrain of power, it lacks modes of political, social, cultural and aesthetic cohesion beyond its political economy.
2. In developing this research, ethical approval was gained for a wider set of surveys and co-creation events, governed by the DMU, Faculty of Health and Life Sciences Research Ethics Committee.

Disclosure statement

No potential conflict of interest was reported by the author(s).

Data availability statement

The data associated with the paper are analysed at: Ansley, L. 2018. *Freedom to Achieve: Project Evaluation Report*. Leicester: De Montfort University. http://hdl.handle.net/2086/16793

ORCID

Richard Hall ⬤ http://orcid.org/0000-0002-1217-5102
Ben Whitham ⬤ http://orcid.org/0000-0001-8494-3257

References

Advance HE. 2019. *Equality in Higher Education: Statistical Report 2019*. Advance HE. Accessed 19 March 2021. https://www.advance-he.ac.uk/knowledge-hub/equality-higher-education-statistical-report-2019.

Advance HE. n.d. *Race Equality Charter*. Advance HE. Accessed 19 March 2021. https://www.advance-he.ac.uk/equality-charters/race-equality-charter.

Ahmed, S. 2004. *The Non-Performativity of Anti-Racism*. University of Kent. Accessed 19 March 2021. https://www.kent.ac.uk/clgs/documents/pdfs/Ahmed_sarah_clgscolloq25-09-04.pdf.

Ahmed, S. 2009. "Embodying Diversity: Problems and Paradoxes for Black Feminists." *Race Ethnicity and Education* 12 (1): 41–52. doi:10.1080/13613320802650931.

Ahmed, S. 2012. *On Being Included: Racism and Diversity in Institutional Life*. Durham, NC: Duke University Press.

Ahmed, S. 2017. *Living a Feminist Life*. Durham, NC: Duke University Press.

American Economics' Association. 2020. "Statement from the AEA Executive Committee." Accessed 19 March 2021. https://www.aeaweb.org/news/member-announcements-june-5-2020.

Andreotti, V., S. Stein, C. Ahenakew, and D. Hunt. 2015. "Mapping Interpretations of Decolonization in the Context of Higher Education." *Decolonization: Indigeneity, Education & Society* 4 (1): 21–40.

Ansley, L. 2018. *Freedom to Achieve: Project Evaluation Report*. Leicester: De Montfort University. Accessed 19 March 2021. http://hdl.handle.net/2086/16793.

Ansley, L. and R. Hall. 2019. "Freedom to Achieve: Addressing the Attainment Gap Through Student and Staff Co-Creation." *Compass: Journal of Learning and Teaching* 12 (1). doi:10.21100/compass.v12i1.946.

Arday, J., D. Z. Belluigi, and D. Thomas. 2020. "Attempting to Break the Chain: Reimaging Inclusive Pedagogy and Decolonising the Curriculum Within the Academy." *Educational Philosophy and Theory* 53 (3): 298–313. doi:10.1080/00131857.2020.1773257.

Bhambra, G. K., D. Gebrial, and K. Nisancioglu. 2018. *Decolonising the University: Understanding and Transforming the Universities' Colonial Foundations*. London: Pluto Press.

Bhopal, K., and C. Pitkin. 2020. "'Same Old Story, Just a Different Policy': Race and Policy Making in Higher Education in the UK." *Race Ethnicity and Education* 23 (4): 530–547. doi:10.1080/13613324.2020.1718082.

Birch, K., M. Chiappetta, and A. Artyushina. 2020. "The Problem of Innovation in Technoscientific Capitalism: Data Rentiership and the Policy Implications of Turning Personal Digital Data into a Private Asset." *Policy Studies* 41 (5): 468–487. doi:10.1080/01442872.2020.1748264.

Blundell, R., M. Costa Dias, R. Joyce, R. and, and X. Xu. 2020. *Covid-19 and Inequalities*. London: Institute for Fiscal Studies. Accessed 19 March 2021. https://www.ifs.org.uk/inequality/wp-content/uploads/2020/06/Covid-19-and-inequalities-IFS-1.pdf.

Curran, J., I. Gaber, and J. Petley. 2019. *Culture Wars: The Media and the British Left*. London: Routledge.

Decolonising DMU. 2021a. *Decolonising DMU*. De Montfort University. Accessed 19 March 2021. https://decolonisingdmu.our.dmu.ac.uk/.

Decolonising DMU. 2021b. *Decolonising DMU: A Working Position*. De Montfort University. Accessed 19 March 2021. https://decolonisingdmu.our.dmu.ac.uk/wp-content/uploads/sites/12/2020/01/Decolonising_DMU_position.20.01.20.pdf.

Dobinson, T., and P. Mercieca. 2020. "Seeing Things as They Are, Not Just as We Are: Investigating Linguistic Racism on an Australian University Campus." *International Journal of Bilingual Education and Bilingualism* 23 (7): 789–803. doi:10.1080/13670050.2020.1724074.

ECU. 2015. *Equality in Higher Education: Statistical Report 2015. Part 2: Students*. London: ECU.

EHRC. 2019. *Tackling Racial harassment: Universities Challenged*. London: EHRC. Accessed 19 March 2021. https://www.equalityhumanrights.com/sites/default/files/tackling-racial-harassment-universities-challenged.pdf.

Erickson, M., P. Hanna, and C. Walker. 2020. "The UK Higher Education Senior Management Survey: A Statactivist Response to Managerialist Governance." *Studies in Higher Education*. doi:10.1080/03075079.2020.1712693.

French, K. B., A. Sanchez, A., and E. Ullom. 2020. "Composting Settler Colonial Distortions: Cultivating Critical Land-Based Family History." *Genealogy* 4 (3): 84. doi:10.3390/genealogy4030084.

Gabriel, D., and S. A. Tate. 2017. *Inside the Ivory Tower: Narratives of Women of Colour Surviving and Thriving in British Academia*. Stoke-on-Trent: Trentham Books.

Garba, T., and S.-M. Sorentino. 2020. "Slavery is a Metaphor: A Critical Commentary on Eve Tuck and K. Wayne Yang's 'Decolonization is Not a Metaphor'." *Antipode: A Radical Journal of Geography* 52 (3): 764–782. doi:10.1111/anti.12615.

Gebrial, D. 2018. "Rhodes Must Fall: Oxford and Movements for Change." In *Decolonising the University: Understanding and Transforming the Universities' Colonial Foundations*, edited by G. K. Bhambra, D. Gebrial, and K. Nisancioglu, 19–36. London: Pluto Press.

Glasener, K. M., C. A. Martell, and J. R. Posselt. 2019. "Framing Diversity: Examining the Place of Race in Institutional Policy and Practice Post-Affirmative Action." *Journal of Diversity in Higher Education* 12 (1): 3–16. doi:10.1037/dhe0000086.

Hall, R. 2018. *The Alienated Academic: The Struggle for Autonomy Inside the University*. London: Palgrave Macmillan.

Hall, R. 2020. "The Hopeless University: Intellectual Work at the End of the End of History." *Postdigital Science and Education* 2: 830–848. Accessed 19 March 2021. doi:10.1007/s42438-020-00158-9.

Harper, S. R. 2020. "COVID-19 and the Racial Equity Implications of Reopening College and University Campuses". *American Journal of Education* 127 (1): 153–162. doi:10.1086/711095.

Heleta, S. 2016. "Decolonisation of Higher Education: Dismantling Epistemic Violence and Eurocentrism in South Africa." *Transformation in Higher Education* 1: 1. doi:10.4102/the.v1i1.9.

Hoofd, I. M. 2017. *Higher Education and Technological Acceleration: The Disintegration of University Teaching and Research*. London: Palgrave Macmillan.

hooks, b. 1982. *Ain't I a Woman?* London: Pluto Press.

hooks, b. 1994. *Outlaw Culture: Resisting Representations*. Abingdon: Routledge.

hooks, b. 2000. *Feminist Theory: From Margin to Center*. 2nd ed. London: Pluto Press.

Icaza, R., and V. Rolando. 2018. "Diversity or Decolonisation? Researching Diversity at the University of Amsterdam." In *Decolonising the University: Understanding and Transforming the Universities' Colonial Foundations*, edited by G. K. Bhambra, D. Gebrial, and K. Nisancioglu, 64–92. London: Pluto Press.

Inge, S. 2020. "UKRI in Row Over Absence of Black PIs in Its Covid-19 BAME Grant." *Research Professional*, August 7. Accessed 19 March 2021. https://www.researchprofessionalnews.com/rr-news-uk-research-councils-2020-8-ukri-in-row-over-absence-of-Black-pis-in-its-covid-19-bame-grant/.

Johnson, A. 2020. "Throwing Our Bodies Against the White Background of Academia." *Area* 52 (1): 89–96. doi:10.1111/area.12568.

Johnson, A., and R. Joseph-Salisbury. 2018. "'Are You Supposed to Be in Here?' Racial Microaggressions and Knowledge Production in Higher Education: Racism, Whiteness and

Decolonising the Academy." In *Dismantling Race in Higher Education: Racism, Whiteness and Decolonising the Academy*, edited by J. Arday and H. S. Mirza, 143–160. London: Routledge.

Kam, B., H. Mendoza, and A. Masuda. 2018. "Mental Health Help-Seeking Experience and Attitudes in Latina/o American, Asian American, Black American, and White American College Students." *International Journal for the Advancement of Counselling* 41 (4): 492–508. doi:10.1007/s10447-018-9365-8.

Kayali, L., and M. A. Walters. 2021. "Responding to Hate Incidents on University Campuses: Benefits and Barriers to Establishing a Restorative Justice Programme." *Contemporary Justice Review* 24: 64–84. doi:10.1080/10282580.2020.1762492.

Leading Routes. 2020. "The Broken Pipeline – Barriers to Black PhD Students Accessing Research Council Funding." Accessed 19 March 2021. https://leadingroutes.org/the-broken-pipeline.

Maldonado-Torres, N. 2017. "The Decolonial Turn." In *New Approaches to Latin American Studies: Culture and Power*, edited by J. Poblete, 111–127. London: Routledge.

McDuff, N., K. Patel, J. Evans, P. Williams, C. Couper, H. Barefoot, and P. Gravestock. 2020. *Use of a Value Added Metric and an Inclusive Curriculum Framework to Address the Black and Minority Ethnic Attainment Gap*. London: Office for Students. Accessed 19 March 2021. https://www.officeforstudents.org.uk/media/c8484f11-ef3f-4c59-9fdb-f9c201b54205/abss-final-project-report-kingston-university.pdf.

McGettigan, A. 2015. "The Treasury View of HE: Variable Human Capital Investment." *Political Economy Research Centre Papers Series 6*. Accessed 19 March 2021. http://www.perc.org.uk/perc/wp-content/uploads/2015/04/PERC-6-McGettigan-and-HE-and-Human-Capital-FINAL-1.pdf.

Meghji, A. 2019. *Black Middle Class Britannia: Identities, Repertoires, Cultural Consumption*. Manchester: Manchester University Press.

Meyerhoff, E. 2019. *Beyond Education: Radical Studying for Another World*. Minneapolis: University of Minnesota Press.

Moosavi, L. 2020. "The Decolonial Bandwagon and the Dangers of Intellectual Decolonisation." *International Review of Sociology* 30 (2): 332–354. doi:10.1080/03906701.2020.1776919.

Morrissey, J. 2015. "Regimes of Performance: Practices of the Normalised Self in the Neoliberal University." *British Journal of Sociology of Education* 36 (4): 614–634. doi:10.1080/01425692.2013.838515.

Murphy, E. 2020. *Arms in Academia: The Political Economy of the Modern UK Defence Industry*. London: Routledge.

Neary, M. 2020. *Student as Producer: How do Revolutionary Teachers Teach?* London: Zero Books.

Nyamnjoh, F. B. 2019. "Decolonizing the University in Africa." *Oxford Research Encyclopedia in Politics*. Accessed 19 March 2021. https://oxfordre.com/politics/view/10.1093/acrefore/9780190228637.001.0001/acrefore-9780190228637-e-717.

Particles for Justice. 2021. "Strike for Black Lives." Accessed 19 March 2021. https://www.particlesforjustice.org/.

Pierce, C. M., J. V. Carew, D. Pierce-Gonzalez, and D. Wills. 1977. "An Experiment in Racism: TV Commercials." *Education and Urban Society* 10 (1): 61–87.

Pimblott, K. 2019. "Decolonising the University: The Origins and Meaning of a Movement." *Political Quarterly* 91 (1): 210–216. doi:10.1111/1467-923X.12784.

Puwar, N. 2004. *Space Invaders: Race, Gender and Bodies Out of Place*. London: Bloomsbury.

Rollock, N. 2019. *Staying Power: The Career Experiences and Strategies of UK Black Female Professors*. London: Universities and Colleges Union. Accessed 19 March 2021. https://www.ucu.org.uk/media/10075/Staying-Power/pdf/UCU_Rollock_February_2019.pdf.

Santos, B. de Sousa. 2017. *Decolonising the University: The Challenge of Deep Cognitive Justice*. Cambridge: Cambridge Scholars Publishing.

Smith, W. 2008. "Higher Education: Racial Battle Fatigue." In *Encyclopedia of Race, Ethnicity, and Society*, edited by R. T. Schaefer, 615–618. London: Sage.

Stein S., and V. O. de Andreotti. 2016. "Decolonization and Higher Education". In *Encyclopedia of Educational Philosophy and Theory*, edited by M. Peters, 1–6. Singapore: Springer. doi:10.1007/978-981-287-532-7_479-1

Sue, D. W., C. M. Capodilupo, G. C. Torino, J. M. Bucceri, A. M. B. Holder, K. L. Nadal, and M. Esquilin. 2007. "Racial Microaggressions in Everyday Life: Implications for Clinical Practice." *American Psychologist* 62 (4): 271–286.

Tannock, S. 2018. "Educational Equality and International Students." *Journal of International Students* 9 (4): 1191–1195. doi:10.32674/jis.v0i0.618.

Thompson, E. P. 1971. "The Moral Economy of the English Crowd in the Eighteenth Century." *Past & Present* 50: 76–136.

Tuck, E., and W. Yang. 2012. "Decolonization is Not a Metaphor." *Decolonization: Indigeneity, Education & Society* 1: 1–40. Accessed 19 March 2021. https://jps.library.utoronto.ca/index.php/des/article/view/18630.

Tuhiwai Smith, L., E. Tuck, and K. W. Yang. 2018. *Indigenous and Decolonizing Studies in Education: Mapping the Long View*. London: Routledge.

University of Bath Press Release. 2020. *New Project Investigates Indigenous People's Experiences of Higher Education Across Latin America*. University of Bath. Accessed 19 March 2021. https://www.bath.ac.uk/announcements/new-project-investigates-indigenous-peoples-experiences-of-higher-education-across-latin-america/.

University of Edinburgh. 2020. *Effects of Microaggressions*. University of Edinburgh. Accessed 19 March 2021. https://www.ed.ac.uk/equality-diversity/students/microaggressions/effects-of-microaggressions.

University of Liverpool. 2020. *Tackling Racial Harassment: Universities Challenged: A University of Liverpool Response*. University of Liverpool. Accessed 19 March 2021. https://www.liverpool.ac.uk/media/a4-equality-and-human-rights-commission-2110.pdf.

University of Sheffield. 2020. *University of Sheffield Recruits Race Equality Champions to Help Students Understand Microaggressions*. University of Sheffield. Accessed 19 March 2021. https://www.sheffield.ac.uk/news/nr/race-equality-champions-help-students-challenge-microaggressions-1.878374.

UUK. 2020. *Tackling Racial Harassment in Higher Education*. London: UUK. Accessed 19 March 2021. https://www.universitiesuk.ac.uk/policy-and-analysis/reports/Documents/2020/tackling-racial-harassment-in-higher-education.pdf.

UUK and NUS. 2019. *Black, Asian and Minority Ethnic Student Attainment at UK Universities: #Closingthegap*. London: UUK. Accessed 19 March 2021. https://www.universitiesuk.ac.uk/policy-and-analysis/reports/Documents/2019/bame-student-attainment-uk-universities-closing-the-gap.pdf.

Walter, M. and M. Guerzoni. 2020. "How a University Can Embed Indigenous Knowledge into the Curriculum and Why It Matters." *The Conversation*, October 15. Accessed 19 March 2021. https://theconversation.com/how-a-university-can-embed-indigenous-knowledge-into-the-curriculum-and-why-it-matters-147456.

OPEN ACCESS

From silence to 'strategic advancement': institutional responses to 'decolonising' in higher education in England

Farzana Shain, Ümit Kemal Yıldız, Veronica Poku and Bulent Gokay

ABSTRACT
Amid the rising calls for a 'decolonised curriculum', scholars and activists have outlined what needs to be done to 'decolonise the university'. Yet in practice, those involved in decolonising work often face considerable backlash and institutional resistance. Drawing on empirical research with students and staff across nine universities in England, this paper sets out to capture the contested terrain of 'decolonising the university'. We draw on qualitative accounts, collected through in-depth interviews with 24 individuals who are engaged in individual and/or group-based decolonial efforts, at discipline/departmental/institutional level to achieve change in their universities. We conceptualise and explore institutional responses to 'decolonising' through three strategies: rejection, reluctant acceptance, and strategic advancement. Presenting a snapshot of decolonising work in England over the period 2014–2021, our findings raise questions about what needs to be done to counter institutional co-option, incorporation, and the dilution of the radical message of decolonising.

Introduction

Global calls to 'decolonise' education have risen significantly in recent years, becoming more pronounced in the aftermath of the Black Lives Matters (BLM) protests following the racist police killing in Minneapolis of George Floyd in May 2020. Since then, universities in the UK[1] and elsewhere have rushed out public statements in which they have made commitments to 'anti-racism' and 'decolonising the curriculum'. Some of these universities have faced backlash for their performative gestures at this time having hitherto done little to respond to decolonising agendas while also failing to effectively address persistent racialised inequalities. Drawing on interviews with students and staff in England, this paper aims to capture the contested terrain of 'decolonising the university'. While scholars argue that '[d]ecolonising involves a multitude of definitions, interpretations, aims and strategies' (Bhambra, Nisancioglu, and Gebrial 2018, 2), within and across a number of universities in the UK, as elsewhere in the colonial metropoles and former colonies, a series of mostly student-led campaigns have drawn attention

---

This is an Open Access article distributed under the terms of the Creative Commons Attribution License (http://creativecommons.org/licenses/by/4.0/), which permits unrestricted use, distribution, and reproduction in any medium, provided the original work is properly cited.

to the Eurocentrism[2] at the heart of Western education systems. Campaigns such as Rhodes Must Fall (RMF) (Cape Town) and RMF (Oxford) have exposed the legacies of empire, colonialism and slavery that reinforce the institutions, their disciplines, policies, curriculum and practices. Calling for the colonial structures of higher education to be dismantled, the campaigns highlight how Western education was, and is still, a key site through which colonialism, and colonial knowledge, is produced, institutionalised and naturalised (Takayama, Sriprakash, and Connell 2016).

Amid the rising calls for a 'decolonised curriculum', scholars and activists have outlined what needs to be done to 'decolonise the university'. Yet in practice, those involved in decolonising work continue to face considerable backlash and institutional resistance (Chantiluke, Kwoba, and Nkopo 2018). We set out to exemplify this institutional resistance as part of our analysis of decolonial efforts within and across university projects. The empirical site for our research is England, where a number of universities make progressive claims about 'decolonising the university'. We draw on qualitative accounts, collected through in-depth interviews with 24 individuals who describe themselves as being involved in 'decolonising work'– that is, they are engaged in individual and group-based decolonising efforts, at discipline, departmental or institutional level to bring about change in their universities. Our analysis builds on the growing body of literature that charts interpretations and practices of decolonisation alongside institutional responses (Ahmed 2012; Battiste 2013; Stein and Andreotti 2016; Gaudry and Lorenz 2018; Blake 2019). As we later discuss, these studies highlight the tensions and contradictions inherent in attempting to decolonise spaces that were customised to advance colonisation and racialisation. While much of the above-mentioned literature is based on discursive analysis, our paper contributes new empirical insights into how decolonising is being defined by student and staff activists as well as universities' senior managers. Drawing on Bell (1980) we highlight the circumstances in which universities have embraced and/or resisted 'decolonising' in England.

The paper is structured as follows: we first explore what it means to decolonise in the contemporary moment when a wave of campus-based activism has re-opened questions about the transformational possibilities of institutions that are steeped in Eurocentrism and coloniality; we then briefly outline the contextual factors that form the backdrop for UK-based decolonising work; following an overview of our research design, we discuss how decolonising is being framed, interpreted, contested and claimed and the measures that have been used to progress or hinder decolonising work agendas. We conceptualise and explore institutional responses through three strategies: strategic rejection, reluctant acceptance, and strategic advancement of 'decolonising' and consider some issues for the future direction of decolonising work in England.

We argue that strategic advancement of 'decolonising' by some university managements is being pursued as universities face pressures to recruit and retain students in the context of economic downturn and the post-Brexit period and as the UK emerges from the Covid pandemic. However, strategic advancement of 'decolonising' can also contribute to an institutional taming or a dilution of the discourse, especially when top-down initiatives and strategies are pursued while leaving intact the structures and processes that perpetuate coloniality. Presenting a snapshot of the contested terrain of decolonising work within and across universities in England over the period 2014–

2021, our analysis poses questions about what needs to be done to counter institutional co-option, incorporation, and the dilution of the radical message of decolonising.

What does it mean to 'decolonise education'?

Postcolonial analyses highlight that while powerful nations may have vacated their former geographical colonies in Africa and Asia, 'they retained them not only as markets but as locales on the ideological map over which they continued to rule morally and intellectually' (Said 1993, 25). Coloniality, a term coined by Quijano (2000) refers to this ongoing logic of domination underlying imperial conquests (in the Americas as well as Asia and Africa) and Eurocentrism in shaping the knowledge and culture of institutions including higher education long after decolonisation or the dismantling of colonial administrations. Following Mignolo (2011), we understand decoloniality as an epistemic, political and pedagogical project that seeks to understand and disrupt coloniality.

Since 2015, campus-based activist projects have drawn attention to the coloniality of higher education. RMF at Cape Town University in South Africa provided a catalyst for the wave of student movements calling on their universities to 'decolonise the curriculum'. In the UK, student-led movements emerged prior to the 2015 RMF movements, taking inspiration from campaigns such as #iTooAmHarvard[3] – a campaign started by Harvard student Carol Powell in March 2014 which, in turn, drew on the long history of struggle by African Americans to achieve equality in American higher education via the campuses of Historically Black Colleges and Universities (Blissett, Baker, and Fields 2020). In 2014, students at University College London (UCL) produced a 20-minute video asking, 'Why Is My Curriculum White?' as they took aim at the 'Whiteness' and Eurocentric domination that has obscured the impact of slavery and colonialism at British universities (El Magd 2016). It galvanised the support of the National Union of Students (NUS) with launches at Warwick and LSE in 2015, Bristol, Birmingham and Manchester in 2016, and an online presence at many more universities. Along with another high-profile NUS campaign, 'Liberate My Degree', these projects generated a national debate about the need to 'decolonise the university'.

In contrast to the NUS-supported and largely student officer-initiated campaigns, some of the more recent student campaigns have met with a lack of support and sometimes opposition from their own students' union. For example, in November 2019, a group of students at Warwick University ended a 30-day occupation of their students' union building in protest at the 'Union's failure to adequately combat racism and structural oppression, and the wider legacies of colonialism at Warwick University' (Warwick Occupy 2019). In July 2019, another group of predominantly Black and racially minoritised students ended a 137-day long occupation of the grade-II listed Deptford Town Hall building in southeast London. Goldsmiths Anti-Racist Action (GARA) was formed following high-profile racist incidents that occurred as part of the students' union elections process which the occupiers argued were left unchallenged within the university. Despite GARA winning landmark concessions from the University including mandatory anti-racist training for all staff and the reinstatement of scholarships for Palestinian students (GARA 2019) many of the agreed changes had not been implemented a year later. For us, these delays, and the lack of support from student bodies signal the sustained effort needed to transform institutions that are so steeped in colonial legacies. They also highlight that concessions are often made not because universities agree with the need for change but to diffuse the impending threat or reputational damage or in other words, because of 'interest convergence' (Bell 1980).

The theory of interest convergence originates in the work of Critical Race Theory scholar, Derrick Bell (1980), who argued that Black people achieved civil rights victories only when White and Black interests converged. Bell argued that the 1954 decision in which the Supreme Court outlawed segregation in public schools in America did not happen because the US wanted to take a moral stance against racism but for reputational reasons. Many in the US administrations linked progress on civil rights to success in America's struggle against Soviet communism during the Cold War in the competition of influencing nations in Africa and Asia. The threat of domestic upheaval was also a factor in the decision. Once the interests diverged, the enforcement of civil rights was curtailed.

Although applied in a different time and space, Bell's theory is helpful for analysing institutional claims and strategies focused on decolonising in England. We draw on 'interest convergence' to ask whether institutional claims made in 2020 reflect genuine advancement of decolonising work or the short-lived victories that Bell referred to when talking about desegregation moves by the US government in the 1960s (Bell 1980). Working with this lens means that our focus cannot be the motivations of individual senior managers. Rather, we draw on the principle of interest convergence to highlight the structural pressures and circumstances that converge at a particular historical movement to underpin a strategic advancement of decolonising by some universities. We next sketch out some of these structural pressures and drivers, also highlighting the persistence of racialised inequalities that have driven students to demand the decolonisation of their universities.

Contextualising decolonising claims of universities in England

Decolonise movements are shaped in each locale both by histories of anti-colonial struggles and by the conditions facing racialised groups in the contemporary moment. In the UK, a new generation of student activism has emerged amid a climate of increasing scrutiny and surveillance of Black and Minority Ethnic (BME) students in universities. This has taken place in the context of more than a decade of austerity and rising nationalism and populism, especially in the run-up to, and aftermath of, the Brexit referendum in 2016 (Virdee and McGeever 2018). The Covid-19 pandemic and 2020 BLM protests have also exposed the depth and persistence of racialised inequalities in wider society and within higher education. Despite rising numbers of BME students applying to and attending UK universities over the last 30 years, they remain less likely to secure places in elite institutions; BME students also continue to achieve lower outcomes, on average, than White students with similar entry grades (Boliver 2013; Noden, Shiner, and Modood 2014).

This picture of structural and systemic disadvantage has been compounded by the hostile environment created by immigration and counter-terror policies in a post-9/11 context. As well as the over-policing, continued surveillance, and racial profiling of BME students through the auspices of Prevent arm of the UK government's counterterrorism strategy (Shain 2011; Miah 2017), in the aftermath of Britain's EU referendum and the rising tide of nationalism, targeted racial harassment on campuses has also increased (Housee 2018).

'Bottom-up' pressure from the student-led decolonising campaigns has been accompanied by a series of national reports providing statistical and empirical evidence of the persistence of racialised inequalities (NUS 2011; EHRC 2019; UUK 2020). However, universities also face intense pressure due to shifting higher education markets globally and changes in the way that UK higher education is funded. With the tripling of tuition fees over the last decade, universities have become more reliant on student fees and loans for their income. Most providers received less than 15% of their income as grant funding in 2015 (Department for Business Innovation and Skills 2016) leaving universities to scramble for student income amid a series of complex rules and regulations including on–off caps on student numbers.

We understand these pressures on higher education as stemming from the economic conditions associated with the 2007–2008 global financial crisis and the continuing economic downturn. The UK has a long-standing comparative advantage in providing education to international students based on the importance of English in the global economy and the high-quality courses its universities offered. It has the second-largest group of international students in the world, after the US, in the number of foreign students it educates, approximately 20% of its entire university student body. There is a risk, however, that the UK will soon be overtaken by Australia. New threats amid the UK's withdrawal from the EU, together with the introduction of harsher visa regulations pose further complications for the UK higher education sector. Although international student numbers have risen in recent years, the UK's overall market share has fallen, and competitor countries are more active in recruitment (Migration Advisory Committee 2018). The rise of the Global East in reshaping global higher education and increasing competition for international students is also worth mentioning here. In the past 30 years, there has been a rapid expansion of 'world-class universities' in Asia. Among the world's top five countries for outbound international students, four are in Asia: China, India, Vietnam and South Korea. While Western countries still attract the most incoming international students, some Asian countries are emerging as regional education hubs (Xu 2021).

These factors and pressures form an important context for our analysis because they provide a backdrop for universities' developing responses to demands for decolonising the curriculum. As we later highlight, universities have responded in a range of ways to student demands for decolonising, but a notable shift occurred from 2020 with universities more readily embracing the language of decolonisation and anti-racism with some moves towards 'mainstreaming' decolonising work – the introduction of top-down senior manager-led initiatives for 'decolonising the curriculum' that are designed to be embedded within institutional processes. We contend that this shift towards 'mainstreaming' can be read through the lens of 'interest convergence' (Bell 1980) as universities face pressures around recruitment in the context of economic downturn and the post-Brexit period. Decolonising work has therefore become strategically important for universities. As they compete for more students, in particular international students from the Global South, they must demonstrate their commitment to university-wide change towards eliminating racialised inequalities. Before presenting our data, we briefly consider some of the literature that has explored institutional responses and the possibilities for decolonising.

Possibilities for institutional transformation

We earlier mentioned the lack of agreement over how decolonising is to be conceptualised and the methods needed to achieve it. This raises questions about the possibilities for 'decolonising'; it also leaves the way open for universities to label as 'decolonising' a range of activities from diversifying reading lists to introducing special modules about decolonisation and/or employing a few more Black staff while leaving intact structures and processes that perpetuate coloniality. Blake argues that this type of inclusion without attention to the histories and structures of oppression justifies the organised abandonment of underrepresented communities (Blake 2019, 309). Battiste (2013) also describes this as an 'add and stir approach', where content about the Global South is added to existing curricular without providing the proper cultural and historical context.

Academics, including Stein and Andreotti (2016, 4), argue that within institutional responses, 'inclusion' is often framed as a benevolent gift, with racially minoritised staff 'expected to perform their gratitude and refrain from further dissent'. Those advancing more radical critiques or demands can be accused of being ungrateful. In this way, 'the boundaries of the institution and of acceptable modes of knowledge production and critique are still firmly policed by White (and capitalist) power structures' (Stein and Andreotti 2016). They argue that the majority of institutional actions around colonialism and race focus on 'inclusion' with little commitment to 'a redistribution of resources' (Stein and Andreotti 2016) so that scholarships and symbolic gestures (renaming buildings) may be offered in place of real structural change that may facilitate a transition to decolonial futures.

Gaudry and Lorenz (2018, 223), writing about the Canadian academy, also set out three possibilities for transformation from 'inclusion' to wholescale reform of institutions. However, they argue that institutions have only started the implementation of the least transformative vision of decolonising which they identify as 'indigenous inclusion'. Scholars, therefore, remain sceptical about the possibilities for decolonising because despite extensive academic critique, proposals and toolkits from scholar-activists, universities seem remarkably resistant to change even as they profess to 'decolonise' (Ahmed 2012; Almeida and Kumalo 2018; Begum and Saini 2019).

Building on the above literature we now present the findings from our research. In the following sections, we briefly explain our methodological approach before exploring how decolonising work is being interpreted and some of the measures that are used by university managements to advance or hinder the work in universities in England.

Research design and methodology

The paper draws on interviews with 24 individuals who are involved in decolonising work within universities in England. The sample includes those who have been part of institutional and/or discipline or unit-level decolonising networks within institutions. A third of our interviewees had been involved in decolonising work across more than one university. We, therefore, captured participants' perspectives across nine universities that were geographically spread across England. Of the 24 individuals interviewed, 8 are, or were, involved in decolonising work as students or student officers including one who was now employed within a professional services role, 11 were academic staff with 5 staff in professional services or managerial roles including 1 ex-student. The sample includes three senior managers, who were operating at dean or head of directorate level. In addition to a diversity of roles and responsibilities the sample was also mixed in terms of racial/ethnic identities with our participants identifying as follows: 4 as Black; a further 4 as Politically Black[4]; 4 as Asian; 2 as a 'Person of Colour'; 4 as 'Mixed'; 6 as White.

All four authors were involved in the collection and analysis of the data with the interviews being conducted between October 2020 and February 2021 during the second and third Covid-19 lockdowns in England. Given the national restrictions at this time, the interviews were conducted online and recorded digitally following ethical approval. All the authors have also been involved in decolonising work with two being founding members of a decolonising network in an English university. Although we collectively understand decolonising as a knowledge project which involves identifying colonial systems, structures and relationships, and working to challenge these both inside and outside the classroom, we did not offer a definition of the term in our interviews. Our aim was to capture the ways in which decolonising was being defined and operationalised within universities. In the next section, we present our findings focusing on the different meanings and interpretations of 'decolonising' for our participants and the institutional measures used by university managements to respond to student and staff-led decolonising work.

Shifting conceptions and contested ownership of decolonising work, 2015–2021

A key theme across the interviews centred on the contested meaning and ownership of 'decolonising' at this moment. In line with the existing academic literature (Tuck and Yang 2012; Bhambra, Nisancioglu, and Gebrial 2018), our research revealed multiple definitions and interpretations of decolonising in operation; this was the case even within the same decolonising groups. For Susi, decolonising work is, and should categorically be, a knowledge project:

> I think it should be about knowledges. I really do not want to see a decol movement degenerate into anti-racism and social injustices and all that. They are associated issues, but to me, decol is about knowledge, knowledge authorisation, legitimisation, construction. (Susi, Academic)

However, for others, the meaning of decolonising was not fixed. Ella, explained how her own understanding of decolonisation was constantly shifting.

> On this particular day … I will have one understanding of decolonisation that could be very different to next year or even yesterday, Right now, I'm really aware that decolonisation can be used in a metaphorical way, … universities can stake claim to doing decolonisation but … what they're really doing is diversifying, which is still good, but it's not decolonisation …. I understand decolonisation [as] …. serving justice, in some cases, reversal, in some cases undoing all the violence, subjugation, purposeful racialisation of human beings, their land, their cultures, their languages, their rights, for the purpose of White Western capitalism instead. (Ella, Academic)

In this case, decolonising is understood as a project which involves exposing and undoing the legacies of colonisation and racialisation. However, for Ella, the goals of this project are constantly being challenged by the evolvement of the discourse of decolonisation. Part of the battle involved preventing decolonisation from being superficially applied as a metaphor (Tuck and Yang 2012) for a range of goals and activities including diversifying reading lists. Here, Ella shared Susi's concerns about decolonising work being claimed for multiple causes. Alongside these notions, decolonisation was also defined by some as 'inclusion' or 'diversifying' and there were critiques of a 'let's market ourselves as a decolonised university' from a 'we are the university' perspective. To explain this, and to set the context for our later analysis, we briefly outline three overlapping phases of decolonisation work drawing from our participants' reflections on developments nationally in the UK from 2014 to 2021.

Student officer-initiated decolonising initiatives: 2014 onwards

We mentioned above the 2014–2016 decolonising campaigns which included the RMF campus-based, and NUS initiated multimedia campaigns such as 'Why Is My Curriculum White?' and 'Liberate My Degree'. Our participants, including Saira, confirmed that these were very much student-officer led:

> Our student union education officer was nothing short of amazing. [T]hey led the campaign 'Why Is My Curriculum White', and it was from that that I got involved and I've been doing that work since then. (Saira, Professional Services)

Among our sample, staff members had also been involved in these early campaigns including Catherine, the head of a professional services unit who led a successful institutional initiative focused on reading lists in her university, inspired by 'Liberate My Degree' and Dev and Helen who were both involved grassroots campaigns since 2016.

'We are the university': 2018 onwards

Overlapping with and building on this initial phase, a second wave of decolonising movements emerged around the University College Union (UCU) industrial action (over pensions) in February–March 2018 which provided a space for discussion of the role and purpose of the university (Collini 2017). Over two months, UCU members flooded social media taking aim at neoliberal policies and cultures that have become embedded within a marketised model of higher education since the 1990s leading to the widespread casualisation of the sector. Drawing on the slogan 'We are the university', staff critiqued various aspects of the neoliberal university. Decolonising featured in the many teach-outs delivered in this period. A key prompt for the focus had been the UCU Black Members-initiated 'Day of Action on Racism' in February 2018 which coincided with one of the strike days. Decolonising groups formed at this time were still predominantly student-led but less directed by student officers and some were staff-led.

'Mainstreaming' decolonising work: 2020 onwards

Our participants mentioned a third wave of 'decolonising' as distinctly different from the grassroots student and staff-led movements. While some university managements were already responding to calls to decolonise, in most cases, a top-down institution-led approach to 'decolonisation of the curriculum' was initiated only in the aftermath of the BLM protests in May 2020. Participants across four of our nine universities recognised their universities as mainstreaming decolonising work through developing such top-down institutional approaches. Alex, a senior manager at one of these universities outlines the aims of his own institution-led project:

> [C]ompared to others that I've observed, we're better at .... We've done more work and achieved more in terms of mainstreaming the work and getting pretty much everyone to have it on their radar ... I don't think there are many universities that've adopted the same kind of systematic approach that we're demanding ... I've written recently to every school, every director and asked them to write back to the Race Equality Group, detailing what specific areas ... they feel they've got the most opportunity to impact on positively. (Alex, Senior Manager)

Alex mentions his attempts to mainstream decolonising under the umbrella of race equality and takes pride in his university having 'done more work' and 'achieved more' than other universities. While Alex's university was gaining a reputation for advancing further and faster than others, some of our participants expressed concerns about potentially superficial tick-box approaches to decolonising within this mainstreaming. For Tara, such institution-led projects represented yet another neoliberal performance indicator that could be worn as a badge of achievement:

> There is a huge level of irony that there is an imposed way to decolonise from the top ... I think because the conversation, nationally, has moved to 'let's decolonise', it has also moved to 'let's tick this box'. ... and suddenly decolonise is a measurable thing according to senior management ... . (Tara, Student)

Alex and Tara's accounts reflect the tensions that arise from the neoliberal corporatisation of UK universities and decolonisation of knowledge projects. One of the issues here is that the neoliberal marketised model of higher education is presented ostensibly as a colour-blind project which is premised on western-centric notions of meritocracy (Bhambra, Nisancioglu, and Gebrial 2018). Within the neoliberal marketised structure of higher education, discussions about race and coloniality come to fore only when there is a business case for advancing them. Alex's comments about being 'better than' other universities imply market advantage and therefore as Tara notes, the discourse of decolonising is deployed as a performance indicator to be measured. This instrumental approach to decolonising was also reflected on by Dev.

> When George Floyd was murdered ... it started the global anti-racist movement ... . Our university, taking the heart of our success on things like [our decolonising publication], made a statement to say 'we've achieved a lot' and ... 'we are a very good, well-ahead, anti-racist university'. When they did that, I'm not using the word backlash, but what happened was people said, 'we don't accept what you've said'. (Dev, Academic)

In Dev's view, the university co-opted the work of the decolonise network in the midst of the BLM protests to make the case that it was, like Alex's university, 'well ahead' of other universities in terms of its commitment to anti-racism. Rather than being seen as a genuine commitment to anti-racism the university was exposed by students as opportunistically advancing decolonising work when under pressure to demonstrate its anti-racist credentials. An open letter from students forced the university in Dev's words, 'to eat humble pie' and to start a formal consultation exercise on how to address race inequalities institutionally. What Dev describes here is also an example of what we term 'reluctant acceptance' of decolonising work by his institution. Having failed to opportunistically pass off existing decolonial efforts as its own, Dev's university was forced by the student and staff response to formally engage with the work to demonstrate its commitment to antiracism. In the next section, we map out this 'reluctant acceptance' alongside other institutional strategies in relation to 'decolonising'.

Institutional responses to staff and student-led decolonising work

Here we explore the institutional measures used by university managements to respond to student and staff-led decolonising work. Although our wider project centred also on student union and departmental responses to decolonising work, our focus here is university management staff with strategic responsibility for teaching-learning and curriculum design. This includes deans, pro-vice chancellors for teaching-learning, heads of departments and directorates for teaching excellence. We highlight the measures that were used to refuse, reject and/or claim decolonial efforts within their institutions categorising these through three related strategies:

1. Strategic rejection of decolonising work
2. Reluctant acceptance of the need to decolonise
3. Strategic advancement of decolonising work

In doing so, we do not suggest that universities moved in a linear way from strategy one to three in the period captured by our research. Instead, we found that universities used all three strategies at various stages so that even in the phase of 'mainstreaming' which required a strategic advancement of decolonising, some universities continued to use tactics of silence/ refusal and 'divide and rule' which we categorise as the strategic rejection of decolonising work.

Strategic rejection

A range of tactics were used by university managements that we count as part of this strategy. The first was to ignore or refuse to engage with decolonising work. In some cases, management-led initiatives were introduced without consultation with existing decolonising networks. For Karima, this silence and refusal was a tool of oppression (Ahmed 2010) 'to continuously remind [Black students] that these spaces were not designed for us' (Karima, Student).

Selina explains that management in her university had reluctantly agreed to meet with her after the students' direct action forced them to. Even so, there was a strategic rejection of the demands they put forward. This was done through the claim that the work was *'already happening'.*

[Senior manager] ... was saying 'We've done this, we've done that' or 'if you checked our website you would see that we've got decol on the website'. Putting it on your website isn't enough, we have to have actual actions. ... Another thing that really upset them was that we wrote our demands down and ... we did not hear the end of that; they kept saying 'Oh, you know, it sounds quite aggressive' and I was like, 'First of all, are you just saying it's aggressive because some of us are Black?' (Selina, Student)

The meeting represented a hesitant acceptance of the need to engage with the network while at the same time the University attempted to refuse the demands of the network. The suggestion that the University was doing the work already could be seen to imply that students should be grateful and not rock the boat (Stein and Andreotti 2016) while the tone-policing invokes colonial stereotypes of Black women as strong and aggressive who need to be contained (Carby 1982). The focus on the *manner* in which the students' message was conveyed instead of the *message* itself can be seen to distract from the structural issues of injustice; it also reasserts the power, dominance and Whiteness of the institution by prioritising the psychological discomfort of the (White senior male) audience.

Reluctant acceptance

We define reluctant acceptance as a containment strategy that was used by institutions when the demands from students and staff could not easily be silenced, especially given the intense public scrutiny of universities and the pressures to avoid income (and reputation) loss, post-Brexit. Participants cited a range of devices used by senior leadership groups to deal with the demands including stalling. As Patricia mentions, almost a year after the agreement was reached to remove colonial statues, her university was still holding talks about the processes needed to make this happen. 'I had an email two days ago saying that we're going to talk about the statues again .... I'm thinking, 'another talk!' She went on to describe the placatory moves that were used in formal meetings with management to discuss action. Meetings were held with plenty of time allowed for discussion, but little was achieved in practice.

When we would be having these long meetings with the deputy VC [who is] very personable, but after a while you think this is part of a strategy that the person will talk and talk and talk ... so you can't get a word in edgeways. (Patricia, Academic)

Like Patricia, Vijay also expressed frustration about the stalling tactics used by university managements to avoid making strategic and structural changes within their institutions. He explained how in his university, budgets for a seminar series were allocated but no commitments were made beyond this. 'We had speakers and [management] would encourage us to have these seminars but that is where it ended'. We identify these as holding tactics as similar to the strategies that were evident following the public and media reactions in the aftermath of George Floyd's murder when Black people were repeatedly asked to share their stories of racism as part of the learning process for White people. Such strategies can be seen as having a stalling effect as Black people's anger was aired while also being contained. The university was seen to be acting through the process of giving funding for seminars, while the structures that perpetuate Eurocentrism and coloniality were left untouched (Ahmed 2012).

Dev also recounted how tactics of delay were compounded by the placing of unnecessary obstacles. He had been tasked with setting up a 'decolonisation exhibition'. However, even after formal sign-off from management, Dev felt that gate-keeping methods (Almeida and Kumalo 2018) were used to delay the work:

> We have one wall which stretches up to ... 15 metres and the height of it is 3 metres ... .On that wall [is one] White artist and that's all ... I said to the library manager 'I would like to use the wall' and there was real resistance about using that wall for the exhibition. There was also the commitment side to give; every little hole had to be made good. (Dev, Academic)

Dev describes after how facing initial refusal and delay he was then reminded to remove any traces of the exhibition. While a legitimate request, our participants gave many examples of how delays and expectations to remove all traces of their work were experienced disproportionally by BME staff and students serving as constant reminders that higher education spaces were not built for them (Ahmed 2012; Almeida and Kumalo 2018).

Strategic advancement

While reluctant acceptance involved universities grudgingly accepting the need to respond to student demands, we define strategic advancement of decolonising as a more proactive strategy driven by a need for the institution to be 'seen to be' responsive in the face of wider pressures and social changes. Although some institutions were already engaged in, or claiming to be decolonising, the key drivers of this response in 2020 were the Covid-19 pandemic and the BLM protest movements along with uncertainty around future student recruitment. Selina and Karima who had struggled to engage senior management over a two-year period, found in the aftermath of the BLM protests that they were now invited to comment, at very short notice, on their university's official anti-racist statement. 'We were really surprised as it was normally us chasing them and not hearing for ages. Mind you, they didn't really give us much time to respond and in the end, we didn't have time to contribute' (Karima, students). Strategic advancement meant that the university made a public commitment to decolonisation in the face of external pressures to declare an anti-racist stance. While the decolonising network was acknowledged, the tokenistic and belated manner in which the chairs of the network were 'included' in the process raised questions about the University's motivations and commitments to actual racial justice.

Michael, responsible for equalities and diversity work in his department, talks below about his university's motivations for decolonising in relation to recruitment needs rather than a commitment to the work, per se.

> I'm sure there are individuals who do care about [it], even at senior management level, but I think overall, it seems to me that there is almost a neoliberal pragmatic aspect to it, namely that universities want to recruit students and be seen as open and inclusive. They need those things, like with Athena Swan, they need the badge or the badges to show off as it were to be accredited. (Michael, Academic)

Michael's reference to 'neoliberal pragmatism', student recruitment and accreditation as reasons for engaging in decolonising, supports our argument about the opportunistic or strategic advancement of decolonising. Like Michael, Ella was also sceptical about her university's motivations for 'mainstreaming decolonising':

> We've shown that we can change things rapidly with Covid; ... It's what the motivation is, and ultimately this is a neoliberal capitalist society. They are only really motivated by money and I think the pressure of the BLM, through the potential loss about international students, the potential loss of all of our Black students, because they don't want to be among racist universities, this is a big economic threat, but then, ... what I'm concerned about with Brexit and with all the economic fallout of the pandemic in the next few years, when the University has to tighten its belt, can it still hold on its diversity agenda and its decolonisation? (Ella, Academic)

Ella's comment signals that her university's advancement of decolonising is a case of 'interest convergence' (Bell 1980) referring to factors such as the potential loss of Black students, she maintains that the Covid-19 pandemic has demonstrated how quickly initiatives can be put into place. However, in her view, only a business case for decolonising prompts universities to take action. Ella's questions about whether the wins gained now would translate into meaningful institutional change or be short-lived also cohere with Bell's theory and we take up this theme in the next section.

Grassroots or top-down decolonisation?

We now turn to a consideration of what the strategic advancement of decolonising might mean for those involved in grassroots' decolonising work. Given the proliferation of projects, participants discussed their ideas for how decolonising might progress given this contested terrain. Most agreed that grassroots decolonial efforts would likely fail without some institutionalised support e.g. funding for students, time for staff, institutional approval of decolonised content, methods and pedagogies or additional resource for new staff or programmes of work. However, there were also concerns about dilution and institutional taming of the discourse and what this might mean for those who have already invested heavily in decolonising work.

Alex, cited earlier, expressed his view that a top-down managerial approach was not the most desirable way forward, but it was important to have a two-way flow of communication between the 'grassroots, bottom-up demands for decolonising' and a management-led approach.

> I suppose it has to be ... a mix and a balance between ... grassroots, bottom-up demands for change from students and staff and the management support ... if it's only management-led, it doesn't have that demand coming from below, then it just becomes managerial ... one of the more interesting and challenging things about all the work is trying to ensure that we still have energy flowing ... from below and above. (Alex, Senior Manager)

What Alex identified as a potentially 'healthy flow of energy' between management-led and staff and student-led approaches was differently constructed by others. For Tara, there was an inherent tension because the relationship between the 'above and below' forces that Alex described, was not operating on an equal power basis. One factor was the scarce financial resource for the bottom-up, decolonise group in Tara's university. As with many decolonising groups nationally, it was often reliant on the unpaid labour of primarily Black and Brown women (Chantiluke, Kwoba, and Nkopo 2018).

Tara and others felt that the group's considerable work was being co-opted without proper recognition within the institution's approach to decolonising. 'They sometimes include a nod to our work, but I don't think it's appropriately credited. (Tara, Student)

The levels of co-option involved in management-led decolonise projects were commented on by other participants. Selina considered this to be a critical moment for the future of decolonising networks. In her new university, a prominent discipline-based group had disbanded as the institution introduced a top-down decolonising initiative because, according to Selina, it became 'an issue of complicity rather than cooperation'. Burnout and exhaustion were also factors for this group of mainly Black female students (Chantiluke, Kwoba, and Nkopo 2018).

For Helen, institution-led approaches risked superficiality or an 'institutional taming' of decolonising.

> With any social movement you have the challenge of institutionalisation and taming... Writers have talked about decolonising being revolutionary; you don't want it to get lost in diversifying ... . Decolonising is about looking at the root ... and [my university] has benefited from slavery, it has that profound history there. (Helen, Academic)

Helen went on to explain the colonial history which was being formally catalogued through the grassroots decolonising network. However, the approach taken by a 'top-down' decolonising led by management threatened erasure of this history and colonial legacies at the expense of more measurable targets for decolonising. In one sense the developments that we have mentioned reflect the impossibility of decolonising institutions that were designed to support colonisation and racialisation (Said, 1993). However, Omer remained optimistic about the prospects for grassroots decolonising work while calling for more clearly defined goals and independence.

> I think this group should remain independent first. I don't want to be part of that [official] structure ... otherwise your power of pressuring will disappear ... and I think this is the urgent task: we should clarify our position. ... *We've* initiated this project, and the university is responding to *this* project. So, we're two separate bodies and this dual-ness, this separation, should be kept. (Omer, Academic)

We end with Omer's account because it enables us to reflect on the current and future direction for decolonising work in higher education. Omer's comments when read alongside the earlier mentioned disbanding of some networks suggest that grassroots decolonising work in England finds itself at a crossroads. Strategic advancement of decolonising may have provided some resource and institutional backing for grassroots networks but has come with costs, not least of which is institutional taming of the radical message of decolonisation. Omer points to the need to reclaim decolonising work from this institutional co-option suggesting that this can be done through first, clearly defining aims/goals second, by maintaining a clear distinction and independence from the formal university structures. However, doing so would require long-term and most likely un-resourced effort which brings us back to issues of burnout and the sustainability of grassroots decolonising work.

Conclusion

We have argued that calls to 'decolonise education' have risen in the UK since 2014, amid a wave of unrest about higher education conditions for staff and persistent racialised inequalities and outcomes for both students and staff. As the campaigns have developed, there has been a proliferation of aims, goals and methods under the umbrella of 'decolonising the curriculum' meaning that 'decolonising' remains a much contested terrain.

We identified three overlapping phases of decolonisation in higher education in England in the short period between 2014 and 2021. Decolonial efforts have mushroomed at this juncture with groups communicating their messages via occupations and through open letters as well as manifestos, zines, academic books, papers and exhibitions. While university managements have actively engaged with decolonial efforts and campaigns, our findings show that there has also been a strategic rejection of this decolonising work through refusal, delay and silencing. Some universities have made claims to decolonising through strategic and often opportunistic advancement. However, these claims have been voiced considerably more loudly in the aftermath of the BLM protests in 2020.

We have argued that strategic advancement of decolonising reflects 'interest convergence' (Bell 1980) as universities face pressures to recruit students in uncertain times and circumstances. While some participants identified strategic advancement of decolonising as necessary and inevitable, they also identified risks: tokenism, superficiality, and a ramping up of the exploitation of Women of Colour, especially, as decolonising is delivered through neoliberal managerial principles of 'more for less'. Institutional taming of the discourse was also associated with the work becoming divorced from a structural focus on coloniality. With some high-profile decolonising groups disbanding because of 'co-option', there would seem to be a sense of decolonising work being at a crossroads.

We ended the previous section with Omer because his account posed an important question for the future of decolonising work: If the movement develops a clear set of aims and goals through connections with other grassroots movements while also maintaining independence from official university processes, then might it be possible to head off institutional co-option, incorporation, and the dilution of the radical message of decolonising?

Notes

1. While the empirical site for our research is England, we refer here to the UK as the sovereign state and heartland of the British Empire. The UK is also referenced when we cite examples of decolonising from the countries that make up the UK and when referring to specific polices or developments that also impact the wider unit of the UK.
2. We understand Eurocentrism as a false universalism based on the claim of European superiority – 'the notion that European civilisation ... has had some unique historical advantage, some special quality of race and culture or environment or mind or spirit, which gives this human community a permanent superiority over all other communities, at all times in history and down to the present'(Blaut 1993, 1). Within a higher education context, we understand Eurocentrism to refer to a form of cognitive imperialism (Battiste 2013) in which European based knowledge and values are centred at the expense of other forms of knowledge.
3. The campaign which spread across 40 universities in the US involved students sharing short videos and photos of themselves on Tumblr with the caption 'I, too, am Harvard'. The project set out to expose the everyday encounters with racism experienced by Black students on campus and the emotional toll it took to deal with these microaggressions (Baker and Blissett 2018).

POSSIBILITIES AND COMPLEXITIES OF DECOLONISING HIGHER EDUCATION 49

4. Political Blackness is an umbrella term used by people who are likely to experience racial discrimination based on skin colour. The UCU uses 'Black' to refer to people who are descended, through one or both parents, from Africa, the Caribbean, Asia (the Middle East to China) and Latin America. It refers to those visible minorities who have a shared experience of oppression.

Acknowledgements

Huge thanks to our participants for agreeing to take part in the research at a particularly challenging time for higher education students and staff. We would also like to thank the two anonymous reviewers for their very valuable feedback on an earlier version of this paper.

Disclosure statement

No potential conflict of interest was reported by the author(s).

References

Ahmed, S. 2010. "Foreword: Secrecy and Silence in the Research Process: Feminist Reflections." *Perspectives: Policy and Practice in Higher Education* 23 (4): 158–161.

Ahmed, S. 2012. *On Being Included: Racism and Diversity in Institutional Life*. London: Duke University Press.

Almeida, S., and S. H. Kumalo. 2018. "(De) Coloniality Through Indigeneity: Deconstructing Calls to Decolonise in the South African and Canadian University Contexts." *Education as Change* 22 (1): 1–24.

Baker, D. J., and R. S. L. Blissett. 2018. "Beyond the Incident: Institutional Predictors of Student Collective Action." *The Journal of Higher Education* 89 (2): 184–207.

Battiste, M. 2013. *Decolonizing Education: Nourishing the Learning Spirit*. Saskatoon: Purich Publishing.

Begum, N., and R. Saini. 2019. "Decolonising the Curriculum." *Political Studies Review* 17 (2): 196–201.

Bell Jr., D. A. 1980. "Brown v. Board of Education and the Interest-Convergence Dilemma." *Harvard Law Review* 93: 518–533.

Bhambra, G. K., K. Nisancioglu, and D. Gebrial. 2018. *Decolonizing the University*. London: Pluto Press.

Blake, F. 2019. "Why Black Lives Matter in the Humanities." In *Seeing Race Again: Countering Colorblindness Across the Disciplines*, edited by K. W. Crenshaw, L. C. Harris, D. M. HoSang, and G. Lipsitz, 307–326. Oakland: University of California Press.

Blaut, J. M. 1993. *The Colonizers' Model of the World*. New York: The Guilford Press.

Blissett, R. S. L., D. J. Baker, and B. Fields. 2020. "When Women Speak Out: Understanding the Motivations for I, Too, Am Mobilization." *Teachers College Record* 122 (3): 1–36.

Boliver, V. 2013. "How Fair Is Access to More Prestigious UK Universities?" *The British Journal of Sociology* 64 (2): 344–364.

Carby, H. 1982. "White Woman Listen! Black Feminism and the Boundaries of Sisterhood." *Centre for Contemporary Cultural Studies* 111–128.

Chantiluke, R., B. Kwoba, and A. Nkopo. 2018. *Rhodes Must Fall: The Struggle to Decolonise the Racist Heart of Empire*. London: Zed Books.

Collini, S. 2017. *Speaking of Universities*. London: Verso.

Department for Business Innovation and Skills. 2016. Case for Creation of the Office For Students. London

EHRC. 2019. *Racial Harassment in Higher Education: Our Inquiry*. London: Equalities and Human Rights Commission.

El Magd, N. A. 2016. *Black Students' Committee*. Postgraduate Rep NUS. Why Is My Curriculum White? Decolonising the Academy. NUSConnect. https://www.nusconnect.org.uk/articles/why-is-my-curriculum-white-decolonising-the-academy

GARA. 2019. "Commitments-signed April 23rd"'. Accessed January 25, 2021. https://drive.google.com/file/d/12l7fBTpsEfybV8g71H-Lqjjc6fA65LxP/view.

Gaudry, A., and D. Lorenz. 2018. "Indigenization as Inclusion, Reconciliation, and Decolonization: Navigating the Different Visions for Indigenizing the Canadian Academy." *AlterNative: An International Journal of Indigenous Peoples* 14 (3): 218–227.

Housee, S. 2018. *Speaking Out Against Racism in the University Space*. Stoke-On-Trent: Trentham Books.

Miah, S. 2017. *Muslims, Schooling and Security*. London: Palgrave Macmillan.

Mignolo, W. 2011. *The Darker Side of Western Modernity: Global Futures, Decolonial Options*. Durham: Duke University Press.

Migraton Advisory Committee. 2018. *Impact of International Students in the UK*. London: Gov.uk. September. https://dera.ioe.ac.uk/32233/1/Impact_intl_students_report_published_v1.1.pdf.

National Union of Students. 2011. *Race for Equality: A Report on the Experiences of Black Students in Further and Higher Education*. London: National Union of Students.

Noden, P., M. Shiner, and T. Modood. 2014. "University Offer Rates for Candidates from Different Ethnic Categories." *Oxford Review of Education* 40 (3): 349–369.

Quijano, A. 2000. "Coloniality of Power and Eurocentrism in Latin America." *International Sociology* 15 (2): 215–232.

Said, E. 1993. *Culture and Imperialism*. London: Chatto and Windus.

Shain, F. 2011. *The New Folk Devils: Muslim Boys and Education in England*. Stoke-on-Trent: Trentham Books.

Stein, S., and V. D. O. Andreotti. 2016. "Decolonization and Higher Education." In *Encyclopedia of Educational Philosophy and Theory*, edited by M. Peters, 1–6. Singapore: Springer Science + Business Media.

Takayama, K., A. Sriprakash, and R. Connell. 2016. "Toward a Postcolonial and International Education." *Comparative Education Review* 61: S1–S24.

Tuck, E., and K. W. Yang. 2012. "Decolonization I Not a Metaphor." *Decolonization: Indigeneity, Education & Society* 1 (1): 1–40.

UUK. 2020. *Tackling Racial Harassment in Higher Education*. London: Universities UK.

Virdee, S., and B. McGeever. 2018. "Racism, Crisis, Brexit." *Ethnic and Racial Studies* 41 (10): 1802–1819.

Warwick Occupy. 2019. "Warwick Occupy Manifesto." Accessed January 25, 2021. https://docs.google.com/document/d/1zhiwsTPDniQ19O1V4AMlQVcS7WNm59vXGj4A7ZHO4tg/mobilebasic.

Xu, Xin. 2021. "What Does the Rise of Asia Mean for Global Higher Education?" *Times Higher Education Supplement*, June 1. https://www.timeshighereducation.com/campus/what-does-rise-asia-mean-global-higher-education.

OPEN ACCESS

Approaching global education development with a decolonial lens: teachers' reflections

Sharanya Menon, Crystal Green, Irène Charbonneau, Elina Lehtomäki and Boby Mafi

ABSTRACT

In this paper, we as the teachers and researchers of a course titled Global education development informed by theories of decoloniality, report on our analysis of our self-critical and constructive dialogue on the course design, its underlying assumptions, expectations, implementation, success and needs for improvement. We centered decoloniality from the beginning of the course, problematised binary-thinking and encouraged our students to look at issues within the field of development and education in pluriversal ways. Our gestures toward decolonial pedagogy in the course were complicated by our own entanglements with coloniality as well as structural factors such as the context of Finland, where the colonial past is seldom addressed. Despite these contradictions and challenges, we aspire to continue thinking through decoloniality to decenter the dominant liberal frameworks within global education development.

Introduction

"Schooling for all has long been an international goal. The idea that all people, wherever they live and however poor they might be, should have the opportunity to develop their capacities to improve their own lives and create better societies has been a key notion articulated by social reformers in many different kinds of society for centuries. Yet history has proved that it is extraordinarily difficult to realize this widely shared aspiration." (McCowan and Unterhalter 2015, 1–2)

Designing and implementing a university course on such a difficult aspiration as global education development seemed a challenging task. As course designers and teachers of a course on 'Global education development[1]', we had to decide on what to cover, how to arrange teaching and learning, what to select as core study material, and moreover, what conceptual and theoretical approaches to select. First, the book *Education and International Development*[2] edited by Tristan McCowan and Elaine Unterhalter (2015) guided the course planning. We shared an interest in understanding education

---

This is an Open Access article distributed under the terms of the Creative Commons Attribution-NonCommercial-NoDerivatives License (http://creativecommons.org/licenses/by-nc-nd/4.0/), which permits non-commercial re-use, distribution, and reproduction in any medium, provided the original work is properly cited, and is not altered, transformed, or built upon in any way.

development in line with Andreotti's (2011) decolonial notion of global mindedness that emphasises seeing 'learning to read the world through other eyes' which requires the acknowledgement of multiple perspectives on reality. In the course design, we planned to engage university students both from Finland and abroad in exploring global education development with a decolonial lens. During the course implementation we recognised the need for and importance of reflecting on our underlying assumptions (defining and discussing education development in whose eyes), teaching and learning processes (decoloniality in interaction and practices), the learning outcomes (students' experiences and achievements).

The course titled 'Global education development' is one of the virtual study courses provided in English by the Finnish University Partnership in International Development (UniPID)[3], a network of universities working with issues related to sustainability and global challenges. The network's virtual courses focus on development studies and are available for degree and exchange students registered in universities in Finland, and from 2021 also to students from the network universities' partner institutions (UniPID 2021). Students may take one course or even complete an amount equivalent to a minor (25 ECTS[4]) credits that can be integrated to their degree. The flexible online learning studies enable students from diverse disciplines, study programmes, universities, and contexts to join.

The course focused on education development across the world rather than in a specific country to study the global connectedness in education, the influence of global governance on educational development and the interaction between local actions and global policies, and to position ourselves, as students and teachers, in the field of educational development. The use of 'global' rather than 'international' was an informed choice, drawing on Unterhalter's (2015) review of perspectives to education development and emphasis on understanding of education 'as a set of ethical ideas about rights, capabilities and obligations which enjoin particular ways of thinking about what we owe each other regardless of our nationality and our particular beliefs' (Unterhalter 2015, 28).

The work of decolonial scholars (Andreotti 2011; de Sousa Santos 2018; Mignolo 2011a, 2011c) inspired the course planning. We wanted students to critically reflect on who sets agendas and defines priorities, what research informs ideas about development, whose voices and knowledges are included in development discourses, and the ways changes in global education development are assessed. Thus, the coursework aimed to critically reflect on educational power structures globally and locally, giving attention to how education is implicated in the colonial matrix of power (Mignolo 2011a; Mignolo and Walsh 2018; Quijano 2000).

In addition to the global context, the decolonial lens in education development seemed important in the context of this Finnish university course because decoloniality has been largely absent in educational research and education development cooperation discourses. In light of Sámi studies, Finland represents a context where the colonial past may be discussed but is seldom critically addressed (Lehtola 2015). In relation to Western colonisation, Finland has an ambivalent position, having been both occupied by foreign kingdoms and built on racialised conception of nationhood.[5] Furthermore, a colonial worldview is maintained through narratives of Nordic benevolent exceptionalism and equality (Pashby and Sund 2020; Vuorela 2009) which is evident, for instance, in the recent education export initiatives that have benefited from the international positive image created around Finnish education following the consecutive successful outcomes in OECD's Programme for International Student Assessment (PISA) from the early 2000s (Schatz 2016). Education export may represent a form of neocolonialism, legitimised by the neoliberal marketisation of excellence and following the complex drives of international development aid work (Juusola 2020; Schatz, Popovic, and Dervin 2017). Such observations alerted us as teachers responsible for the course Global education development to address education development with a decolonial lens.

Throughout the course, as course designers and teachers, we critically reflected on the theoretical approaches we took as well as the worldview our course represented and may have reinforced. Following McCowan (2015), teachers need to be aware of the theories they use for understanding the underpinnings of policies and practices in education development to allow them to teach and encourage students to engage, critique and recast (dominant) theories. This task challenges us to review our own thinking and approaches. After the first round of the virtual course was completed in April 2020, we teachers and researchers reflected on the design and pedagogy in a series of reflective group discussions. In this paper, we analyse our gestures towards decolonial theory in the course on Global education development. The research questions guiding our paper are:

(1) How has our understanding of decoloniality informed the planning and execution of the first offering of the virtual course on Global education development?
(2) What have we learned as university teachers and researchers about the possibilities and challenges of introducing decoloniality in Global education development?

There are multiple views of the gesture of decoloniality, and we do not intend to make available a prescriptive model or an example of good practices. Instead, our goal is to offer situated insights about our experiences and learning using decoloniality in curricula and teaching of global education development.

Theoretical framings

Decoloniality is an endless process and practice of challenging and transforming the relations of colonial domination (Legg 2017). This means relentlessly aiming to delink from the cloak of coloniality disguised under the rhetoric of modernity (progress, growth) which has and continues to be seen as the natural order of things due to Europe claiming a dominant position geo-politically and epistemically in order to open up decolonial options (Mignolo 2011a, 2011b). The epistemic hegemony of Western knowledge disregards and invisibilises other ways of being, knowing, and living and encourages material domination of those who are outside the Eurocentric norm (Stein 2019). Decoloniality is not meant to supplant the dogma of the Western episteme within higher education with another, singular and totalising decolonial episteme. It rather *de-centers* the West and affirm the re-emergences, re-existences and liberation of people dominated by the global westernising project. In this way, it secures and re-links with memories, modes of existence and legacies that people have reason to value but have been destituted by modernity (Mignolo 2016).

Decolonising the ideologies of development also requires decolonising development education and its pedagogies (Rutazibwa 2018; Sultana 2019). Decolonial pedagogy approaches teaching by thinking from the outside. We approach our teaching sitting at the border, trying to learn from indigenous and non-western traditions and cosmologies. Decolonial pedagogy is also a commitment to working without fixed hierarchies and beyond the student/teacher binary. In this way, decolonial pedagogy is pragmatic, involving decentring dominant practices and voices (Atehortúa 2020; De Lissovoy 2010; Silva 2018). In addition, decolonial pedagogy is dialogic. It is a process of conscientisation (Freire 1970) as the students become able to recognise their own entanglements in the colonial matrix of power (Walsh 2015). Decolonial pedagogy is therefore also a reflexive learning process in which students reflect not only on colonial histories and geographies, but also their own personal biographies.

Dialogic inquiry framed both our pedagogical practice and our methods in writing this paper. We see dialogic inquiry and reflective practice as essential in decolonial gestures – it is a way of developing dialogical forms for the construction of knowledge (Cusicanqui 2012). Reflecting on our own teaching we also engage in dialogue which helps us to decolonise our own ways of thinking and open up possibilities for (re)learning through our practice in new ways.

Methods

The data for this paper was generated in a series of three recorded teacher-researcher dialogues between us, the teachers and researchers of the Global education development course. The core team of the course Global education development course consisted of Elina (Professor of Education), Boby (PhD researcher with years of teaching experience) and Sharanya (PhD researcher with some teaching experience). Additionally, the authors include Crystal (postdoctoral researcher with teaching experience) who was one of the visiting scholars of the course and Irène who worked with the team as an intern to collect and analyse data on the course implementation and examine how social presence was experienced, negotiated and perceived by students. The authors of the paper are all living and working between worlds. As scholars with the experience of working in diaspora, our sense of our own positionalities cannot be fixed nor unitary but become salient in relation to changing contexts and relationships. In our reflections and discussion, we open up the complexity of our positionalities. We followed a dialogic inquiry and collaborative reflective discussions in these dialogues to engage and learn from each other. All the three teacher-researcher dialogues were 60–90 min long. They were recorded on Zoom and were transcribed by the authors. Crystal, Sharanya and Irène analysed the contents of the transcripts individually and collaboratively and devised the themes. These themes were refined further in discussion with Elina. The themes that were identified in our analysis of the first two discussions were used to guide the third discussion.

The decolonial methodological orientation of this paper is based on a humanising aspiration; it is a collaborative sense-making experience that is creative and edifying (Boveda and Bhattacharya 2019). We attempt to use a transformative methodology which will have implications for our own transformation and for our decolonial praxis in the course. Since we are writing this paper as a collaborative reflection, we have opted to use 'we' in presenting the findings. We have also chosen to write parts of our dialogues directly, rather than using pull quotes from the transcripts to demonstrate the authenticity of our interpretation of the data. When relevant, the name of the author whose perspective is elaborated is indicated.

This paper focuses on our reflections on the course Global education development offered in the 2020 spring semester by the University of Oulu in collaboration with the UniPID Network. The 5 ECTS masters level course lasted 12 weeks and included 5 synchronous discussions as well as several asynchronous discussions in Moodle forums. The course was divided into six modules (see Figure 1). After each module, students were also asked to write in a learning diary. Sixty-seven students registered for the course and thirty-five completed. Out of the thirty-five students, sixteen were Finnish students and nineteen were international master's students or exchange students in Finland. Out of the nineteen international students, eleven came from countries categorised under the Global North and nine were from countries placed under the Global South. In the course, students explored the themes of interconnectedness among humans and the environment within the fields of global education and international development, raising critical questions around belonging, access and quality living for all.

Our reflections

The primary goal of this reflective paper is to offer insights on how our understanding of decoloniality informed the planning and execution of the virtual course on Global education development. In addition, we also want to highlight some of the possibilities and challenges that we as teachers experienced while working with decolonial perspectives. In the reflections, we analyse the choices made in the course design, our perceptions of students' engagement with the course and our learnings based on the teacher-researcher dialogues. The results of our dialogic inquiry are presented in three parts, following a chronological order, starting with the beginning of the course, moving to the process throughout the course, to finally focusing on the end of the course.

Beginning with decoloniality

We start by considering how we interpreted the ways in which the students initially engaged with decolonial theory and how this related to our own experiences of the course and decoloniality. In the course design, we foregrounded decoloniality to make

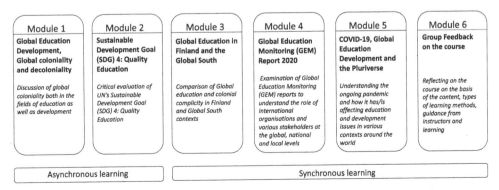

Figure 1. Overview of the Global Education Development Course Spring 2020.

our students think deeply about their socially situated realities in relation to the course content, destabilise the authority of the Eurocentric perspectives and begin thinking and engaging with pluriversality. For this reason, we begin a consideration of global education development by asking, where *do we start the story?* Beginning with Finland's colonial entanglements in international development is an effort to remedy what Rutazibwa (2018) calls 'colonial amnesia' and, in Finland's case, what Vuorela (2009) calls 'colonial complicity'.

In the first module of the course, students read Zavala's (2016) article *Decolonial methodologies in education*[6], and watched a video featuring scholar Vanessa Andreotti titled *Shouldering our colonial backpack*[7] (2016) along with Nygaard and Wegimont's (2018) paper on *Global Education in Europe ... Development.*[8] Highlighting decolonial and postcolonial scholarship from the start was inspired by the way Morreira (2017) started her course on social sciences with Steven Biko's work, a South African anti-apartheid activist, as opposed to the works of Euro-American scholars highly regarded in the field. By juxtaposing decolonial reading of education with the dominant perspectives on Global education development, we hoped students would begin questioning why certain models of education and development are privileged over the others. After engaging with the content individually, the students were asked to reflect on the question, '*What are your thoughts on thinking about Global education development through the lens of decoloniality?*' in a Moodle forum and in their individual reflective learning diaries.

In students' responses, we felt like students experienced both the possibilities and challenges of embracing decolonial theory. Firstly, we were surprised to read that very few of them had prior opportunities to engage with decolonial/anti-colonial literature, yet they thought it was relevant to global education development. They deliberated on the need for decolonial methods as they felt that some prevalent ideas and concepts within education development such as indicators under Sustainable Development Goal (SDG) number 4 (ensure inclusive and equitable quality education and promote lifelong learning opportunities for all) do not really take into consideration the local contexts. One student raised in the Latin American context reflected on how the contents of this module made them reflect on the lack of spirituality and connection to nature in their education. As a teacher, this reflection evoked an emotional response in Sharanya as the student described how our relationality with the environment profoundly impacts how we perceive and think about nature and creates possibilities for radical change (or not). We were quite happy to read students' critical stance on some of the issues within Global education development and hoped they would go deeper than simply reject the SDGs by the end of the course.

Secondly, in their responses to the course content, students wondered if border thinking and decolonial methods could truly emerge from the margins within Global North and the West, querying whether that would be considered misappropriation. As course teachers, we responded to these questions by asking if the onus of expanding decolonial thought should be placed solely on margins of the Global South. We wanted them to consider the implications of working with theories coming from the margins and the responsibilities that come with adopting and adapting something which did not originate from a context or social reality that they are familiar with. In our teacher-researcher dialogue, Boby described this process as 'productive tension' i.e. ways of engaging with the course material which makes us uncomfortable yet inspires us to think, reflect further and make room for cognitive dissonance. We wanted the students in our course to develop a philosophical inquiry so that they are able to sit with their discomfort and express their learning and reflexive processes through the learning diaries.

Finally, there was also a general sentiment among the students about how challenging it is to actually *de-link* from one's own Eurocentric ways of thinking about education and development. One student described how the relational nature of decolonial methodologies makes it difficult to form connections with global education development without falling into the 'trap' of epistemological and ontological colonialism. In our teacher-researcher dialogues, we discussed at length about this 'trap' as being the most challenging part of engaging with decoloniality in education. We wonder how to inhabit and work within colonial structures in education while desiring the decolonial? How do we collectively desire non-dominant approaches in global education development? How do we pull the rug of colonialism from under our feet, while standing on it knowing that part of us still desires the comfort it provides us? How do we authentically engage with decoloniality while not becoming desolately hopeless? This metaphor of the 'trap' is a reminder for us to be reflexive of our seemingly decolonial aspirations. Some students also described the struggles of working with decolonial methodologies, especially dealing with issues of race and 'white guilt'. This is an important topic to consider in the Finnish context because there are silences around issues of race due to a lack of acknowledgement of Finland's racist past (Rastas 2004).

We as teachers and researchers shared the same sentiment about the challenges of completely embracing decoloniality within the context of our institution. Indeed, we are all implicated in structures larger than us and resisting structural forces requires courage and patience. Engaging with decolonial pedagogy is an arduous task because if the institutional structures do not support you there are many tensions (some more palpable than others) that arise. In the course design, we aspired to move away from certain normative practices inspired by decolonial thought. For instance, we thought of reflective learning diaries as an opportunity for the students to engage reflexively with the course content and not write a term-end paper. However, these diaries were also graded per the university requirements and only those students who completed all the learning tasks were able to receive the five ECTS credits for the course. Elina had proposed that the students who completed a portion of the coursework could receive a portion of the ECTS credits, however we were not able to negotiate that with the stakeholders. This required assessment felt like a departure from the idea of engaging in epistemic disobedience in more meaningful and creative ways.

Another example of this tension is the way we had to set criteria for critical thinking to assess students' assignments. We evaluated the extent to which students used multiple sources (usually peer-reviewed sources) to justify their claims or arguments in the paper. One of the students pointed out in the feedback that they found it ironic that they had to reflect personally in the diary entries but at the same time follow a rubric (e.g. connections to material assigned, critical argumentation, APA style citation[9]). As teachers and researchers, we later reflected on how this evaluation was based on the dominant way of conceptualising critical thinking in higher education, that is, defining critical thinking as a rhetorical strategy of citing from established literature often produced in and for the Global North. We realised that we could have looked at other non-dominant ways in which criticality and critical thinking are conceptualised as culturally situated and socially constructed practices (Vaidya 2016; Vandermensbrugghe 2004). Finally, our perceptions of students' engagement with the course made us wonder – by asking them to question their positionality in relation to the course content, have we managed to create opportunities to engage with the concept of coloniality/decoloniality not only intellectually but also emotionally, ethically and spiritually?

Problematising the binaries within Global education development

After students initially engaged with decolonial theory, several activities were organised in Module 2 to help them problematise binary thinking in, for instance, defining quality education. Our course had a strong emphasis on SDG 4 and the global policy frameworks such as the Global Education Monitoring Reports.[10] Yet, we wanted to emphasise the diverse ways in which we can interpret and understand, agree, and disagree on what constitutes 'quality education'. While most of our students agreed that local narratives and initiatives should be privileged, some of them asked if the term 'global' in global education development itself is colonial as it implies some form of uniformity or consensus. We were pleased to read that students were beginning to question the content and not uncritically accept what we assign as part of their course material.

This was further examined in Module 3 on Global education development in Finland and other contexts, designed with the intention of giving the students an opportunity to start engaging with the politics of the local vs the global. Students read Vuorela's (2009)[11] post-colonial reading of Finland's colonial complicity. They were then asked to link it to another area in global education in Finland (e.g. developmental aid, education export, Finnish curriculum, academic research) to begin thinking about the ways in which coloniality could operate in these areas. Through these readings, we were hoping to make the abstract concepts of colonial/decolonial more apparent and visible in the Finnish context. The learning diary prompt for this Module was: *'Did you find any connections between the article 'Colonial Complicity: The 'Post- colonial' in a Nordic context and the second reading you chose?'*. Elina considers this deliberation over these binaries to be important particularly in Finland as there is an uncritical acceptance of the Finnish education system. Finnish teachers are considered to be the 'best' in the world without taking into account the (political, security, cultural, social) variables that have been in influential in the ways Finnish education system is perceived as it is today. As course teachers, we were curious to know how students from Finland interpret colonial division of labour within global education development as compared to international students born and raised in non-western contexts in their learning diary reflections.

Our general perceptions of the students' reflections were that many of the international students from non-western contexts were able to resonate with Vuorela's (2009) article at a personal level in comparison to the Finnish students whose reflective diary responses were quite neutral. After the course, when we discussed in the teacher-researcher dialogues, we talked about the ways in which we could have opened up about our own positionalities and ways in which we could make the students, especially Finnish students think about how their neutrality might be linked to colonial complicity. One student touched on this complicity by evoking the challenges of bringing about change without participating in the circles of power that they often critique and question.

In similar vein, in our teacher-researcher dialogues, we discussed that engaging with decolonial theories at the university feels like a kind of cognitive dissonance; there is an instability in knowing the limitations of the university as a colonial space and still engaging in decolonial practice, building a career within academia on the premise of deconstructing the institution. This begs the question – can the university and courses offered through the university truly be a space for engaging in decolonial work?

For the students to investigate the issue of binaries within Global education development further during the course, we invited colleagues who had experiences working in the field of international education and development from Brazil, Ethiopia, India, Sweden and the United States for a panel discussion. The topic for the discussion centered on what global education development meant in their respective contexts and what could a decolonial global education development look like based on their experiences in the field. We hoped that listening to diverse perspectives from around the world would help students think outside of the contexts they are most familiar with, especially our Finnish students who had mentioned that this course was the first time they were encountering perspectives on anticolonial literature.

All of the speakers emphasised the importance of understanding the diversity within binaries such as the 'Global North' and 'Global South' so as to create a circulation of ideas and build solidarities between marginalised peoples. One of the speakers talked about *Nai Talim (New education)* – a Gandhian philosophy of education for the head, heart and hand that questions boundaries between education and work, knowledge and skills. They gave an example of how food and food systems are taught in schools in India by only focusing on the 'facts' about food (e.g. nutritional value, constituents) without taking into consideration other contributing issues such as availability, affordability, available technology, traditions of preservation, and the social realities of children. These examples highlight how education systems do not offer a platform to engage with different topics within education with nuance. The speakers concluded that to move beyond binaries we need to create small ruptures of change in the spaces we occupy and traverse. We speculated how we could have created more possibilities for the students to participate in creating ruptures or participating in what Mignolo (2011b) calls 'epistemic disobedience'.

Reflecting on the binaries was quite challenging even for us as teachers and researchers. If we came up with new terms to talk about the binaries such as the 'Global North' and 'Global South', we fear that it would lead to a sanitisation around conversations about inequalities within Global education development. While certain terms and concepts are certainly problematic, by completely doing away with them we may avoid the reconciliation process which is of paramount importance for groups that have been wronged because of coloniality.

Gesturing towards the pluriverse: challenges and possibilities

In the fifth Module of the course, we asked students to work together in groups and read essays from *Pluriverse – a post-development dictionary*[12] by Kothari et al. (2019). We hoped that this book would give the students an opportunity to pause and think collectively about alternatives to mainstream models of global education development amidst the Covid-19 pandemic. The students had to select an approach outlined in *Pluriverse* and think about ways to address a current issue in education exacerbated by the pandemic and present it in any format they like to their course mates. Students chose to discuss two key issues in education during Covid-19 – school meals and inequitable access to technology. Food sovereignty, low-tech educational tools and civilisational transitions were the most common approaches from Pluriverse cited by the students to address these issues. All these alternative approaches call for a systemic change. While the students in our course were hopeful, they were not optimistic about the world system changing from 'capitalistic-heteropatriarchal' to a place where multiplicity is allowed and celebrated.

We wanted to encourage pluriversality in thought through this course but sometimes we as teachers felt like we were pushing for one way of looking at issues. For example, during one of the synchronous discussions, Boby recalled being surprised by his own reaction after one student, a priest of the African Orthodox church, raised the issue of religion in the context of global education. Boby's initial reaction was to dismiss the topic of religion outright. He described his way of thinking that we should 'do away with religion' as 'a standard kind of thinking.' In our teacher-researcher dialogues, we recognised that our omission of the role of religious institutions in Global education development, despite its historical and contemporary importance, indicates our collective implicit affirmation of modern secularism. Yet a commitment to pluriversal options holds space for discussing religion and spirituality as viable onto-epistemic orientations to the world. On reflection, Boby challenged himself to think about religion in terms of pluriversality and to problematise decolonial translations within the context of religion.

This idea of pluriversality is further convoluted because of a lack of consensus among us as course organisers. For Boby, giving equal importance to various perspectives in global education and international development meant being open to a high level of uncertainty and unknown ways of engaging with these topics. Sharanya, on the other hand, wonders how we can talk about underrepresentation of people from the Global South in Finnish higher education when indigenous Sámi and Roma scholars' voices are absent in the field. Finally, for Elina incorporating pluriversality meant highlighting scholarship from the Global South and placing it at the core of the course which is rarely seen in Finnish higher education courses. This conception of pluriversality was translated in the course by giving the stage to scholars from the Global South in order to increase representation and incorporate diverse perspectives. However, this bore the risk of scholars from the Global South, such as Sharanya and Boby, being pressured to perform for the Finnish students as token experts. We shared a concern that Sharanya's and Boby's experiences would be taken by Finnish students as authoritative examples of the experiences of all South Asian or African people.

We also reflected on the power dynamics between teachers and students, specifically in relation to the expectation of students' vulnerability and openness to unknown ways of engaging in learning. We encouraged the students to share personal reflections on their own lives, exploring the raw and tender aspects of themselves. We evaluated students based on the extent to which they showed themselves as vulnerable or vulnerable enough to fulfill the criteria of our grading rubric. Vulnerability was therefore not reciprocal, but hierarchically observed. Yet, as course teachers we realised that, even though we stated our positionalities, we did not open up to the students about our lived experiences as individuals struggling with the issues, they raised in the learning diaries such as class, race and gender. The format of the virtual course made it difficult for us to share our vulnerabilities with the students. Elina shared that her openness with the students was hindered in part by the frequency of online synchronous meetings. Thus, we ask ourselves how as course teachers we can show up authentically with our entanglements with coloniality and engage in non-hierarchical dialogue with our students?

We also faced the complexity of addressing students' multiple resistances towards decoloniality. We felt our students lacked an awareness of their own racialisation as being white in Finland, as part of race blindness in the Nordics (Rastas 2019), demonstrated by their neutral responses to Vuorela's (2009) article. In retrospect, we realised that we could have included more conversations about race and colonial complicity in Finland. Currently, Finland has higher rates of incidents and experiences of racial discrimination, harassment speech and gestures than 12 other European countries (European Union Agency for Fundamental Rights 2019). We wonder, how do we have nuanced conversations about race in Finland with our students by not just looking at it as an abstract historical concept but engaging with it at a deeper level – as a tender, lived experience?

In one of the teacher-researcher dialogues we discussed our defensiveness when faced with our students' resistances. We see the students' resistance as a natural part of all learning processes. Fear, resistance and rejection are common responses to uncertainty and the unknown. This resistance also manifested in students' desire for stability and consensus. They expressed their sense that we cannot move away from the universal and still have a peaceful world. Similarly, the students preferred to rely on their traditional academic habits, even when provided with spaces to explore non-standard options. In the group task based on the alternative approaches to education, students were encouraged to display their work in other formats (e.g. infographics, podcast, vlog). But most students chose common formats used in academia such as PowerPoint presentations and standard essays. While we acknowledge that some other formats might be becoming increasingly popular in higher education, they are not given the same status as traditional academic essays backed by peer-reviewed sources. To conclude, we want to encourage our students to challenge the status-quo and think about alternatives but at the same time be mindful of their actions and not just accept a new way of doing something without thinking through it thoroughly.

Our learnings

By approaching Global education development with a decolonial lens, we hoped to introduce various possibilities for disentangling from hegemonic Western ideologies and with methods and materials that decenter Eurocentric knowledges and ways of being (Sultana 2019). The 'anchor of decolonial epistemologies' is starting from 'I am where I do and think' (Mignolo 2011a), in our case, meant locating a course about Global education development in Finland. In our reflections, we deliberated on the ways in which our decolonial ambitions were not fully realised because of certain structural factors as well as coloniality within us. As we are beneficiaries of funding from UniPID and the university, we are therefore beholden to certain stipulations. We also recognise the paradox that the university, as an institution with colonial roots, is the institution which funds our decolonial initiative. Making structural changes to the assessment and organisation of the course would mean asking UniPID and the university to rethink how courses are envisioned and to invite dialogue with our colleagues, especially those in leadership positions, which would require much more time and collective effort.

By centering decoloniality in this course on Global education development we aspired to move away from the banking model of education to a problem-posing method where students had to engage with a major portion of the content independently without being coddled by the teachers (Freire 1970). We expected our pedagogy, which allowed the students a great deal of independence in determining the times and materials they used to engage with the course, to disrupt the teacher-student hierarchy that traditionally exists in higher education. However, our experience was that the students in fact felt like they were isolated because of the limited synchronous sessions and interactions with other participants (Charbonneau 2020). In contrast to the isolation the students felt, we as teachers and researchers experienced a growth in our coalitions, coalescing with each other and bringing together researchers and scholars from other contexts to participate in the course. On the basis of our reflections and Charbonneau's (2020) study, we wonder about the ways in which we can build trust, a sense of community and be vulnerable with students, particularly in virtual courses (Mangione and Norton 2020) and especially when for the students the course runs over a period of weeks, while our teacher-researcher collaborations have developed over years. Although we did not share our struggles and dilemmas with the students, in our discussions with one another, we shared them quite openly. Our ambivalence about the practice of vulnerability was connected to our roles in preserving the institutional power structures of the university.

In our dialogues, we noted that the lack of Sámi and Roma scholarship from this course continue decolonial patterns of omissions, silence and absence. We were not successful in incorporating the voices of the indigenous scholars based in Finland though we coalesced with individuals from different contexts in the course. We could have made more effort to include their epistemologies and ontologies as we imagine a decolonial development education to participate in acknowledging the harm done to indigenous people and ways in which development education can genuinely work towards restitution (Legg 2017; Mignolo and Walsh 2018). We see decolonial pedagogy as being about our role as teachers in the cultivation and construction of knowledge. This includes thinking about who gets to speak authoritatively about education development and whose accounts are presented in class as worthy of investigation, comparison and interrogation. As the decolonial school of thought presents critiques and proposals of liberation from the margins rather than privileged sites of knowledge production such as the university, we recognise that we could have done more to invite and collaborate with individuals working on decolonial options outside academic circles (Asher 2013).

As Tuck and Wayne Yang (2012) remind us, decolonisation always involves affirmative practice; in the case of development education this includes engagement in a constant struggle to address 'both the material and discursive aspects of representation and politics in curricula, among students and educators, and beyond the classroom' (Sultana 2019, 38). Our work therefore is a practice of the possible, and we recognise that we have benefited from a supportive climate at the university: working within the Faculty of Education at the University of Oulu allowed us the possibility to include the non-dominant approach of decoloniality in our course because of the precedent set by critical and intercultural scholars in our faculty.

For us the question remains, can we de-link from coloniality in a course on global education development when the SDGs are the central reference point and pillar of the course? From the liberal perspective, racialisation and capitalism have become emancipatory perspectives from which to critique the normative universal framework. To embrace the decolonial option would be to begin otherwise, deconstructing the axes of race and capitalism which undergird the colonial matrix of power.

Epilogue

At the time of writing this dialogic inquiry it has been almost a year since we offered the first course on global development education through the UniPID network, which was the focus of this paper. There have been two more iterations of the course and we are currently working with our third cohort of students. These three offerings of the course have provided us teachers with so many opportunities to think with our students about what it means to think about education development with *other eyes*. We have made a conscious attempt to listen to the students' feedback and have modified the course in various ways. In the second offering of the course, we invited guests to respond to some of the major themes arising from students' learning diaries to maintain a continuity in the dialogue in terms of their reflections. To build a sense of community within the course, we have now organised biweekly reflective reading sessions. We have had opportunities to coalesce with colleagues including indigenous scholars from the Nordics and other parts of the world. We have also had poetry reading as part of these sessions which opened possibilities to talk about our positionalities and has in turn inspired some of the students to reflect more deeply on issues that they are passionate about in the field of education development. We continue to struggle, reflect and learn from our entanglements with coloniality and the intricate and contradictory nature of how we understand and interpret decoloniality as part of the university structure, and moreover of university teaching and learning.

Notes

1. In this paper, we use 'Global education development' to refer to our course and 'global education development' to refer to the concept in a broader sense.
2. 'Education and International Development: An Introduction' edited by Tristan McCowan and Elaine Unterhalter was the course textbook which provides an overview, historical origins of education development and the major trends in the field.
3. For more information on the virtual courses offered by UniPID, check https://www.unipid.fi/students/virtual-studies/
4. ECTS is the European Credits Transfer and Accumulation System in which 1 ECTS credit correspond to 25–30 h of study. In Finland, 1 ECTS credit = 27 h of study; 25 ECTS is the equivalent of 675 h of study
5. Finland has an ambivalent relation to colonization, for being both occupied by foreign kingdoms and built on racialized conception of nationhood. Under the Swedish rule, Finns were subject to racialized stereotypes and a lower status in the hierarchy as being descendents of the Mongols. Later, the Fennoman movement, emerging as a movement for nationhood and autonomy, produced the imaginary of Finland as a unified nation of people, and also

explicitly defines this as a nation of white europeans speaking the Finnish language. This meant the exclusion of the indigenous Sàmi people and Roma people. It has been later coupled with the marginalization of racialized immigrant communities since the 1990s.

6. In 'Decolonial methodologies in education', Zavala (2016) elaborates on three decolonial strategies used in education – 1) Counter/Storytelling 2) Healing 3) Reclaiming. All these strategies emphasise community self-determination and includes generative praxis that brings ancestral knowledges together with local, endogenous knowledges to create decolonial educational spaces.

7. 'Shouldering our colonial backpack' (2016) is a video produced by Center for Global Learning in Schools where post/decolonial scholar Vanessa Andreotti is interviewed by Sonja Richter. The conversation focuses on the implications of using postcolonial theory in education and thereby understand the ways in which educators can engage with the discomfort of unlearning harmful patterns of colonialism within education.

8. 'Global Education in Europe … Development' by Nygaard and Wegimont (2018) is a policy paper written for the Global Education Network Europe (GENE) which outlines how Global Education is defined and conceptualised by international organisations as well as the different EU member states.

9. This feedback by the student made us reflect on the citational politics. While we understand that the mechanical process of APA-style citation which is commonly used in our faculty is not colonial in itself, it makes us reflect on which types of work/knowledge that attains the status of legitimacy to be included in peer-reviewed journals and thereby be part of courses like Global education development.

10. *The Global Education Monitoring Report* (GEM Report) prepared by an independent team of scholars is published by UNESCO. It monitors progress towards SDG 4. The annual GEM Report provides an evidence-based overview of education development globally with the emphasis on quality. https://en.unesco.org/gem-report/about

11. The article 'Colonial Complicity: The 'Post-colonial' in a Nordic context' by Vuorela (2009) discusses the ways which Finland participated and benefited from the colonial system even though there is a general perception of Finnish colonial innocence as Finland did not officially colonise countries and was colonised by Sweden and Russia. Vuorela (2009) gives the examples of story books, anthropology research, development work and joining the European Union (EU) to highlight how dominant colonial worldview is perpetuated in Finland through these different sources.

12. 'Pluriverse: A Post-Development Dictionary' by Kothari et al. (2019) consists of over one hundred essays focusing on alternatives to current hegemonic models of development around the world with contributions from multiple contexts. The book argues that unless we staunchly challenge the liberal idea of the linear progression of development, we will not be able to think and open pathways for alternative ways of living and being in harmony with the environment.

Disclosure statement

No potential conflict of interest was reported by the author(s).

ORCID

Elina Lehtomäki ⓘ http://orcid.org/0000-0002-3733-0578

References

Andreotti, Vanessa de Oliveira. 2011. "(Towards) Decoloniality and Diversality in Global Citizenship Education." *Globalisation, Societies and Education* 9 (3-4): 381–397.

Asher, Kiran. 2013. "Latin American Decolonial Thought, or Making the Subaltern Speak." *Geography Compass* 7 (12): 832–842.

Atehortúa, Juan Velásquez. 2020. "A Decolonial Pedagogy for Teaching Intersectionality." *Nordic Journal of Comparative and International Education (NJCIE)* 4 (1): 156–171.

Boveda, Mildred, and Kakali Bhattacharya. 2019. "Love as de/Colonial Onto-Epistemology: A Post-Oppositional Approach to Contextualized Research Ethics." *The Urban Review* 51 (1): 5–25.

Charbonneau, Irène. 2020. "Social Presence And Educational Technologies In An Online Distance Course In Finnish Higher Education - A Social-Constructivist Perspective." (Masters thesis) Stockholm University, http://su.diva-portal.org/smash/get/diva2:1506466/FULLTEXT01.pdf

Cusicanqui, Silvia Rivera. 2012. "Ch'ixinakax Utxiwa: A Reflection on the Practices and Discourses of Decolonization." *South Atlantic Quarterly* 111 (1): 95–109.

De Lissovoy, Noah. 2010. "Decolonial Pedagogy and the Ethics of the Global." *Discourse: Studies in the Cultural Politics of Education* 31 (3): 279–293.

de Sousa Santos, Boaventura. 2018. *The end of the Cognitive Empire: The Coming of age of Epistemologies of the South.* Durham: Duke University Press.

European Union Agency for Fundamental Rights. 2019. "Being Black in the EU: Second European Union Minorities and Discrimination Survey." https://fra.europa.eu/en/publication/2018/being-black-eu.

Freire, Paulo. 1970. "The Adult Literacy Process as Cultural Action for Freedom." *Harvard Educational Review* 40 (2): 205–225.

Juusola, Henna. 2020. "Perspectives on Quality of Higher Education in the Context of Finnish Education Export." (PhD dissertation) Tampere University. https://trepo.tuni.fi/bitstream/handle/10024/123165/978-952-03-1679-2.pdf?sequence=2&isAllowed=y

Kothari, Ashish, Ariel Salleh, Arturo Escobar, Federico Demaria, and Alberto Acosta. 2019. "Pluriverse." *A Post-Development Dictionary. New Dehli: Tulika Books.*

Legg, Stephen. 2017. "Decolonialism." *Transactions of the Institute of British Geographers* 42 (3): 345–348.

Lehtola, V. 2015. "Sámi Histories, Colonialism, and Finland." *Arctic Anthropology* 52: 22–36.

Mangione, Daniela, and Lin Norton. 2020. "Problematising the Notion of 'the Excellent Teacher': Daring to be Vulnerable in Higher Education." *Teaching in Higher Education* 1–16. https://doi.org/10.1080/13562517.2020.1812565.

McCowan, Tristan. 2015. "Theories of Development." In *Education and International Development: An Introduction*, edited by Tristan McCowan, and Elaine Unterhalter, 31–48. London: Bloomsbury Publishing.

McCowan, Tristan, and Elaine Unterhalter, eds. 2015. *Education and International Development: An Introduction.* London: Bloomsbury Publishing.

Mignolo, Walter. 2011a. *The Darker Side of Western Modernity: Global Futures, Decolonial Options.* Durham: Duke University Press.

Mignolo, Walter D. 2011b. "Epistemic Disobedience and the Decolonial Option: A Manifesto." *Transmodernity* 1 (2): 3–23.

Mignolo, Walter D. 2011c. "Geopolitics of Sensing and Knowing: on (de) Coloniality, Border Thinking and Epistemic Disobedience." *Postcolonial Studies* 14 (3): 273–283.

Mignolo, Walter D., and Catherine E. Walsh. 2018. *On Decoloniality: Concepts, Analytics, Praxis.* Durham: Duke University Press.

Morreira, Shannon. 2017. "Steps Towards Decolonial Higher Education in Southern Africa? Epistemic Disobedience in the Humanities." *Journal of Asian and African Studies* 52 (3): 287–301.

Nygaard, Arnfinn, and Liam Wegimont. 2018. "Global Education in Europe–Concepts, Definitions and Aims in the Context of the SDGs and the New European Consensus on Development." *Global Education Network Europe* 1–54.

Pashby, Karen, and Louise Sund. 2020. "Decolonial Options and Challenges for Ethical Global Issues Pedagogy in Northern Europe Secondary Classrooms." *Nordic Journal of Comparative and International Education* 4 (1): 66–83.

Quijano, Anibal. 2000. "Coloniality of Power and Eurocentrism in Latin America." *International Sociology* 15 (2): 215–232.

Rastas, Anna. 2004. "Am I Still 'White'? Dealing with the Colour Trouble.".

Rastas, Anna. 2019. *"The Emergence of Race as a Social Category in Northern Europe." In Relating Worlds of Racism, pp. 357-381.* Cham: Palgrave Macmillan.

Rutazibwa, Olivia. 2018. "On Babies and Bathwater: Decolonizing International Development Studies." In *Decolonization and Feminisms in Global Teaching and Learning*, edited by Sara de Jung, Rosalba Icaza, and Olivia Rutazibwa, 158–180. London: Routledge.

Schatz, Monica. 2016. Education as Finland's Hottest Export." In *A Multi-Faceted Case Study on Finnish National Education Export Policies Helsingin Yliopisto.*

Schatz, Monika, Ana Popovic, and Fred Dervin. 2017. "From PISA to National Branding: Exploring Finnish Education*." *Discourse: Studies in the Cultural Politics of Education* 38 (2): 172–184.

Silva, Janelle M. 2018. "and Students for Diversity Now. "#WEWANTSPACE: Developing Student Activism Through a Decolonial Pedagogy."." *American Journal of Community Psychology* 62 (3-4): 374–384.

Stein, Sharon. 2019. "Beyond Higher Education as we Know it: Gesturing Towards Decolonial Horizons of Possibility." *Studies in Philosophy and Education* 38 (2): 143–161.

Sultana, Farhana. 2019. "Decolonizing Development Education and the Pursuit of Social Justice." *Human Geography* 12 (3): 31–46.

Tuck, Eve, and K. Wayne Yang. 2012. "Decolonization is not a Metaphor." *Decolonization: Indigeneity, Education & Society* 1 (1): 1–40.

"UniPID" Finnish University Partnership for International Development. 2021. Accessed March 1, 2021. https://www.unipid.fi/.

Unterhalter, Elaine.. 2015. "Education and International Development: A History of the Field." In *Education and International Development: An Introduction*, edited by Tristan McCowan and Elaine Unterhalter, 13–29. London: Boomsbury Publishing.

Vaidya, A. 2016. "Does Critical Thinking Education Have a Western Bias? A Case Study Based on Contributions from the Nyāya Tradition of Classical Indian Philosophy." *Journal of Philosophy of Education* 50 (2): 132–160.

Vandermensbrugghe, Joelle. 2004. "The Unbearable Vagueness of Critical Thinking in the Context of the Anglo-Saxonisation of Education." *International Education Journal* 5 (3): 417–422.

Vuorela, Ulla. 2009. "Colonial Complicity: The 'Postcolonial' in a Nordic Context." In *Complying with Colonialism: Gender, Race, and Ethnicity in the Nordic Region*, edited by Suvi Keskinen, Salla Tuori, Sari Irni, and Diana Mulinari, 19–33. Farnham: Ashgate.

Walsh, Catherine E. 2015. "Decolonial Pedagogies Walking and Asking. Notes to Paulo Freire from AbyaYala." *International Journal of Lifelong Education* 34 (1): 9–21.

Zavala, Manuel. 2016. "Decolonial Methodologies in Education." *Encyclopedia of Educational Philosophy and Theory* 361–366.

Refusal as affective and pedagogical practice in higher education decolonization: a modest proposal

Michalinos Zembylas

ABSTRACT

The questions driving this paper are: What sort of affective (dis)investment is needed in higher education to refuse the colonial university? How can educators and students in higher education invent 'pedagogies of refusal' that function affectively to challenge colonial futurity? What do pedagogies of refusal look like? This paper theorizes *refusal* as an affective practice that produces political effects and desires that challenge normative manifestations of power and control. It is argued that refusal may constitute a fruitful avenue toward decolonization of higher education, because it directs attention to the affective (dis)investments from/in desires that can be fulfilled by the university. To this end, the paper suggests that if the aim is to disrupt the seductive workings of colonial power in its most intimate dimensions, then it is crucial to invent pedagogies that engage with the affective (dis)investments of students and educators in colonial relations.

Introduction

What forms of intimacies do we need to develop to truly realize social transformation? (Alexander 2001, 6)

What happens when we refuse what all the (presumably) 'sensible' people perceive as good things? What does this refusal do to politics, to sense, to reason? When we add Indigenous peoples to this question, the assumptions and the histories that structure what is perceived to be 'good' (and utilitarian goods themselves) shift and stand in stark relief. The positions assumed by people who refuse 'gifts' may seem reasoned, sensible and in fact deeply correct. Indeed, from this perspective, we see that a good is not a good for everyone. (Simpson 2014, 1)

A theme that has recently emerged in contemporary literature on decolonization in higher education is *refusing* the (colonial) university (Grande 2018; Metcalfe 2019; Tuck and Yang 2014a, 2014b, 2018). The university historically 'functioned as the institutional nexus for the capitalist and religious missions of the settler state, mirroring its histories of dispossession, enslavement, exclusion, forced assimilation and integration' (Grande 2018, 47–48). Hence, refusing the university means taking a political stance and action 'within, against, and beyond the university-as-such' (Grande 2018, 51). The notion of 'refusal', which is rooted in cultural anthropology (McGranahan 2016) and Indigenous studies (Coulthard 2014; Simpson 2007, 2014, 2016), marks a political ethos and praxis that denies, resists, reframes and redirects colonial and neoliberal logics, while asserting diverse sovereignties and lifeworlds (Wright 2018). Refusal is a kind of 'disinvestment' from certain rules and relations (Bhungalia 2020) such as those that enable colonialism and an 'affirmative investment' (Weiss 2016, 352) to possibilities that invoke decolonization.

While some accounts on the politics of refusal acknowledge the affective modes of legitimating and reproducing colonial hegemony (e.g. see Coulthard 2014; Simpson 2016), scholarship on decolonization in higher education has not paid enough attention to theorizing the *affective* contours of refusing the colonial university. Drawing on Alexander's quote (2001) in the epigraph of this paper, then, I ask in this paper: What sort of affective (dis)investment is needed in higher education to refuse the colonial university? In particular, how can educators and students in higher education invent 'pedagogies of refusal' (Rodríguez 2019; Tuck and Yang 2014a) that function affectively and politically to challenge colonial futurity? What do pedagogies of refusal look like? As Stein (2019b) has pointed out, our intellectual analysis of the university's colonial history as harmful does not necessarily 'translate' into an affective disinvestment from desires that perpetuate colonial violence in higher education. Hence, it is important to explore what it means for educators and students in higher education to invest in forms of feeling and relating that refuse the colonial university and work towards its 'abolition' (Moten and Harney 2004).

'Affects' are generally understood as relational and embodied intensities (Seigworth and Gregg 2010) that circulate in 'affective economies' in which feelings are mobilized to create particular affective attachments (Ahmed 2004) that mark the ways in which things become significant and relations are lived (Anderson 2014). It is suggested, then, that affects are 'forces of encounter' which are intertwined with discourse, power, and the body (Zembylas 2019). In this sense, 'refusal' may be conceptualized as an 'affective practice' (Wetherell 2012) which produces political effects and desires that challenge normative manifestations of power and control. As Mühlhoff argues, '*Every* political movement and every critical project is driven by affects, so the point is not *whether* or not affect is relevant, but *how* it is involved' (in Kemmer et al. 2019, 26, original emphasis). What I am interested in this paper, therefore, is how refusal may constitute a fruitful avenue toward decolonization of higher education precisely because it directs attention to the affective (dis)investments from/in desires that can be fulfilled by the university.

The main objective of this article, then, is to discuss the affective contours of refusing the colonial university and articulate what this analysis implies for pedagogies of refusal in higher education decolonization. The discussion proceeds as follows: the first section situates the project of higher education within the history and politics of colonization and discusses how the university has facilitated the integration of state technologies of settler colonialism and racial capitalism. The second section provides a theorization of refusal in cultural anthropology and Indigenous studies, focusing in particular on how refusal may be conceptualized in the terms of affective economy and affective practice. The third section takes McGranahan's (2016) theorization of refusal in generative ways as a point of departure to outline three affective modes of decolonial refusal that challenge the colonial university: refusal as social and affiliative; refusal as distinct from resistance; and, refusal as hopeful and willful. The last section of the paper concludes by outlining how these affective modes 'translate' into an ethos of pedagogies of refusal for decolonization in higher education.

Situating the project of higher education: its colonial legacies

Any effort to make sense of the project of higher education today has to be situated in the long history of colonialism (Wolfe 2006). Wolfe argues that for many centuries from the establishment of the early universities of medieval Europe to the beginning of the twentieth century, higher education was at the service of the nation-state (see also, Luke and Heynen 2019; Stein 2020). The European university model, grounded in Eurocentric epistemologies and colonial principles, has been imposed across the colonies in other continents – the Americas, Asia, Africa, and the Pacific (Mignolo 2011). Hence, it is important to acknowledge how the establishment of universities in many Western societies and colonies has been inextricably linked to colonial processes and practices that continue to shape contemporary higher education (Stein 2020). Unless, the project of higher education recognizes, confronts *and* undoes its colonial legacies, it is difficult to imagine how the terms of current academic and political debates about the future of higher education will change (Patton 2016; Wilder 2013).

My point of departure is recognizing how settler colonialism and the frontier logic have been central to the institutionalization of universities to facilitate the integration of land and capital accumulation (Wolfe 2006). Settler colonialism is generally understood as a set of social and material relations, policies and practices through which colonizers assert their power and ownership over and against colonized (i.e. Indigenous) peoples (Coulthard 2014). Also, the frontier logic reflects a combination of economic, geographical and historical claims that justify the expansion and settlement of colonizers; these claims are grounded in the assumption that land is free and that development justifies its conquest to produce capital and secure state sovereignty (Luke and Heynen 2019). Although colonialism is understood as a temporal period of oppression that has come and gone, coloniality is the underlying logic that places peoples and knowledge into a classification system such that all that is European is valorized – a system which is still very much with us today (Grosfoguel 2007; Maldonado-Torres 2007).

Critiques of the modern western university by critical Indigenous, Black, and other de-/anti-/post-colonial theorists have identified higher education as central to settler colonialism and the frontier logic (Andreotti et al. 2015; Grande 2018; Grosfoguel 2007; Luke and Heynen 2019; Maldonado-Torres 2007; Stein 2019a, 2020; Stein and Andreotti 2017). As Luke and Heynen assert, the institutionalization of higher education as a key site of settler colonialism and the frontier logic has been facilitated through three intertwined processes:

> First, university involvement in Indigenous removal and ongoing dispossession through occupation of Indigenous land; second, the advancement of empire-building research and teaching agendas to commercialize and modernize neo-plantation agriculture; and finally, the contribution to shaping a racialized labor system in the exclusion of potential students deemed alien, illegal, or non-citizen. (2019, 3)

Historically, then, the university has functioned as the institutional nexus for the capitalist and imperialist expansion of the settler state and its efforts to instigate dispossession, enslavement, exclusion and oppression (Grande 2018; Patton 2016).

In particular, American universities reproduced slavery to the extent that they served as key sites in the production, legitimation and dissemination of ideas that justified and proliferated scientific racism and racial capitalism (Wilder 2013). As Wilder writes:

> American colleges were not innocent or passive beneficiaries of conquest and colonial slavery. The European invasion of the Americas and the modern slave trade pulled peoples throughout the Atlantic world into each other's lives, and colleges were among the colonial institutions that braided their histories and rendered their fates dependent and antagonistic. The academy never stood apart from American slavery – in fact it stood beside church and state as the third pillar of a civilization built on bondage. (2013, 11)

In fact, points out Wilder, universities served as 'instruments of Christian expansionism, weapons for the conquest of indigenous peoples, and major beneficiaries of the African slave trade and slavery' (2013, 17) as well as 'imperial instruments akin to armories and forts, a part of the colonial garrison with the specific responsibilities to train ministers and missionaries, convert indigenous peoples and soften cultural resistance, and extend European rule over foreign nations' (2013, 33).

The model of the modern university, then, has its roots to religious expansionism and the Enlightenment values of Western modernity (e.g. freedom, democracy, citizenship). Yet the irony is that this model has operated within a set of fundamental contradictions – such as promising education to all students, yet excluding those who have been historically disenfranchised (e.g. the landless, women, Indigenous peoples, people of color), and advocating humanistic values for all, yet dehumanizing colonized peoples (Chatterjee and Maira 2014). Higher education, therefore, functioned as a key technology not only of colonial expansion in various continents, but also in being complicit in social reproduction for capital accumulation and capital expropriation (Boggs and Mitchell 2018). In fact, in the name of market-based ideologies, such as 'democracy' and the 'public good,' higher education has been historically complicit in the further establishment of racialized, hegemonic, settler capitalism (Labaree 2017).

As suggested by several scholars, the 'neoliberal university' and the internationalization of higher education have evolved out of this ethos of coloniality and disenfranchisement (Luke and Heynen 2019; Shahjahan and Morgan 2016; Stein 2017). These trends in contemporary higher education risk reproducing already uneven geopolitical relations and ultimately contribute to expanding social and economic injustices and furthering coloniality in the world. This is why it is important to scrutinize the colonial roots of the continued hegemonic model of contemporary higher education, if we wish to adequately grasp and respond to the dire consequences of these trends (Stein 2020). The dominant 'academic model', explains Stein (2019a), 'is not only thoroughly Eurocentric in its regimes of sanctioned knowledge and socialization, but also capital-and nation-state-centric; in other words, it is thoroughly colonial' (149).

The contemporary university, then, functions in a space full of paradoxes, tensions, and complexities. On the one hand, it faces the rise of 'academic capitalism' and the corporatization of higher education (Boggs and Mitchell 2018); the hegemonic reign of these trends preclude other educational possibilities from happening, such as broadening access to those who have been excluded, democratizing the university space, or contributing to confronting inequality and injustice in the world. On the other hand, if within the colonizing university there is also a decolonizing education (la paperson 2017), then it is important to engage in efforts that build new modes of academic practices and alliances which not only recognize, analyze and confront the university's complicity in coloniality but also re-claim the academy as a decolonizing space (Luke and Heynen 2019; Stein 2019a; Zembylas 2020b). This is where refusal as a political ethos and practice may have a crucial contribution. The next part of the paper provides a theorization of refusal, highlighting, in particular, a neglected aspect, namely, how refusal may be conceptualized through the lens of affect.

Theorizing refusal as affective economy and practice

The notion of 'resistance' has monopolized theoretical interest across the social sciences for decades now (Bhungalia 2020) – ranging from Scott's (1985) account on 'everyday' or 'invisible' acts of resistance to Foucault's (2009) theorization of 'counter-conduct.' Despite considerable disagreements as to what exactly it denotes (Hollander and Einwohner 2004), resistance is generally understood as an oppositional act (Johansson and Vinthagen 2016). Refusal, however, is distinguished from resistance as it does not always entail an act of opposition, but rather it is 'a kind of abstention, a disinvestment from rules of engagement' (Bhungalia 2020, 390). Whereas resistance, suggests McGranahan (2016), consciously defies or opposes superiors, albeit in a context of differential power relations, refusal 'rejects this hierarchical relationship, reposting the relationship as one configured altogether differently' (McGranahan 2016, 323). In this sense, refusal is generative as it 'moves away from default negative connotations into spaces that might be more social than antisocial' (McGranahan 2016, 322).

As Simpson (2014) explains in her landmark ethnography of Mohawk political life and the Indigenous relations to the settler state, refusal operates very differently from resistance. Whereas resistance may reinscribe the weakness of the colonized in the power relations with the colonizer (settler state), refusal interrupts the smooth operation of power relations, denying the authority of the settler state and remaking the rules of engagement. Refusal, then, does not stand in opposition to repressive power and authority, as resistance does; instead, refusal is a political stance and action that denies the very legitimacy of power over the subjugated, seeking alternative forms of legitimacy (Bhungalia 2020). As Simpson (2014) argues,

> there is a political alternative to "recognition," the much sought-after and presumed "good" of multicultural politics. This alternative is "refusal," [...] as a political and ethical stance that stands in stark contrast to the desire to have one's distinctiveness as a culture, as a people, recognized. Refusal comes with the requirement of having one's political sovereignty acknowledged and upheld, and raises the question of legitimacy for those who are usually in the position of recognizing. (11)

Liberal recognition in multicultural politics, according to Simpson, is refused on the grounds that it is limited to the mere recognition of cultural difference, not to mention that it fails to acknowledge the heterogeneity of Indigenous peoples. Most importantly, though, liberal recognition excludes political or land rights, thus it is of little use in decolonization struggles (Burman 2016). The political regime of recognition, emphasizes Simpson (2016), is rooted in colonial practices that enforced Indigenous dispossession and then granted freedom through the legal tricks of consent and citizenship. Hence, refusing liberal recognition is a practice that contributes toward decolonization because it insists on highlighting the lived experiences and desires of the oppressed and colonized (Murdock 2019). Practically, refusal is manifested in various activities such as refusing to vote, pay taxes or travel on settler nation documents (Simpson 2014). In tracing these refusals, Simpson invites us to consider what happens when consent is withdrawn and the ontological fixity of the settler state is unsettled (Bhungalia 2020).

In a similar vein, Coulthard (2014) critiques the politics of recognition in the settler state's efforts for reconciliation, and questions the 'specific modes of colonial thought, desire and behavior that implicitly or explicitly commit the colonized to the types of practices and subject positions that are required for their continued domination' (16). For Coulthard, refusal is the starting point for prefiguring 'radical alternatives to the structural and subjective dimensions of colonial power' (Coulthard 2014, 18). He advocates Indigenous resurgence and thus recommends to 'redirect our struggles *away* from a politics that seeks to attain a conciliatory form of settler-state recognition for Indigenous nations toward a *resurgent politics of recognition* premised on self-actualization, direct action, and the resurgence of cultural practices' (Coulthard 2014, 24, original emphasis). In other words, for Coulthard, refusal is a positive rather than a negative stance – one that is less oriented around affirmative forms of settler colonial state recognition, and more about reevaluating, reconstructing and redeploying culture and tradition in the Indigenous practices of living. In this way, Coulthard reorients the project of decolonization to place Indigenous liberatory practices at the center of political transformation (Burman 2016).

Undoubtedly, refusal is a political stance and praxis, as the works of McGranahan, Simpson, and Coulthard show. Importantly, 'The political describes distributions of power, of effective and *affective* possibility,' points out Simpson (2016, 326, added emphasis). Similarly, Coulthard (2014) writes about the significance of the 'psycho-affective attachment' to colonialist forms of recognition and the ways in which colonial desires are cultivated and internalized. One of the aspects of coloniality that is gradually coming to the forefront of discussions in recent years, then, is the colonial legacies of affects and emotions, that is, how affectivity plays a major part in relations of coloniality and oppression just as in seeking alternative relations and liberatory practices (Cvetkovich 2012). Not only there is no escape from the emotional history of the past and the present rooted in coloniality, but also the achievement of social justice and the dismantling of colonial relations have been linked in part with the need to invent new affects and affective relations (Pedwell 2016).

Hence, theorizing refusal not only as political but also as affective practice is valuable in turning our attention toward the production of those affective practices that could challenge colonial practices and enable decolonization. In general, affective practices are understood as forms of activity that understand and mobilize affect as a central part of practice (Wetherell 2012). As Wetherell explains, 'An affective practice is a figuration where body possibilities and routines become recruited or entangled together with meaning making and with other social and material figurations' (2012, 19). Through the lens of affect theory, then, all political practices are also affective ones. Viewing refusal as a form of affective practice helps us pay attention to the ways in which forms and structures of refusal come to be conceivable, how they are articulated and legitimated, and how they contribute to the reproduction or interrogation of colonial practices. The patterning of refusal as affective practice, then, is inevitably embedded within particular socio-political settings (see Breeze 2019).

Similarly, Ahmed (2004) theorizes the production of affective attachments as economies that circulate and invest in particular feelings of desire. Her analysis views emotions as cultural and political, that is, not as individual feelings residing 'within' subjects and then moving outward toward objects, but rather as forms of capital 'produced as an effect of its circulation' (45). In affective economies, according to Ahmed, emotions are relations and they *do things*; in particular, emotions align individuals with communities through the very intensity of their attachments. Agathangelou, Bassichis, and Spira (2008) have specifically used the notion of affective economies in reference to 'the circulation and mobilization of feelings of desire, pleasure, fear, and repulsion utilized to seduce all of us into the fold of the state' and become 'invested emotionally' in the 'false promises' of capitalism and the empire (122). For example, the desire for recognition cultivated by liberal politics is invoked as an affective economy that works through an 'imperial project of promise and non-promise' (Agathangelou, Bassichis, and Spira 2008, 128); some are included in these promises and become complicit to the imperial regime that makes them, while others (e.g. Indigenous peoples) are systematically excluded and persistently suffer the consequences of colonization.

All in all, then, theorizing refusal as an affective practice and economy helps us understand the ways in which alternative practices – e.g. Indigenous liberatory practices, as Coulthard (2014) would say – may be invoked to challenge colonial relations. Intellectual analysis and critical consciousness are not enough to identify how harmful colonial practices are in the field of education and beyond; these practices need to be accompanied by actions that create affective disinvestment from those desires that perpetuate coloniality – such as autonomy, certainty, and accumulation of capital (Stein 2019b). In the context of higher education, in particular, as I show next, refusal also requires the cultivation of new affective economies and practices that not only identify complicity in reproducing harmful promises and colonial effects, but also establish new solidarities, commitments, and possibilities for decolonization.

Three affective modes of decolonial refusal in higher education

An analysis of different modes of refusal examines the ways in which refusal as both political and affective practice can make contributions to higher education decolonization. More importantly, this analysis could identify pedagogical spaces and practices of 'affective counterpolitics' (Massumi 2015) at the university, namely, spaces and practices of decolonial refusal that invoke 'hopeful criticism' (Anderson 2017) – that is, criticism which is not merely negative but rather affirmative, creating opportunities of hope for social transformation (Zembylas 2020a). In particular, I focus on three affective modes of decolonial refusal that emerge from McGranahan's (2016) theorization of refusal in cultural anthropology. McGranahan, who draws on Simpson's (2007, 2014, 2016) work, details three aspects of refusal: refusal as social and affiliative; refusal as distinct from resistance; and, refusal as hopeful and willful. I argue that these three aspects may also constitute affective modes of decolonial refusal in higher education, and I explain below how and why this is so.

The first aspect, according to McGranahan (2016), is that refusal is social and affiliative. This aspect suggests that by refusing the colonial state's structures of social and cultural organization, practices of refusal enable the production of new forms of community and relationality (Jafri 2020). In relation to the colonial university, Grande (2018) suggests that the prospect of refusal raises a fundamental question in debates of higher education decolonization: 'What kinds of solidarities can be developed among peoples with a shared commitment to working beyond the imperatives of capital and the settler state?' (59-60). Previous attempts at alliance-building within and across, for example, feminism, anti-war, and anti-capitalist movements, have shown that these solidarities are also sites of power differential and struggle; hence, a question here is how affective refusal may confront some of these sticky but important issues within the higher education context. Making more explicit the link between affective refusal and solidarity, this question may be re-phrased as follows: What kind of 'affective solidarities' (Hemmings 2012) can be developed at the university so that peoples who work on various social justice projects (e.g. anti-racist, anti-capitalist projects) 'stand with' (TallBear 2014) those struggling for decolonization?

To address this question, it is important first to acknowledge that there are two fundamental dimensions of promise and recognition promoted by the empire (Agathangelou, Bassichis, and Spira 2008). On the one hand, there are those peoples for whom 'pleasures and rights are being forever promised [...] at the expense of compliance with, or perhaps a distraction from, the larger structural underpinnings of social relations and processes' (Agathangelou, Bassichis, and Spira 2008, 137). On the other hand, there are those for whom the same promise has not been issued, the colonized and oppressed peoples (e.g. Indigenous peoples) whose sufferings are recognized only at a superficial level. Decolonial refusal as an affective economy and practice, then, takes different trajectories for these groups. While refusal for the colonized emerges directly from conditions of dispossession and violence produced by settler colonialism, a refusal for those who are privileged requires the development of a critical and affective consciousness around complicity in ongoing colonization (cf. Jafri 2020).

Decolonial refusal, therefore, is manifested differently for different groups, yet the new openings emerging have the potential to create pedagogical and political spaces at the university that could inspire *anti-complicity* praxes *for all* – that is, actions that actively refuse to commit any social harm in everyday life (Zembylas 2020c). In other words, affective refusal may confront some of the thorny issues of solidarities across different movements by creating a common ground that refuses to sustain complicity. For example, a university instructor could be concerned with how to make students understand complicity as situated – that is, how power relations and affective infrastructures in their specific setting constellate to formulate complicity, what it would take to recognize this complicity (politically and emotionally; collectively and individually) and engage in actions that refuse to perpetuate it. The notion of refusal as social, affiliative *and* affective offers a productive point of departure to begin articulating the ways in which our differential affective attachments to the colonial project – our fears, desires, and so on – can be mobilized to produce solidarities 'not premised upon exploitation, profit, or death'

POSSIBILITIES AND COMPLEXITIES OF DECOLONISING HIGHER EDUCATION 75

(Agathangelou, Bassichis, and Spira 2008, 137). Hence, affective refusal in higher education can make an important contribution to solidarities and alliance building, despite differential motivations to decolonial refusal.

The second aspect of refusal, according to McGranahan (2016), is its distinction from resistance. As Simpson (2016, 330) points out, resistance 'overinscribe[s] the state with its power to determine what matter[s].' Approaching Mohawk refusals as both political stance and theory, Simpson (2014) argues that the concepts of resistance or recognition – which have been predominantly used in social and political theory – are insufficient to account for refusing the place of the state. Whereas resistance reaffirms the rules of engagement set by the state, refusal not only critiques them, but it also produces new rules and forms of relationality. As such, a critical and affective consciousness of refusal constitutes a form of *revenge* against the deep inequities and injustices that structure colonial relations (Simpson 2016). However, as Simpson explains, 'Revenge does not mean individuated harm inflicted on a perpetrator in a transaction that renders justice' but rather 'avenging a prior of injustice and pointing to its ongoing life in the present' (Simpson 2016, 330). It is a 'refusal to let go, to roll over, to play this game,' (Simpson 2016) adds Simpson.

These insights are relevant to the state of neoliberal and neocolonial higher education, because they highlight not only the intellectual but also the deep affective commitment that is required for decolonial refusal. If we – educators and students, Indigenous and non-Indigenous alike – are affectively invested in the status quo, the empty promises or the complicity of those of us who benefit from this system, then unless we become affectively disinvested in this system, we run the risk of reproducing the colonized economies of affect 'that fortify so much of conservative, liberal and even radical praxis' (Agathangelou, Bassichis, and Spira 2008, 137). Hence, resistance may indeed not be enough in some circumstances; refusal has to take the front seat and drive decolonization efforts in higher education. Here, then, I am extending previous discussions that recognize the affective dimensions of resistance and its educational implications (Zembylas 2019), and I argue that educators and students in higher education need to also learn how to refuse emotional participation to *all* forms of colonial violence that impact us *all*.

A point that merits some further clarification here is what to do with anti-capitalist movements calling for resistance to the neoliberal university. While such movements and their importance cannot be dismissed, my argument is that affective refusal moves a step forward compared to resistance, because it refuses to play the game of legitimating colonial structures and seeks to find new ways to dismantle its power. Needless to say, as I point out later, refusal creates space for resistance, therefore, resistance cannot be completely dismissed as a pedagogical strategy. After all, resistance and refusal are connected, as both are tactics of negation that struggle to dismantle neoliberal and neocolonial structures, albeit from different trajectories and intensities. Hence, once again, the notion of 'common ground' between the two tactics may reconcile concerns whether resistance should be completely dismissed.

Finally, the third aspect of refusal, according to McGranahan (2016), is that refusal is hopeful and willful. This refers to how 'Hope combines with will to refuse authorized anticipations' (McGranahan 2016, 323), namely, that which is usually expected, 'thus moving away from the probable into the possible' (McGranahan 2016). In other words, hope is understood as an affective practice, just like refusal, that is generated, mobilized, sustained and/or transformed (Kleist and Jansen 2016) for equality, decolonization or simply for a better life (Coleman and Ferreday 2010). Hence, I argue here that it is crucial for educators and students in higher education to imagine alternative ways to feel and hope that are not stuck in default negative connotations of refusal but rather speak forcefully of the desire for decolonization. In this sense, decolonial refusal is combined with hope to highlight the visions, mournings, memories, voices, and spaces that have been relegated to silence as a result of coloniality.

To challenge colonial relations in higher education without paying attention to the affective entanglements of refusal and hope – including their potential impact on social relations and processes – may ultimately prove unproductive as it will miss accounting for the complex ways in which these affects (and others) may be embodied differentially in different peoples and sites. The need to begin the restorative processes required to facilitate the move away from colonial relations and structures in higher education can be inspired by and oriented around the cultivation of hope that gives rise and materializes new capacities to aspire a decolonial futurity. Yet, this hope is not an empty or sentimental hope, but rather a *material hope*, deeply informed by the affectivity and materiality of the 'land *as a system of reciprocal relations and obligations*' (Coulthard 2014, 13, original emphasis). This radical assertion of the land in discourses and practices of refusing the university (Grande 2018) is necessary to confront colonial relations. However, this means that the changes that need to happen at the university to become a place that reformulates the rules of engagement with the land and Indigenous peoples should not be limited to hollow performances of recognition such as routine-like territorial acknowledgments which are quickly forgotten (Daigle 2019). These changes need to be forged as a fundamental disruption of the colonial affective logics that are manifested in all aspects of higher education – from the systems of access and management in universities, the systems of authoritative control, standardization, classification, commodification, accountancy, and bureaucratization reflected in the organizational structures, the teaching methods and assessment mechanisms of students and faculty alike, the research practices and publishing norms, to the curricular content and design of courses (Mbembe 2016). In the last part of this paper, I will focus on one of these aspects: how to cultivate an affective ethos of refusal in higher education pedagogies.

Pedagogies of refusal in higher education decolonization

As I have argued so far, affect is key to refuse colonial relations at the university and beyond. If it is true that our deepest desires and emotions 'are tapped into for imperial production,' then it is crucial to ask 'how we might organize, mobilize and form alternative intimacies and desires' (Agathangelou, Bassichis, and Spira 2008, 139) that embody an ethos of refusal in higher education pedagogies. But how do the affective modes of decolonial refusal mentioned earlier 'translate' into an ethos of refusal in higher education pedagogies? In other words, how do refusal as social and affiliative, refusal as distinct from resistance, and, refusal as hopeful and willful formulate collectively an affective ethos of refusal in higher education pedagogies? The vision of pedagogies of refusal in higher education decolonization would be nothing less than the potential to create abolitionist students and educators (Moten and Harney 2004), who would not stop at the recognition of the harm caused by settler colonialism, but would rather move beyond recognition toward decolonial action (Rodríguez 2019). If Spivak (2004) is right that education is 'the uncoercive rearrangement of desires' (526), then there is no guarantee that pedagogies of refusal will form alternative intimacies and desires; nevertheless, it is crucial to begin sketching how such pedagogies might look like. Importantly, the paper's aim is not discuss the practical aspect of pedagogies of refusal, but rather to offer some reflections on how to cultivate an ethos of affective refusal in the academy.

First of all, I understand *pedagogies of refusal* (Tuck and Yang 2014a; Rodríguez 2019) to be those pedagogies that empower students – many of whom experience forms of colonial violence on a daily basis and others who are complicit to this violence – to not only recognize these forms of colonial violence but also disrupt, refuse and displace them with alternative relations that affirm decolonizing imaginaries. I turn to Alexander's (2001) definition of 'pedagogies' in her book *Pedagogies of Crossing*, because it allow us to see how our pedagogical practices may embody an ethos of refusal. As Alexander writes: 'I came to understand pedagogies in multiple ways [...] as in breaking through, transgressing, disrupting, displacing, inverting inherited concepts and practices [...] so as to make different conversations and solidarities possible' (7). Alexander's notion of pedagogies includes transformative teaching that compels students to think about colonial trauma and white complicity, renewed relationships with the 'self' and 'others', and engagements with genealogies of Indigenous peoples that break through inherited boundaries, allowing students 'to "cross" into future imaginings for social change' (Hanna 2019, 232).

Teaching the practice of refusal, write Tuck and Yang (2014a) 'is unsettling both because students may first consider refusal to be undesirable, as failure, and also because it can feel like explaining refusal requires exposing that which ought not to be exposed' (815). Although refusal is unsettling, it can also be generative, because it creates pedagogical spaces to examine that which is being refused (Rodríguez 2019). In particular, writes Rodríguez,

> Refusal helps us unmask seemingly benevolent relations and the function of affect in creating institutional buy-in. Our refusal creates space for resistance to incorporation while simultaneously opening space for us to turn toward another possibility. Our refusal lets us recognize that we are each other's possibility. Through our refusal we challenge normalized coercive violence (e.g. the capitalist reproduction of death, prisons, the dispossession of Indigenous lands). Our refusal delegitimizes that which has gained legitimacy by force. As such, our embodied refusal constitutes a decolonial potential. (2019, 6)

Teaching the practice of decolonial refusal, then, entails the cultivation of embodied and affective refusal that challenges all forms of coercive violence. Hence, it is crucial, according to Grande (2018), to find 'common ground' among parallel social justice projects that aim to undermine colonial relations and practices (e.g. anti-capitalist, anti-racist, anti-colonial projects). The 'common ground' here, suggests Grande, 'is not necessarily literal but rather conceptual, a corpus of shared ethics and analytics: anti-capitalist, feminist, anti-colonial. Rather than allies, we are accomplices – plotting the death but not the murder of the settler university' (2018, 60–61). I have argued throughout this paper that this common ground is, importantly, deeply affective too; teaching and learning how to become accomplices with others against all forms of violence entails the production of affective solidarities that 'engage the traumas *as well as* the yearnings of our pasts and out futures' (Agathangelou, Bassichis, and Spira 2008, 139, original emphasis). Given the necessity and value of forming such affective solidarities, it would be unwise, in my view, to create a 'competition' among different social justice projects or distinguish between those which are explicitly decolonial and others which are 'less' so.

Furthermore, attending to affect in pedagogies of refusal brings into view the micropolitical dimension through which knowledge production takes place at the university. A micropolitical dimension is a constitutive dimension of all political activity, argues Anderson (2017). Knowledge production and legitimation at the university is one such activity; teaching that compels students to critique colonial relations and their consequences is another. Yet, both of these activities are intertwined and affectively grounded. Paying attention to the micropolitics of colonial relations enable us – researchers and educators in higher education – to see how the affective segmentations of life in the classroom can be as harmful as rigid colonial structures (Zembylas 2020a). In other words, it is crucial not to underestimate, or worse to dismiss the entanglement of affective power between the micro- and macro-political level (Protevi 2009).

For example, in the case of universities located on stolen lands – actively supportive of the ongoing dispossession of Indigenous lands (Daigle 2019) – power works affectively and micropolitically to increase a body's docility and achieve an affective mode of governance (Anderson in Kemmer et al. 2019). Therefore, a point of departure for pedagogies of refusal is for educators to understand how affective dynamics function micropolitically to organize, mobilize and form Indigenous and non-Indigenous students' responses toward the issue of land dispossession and under which circumstances there can be an antidote to the affective ideology of colonial relations and practices in everyday university life. A key pedagogical question, then, is: How and with which resources can educators and their students first identify the forms of damage and harm that are reproduced by colonial relations micropolitically, and then explore different manifestations of decolonial action that would bring the desired transformations within or beyond the university? A set of relevant questions to explore with/in the university has been suggested by Stein (2020) such as:

> How can we prepare learners to work with and through the difficulties, failures, uncertainties, and anxieties that are a central part of social change, without fear? What kind of curriculum can encourage learning from feelings and experiences of discomfort, complicity, and disillusionment? (225)

If educators in higher education want to move beyond recognition-based practices taking shape across universities in settler colonial contexts, then pedagogies of refusal need to identify the ways that recognition-based practices perpetuate 'cruel optimism' (Berlant 2011). Cruel optimism, according to Berlant, exists 'when something you desire is actually an obstacle to your flourishing' (1). Affective attachment to the false promises of capitalism and empire involves an inclination to return to fantasies that will never fulfill the transformation people desire; this is coupled with the production of feelings of 'reconciliation' as a remedy to past injustices, wrongs and sufferings of Indigenous peoples (Daigle 2019). Pedagogies of refusal, then, can help educators and students refuse the fraught scripts of optimism and relationality that function as 'containment and appeasement mechanisms' (Rodríguez 2019, 6) and try to listen deeply to each other's stories and struggles (Tuck and Yang 2014a); and, to enable non-Indigenous students to understand their own complicity and how colonial logics constrain their ability to affectively connect with Indigenous worldings and forms of knowledge (see Wright 2018). Therefore, pedagogies of refusal in higher education are not negative, but rather affirmative practices highlighting 'positive' and hopeful stories of alternative relationalities that embody the hope for decolonial futurity. All in all, pedagogies of refusal that are grounded in the affirmative elements of refusal (e.g. as social and affiliative; as hopeful and willful) create the potential to cultivate a decolonial ethos in higher education – a much needed ethical and political orientation towards the long and difficult processes of higher education decolonization.

Concluding remarks

In this article I have discussed how a politics and an affective pedagogy of refusal could provide openings in higher education to offer first a disruption of empire's seductive promises and then a hope and desire to form new solidarities and intimacies for decolonization. Refusal, I have pointed out, invokes a vision for both a decolonizing and affective approach that serves as public and political pedagogy, methodology, and intellectual analysis within and outside the university (see Hundle 2019). To build on Hundle's theorization, such a pedagogy, methodology and intellectual analysis is derived from careful engagement with anti-colonial thought and its histories, theories, and practices of decolonization that are based on the entanglements of the political, the intellectual, and the affective. While many scholars in higher education decolonization have framed refusal as foremost a methodology, political pedagogy and intellectual analysis, I argue that its affective elements and the transformative possibilities emerging from this acknowledgment remain ignored. To this end, I suggest that it is crucial to focus on and enact pedagogies of refusal that engage with the affective (dis)investments of students and educators in colonial relations, if we are to disrupt the seductive workings of colonial power in its most intimate dimensions (Agathangelou, Bassichis, and Spira 2008).

Amid the apparent power of the neoliberal and neocolonial university, some may argue that pedagogies of refusal are utopian, as they invoke the idea of decolonial desires. However, as la paperson (2017) reminds us:

> My position is impossible, a colonialist-by-product of empire, with decolonizing desires. I am, and maybe you are too, a produced colonialist. I am also a by-product of colonization. As a colonialist scrap, I desire against the assemblage that made me. This impossibility motivates this analysis, which seeks not to resolve colonialist dilemmas, but to acknowledge that they include specific machined privileges that may be put to work in the service of decolonizations. (xxiii)

la paperson emphasizes that decolonial desires and visions are crucial in efforts to disrupt coloniality; it goes without saying that such desires by themselves will not dismantle colonial relations and structures. Yet, every position of impossibility also holds some kind of possibility; these impossibilities and possibilities coexist and are part of the potential of higher education decolonization. Crucially, decolonizing higher education is not the sole work of educators, students or administrators in universities; work outside the university is equally important. However, if there is one major argument emerging from this paper is that it becomes crucial to continue exploring how universities are sites of both estrangements and intimacies – that is, affective sites of struggles against coloniality. As such, pedagogies of refusal – within and beyond the university – have an important contribution to seize the possibilities emerging for breaking down empire's seductive promises.

Disclosure statement

No potential conflict of interest was reported by the author(s).

ORCID

Michalinos Zembylas ⓘ http://orcid.org/0000-0001-6896-7347

References

Agathangelou, A., M. D. Bassichis, and T. L. Spira. 2008. "Intimate Investments: Homonormativity, Global Lockdown, and the Seductions of Empire." *Radical History Review* 2008: 120–143.

Ahmed, S. 2004. *The Cultural Politics of Emotion*. Edinburgh: University of Edinburgh Press.

Alexander, M. J. 2001. *Pedagogies of Crossing: Meditations on Feminism, Sexual Politics, Memory and the Sacred*. Durham, NC: Duke University Press.

Anderson, B. 2014. *Encountering Affect: Capacities, Apparatuses, Conditions*. Aldershot: Ashgate.

Anderson, B. 2017. "Hope and Micropolitics." *Environment and Planning D: Society and Space* 35 (4): 593–595.

Andreotti, V., S. Stein, C. Ahenakew, and D. Hunt. 2015. "Mapping Interpretations of Decolonization in the Context of Higher Education." *Decolonization: Indigeneity, Education & Society* 4 (1): 21–40.

Berlant, L. 2011. *Cruel Optimism*. Durham: Duke University Press.

Bhungalia, L. 2020. "Laughing at Power: Humor, Transgression, and the Politics of Refusal in Palestine." *EPC: Politics and Space* 38 (3): 387–404.

Boggs, A., and N. Mitchell. 2018. "Critical University Studies and the Crisis Consensus." *Feminist Studies* 44 (2): 432–463.

Breeze, R. 2019. "Emotion in Politics: Affective-Discursive Practices in UKIP and Labour." *Discourse & Society* 30 (1): 24–43.

Burman, J. 2016. "Multicultural Feeling, Feminist Rage, Indigenous Refusal." *Cultural Studies ↔ Critical Methodologies* 16 (4): 361–372.

Chatterjee, P., and S. Maira, eds. 2014. *The Imperial University: Academic Repression and Scholarly Dissent*. Minneapolis, MN: University of Minnesota Press.

Coleman, R., and D. Ferreday. 2010. "Introduction: Hope and Feminist Theory." *Journal for Cultural Research* 14 (4): 313–321.

Coulthard, G. S. 2014. *Red Skin, White Masks: Rejecting the Colonial Politics of Recognition*. Minneapolis: University of Minnesota Press.

Cvetkovich, A. 2012. *Depression: A Public Feeling*. Durham: Duke University Press.

Daigle, M. 2019. "The Spectacle of Reconciliation: On (the) Unsettling Responsibilities to Indigenous Peoples in the Academy." *Environment and Planning D: Society and Space*, 37 (4): 703–721.

Foucault, M. 2009. *Security, Territory, Population: Lectures at the Collége de France 1977-1978. Vol.4*. New York: Macmillan.

Grande, S. 2018. "Refusing the University." In *Toward What Justice?: Describing Diverse Dreams of Justice in Education*, edited by E. Tuck, and K. W. Yang, 47–65. New York: Routledge.

Grosfoguel, R. 2007. "The Epistemic Decolonial Turn: Beyond Political-Economy Paradigms." *Cultural Studies* 21 (2-3): 211–223.

Hanna, K. B. 2019. "Pedagogies in the Flesh: Building an Anti-Racist Decolonized Classroom." *Frontiers: A Journal of Women Studies* 40 (1): 229–244.

Hemmings, C. 2012. "Affective Solidarity: Feminist Reflexivity and Political Transformation." *Feminist Theory* 13 (2): 147–161.

Hollander, J. A., and R. L. Einwohner. 2004. "Conceptualizing Resistance." *Sociological Forum* 19 (4): 533–554.

Hundle, A. K. 2019. "Decolonizing Diversity: The Transnational Politics of Minority Racial Difference." *Public Culture* 31 (2): 289–322.

Jafri, B. 2020. "Refusal/Film: Diasporic-Indigenous Relationalities." *Settler Colonial Studies* 10 (1): 110–125.

Johansson, A., and S. Vinthagen. 2016. "Dimensions of Everyday Resistance: An Analytical Framework." *Critical Sociology* 42 (3): 417–435.

Kemmer, L., C. H. Peters, V. Weber, B. Anderson, and R. Mühlhoff. 2019. "On Right-Wing Movements, Spheres, and Resonances: An Interview with Ben Anderson and Rainer Mühlhoff." *Distinktion: Journal of Social Theory* 20 (1): 25–41.

Kleist, N., and S. Jansen. 2016. "Introduction: Hope Over Time—Crisis, Immobility and Future-Making." *History and Anthropology* 27 (4): 373–392.

Labaree, D. F. 2017. *A Perfect Mess: The Unlikely Ascendancy of American Higher Education*. Chicago: University of Chicago Press.

la paperson. 2017. *A Third University is Possible*. Minneapolis: University of Minnesota Press.

Luke, N., and N. Heynen. 2019. "Abolishing the Frontier: (De)Colonizing 'Public' Education." *Social & Cultural Geography*, doi:10.1080/14649365.2019.1593492.

Maldonado-Torres, N. 2007. "On the Coloniality of Being." *Cultural Studies* 21 (2-3): 240–270.

Massumi, B. 2015. *Q & A With Brian Massumi, by Laura Sell*. Duke University Press Blog. https://dukeupress.wordpress.com/2015/08/19/qa-with-brian-massumi/.

Mbembe, A. 2016. "Decolonising the University: New Directions." *Arts and Humanities in Higher Education* 15 (1): 29–45.

McGranahan, C. 2016. "Theorizing Refusal: An Introduction." *Cultural Anthropology* 31: 319–325.

Metcalfe, A. S. 2019. "Thinking in Place: Picturing the Knowledge University as a Politics of Refusal." *Research in Education* 104 (1): 43–55.

Mignolo, W. 2011. *The Darker Side of Western Modernity: Global Futures, Decolonial Options*. Durham, NC: Duke University Press.

Moten, F., and S. Harney. 2004. "The University and the Undercommons: Seven Theses." *Social Text* 22 (2): 101–115.

Murdock, E. 2019. "Sites of Epistemic Friction: Are Decolonial Desires Entitled to Opacity?" *Journal of World Philosophies* 4: 87–91.

Patton, L. D. 2016. "Disrupting Postsecondary Prose: Toward a Critical Race Theory of Higher Education." *Urban Education* 51 (3): 315–342.

Pedwell, C. 2016. "Decolonizing Empathy: Thinking Affect Transnationally." *Samyukta: A Journal of Women's Studies* XVI (1): 27–49.

Protevi, J. 2009. *Political Affect: Connecting the Social and the Somatic*. Minneapolis, MN: University of Minnesota Press.

Rodríguez, Y. 2019. "Pedagogies of Refusal: What it Means to (Un)Teach a Student Like Me." *Radical Teacher* 115: 5–12.

Scott, J. 1985. *Weapons of the Weak—Everyday Forms of Peasant Resistance*. New Haven, CT: Yale University Press.

Seigworth, G., and M. Gregg. 2010. "An Inventory of Shimmers." In *The Affect Theory Reader*, edited by M. Gregg, and G. Seigworth, 2–25. Durham, NC: Duke University Press.

Shahjahan, R., and C. Morgan. 2016. "Global Competition, Coloniality, and the Geopolitics of Knowledge in Higher Education." *British Journal of Sociology of Education* 37 (1): 92–109.

Simpson, A. 2007. "On Ethnographic Refusal: Indigeneity, 'Voice' and Colonial Citizenship." *Junctures* 9: 67–80.

Simpson, A. 2014. *Mohawk Interruptus: Political Life Across the Borders of Settler States*. Durham, NC: Duke University Press.

Simpson, A. 2016. "Consent's Revenge." *Cultural Anthropology* 31: 326–333.

Spivak, G. 2004. "Righting Wrongs." *South Atlantic Quarterly* 103 (2/3): 523–581.

Stein, S. 2017. "Internationalisation for an Uncertain Future: Tensions, Paradoxes, and Possibilities." *The Review of Higher Education* 41 (1): 3–32.

Stein, S. 2019a. "Beyond Higher Education as we Know it: Gesturing Towards Decolonial Horizons of Possibility." *Studies in Philosophy and Education* 38: 143–161.

Stein, S. 2019b. "Navigating Different Theories of Change for Higher Education in Volatile Times." *Educational Studies* 55 (6): 667–688.

Stein, S. 2020. "A Colonial History of the Higher Education Present: Rethinking Land-Grant Institutions Through Processes of Accumulation and Relations of Conquest." *Critical Studies in Education* 61 (2): 212–228.

Stein, S., and V. Andreotti. 2017. "Decolonisation and Higher Education." In *Encyclopaedia of Education Philosophy and Theory*, edited by M. Peters, 1–6. Singapore: Springer Science + Business Media.

TallBear, K. 2014. "Standing With and Speaking as Faith: A Feminist-Indigenous Approach to Inquiry." *Journal of Research Practice* 10 (2): Article N17. Accessed May 22, 2020. http://jrp. icaap.org/index.php/jrp/article/view/405/371.

Tuck, E., and K. W. Yang. 2014a. "Unbecoming Claims: Pedagogies of Refusal in Qualitative Research." *Qualitative Inquiry* 20 (6): 811–818.

Tuck, E., and K. W. Yang. 2014b. "R-Words: Refusing Research." In *Humanizing Research: Decolonizing Qualitative Inquiry with Youth and Communities*, edited by D. Paris, and M. T. Winn, 223–247. Thousand Oaks, CA: Sage Publications.

Tuck, E., and K. W. Yang. 2018. "Introduction: Born Under the Rising Sign of Social Justice." In *Toward What Justice?: Describing Diverse Dreams of Justice in Education*, edited by E. Tuck, and K. W. Yang, 1–18. New York: Routledge.

Weiss, E. 2016. "Refusal as Act, Refusal as Abstention." *Cultural Anthropology* 31: 351–358.

Wetherell, M. 2012. *Affect and Emotion: A New Social Science Understanding*. London: Sage.

Wilder, C. S. 2013. *Ebony and Ivy: Race, Slavery, and the Troubled History of America's Universities*. New York: Bloomsbury Press.

Wolfe, P. 2006. "Settler Colonialism and the Elimination of the Native." *Journal of Genocide Research* 8 (4): 387–409.

Wright, S. 2018. "When Dialogue Means Refusal." *Dialogues in Human Geography* 8 (2): 128–132.

Zembylas, M. 2019. "The Affective Dimension of Everyday Resistance: Implications for Critical Pedagogy in Engaging with Neoliberalism's Educational Impact." *Critical Studies in Education*, doi:10.1080/17508487.2019.1617180.

Zembylas, M. 2020a. "From the Ethic of Hospitality to Affective Hospitality: Ethical, Political and Pedagogical Implications of Theorizing Hospitality Through the Lens of Affect Theory." *Studies in Philosophy and Education* 39 (1): 37–50.

Zembylas, M. 2020b. "Toward an Ethics of Opacity in Higher Education Internationalisation." *Philosophy and Theory in Higher Education* 2 (1): 91–115.

Zembylas, M. 2020c. "Re-conceptualizing Complicity in the Social Justice Classroom: Affect, Politics and Anti-Complicity Pedagogy." *Pedagogy, Culture, & Society* 28 (2): 317–331.

Understanding the challenges entailed in decolonising a Higher Education institution: an organisational case study of a research-intensive South African university

Anwar Shaik ⓘ and Peter Kahn

ABSTRACT
Decolonisation is being embraced as an imperative within Higher Education, yet many institutions have struggled to formulate a coherent response. This article reports on a case study of a research-intensive South African university where the call for decolonisation emerged amidst considerable conflict on campus. The research takes as its departure point the notion that the discourse on decolonisation, thus far dominated by calls to re-examine Western ways of knowing, would nonetheless benefit from perspectives grounded in the paradigm of critical realism and from a social realist analysis. It found that an intellectual and cultural solipsism, as a form of fractured reflexivity, rooted in social and cultural identity, played a causal role in constricting the collective reflexivity of the corporate agents that shape the Western academic environment, resulting in a reproduction of an exclusionary intellectual and cultural environment.

Introduction

The broad-ranging extent of the cultural and intellectual legacy of colonialism is encapsulated in the term coloniality, which refers to ' ... long-standing patterns of power that emerged as a result of colonialism ... maintained alive in books, in the criteria for academic performance, in cultural patterns, in common sense, in the self-image of peoples [and] in aspirations of self ... ' (Maldonado-Torres, citing Quijano 2007, 243). Cultural and intellectual 'othering' is an often-mentioned feature of coloniality by which the culture and intellectual tradition of the colonised people is invalidated (Ashcroft, Griffiths, and Tiffin 2009; Mbembé 2001; Pwiti and Ndoro 1999). Ashcroft et al. state that 'The self-identity of the colonising subject, indeed the identity of imperial culture, is inextricable from the alterity of colonised others, an alterity determined, according to Spivak, by a process of othering' (2009, 10). Focusing on the effects of othering on the privileged, Field (2013) describes the Western elite as those who generally assume themselves to be well-behaved, appropriately dressed and professing liberal conceptions of personal dignity and impartial justice. Addressing the concept 'whiteness',

Steyn (2001) describes it as a form of unconsciousness of its own exclusionary nature. Manganyi (1973), indeed, first raised the idea of 'Black Consciousness' to counter the white oblivion that existed in relation to blacks. Biko (1987) saw this state of oblivion in which whites typically exist with regard to black suffering as a key challenge for the liberation process. Moon (1999) identifies this form of unconsciousness as an appropriation of the entire frame of human experience into what she calls 'whiteness'. Cultural and intellectual othering and its prolonged effect on the reflections and the actions of subjects of colonialism has been a central theme in this study.

Much is written on othering as intellectual and particularly epistemic exclusion. Paulo Freire (2000) theorises the relationship between epistemology, identity and exclusion, and sees these as necessarily needing to be congruent in order to avoid alienation and exclusion of the learner. More recently, Mbembe (2016) argues for the decolonisation of knowledge, while Asante (2012) calls for redesigning curricula from an Afro-centric perspective and Luutu (2012) calls for greater local relevance of curricula. For knowledge to be decolonised, Mbembé sees a need for the university to move beyond accepted epistemologies and redefining and reprioritising study disciplines towards reflecting the needs of a newly liberated South Africa. The idea of revising the very purpose of the university, with its epistemic and structural change implications, is also advanced by (Msila 2017). Abdullah spells out what is meant by epistemic decolonisation when he states decolonisation means 'For us [subjects of colonialism] to have our own independent world-view of knowledge and world-view of university, in terms of its role, philosophy, aims, and goals' (Abdullah 2012, 23). Nonetheless, where they have been tried, significant challenges have been experienced in realising such agendas within universities (Santos 2017; Bhambra, Nişancıoğlu, and Gebrial 2018). Those who have assessed decolonisation efforts over the past two decades have found that the very normalisers of colonial structures cannot be relied on to deliver real decolonisation and have continued to act in defence of both their privilege and colonised structures (Stein and Andreotti 2017).

What is not in evidence are studies that explore the influence of historical exclusion and alienation on the part of those responsible for maintaining universities in colonised manifestations. Postcolonial studies – being closely associated with postmodern research – typically explore the problem in terms of the narrative of the victims while avoiding broad systemic analyses. They consequently suffer the disadvantage of hindering a systemic response to the problem. This then leads to research schism and programmes that suffer from a lack of objectivity and broad institutional acceptance (Winter 2009; Macfarlane 2012). In seeking a novel and coherent way forward in relation to this gap, this study turns to the paradigm of critical realism. The introduction of a critical realist perspective sets this present study apart from postcolonial investigations that typically define the reality of coloniality solely in terms of the perspectives of the human subjects. In terms of decolonisation, this can result in having to compromise on the broad, objective validity of the emancipatory agenda. An emancipatory agenda with objective and independent validity is central to critical realism. It is encapsulated in what Bhaskar and Hartwig call 'concrete utopianism' (2010, 20). Emphasising the importance of emancipatory power within research, Roy Bhaskar, states 'It is my contention that … liberation … is both causally presaged and logically entailed by explanatory theory, but that it can only be effected in practice' (Bhaskar 2009, 177). While upholding ontological reality, critical realists avoid the pitfall created by positivist research which reduces all reality to what is empirically observable or deducible. They, therefore, assume a domain of causality that transcends and eludes empirical observation. This study, which revisits central postcolonial concepts such as 'othering' and Eurocentrism, therefore, has proceeded with the assumption that empiricism can only offer a partial glimpse into the reality of coloniality and that causality, located beyond empirical observation, may need to be inferred.

Within the paradigm of critical realism, the realist social theory of Archer (1995) and others, offer some important concepts with which to pursue a new analysis of coloniality in its observed manifestations. Archerian concepts such as fractured reflexivity or what Flam (2013) describes as the repressed reflexivity can be helpful in such an analysis. Archer finds that fractured reflexives experience an inhibition in 'their capacity to hold an internal conversation about themselves in relation to their circumstances, which has any efficacy' (Archer 2003, 298). Indeed, one can question the role that agency and reflexivity play within intellectual and cultural exclusion. For this study, the impact of fractured reflexivity has, therefore, been considered within the university, particularly for those with the collective power to shape its context. Known in social realist theory as the corporate agents, these include 'the management, support staff, professional associations, funders, academic disciplinary groups' within the university that shape the academic and cultural context reflexively (Williams 2015, 309). Referring to a form of fractured reflexivity as a pathology of those at the political helm, Donati theorises 'a form of 'strategic-tactic reflexivity' which, particularly in post- modern societies, produces fractured people' (2013, 151). The end-result is that the agents conflate the 'I', as shaped by functional and social status concerns with the 'we', within which is included the 'other' as the non-corporatised social agents (Donati 2013). Such theories within social realism, therefore, provide new ways of understanding coloniality. A concept that is central in recent decolonial literature is the idea of Eurocentrism. It denotes an attitude of evaluating all values and social practices in terms of Western culture (Murrey 2018; Santos 2014). Central to the eventual findings in this study was therefore the interpretation of the concept Eurocentrism, through the lens of social realism. As can be seen later on in this paper, the concept of the Intellectual and Cultural Solipsism (ICS) emerged from the analysis as such a causal mechanism.

Research design

The study took the form of a single case study of a South African university that was severely shaken by demands for it to be decolonised. A period of conflict continued intermittently on campus between 2015 and 2017 and resulted in the disruption and closure of the university on multiple occasions (Booysen 2016; Langa 2017). The campus used for the case study experienced the burning of campus property and ongoing police or security intervention on campus. It followed the pattern of other South African campuses that had previously been majority white under Apartheid, and where a transition to a black majority had taken place. The conflict spurred a myriad of interviews, articles, speeches, campus meetings, videos and open letters in the public domain. This body of published work, representing a vibrant discourse record, compressed within two years, created an ideal body of evidence for a study on coloniality. As the institution was an English medium, globally well-ranked, research-intensive modern university, it also meant that any research outcomes might prove useful to institutions beyond the immediate research setting.

The case study format offered an ideal research design format for this type of research. The ontology advanced by critical realism requires that the researcher assumes an 'observer role', employing an empirical research methodology (Cohen, Manion, and Morrison 2007, 7). The organisational case study research design has been found to fulfil this purpose effectively (Williams and Wynn 2012). Even more relevant to this study, Williams and Wynn cite a number of critical realist researchers whom they state 'have identified the case study method as the best approach to explore the interaction of structure, events, actions, and context to identify and explicate causal mechanisms' (2012, 795). Additionally, the case study has also been found to be effective for organisational and managerial research (Edwards, O'Mahoney, and Vincent 2014; Vincent 2014). A case study was hence developed by means of an analysis of texts generated in the heat of, or in the immediate aftermath of the protests and conflict between 2015 and 2017.

Assuming the research paradigm of critical realism meant assuming an ontologically Real cause behind coloniality being empirically un-observable. That meant that all empirical observations could only be limited to causal effects. These effects were to be detected from within the body of sampled texts. Recognised methods of textual and discourse analysis were used to enable such detection. The sample of text used included speeches, interviews and articles – authored or recorded between the years 2015 and 2018 by players directly connected to the university. These players turned out to be official structures of the institution, campus formations, individual lecturers, officials, students, administrators and alumni. The only criterion was that the textual item had to be found in the public domain. No private unpublished perspectives were solicited, and no publicly available perspective was filtered out. The process of gathering the texts included an exhaustive searching of the official online university portal, and thereafter a search of three other major search engines, using relevant search terms. The only criteria used to filter out items was duplication and relevance. Since the main intention was to discover the manifestations of coloniality at the university, the focus did fall on texts that espoused decolonisation. Texts that seemed to argue against decolonisation were very rare and are cited in the broader discussion. Although the choice of including items did fall on the primary researcher alone, the diverse list of perspectives, as tabulated in the findings section, serves as evidence of the broad range of perspectives that were included. Audio and visual items were treated as textual material since the inclusion of audio-visual records as part of a general textual analysis has been a generally accepted (see Riasati and Rahimi 2011; Wodak and Meyer 2001). A set of 23 items eventually constituted the body of evidence. These 23 items, deemed to be reflective of the broadest range of perspectives, are listed in Table 1. The items are not tagged sequentially since a greater set of items was collected for the greater original research project.

To avoid relying solely on the documentary items, two interviews with institutional actors were also included in the dataset. A small set of interviews can be effective when used in conjunction with a large documentary sample (Paulsen 2016). The special interviews were used specifically to test the explanatory theory that was developed later on in the research process. The two interviewees were members of the university senior executive (between 2015 and 2017).

A content analysis was initially undertaken to consolidate and summarise an enormous body of textual data to arrive at a manageable dataset (Ahmed 2010; Miles,

Table 1. List of textual items and interviews.

Number	Tags	Brief description
1	Item 07	Article that sets out a process for decolonising knowledge published online, authored by a professor at the university
2	Item 09	Video recording of a panel discussion by a group of black academics and activists
3	Item 14	Online article by an academic that explores a four-year degree as part of transforming the curriculum
4	Item 27	Article published online by a professor critically discussing the present crisis on campus
5	Item 34	Blog posting by an academic on the nature of scholarship in an African setting
6	Item 35	Short article collaboration between editors and academics covering transformation of the curriculum
7	Item 36	An op-ed article by a senior member of the executive that reviews some transformation efforts
8	Item 41	Paper written by a professor on campus discussing to the toxic climate on campus
9	Item 48	An official institutional review for the period 2008–2018
10	Item 50	An official institutional yearbook for 2016
11	Item 53	Comment on a curriculum change document, jointly submitted by some staff members
12	Item 58	Suggestions by an academic on how academics can decolonise their classrooms
13	Item 60	An official report published by a key institutional transformation unit
14	Item 65	A document by a student ad-hoc group that addresses the crisis on campus and sets out some proposals
15	Item 68	A composite article reflecting the views of various academics on the topic of decolonisation
16	Item 71	A formally published curriculum change framework document commissioned by the institution
17	Item 72	A video of a university assembly with numerous students strongly voicing their views
18	Item 73	National radio interview with a prominent Africanist academic
19	Item 77	Statement released by a group of academics around the crisis
20	Item 78	A paper authored by academics on how to transform Humanities disciplines
21	Item 79	Video of various members of a black campus academic formation presenting formal testimony
22	Item 81	Open letter published by a professor that critically discusses the crisis
23	Item 84	A personal reflection by a black student on the crisis on campus, published online
	Interviewee 1	A member of the senior executive of the university during the period 2015–2018
	Interviewee 2	Another member of the senior executive of the university during the period 2015–2018

Huberman, and Saldaña 2020). The content analysis technique set out by Carley (1993) was used. This process entailed coding along with predefined theoretical categories as well as by adding newly identified theoretical categories in the process of reviewing the texts (Carley 1993, 83). The first phase of the analysis resulted in a set of themes. Secondly, a process of drawing out meaning was used, by applying aspects of Critical Discourse Analysis (Fairclough 1993, 2016). The CDA entailed looking at each theme and its accompanying excerpts emanating from Phase 1 and drawing out the central idea or sub-discourse that was conveyed by it. This second stage resulted in six sub-discourses, which were termed 'elements of the discourse' on decoloniality. In effect, the elements of the discourse represent the empirically observable manifestations of coloniality.

Following the content analysis, and the identification of a set of clear discursive elements, a process of inferencing was undertaken. Because critical realism assumes the existence of such powers of causation, located beyond direct observation, it depends on the expanded logical tool of inferencing, beyond simple logical deduction (Burnett 2007; Edwards, O'Mahoney, and Vincent 2014; Fletcher 2016). The task during the inferential phase of the study was therefore to relate a set of discursive elements or social effects, back to a postulated causal mechanism. This relating of observed effects back to a reasonably explainable causal mechanism relied on the logical tool of retroduction (Fletcher

2016). Retroduction seeks to meaningfully relate identified regularities back to an original and independent condition. A model of causality behind coloniality was thus developed and then tested. The objective was to arrive at an explanatory model of cultural and intellectual coloniality that could guide emancipatory action.

Findings

The 23 items that formed part of the textual analysis spanned official university reports, student mass meetings, commentaries, interviews, opinion pieces and radio interviews from campus groups, academics, officials and students. These collectively were assumed to constitute a fair reflection of the discourse on coloniality on campus during the protests, upheaval and disruptions which raged between 2015 and 2017. The textual analysis culminated in a set of six elements of the discourse on decoloniality, which are listed here.

Epistemicide

The first element is Epistemicide, which relates to black scholarship, indigenous epistemologies and approaches to knowledge being shifted to the margins and even beyond the scope of academia. A view that comes out clearly on the part of the authors of many of the items is that Eurocentrism invalidates African identity and African scholarship. The term epistemic violence' and 'epistemicide' are used to refer to this phenomenon in the texts. Item 48 states that Western epistemology and the paradigms for knowledge production are Western-based and alienating to Africans. Item 68 claims that certain methods in science have been abused to denigrate Africans and these scientific methods are irrelevant to Africa's needs and must be replaced. Item 7 contends that the very epistemic foundations are regarded as Eurocentric and dismissive of the knowledge contribution as well as the pathways to knowledge stemming from Africa. A formal institutional report released in 2019 refers to 'epistemic violence by marginalising black scholars and scholarship' (Item 60; Item 78). Testifying to the personal impact of epistemic Eurocentrism, an academic staff member, in a radio interview, mentions being made to feel unworthy as an academic and, as an African, denied real membership of the Western scholarly and knowledge fraternity (Item 73). This sense of having one's ideas seen as unworthy is a widely held sentiment within black student and academic ranks (see, for example, Item 73; Item 72; Item 84). A corollary idea that emanates from the discourse is that African scholarship based on an Afrocentric curriculum could be a viable alternative to Eurocentrism. The prevalent view of Afrocentricity seems to be the placing of African and South African ideas and ideals at the centre of the knowledge creation project (Item 34; Item 71; Item 14). In this sense, a move towards African scholarship refers to a 'decentering' of Western knowledge disciplines, and a centring of knowledge which is developed from within a perspective of African ideas and ideals (Jansen 2017; Msila 2017). Decolonisation is also said to be about indigenous African means of knowledge creation (Item 27) that centres Africa's needs (Item 50).

Inequality

The second element of the discourse is Inequality. It refers particularly to the entrenchment of economic and other forms of inequality as a result of Eurocentrism's being firmly rooted within neo-liberalism and capitalism. Eurocentrism is further indicated in that it drives the commodification of knowledge and research, thereby sustaining global economic inequality. The university is seen as a product of colonialism which continues to serve a foreign agenda of economic domination (Item 71) and, in particular, the ends of capitalism and colonial hegemony (Item 09). As such, it remains committed to the commodification of knowledge (Item 73). Eurocentrism preferences some bodies of knowledge over others, and so also the identities associated with those forms of knowledge (Item 71). It therefore perpetuates current unequal social power relations (Item 34; Item 71). Coupled with this commodification of knowledge is the view that *Eurocentrism reproduces historical power relations*. This view on Eurocentrism of the episteme, beyond its role in sustaining capitalism, is its reproduction of a range of socially oppressive power hegemonies. Western hegemony is covered extensively in the texts. This is often mentioned as the historically entrenched, uneven distribution of power that exists at a personal, cultural, economic and political level. Such uneven distribution is discussed in terms of economic power (Item 65), personal power – articulated as a coloniality of being (Item 34) and cultural power (Item 68). Counting amongst these oppressions are heteronormativity, homophobia, transphobia and ableism (Item 77; Item 71). A project of decolonisation entails essentially a deconstruction of patriarchy, deconstructing modernity and deconstructing all forms of hegemony, while reserving for the subaltern – the subaltern scholar in the case of the institution – a special role to shape a new deconstructed learning environment.

Elitism

Academic Elitism and the grip that a historical academic elite continues to have on the formal academic programme at the university is the third element identified from the discourse. Key aspects of the curriculum continue to be controlled by an entrenched elite, aligned to established disciplines, who use their control as a means of perpetuating traditional power (Item 53). The strict discipline-based approach is also seen as perpetuating Eurocentrism and denying the African identity (Item 09; Item 71; Item 07). The present curriculum therefore reproduces a Western agenda at the expense of local needs and interests. The result is that the existing Western paradigm is a means of exercising a restraining power on change and creates a challenge when contemplating a transformation to an Afrocentric curriculum. From the texts, the view emerges that in order to counter this historical control structure, an African centring in the structuring of the curriculum is needed that recognises and serves a local agenda primarily (Item 35; Item 36; Item 48). The curriculum must respond to and incorporate local needs and civic engagement while bearing in mind the global context (Item 48). The university must seek ways of incorporating African values, knowledge and identities into the curriculum (Item 50).

Misalignment

Cultural and Intellectual Misalignment of Programmes, seen in the absence of the indigenous and local experiences in the development of curricula, resulting in these being less relatable to the non-Western student than to the Western student. Content and frames of references should consider the reality of students (Item 71). Choices about cases and examples used to teach content are often strange to students, and they often have difficulty relating to these. One student articulates this as follows 'External theories must be domesticated. This will make them meaningful to African situations and, more importantly, contribute towards solving local challenges' (Item 35). In a workshop with law students, reported on in Item 71, students felt there was 'the need for a law and a constitution that is from an African sensibility and philosophy of Ubuntu' (Item 71). That knowledge is felt as lacking meaning for those coming from an African or non-Western background, is therefore one likely reason that frustration sets in. Examples mentioned are the Western benchmarks used in the faculty of health sciences and the Western music frames of reference within the college of music. Objections to the curriculum also include the sciences and mathematics, which are said to minimise or ignore African contributions and approaches.

Aesthetics

Aesthetic Estrangement was seen in the lack of African and indigenous iconography while aesthetics in the classroom results in the classroom being an alienating experience to the black student and finally. Black students experience the classroom as a place where no or little effort is made to incorporate examples, case studies, symbols, real-life applications of theory, texts, images, icons, sounds or problem scenarios that make the content or learning objectives more culturally relatable and meaningful to them. There is a rarity of black iconography, stories, illustrations or cases studies in any syllabus, working space or official literature of the institution, with the exception of the African Studies Department. That means that the stories, examples and cases that are hard coded into the syllabi, the official discourse and the artefacts of the university at large, are mainly European and white. In light of this, there is a call for teaching choices to be revised to prevent a reproduction of the status quo (Item 71, 61) and learning material to contain local imagery and examples (Item 71). Language is furthermore seen as an exclusionary factor and plays a significant role in maintaining hierarchies of power and privilege (Item 71, 48). Excluding local languages leads to the excluding local ideas and stories (Item 58). Non-English speakers feel ridiculed and othered (Item 84, 112). The university, in its physical milieu and infrastructure, including the architecture, aesthetics and attitudes, is seen as a culturally alienating place for black people. Campus artworks are seen as foreign and the most telling indication of the rejection of traditional artefacts on campus was 'the burning of portraits and artworks' in April 2016 (Item 48, 199).

Racism

Racism, experienced by the black members of the community mostly in a subtle form, but at times even overtly. These words from a student at a university assembly are telling in this regard

> Comrades, I feel traumatised, [...] not because they called me a monkey or insulted me in some overt manner. Because institutional racism is not like that [...] It's about those educated people who use rationalisations to silence your experiences [loud crowd applause]. (Item 72)

Overt cases were in evidence, however. A black lecturer, for example, testifies at a hearing that a derogatory racist insult was muttered to him by a white staff member (Item 79). What is also found is that black students and academics seem to experience whites as distant and indifferent and that their resentment of blacks takes a more nuanced form at the institution (Item 79; Item 84; Item 72). This takes the form of insensitivity to their needs, an overly strict and hurried resorting to the rules and to authority, and a complete refusal to make any minor gestures of welcoming or acceptance of blacks (Item 79). It often takes the form of singling out blacks and reproaching them for petty offences (Item 73; Item 79). Racism also been described as 'institutional racism' (Item 81; Item 77) which seems to refer to the sense that rules and procedures are applied more robustly against black students and staff.

These six elements of the discourse have, for the purpose of this study, been regarded as the manifestations of coloniality on the part of those linked to the university. Opposing perspectives, aside from a few individuals (Item 41), have largely been absent within the broader discourse. These elements, therefore, constitute an articulation of what coloniality means and formed the basis of the inferencing part of the study.

Inferencing: ICS as a model of causality

As stated in the introduction, the study of coloniality stands to benefit from a social realist analysis. It is such an analysis that frames and underpins the retroductive argument followed in drawing inferences from the empirical findings. The causal condition behind coloniality has generally been inferred as Eurocentrism (Murrey 2018; Santos 2014). The observed elements of coloniality in our case study corresponded with the literature in terms of how Eurocentrism works to perpetuate coloniality. The means by which Eurocentrism operates has however not been adequately explained. Our objective for this study was to pursue a richer explanation of Eurocentrism, from social realism. The task was to describe an objectively real causal mechanism behind coloniality, which could lead to transcendent systemic emancipatory action. Retroduction entails the relating of effects – the elements of the discourse in the case of this study – back to a cause (Danermark et al. 2001). From retroduction, Intellectual and Cultural Solipsism (ICS), is advanced as the causal mechanism behind the observed elements listed in the previous section.

Theorising ICS

Moon (1999) uses the term 'solipsism' to refer to an elite unconsciousness in which existence in general relates to one's own existence and consciousness. The term ICS constitutes an extrapolation of individual solipsism to the socio-cultural world. An ICS may thus be defined as the shared group delusion that, 'what makes sense' means what makes sense for my group and in terms of my group's forms of cognition. One is rendered unable to make proper sense of any idea or experience emanating from outside its ideational boundaries and limitations. It is important, however, to draw a distinction between ICS and personal solipsism, which refers to a radical denial of the existence of the other. What we instead refer is more akin to the epistemic solipsism which Fanon, cited in Bulhan (2010), speaks of as the denial of any intelligence outside of Western experience. ICS is therefore not advanced as merely racism or chauvinism, but rather an acquired fractured reflexivity. The idea of ICS is akin to the hermeneutic gap in the classroom that has been raised by Luckett (2016) and also mentioned in Carnell and Fung (2017). The attribution of a form of solipsism to Western culture is not a completely novel concept in itself (Bulhan 2010).

As stated, a deeper and productive exploring of ICS is undertaken using the tools provided by leading social realist theorists such as Margaret Archer. In terms of social realism, structure imposes a historical conditioning on the agents with which they attempt to confront present realities (Archer 1995; Porpora 2013; Sayer 1992). Instead of therefore taking structure as the only site of analysis, the agents can be independently analysed. This was applied here to explain the concept of ICS. A basic understanding of the reflective process which shapes the actions of the agents is needed firstly. Agents act reflexively through a thought process that juxtaposes their own core concerns with the real-world situation which confronts them. Agents formulate a stance based on what is of ultimate concern to them (Archer 2003). These concerns are tied in with the social identity, implying that agentic stance and action are tied in with identity (Archer 2003). According to Archer, inner conversation makes possible the meaningful engagement of the individual with the social structure. For Archer, collective reflexivity arises when individuals share their own inner conversations with others (Archer 2013). Collective reflexivity sustains corporate agency, in which a group of people formulate shared interests that are in a sense 'ultimate concerns' for them and organise together in furtherance of those concerns. These ultimate concerns transcend functional concerns and include the culturally embedded concerns tied to the group's social identity. If collective reflexivity does not take place in a productive way, however, it prevents the group from formulating a constructive course of action. Problems with the reflexivity amount to unproductive self-talk, leading to an unproductive agentic stance. Unproductive reflexivity, leading to an unproductive agentic stance, is generally referred to as fractured reflexivity (Archer 2000; Flam 2013; Maccarini 2013).

A type of fractured reflexivity is suggested here that refers to a constriction in the imaginative ability of the agents to make sense of an idea or experience. With this in mind, ICS is a condition that arises when, due to structural and cultural conditioning, the corporate agents encounter a real-world situation for which they fail to formulate a productive agentic stance. This failure comes as a result of two reflexivity problems. The first problem occurs when the core concerns of the agents are not being activated at all while the second problem occurs when concerns are activated that are subjective and in furtherance of the status quo. When these social agents encounter an 'outside' idea or experience, the two problems result in two scenarios, respectively. Due to their constricted ability to make sense of the experience, such agents are either wholly unable to make any sense of it (Scenario 1) or misconstrue the experience (Scenario 2).

What happens reflexively in Scenario 1 when agents encounter an idea that exceeds their sensemaking boundaries? Such ideas often come in the form of a set of demands that are forcefully and even violently expressed by a student or other formation and where the institution finds itself obliged to formulate a response. Because no sense is made of the idea, no ultimate concern is activated within the agents and the demand is trivialised as irrational or unjust, leading to short-term appeasement or other forms of circumvention. In the case of Scenario 2, concerns are indeed raised within the corporate agents, but due to their mis-construal of the idea, their actions become inappropriate or misdirected. Misconstruing of an idea or experience might take place even with decolonising efforts within universities, when the corporate agents, (who are predominantly Western conditioned), attempt to steer these initiatives. Decolonisation the curriculum, for example, may then end up being pursued from within the same old curricular paradigm (Stein and Andreotti 2017).

Figure 1 shows an explanatory model of ICS and how it constitutes the causal mechanism behind the perpetuation of coloniality. It proposes a causal model, showing both Scenario 1 and Scenario 2 problems that are caused by the structure. The left-hand side of Figure 1 shows how collective reflexivity is affected when the constricted reflexives cannot make sense of an idea or experience. Within Scenario 1, when the corporate agents cannot make sense of a demand and fail to act productively, it is experienced by the non-corporate agents as dismissive or uncaring behaviour. The charges of marginalisation of non-Western cultures and even charges of racism can be regarded as symptoms of Scenario 1. In the eyes of the 'other', those in power are seen as aloof and dismissive of their plight.

The right-hand side of Figure 1 illustrates how the constricted reflexive's misconstruing of an experience translates into unproductive social action. In response, the corporate agents may reflexively formulate a programme of action, but such a programme is based on their own subjective or false interpretation. In Scenario 2, the corporate agents do formulate a stance and do orchestrate real corporate action in response to the demand but strictly from their limited intellectual and cultural frame. The end-result is that the core grievances and the core elements of coloniality are not addressed. The creation of new departments focusing on indigenous studies, without changing the overall structure of

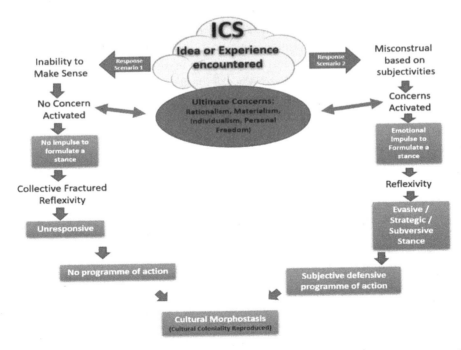

Figure 1. A model of Intellectual and Cultural Solipsism (ICS) as the causal structure of coloniality.

the institution is a good example of this type of inadequate response. Another response within Scenario 2 is for the corporate agents to interpret a demand as antithetical to their core concerns. A demand such as for the abolition of key cultural symbols may then be met by a strong oppositional stance.

In summary form, Intellectual and Cultural Solipsism (ICS) through the mediation of constricted corporate agency, is suggested as the causal mechanism that brings into being the social reality of intellectual and cultural coloniality. This was arrived at by rationally relating the six elements of the discourse back to a single causal condition. ICS in the university implies that the corporate agents, which includes management forums, support staff, professional associations, funders and academic disciplinary groups, have been contributing to the perpetuation of an exclusionary cultural and intellectual environment as a result of a constriction in their reflexivity. This is the causal mechanism that drives a defensive stance towards the status quo and various other evasive and misdirected actions. In the end, it is what prevents them from shaping any future which transcends their own limited imaginary. It constitutes a void that is not knowledge-based, but instead rooted, not in race or ethnicity, but in the social and cultural identity of the agents.

Testing for ICS

The advanced causal explanation is here interpreted in relation to the six elements of the discourse in order to assess its explanatory power. Additionally, the two interviews with the two senior executives are interpreted in terms of the model, to seek further support for the model.

(1) The first element, Epistemicide, generally refers to the alienation of indigenous scholarship and approaches to knowledge. The model explains this in terms of Type 1 and 2 reflexive scenarios that occur as part of ICS. Indigenous scholarship and approaches to knowledge would often, in terms of the historical conditioning of the agents, be misunderstood or devalued. This results in an agentic stance of inaction or active opposition when confronted with the call for greater indigenisation of knowledge and scholarship. (2) Social and economic Inequality is a basic feature that has been historically accepted within neo-liberal capitalist societies. When the agents embrace the free market and neoliberalism as part of their core concerns, they will be conditioned to accept social inequality and the suffering that comes with it. Calls for social justice may be evaluated in terms of those concerns and the agentic stance shaped accordingly. They may then act to defend the established social and economic order. (3) Academic Elitism can be ascribed to the maintenance of traditional professional identities and the agentic concerns that are activated around the preservation of those identities. (4) Cultural and Intellectual Misalignment of Programmes can be explained in terms of the limited experience and sensibility on the part of those who created those programme historically in respect of the experiences of the 'other'. Calls to re-align content and pedagogies to different life experiences are therefore devalued or ignored. (5) The problem of Aesthetic Estrangement and the call for greater indigenous aesthetics will fail to raise any core concerns and result in a stance of trivialising and diminishing such calls. To the estranged, it amounts to a denial of their identity, which will trigger powerful concerns. (6) Racism, rather than being explained as exclusively chauvinistic, can be explained in

terms of the conditioned agents relating to the 'other' on their own cultural and intellectual terms instead of in mutual terms.

The transcripts of the two interviews with two senior executives who served at the institution during the period under consideration were additionally useful in testing the model. The interviewees are diverse in terms of race and gender. Both these executives were centrally involved in the conflict on campus and had to take the lead in responding to demands for the decolonisation of the university. Interestingly, Interviewee 1, even after prompting, failed to raise any of the elements that were ubiquitous in decolonial discourse such as epistemicide or cultural othering, illustrating a clear disjuncture between the core concerns of the corporate agents and non-corporate agents. If ICS describes a constriction in reflexivity, then Interviewee 1 confirms such a gap in the corporate agency of the institution. The interviewee furthermore interpreted the call for decolonisation as being driven solely by group interests and ignored the possibility that decolonisation demands could be associated with a denial of identity. The interviewee dismissively states 'I think that it [the idea of decolonisation] hasn't gotten traction really outside of academia'.

Interviewee 2 raised issues of coloniality and the campus initiatives taken in response to the call for decolonisation. The interviewee states that it was merely a small proportion of the overall curriculum that required decolonisation and that the majority of courses and programmes were aligned with global and technical standards that made serious change unfeasible and also unnecessary. This excerpt from the interview transcript is telling in this regard:

> It's the same curriculum you will study in America or Britain. It's the same if you were studying Statistics, if you were studying Physics or if you were studying Electrical Engineering ... why would you want it to be different? So, I would say that for 80% of what we teach, the question doesn't really arise.

In summary, the second interviewee's perspective on coloniality, the violent protests and transformation are clearly shaped by concerns rooted in his/her cultural and social identity. Both interviews can be said to support the reality of constricted agency by the corporate agents, brought about by ICS, leading to an uncritical projection of a western social and cultural identity onto the institution.

Conclusions

The most important finding of this study is that problems of agency lie at the root of challenges entailed in decolonising the university and that epistemic considerations play a role in significant part because of the ways in which reflexivity is impacted. A social and cultural solipsism was found to play a causal role in constricting both the personal and the collective reflexivity of those shaping the university's Western academic environment. A solipsism represents an acquired hermeneutic void, and it can understand as the inability of those within a group (in this case a university grounded in Western ways of being) to act as corporate agents in relation to ideas or experiences that lie outside of their own social and cultural imaginaries, superior as these imaginaries are perceived to be to those that ground alternative African ways of being. Almost all cases of constricted agency are founded in an exclusive commitment to values which form the basis of the

Western identity such as individualism, materialism, personal freedom and rationalism (Hitlin and Piliavin 2004; Taylor et al. 2003). A constricted collective reflexivity was causally seen to be connected to charges of racism, epistemic exclusion, cultural othering and other known symptoms of coloniality. It can also be related to the acrimony and undue tensions that have been witnessed at many university campuses in recent years.

In contemplating emancipatory action, decolonisation must entail a change in the form of reflexivity that drives agency within the institution. One way of proceeding is offered by Donati (2013), who proposes a type of relational reflexivity that must surpass the functional. This will require the building of networks of relations between 'incongruous' corporate agents instead of maintaining networks of functionally 'congruous' individuals. Practically, in the cases of the charge of epistemicide and inequality, for example, it could mean encouraging and even systematising ongoing dialogue and working relations between established academic disciplines and the drivers of new African-centered approaches. Such relational networks will stir new forms of meta-reflexivity which will transcend the fractured or constricted reflexivity that is created by the present approach. They also have the potential of penetrating traditional insular networks which have hitherto been the main preservers of privilege.

A programme of decolonisation at a university must overcome limiting and partisan identities and foster an inclusive institutional identity. The findings of the study suggest that the present debate around decolonisation within Higher Education is too narrowly framed in terms of knowledge and that a wider vision is required if one is to develop expressions of corporate agency that span ascendant and marginalised populations.

Disclosure statement

No potential conflict of interest was reported by the author(s).

ORCID

Anwar Shaik ⓘ http://orcid.org/0000-0003-0609-5437

References

Abdullah, Saifuddin. 2012. "Our Own World-View of the University." In *Decolonising the University. The Emerging Quest for Non-Eurocentric Paradigms. Special Publication Series*, edited by Claude Alphonso Alvares and Shad Saleem Faruqui. Glugor: Penerbit Universiti Sains Malaysia.

Ahmed, Jashim Uddin. 2010. "Documentary Research Method. New Dimensions." *Indus Journal of Management & Social Sciences* 4 (1): 1–14.

Archer, Margaret S. 1995. *Realist Social Theory*. Cambridge: Cambridge University Press.

Archer, Margaret Scotford. 2000. *Being Human. The Problem of Agency*. Cambridge: Cambridge University Press.

Archer, Margaret Scotford. 2003. *Structure, Agency, and the Internal Conversation*. Cambridge: Cambridge University Press.

Archer, M. S. 2013. "Introduction: The Reflexive Re-turn." In *Ontological Explorations: 2013: 1. Conversations About Reflexivity*, edited by M. S. Archer, 1–14. London: Routledge.

Asante, Molefi Kete. 2012. "4. Reconstituting Curricula in African Universities. In Search of an Afrocentric Design." In *Decolonising the University. The Emerging Quest for Non-Eurocentric*

Paradigms. Special Publication Series, edited by Claude Alphonso Alvares and Shad Saleem Faruqui. Glugor: Penerbit Universiti Sains Malaysia.

Ashcroft, Bill, Gareth Griffiths, and Helen Tiffin. 2009. *Post-colonial Studies. The Key Concepts.* 2nd ed. London, New York: Routledge.

Bhambra, Gurminder K., Kerem Nişancıoğlu, and Dalia Gebrial. 2018. *Decolonizing the University.* London: PlutoPress.

Bhaskar, Roy. 2009. *Scientific Realism and Human Emancipation.* New York: Routledge.

Bhaskar, Roy, and Mervyn Hartwig. 2010. *The Formation of Critical Realism. A Personal Perspective*, edited by Mervyn Hartwig and Roy Bhaskar. London: Routledge.

Biko, S. 1987. I Write What I Like. African Writers Series. Vol. 217. London: Heinemann.

Booysen, Susan. 2016. *Fees Must Fall. Student Revolt, Decolonisation and Governance in South Africa / Susan Booysen.* Johannesburg: Wits University Press.

Bulhan, Hussein Abdilahi. 2010. *Frantz Fanon and the Psychology of Oppression.* New York: Plenum Press. Path in psychology.

Burnett, Nick. 2007. "Critical Realism. The Required Philosophical Compass for Inclusion?" AARE Annual Conference. Australian Association for Research in Education, Freemantle.

Carley, K. 1993. "Coding Choices for Textual Analysis: A Comparison of Content Analysis and Map Analysis." *Sociological Methodology* 75–126.

Carnell, Brent, and Dilly Fung. 2017. *Developing the Higher Education Curriculum. Research-Based Education in Practice.* [Place of publication not identified]: UCL Press.

Cohen, L., L. Manion, and K. Morrison. 2007. *Research Methods in Education.* 6th edn. London: Routledge.

Danermark, Berth, Mats Ekstrom, Liselotte Jakobsen, Jan Ch Karlsson, and Roy Bhaskar. 2001. *Explaining Society.* London: Taylor & Francis.

Donati, Pierpaolo. 2013. "Reflexivity After Modernity: From the Viewpoint of Relational Sociology." In *Conversations about Reflexivity. Ontological Explorations*, edited by Margaret S. Archer, 1st ed., 144–164. London: Routledge.

Edwards, P. K., Joe O'Mahoney, and Steve Vincent. 2014. *Studying Organizations Using Critical Realism. A Practical Guide.* 1st ed. Oxford: Oxford University Press.

Fairclough, N. 1993. "Critical Discourse Analysis and the Marketization of Public Discourse: The Universities." *Discourse & Society* 4 (2): 133–168.

Fairclough, N. 2016. "Discourse Analysis in Organization Studies: The Case for Critical Realism." *Organization Studies* 26 (6): 915–939. http://journals.sagepub.com/doi/pdf/10.1177/0170840605054610.

Field, G. Lowell. 2013. *Elitism. Routledge Revivals.* Routledge.

Flam, H. 2013. "Emotion, and the Silenced and Short- Circuited Sel." In *Conversations about Reflexivity, Ontological Explorations*, edited by Margaret S. Archer, 1st ed., 187–205. London: Routledge.

Fletcher, A. J. 2016. "Applying Critical Realism in Qualitative Research: Methodology Meets Method." *International Journal of Social Research Methodology* 20 (2): 181–194. doi:10.1080/13645579.2016.1144401.

Freire, Paulo. 2000. *Pedagogy of the Oppressed.* 30th Anniversary ed. New York: Continuum.

Hitlin, Steven, and Jane Allyn Piliavin. 2004. Values. Reviving a Dormant Concept 30.

Jansen, J. D. 2017. *As by Fire. The End of the South African University. First Edition (Kindle Edition).* Cape Town South Africa: Tafelberg.

Langa, Malose. 2017. *#Hashtag. An Analysis of the #FeesMustFall Movement at South African Universities.* Johannesburg: CSVR.

Luckett, Kathy. 2016. "Curriculum Contestation in a Post-colonial Context. A View from the South." *Teaching in Higher Education* 21 (4): 415–428. doi:10.1080/13562517.2016.1155547.

Luutu, B. Mukasa. 2012. "7. Bringing the Community Back In. A New University on Affikological Principles and Practices." In *Decolonising the University. The Emerging Quest for Non-Eurocentric Paradigms. Special Publication Series*, edited by Claude Alphonso Alvares and Shad Saleem Faruqui. Glugor: Penerbit Universiti Sains Malaysia.

Maccarini, Andrea M. 2013. "The Morphogenetic Approach and the Idea of a Morphogenetic Society. The Role of Regularities." In *Social Morphogenesis*, edited by Margaret S. Archer, 39–100. Dordrecht: Springer Netherlands.

Macfarlane, Bruce. 2012. "The Higher Education Research Archipelago." *Higher Education Research & Development* 31 (1): 129–131. doi:10.1080/07294360.2012.642846.

Manganyi, N. C. 1973. *Being Black in the World: Rock Art From Southern Africa*. Braamfontein: SPRO-CAS/RAVAN.

Mbembé, J. A. 2001. On the Postcolony. Studies on the History of Society and Culture. Vol. 41. Berkeley, CA: University of California Press.

Mbembe, Achille Joseph. 2016. "Decolonizing the University. New Directions." *Arts and Humanities in Higher Education* 15 (1): 29–45. doi:10.1177/1474022215618513.

Miles, Matthew B., A. M. Huberman, and Johnny Saldaña. 2020. *Qualitative Data Analysis. A Methods Sourcebook*. 4th ed. *International Student Edition*. Los Angeles: SAGE.

Moon, Dreama. 1999. "White Enculturation and Bourgeois Ideology." In *Whiteness: The Communication of Social Identity*, 177–197.

Msila, Vuyisile. 2017. "African Philosophy and African Renaissance." In *Decolonising Knowledge for Africa's Renewal. Examining African Perspectives and Philosophies*, edited by Vuyisile Msila, 21–34. Randburg: KR Publising.

Murrey, Amber. 2018. "'When spider Webs Unite They Can Tie Up a Lion'. Anti-racism, Decolonial Options and Theories from the South." In Routledge handbook of South-South relations. Routledge International Handbooks, edited by Elena Fiddian-Qasmiyeh and Patricia Daley, 1st ed., 59–76. London: Routledge.

Paulsen, M. B. (Ed.) 2016. *Higher Education: Handbook of Theory and Research*. Higher Education: Handbook of Theory and Research. Vol. 31. Cham: Springer.

Porpora, Douglas V. 2013. "Morphogenesis and Social Change." In *Social Morphogenesis*, edited by Margaret S. Archer, 25–37. Dordrecht: Springer Netherlands.

Pwiti, Gilbert, and Webber Ndoro. 1999. "The Legacy of Colonialism. Perceptions of the Cultural Heritage in Southern Africa, with Special Reference to Zimbabwe." *African Archaeological Review* 16 (3): 143–153. doi:10.1023/A:1021624632398.

Quijano, A. 2007. "Coloniality and Modernity/Rationality." *Cultural Studies* 21 (2–3): 168–178. doi:10.1080/09502380601164353.

Riasati, Mohammad Javad, and Forough Rahimi. 2011. ": Critical Discourse Analysis: Scrutinizing Ideologically-Driven Discourses." *International Journal of Humanities and Social Science* 1 (16): 107–112.

Santos, Boaventura de Sousa. 2014. *Epistemologies of the South. Justice Against Epistemicide*. London: Routledge; Paradigm Publishers.

Santos, Boaventura de Sousa. 2017. *Decolonising the University. The Challenge of Deep Cognitive Justice.*. Newcastle upon Tyne: Cambridge Scholars Publishing.

Sayer, R. Andrew. 1992. *Method in Social Science. A Realist Approach*. 2nd ed. London: Routledge.

Stein, Sharon, and Vanessa de Oliveira Andreotti. 2017. "Decolonization and Higher Education." In *Encyclopedia of Educational Philosophy and Theory*, edited by M. Peters. Singapore: Springer.

Steyn, M. E. 2001. *Whiteness Just Isn't What is Used to be: White Identity in a Changing South Africa. SUNY Series, Interruptions – Border Testimony(ies) and Critical Discourses*. Albany: State University of New York Press.

Taylor, Charles, Dilip Parameshwar Gaonkar, Jane Kramer, Benjamin Lee, and Michael Warner. 2003. *Modern Social Imaginaries*. Durham: Duke University Press (Public Planet Books). http://gbv.eblib.com/patron/FullRecord.aspx?p=1168038.

Vincent, Steve. 2014. Critical Realism and the Organizational Case Study. In *Studying Organizations Using Critical Realism. A Practical Guide*, edited by P. K. Edwards, Joe O'Mahoney, and Steve Vincent, 1st ed. Oxford: Oxford University Press.

Williams, Kevin. 2015. "Rethinking 'Learning' in Higher Education." *Journal of Critical Realism* 11 (3): 296–323. doi:10.1558/jcr.v11i3.296.

Williams, Clay K., and Donald Wynn. 2012. "Principles for Conducting Critical Realist Case Study Research In Information Systems." *MIS Quarterly* 36 (3): 787–810., checked on 5/9/2018.

Winter, Richard. 2009. "Academic Manager or Managed Academic? Academic Identity Schisms in Higher Education." *Journal of Higher Education Policy and Management* 31 (2): 121–131. doi:10.1080/13600800902825835.

Wodak, Ruth, and Michael Meyer. 2001. *Methods of Critical Discourse Analysis. Introducing Qualitative Methods.* London: SAGE.

'Pillars of the colonial institution are like a knowledge prison': the significance of decolonizing knowledge and pedagogical practice for Pacific early career academics in higher education

Marcia Leenen-Young ⓘ, Sereana Naepi ⓘ, Patrick Saulmatino Thomsen ⓘ, David Taufui Mikato Fa'avae ⓘ, Moeata Keil ⓘ and Jacoba Matapo ⓘ

ABSTRACT

For Pacific early career academics (PECA) in Aotearoa, there is a tension between the Indigenous knowledges inherited from our Pacific ancestors and those we have been taught within the western education system. As Pacific educators teaching an increasingly Pacific student-body, we have sought to define our own spaces within the lecture theatre where we can prioritize our knowledges and counter standard didactic western pedagogical practices. This paper is a collaboration from six PECA who use as a framework of analysis Andreotti et al.'s [Andreotti, Vanessa de Oliveira, Sharon Stein, Cash Ahenakew, and Hunt. Dallas. 2015. "Mapping Interpretations of Decolonization in the Context of Higher Education." *Decolonization: Indigeneity, Education & Society* 4 (1): 21–40.] *Cartography of Decolonization* to discuss their decolonizing pedagogies. It will explore the successes and challenges faced in making this pedagogical shift, including stories from PECA who have struggled due to disciplinary concepts of what constitutes 'knowledge'. It involves critical reflection on pedagogical praxis, asking throughout what can be considered decolonizing and whether it is indeed possible within the system of higher education in Aotearoa.

Introduction

There is a tension for Pacific early career academics (PECA) between being Pacific and operating pedagogically within a western system of education that was not made for either us or our Pacific students. We ourselves, as PECA, are products of this system, but we have also inherited our ancestral knowledge systems. Our concepts of what knowledge is are not solely the product of a western system. As such, we seek to embrace the different knowledges that embody us as Pacific academics and redefine the educational space by prioritizing our Pacific knowledges as valid and significant ways of knowing and being (Thomsen et al. 2021a). This is not always an easy task within an institution that does not recognize these knowledge systems and can actively punish you for engaging in pedagogies that threaten the institution itself (Koya-Vaka'uta 2017; Naepi 2021). What this means for each of us is different. We share a sense of tension when attempting to practice Pacific decolonial pedagogies; we are almost limited to personal acts of decolonization while the wider structural and foundational coloniality of the institution remains intact.

Pacific peoples within New Zealand universities continue to be excluded. Our students are under-served (Naepi et al. 2020a, 2021), our academics are under-represented making up only 1.7% of all academics (Barber and Naepi 2020; McAllister et al. 2020; Naepi 2019; Naepi et al. 2020b), our Pacific women are under-paid at $.85 to every $1 a non-Maori and Pacific male makes and under-promoted at a 25% promotion rate to professor compared to 39% for non-Maori and Pacific males (McAllister et al. 2020), and our knowledges are undervalued (Ahenakew and Naepi 2015; Anae et al. 2001; Barber and Naepi 2020; Hau'ofa 1993; Naepi 2019; Thaman 2003). However, in spite of this, Pacific peoples continue to engage with universities as we maintain hope that these institutions can be used to further our community aspirations (Naepi 2020). This hope means that as Pacific early career researchers we find ways to bring the Pacific into our classrooms through decolonizing Pacific pedagogies in an attempt to change current patterns of under-serving by our universities.

This paper is a collaborative exploration by six PECA on how we actively attempt to decolonize our learning environments and pedagogical praxis in different disciplinary backgrounds, specifically Education, Sociology, and Pacific Studies. It will explore the successes and challenges faced in making these pedagogical shifts, including stories from PECA about how they engage in Pacific decolonizing pedagogies within western universities. In order to do this, we review the literature and outline our written talanoa method of collaboration. After establishing our method and framing, we present our findings and engage in a talanoa of our experiences in implementing Pacific decolonizing pedagogies and what they mean for the future of the academy.

In exploring the concept of decolonization in higher education, we have utilized Andreotti et al.'s (2015) *Cartography of Decolonization* as a framework of analysis. This allowed us to collaboratively reflect on our own pedagogical practices as Pacific educators within higher education and how we actively strive to shift our teaching praxis beyond the western frame of education we ourselves were socialized into. In doing so, we seek to create environments for our students that validate and embrace Pacific knowledges. This paper has allowed us to push this discussion and consider the ways our pedagogical practices could be considered decolonizing. It has forced us, in reflecting on our own practices, to consider the question, what is decolonizing and whether this is possible within the existing structures of University education? While it is evident that there are significantly varying degrees of decolonizing pedagogical praxis amongst us, the challenge of seeing beyond the University structures and imagining a decolonized learning environment is one that we are collectively still to imagine beyond the theoretical, although we are filled with hope. Of central importance as PECA, however, is the act itself of shifting away from the traditional western models of teaching and learning as a culturally affirming act that strengthens identity and eases the tension PECA feel within the academy (Baice et al. 2021; Thomsen et al. 2021a).

Although the authors lay claim to indigeneity, our diverse conceptualizations reflect our relational positionalities and kinship connections within the diaspora (Fa'avae 2019). Our diasporic indigeneity is associated with where we live and work, as we benefit from a settler state that has built itself off the lands of our extended family. As Pacific people, we have ancient ties to Māori but need to also acknowledge that despite multiple migrations back and forth before colonization, our current existence within Aotearoa is legitimized by a settler state that traverses Eurocentric economic and educational motivations (Fleras and Spoonley 1999; Macpherson, Anae, and Spoonley 2001; Spoonley and Macpherson 2004; Somerville 2012). This sits in contrast to Indigenous solidarity movements that we perhaps could lay claim to in earlier pre-colonial migration stories. Therefore, while we see our pedagogies as decolonizing, we need to remain aware that there is decolonizing for the Pacific diaspora and then there is decolonizing as tauiwi existing as Indigenous diaspora on other Indigenous people's lands, and that each involves different responsibilities and actions. As Tuck and Wayne Yang (2012) have expressed, decolonization is solely about giving land back and anything else is a distraction. Therefore, decolonial Pacific pedagogies must also amplify the message that nothing is more critical than supporting movements to return confiscated or stolen land. As a collective, we believe this is an important acknowledgement and invite others to join us in conversation around how we can best navigate these tensions.

Pacific pedagogies

The push in education to move beyond the pedagogical norms of western institutions to include Pacific knowledges emerged in New Zealand in the late twentieth century out of the agitative efforts of Pacific academics. They advocated for the explicit creation of spaces for Pacific learners as a response to an education system that had come to recognize its own failure to address the needs of Pacific students (Benseman et al. 2002; Coxon et al. 2002; Ministry of Education 2001; Pasikale, George, and Fiso 1996). Literature on Pacific education and Pacific pedagogies frequently acknowledge the need for culturally informed learning environments that focus on relationality and connections between students and teachers (Airini et al. 2010; Alkema 2014; Chu, Abella, and Paurini 2013; Luafutu-Simpson et al. 2015; Sterne 2006). Koloto, Katoanga, and Tatila (2020) discuss Pacific pedagogies as unique and informed by Pacific 'values, worldviews, knowledge, and experience' (4). Research with Pacific students clearly demonstrates what is needed within the tertiary system of education in Aotearoa in order to support Pacific student success: for example, culturally-informed learning environments, student-centered teaching, engagement, commitment to success, pastoral care, role models, and access to resources, to name a few (Alkema 2014; Chu, Abella, and Paurini 2013; Luafutu-Simpson et al. 2015; Reynolds 2016; Sterne 2006; Tuagalu 2008).

Moreover, recent research also demonstrates that Pacific peoples have a history of robust ways of learning outside the university that should be embraced by those who teach Pacific students in tertiary education (Leenen-Young 2020). Scholarship on Pacific pedagogies and how they contribute to success for Pacific students is prevalent within higher education dialogues in Aotearoa, with the central argument that inclusion of Pacific worldviews is *the solution* to Pacific student under-achievement (for example, Airini et al. 2010; ; Hawk et al. 2002; Mackley-Crump 2011). However, while there has been a lot of research on Pacific pedagogies and the need to include Pacific knowledges and worldviews within the tertiary education system, there has still not been a foundational shift in the way we teach in universities.

Decolonial pedagogies

Decolonization is a contested term, as Andreotti et al. (2015) noted, 'decolonization has multiple meanings, and the desires and investments that animate it are diverse, contested, and at times, at odds with one another' (22). Disciplinary and geographical boundaries mean there is no one way Indigenous academic decolonization can be achieved in higher education. This can be seen through analyzing the arguments of Marie Battiste, a Potlotek First Nation scholar, and Konai Helu-Thaman, a Tongan Scholar, who both work on decolonizing pedagogies. Battiste's book on *Decolonizing Education* (2013) argues that:

> educators must reject colonial curricula that offer students a fragmented and distorted picture of Indigenous peoples, and offer students a critical perspective of the historical context that created that fragmentation. In order to effect change, educators must help students understand the Eurocentric assumptions of superiority within the context of history and to recognize the continued dominance of these assumptions in all forms of contemporary knowledge. (186)

Battiste (2013) is describing decolonization where the Eurocentric assumptions that continue to deny Indigenous peoples their lives are called into question and action is taken to deconstruct these assumptions. This is an argument that challenges the unspoken hierarchies of knowledge baked into the system and makes known the inertia that can allow for continued colonial domination. Thaman (2003) argues that

> Decolonizing formal education involves accepting indigenous and alternative ways of seeing the world. For academics, it means accepting Pacific perspectives, ways of knowing, and wisdom, and encouraging efforts by staff and students alike to reclaim indigenous knowledge as well as philosophies of teaching and learning that encompass the multiple experiences of Oceanic peoples. (10–11)

Thaman (2003) is discussing centering Pacific ways of knowing and doing within pedagogical practice. Both scholars show the need for decolonization in education for Indigenous peoples but have different approaches to achieving these aims. Thaman's idea of an inclusive curricula is a form of decolonization that can be seen to be more adaptable within the current system of education without deconstructing the assumed knowledge that the university is built upon; however, it does disrupt the accepted norms and privileges of Pacific knowledges.

The variation in decolonizing pedagogies demonstrated here is an indication of the varying frameworks through which scholars view decolonization in education – although both arguments are equally valid interpretations of decolonizing pedagogies. This disparity can be seen in this paper, particularly in the difference between theoretical and operational decolonization demonstrated through the experiences and efforts of the PECA.

Method

This article is part of a collective of papers where PECA are raising our voices and sharing our stories in an effort to communicate the realities of working within the New Zealand higher education space (Naepi et al. 2020a; Thomsen et al. 2021a, 2021b). Our voices are being added to an already established chorus of Pacific researchers we refer to as our Pacific academic and scholarly elders (for example, Airini et al. 2010; Anae and Suaalii 1996; Benseman et al. 2002; Chu, Abella, and Paurini 2013; Manu'atu 2000; Pasikale, George, and Fiso 1996; Samu 2006; Thaman 2009). As with our other papers (Thomsen et al. 2021a, 2021b), we define PECA as

> someone of Pacific heritage employed in a full-time permanent position at the university who has transitioned into this role within the past five years. This limited definition acknowledges that PECAs in precarious employment do not have the benefit of protection around freedom of speech that permanent academics do. We are mindful of how this may impact career progression for those without permanent contracts. (Thomsen et al. 2021a, 53)

As with our other PECA talanoa papers, we draw on the idea of a written talanoa (relational narrative inquiry or dialogue) (Naepi et al. 2020a; Thomsen et al. 2021a, 2021b) to explore our experiences as PECA engaging in decolonizing Pacific pedagogies. Although as a cultural practice talanoa is oral, we argue that as a methodology it is centered on creating and reinforcing relationships (Thomsen 2019, 2020). As PECA this practice of writing with, to, and around each other, builds and strengthens our relationships as we engage in shared experiences and reflect on the ways that these experiences speak to each other. To begin, we have had opportunities to talanoa in person before opening up to a written talanoa space where individual PECA added their thoughts on decolonial Pacific pedagogies within each of our framing spaces discussed below based on Andreotti et al.'s (2015) cartography of decolonization. From here we openly constructed and contributed to the written talanoa presented in this paper.

Talanoa framing

In order to trace the different decolonizing Pacific pedagogies that we engage in we utilized Andreotti et al.'s (2015) *Cartography of Decolonization* to frame our discussions. This enabled us to both acknowledge what is possible and impossible within institutional spaces. Andreotti et al. (2015) identify three reform spaces that are commonly enacted when people are 'decolonizing' in higher education. The first space is the soft reform space, which focuses on inclusion through personal or institutional transformation and assumes that this inclusion can be achieved 'without any social conflict or significant change in structure, subjectivities, or power relations' (Andreotti et al. 2015, 26). The inclusion space is common in New Zealand universities, where diversity and inclusion are collapsed into numeric representation through national policies and targets set by the Tertiary Education Commission and Ministry of Education (Naepi et al. 2017). However, 'there is no substantive recognition of white/European epistemological dominance and no demand for deep structural change' (Naepi et al. 2017, 90). As a result, decolonial movements within New Zealand universities often focus on an 'inclusion' that does not challenge, shift or transform the colonial and Eurocentric foundations (Ahmed 2012) that have historically excluded and devalued Pacific peoples.

The radical-reform space offers a slightly more critical decolonization process. Within the radical reform space, there is 'recognition of how unequal relations of knowledge production result in severely uneven distribution of resources, labor, and symbolic value' (Andreotti et al. 2015, 26). Radical reform aims to transform aspects of our current system by "giving voice', recognition, representation, redistribution, reconciliation, affirmative action, reentering of marginalized subjects' (Andreotti et al. 2015, 26). Pacific peoples in New Zealand universities could be understood to be engaging with the radical when they engage in enabling pluriversities (Grosfoguel 2012, 2013), which calls into account how different knowledge systems are valued within New Zealand universities. It is a position that 'explicitly names the dynamics of racism and colonialism and articulates its commitment to resist these' (Naepi et al. 2017, 91). Decolonization within the radical reform space involves disrupting the system in ways that often focus a single issue that if fixed will 'solve' systemic problems, which in many cases disables the ability to engage in alternatives to the current system.

The beyond-reform space recognizes the role of ontological domination in ensuring that even with other ways of knowing (such as pluriversities) grafted onto our current system (Ahenakew and Naepi 2015) we will be unable to engage in other ontologies (ways of being) whilst we are still within this system. Andreotti et al. (2015) argue that there are three responses within this critique; system walk-out (opting out of the current system), hacking (using the system against itself), and hospicing (helping the system to die). It is perhaps when we delve into this space as Pacific Early Career researchers that we begin to feel angry and toy with the idea of system walk-out as we see in our everyday life that when we attempt to bring different ways of being in the university there is no space for it (Thomsen et al. 2021a).

Talanoa discussion

Soft-reform

Overall PECA noted that soft reform consisted of common decolonial pedagogical practices; however, there was unease expressed about the limitations of soft reform and its ability to provide an overarching solution to the colonial university, if in fact there is one. Each PECA was able to identify at least one soft reform pedagogical practice that provided an opportunity to engage Pacific pedagogical practices and epistemologies in the colonial institution. However, much of the focus in the talanoa was on the tensions felt about how their efforts did not make a significant impact in decolonizing the institution at the structural level.

Inclusion is a central tenet of soft reform, and PECA discussed multiple inclusions within their efforts for soft reform. Including Pacific knowledges and prioritizing them as valid and academically robust was a central focus of the talanoa from PECA. The push to prioritize, affirm and embrace Pacific ontologies and epistemologies within an institution that values western forms of knowledge was something each PECA strove for in their own pedagogical practice (Thomsen et al. 2021a). The benefit of adopting pedagogy that focuses on relationality and connection for both Pacific and non-Pacific students has been well documented (Allen, Taleni, and Robertson 2009; Manuel et al. 2014) and is reaffirmed by the following talanoa:

> As a Pasifika academic, in practice there are tensions that I have to navigate daily. I am conscientious of my role in seeking opportunities for teaching and learning that affirm Pacific

indigenous knowledges, at the same time ensuring that all students including those who are non-Pacific understand the value of these knowledge systems against the grain of the Western education canon. There is always more that can be done; however, it cannot be carried by Pacific staff only.

PECA pointed out that the pedagogical movement from western frameworks of learning towards pedagogies that embrace multiple knowledges is one that cannot be the sole responsibility of the limited numbers of Pacific academic staff. Research shows us that there is a significant under-representation of Pacific academics within universities in Aotearoa (Naepi 2019; Naepi et al. 2020a). We also know that the student body is an increasingly Pacific one that must be recognized and anticipated if the aim is to effectively teach Pacific students (Salesa 2017). This is a significant tension for PECA who are often isolated within western-based institutions feeling as though they are the only ones in their discipline working against old pedagogical models of teaching.

> It is more important to me that I create a culturally inclusive and responsive space in all of my classes. I do this by centering my classes around Pacific and Indigenous content, thinkers, examples, worldviews, as well as by investing time in building relationships and connecting with my students. I do this because I am Pacific and it aligns with my cultural norms, values and practices. However, I also make a conscious and greater effort because I don't know how much of this they will get in their other classes – so it's also an attempt to compensate for the institutional lack.

In talanoa, PECA commented on inclusion in a number of different ways as soft reform: inclusion of communities, families, and students into the teaching and learning space. The inclusion of Pacific curriculum in the form of mandating the study of Pacific thinkers within their courses was one-way PECA sought to decolonize their practice and seek to normalize Pacific knowledges within the learning environment (Matapo and Baice 2020). Similarly, PECA commented on the act of transforming colonially accepted forms of knowledge by introducing Pacific ways of transmitting knowledge and validating them equally within the traditionally accepted practices of the academic discipline (Matapo 2021; Siilata 2014). This welcomes familial, community and cultural knowledge into the university as a counterpart to western modes of creating, recognizing, and sharing knowledge.

> Their cultural and inherited knowledge is valuable and significant within my lecture theatre, so I ask them to tell oral histories that have been handed down to them … … When student's include the history of their ancestors in their assignments or essays, that is a win for me because it means they are seeing their whakapapa or gafa (ancestral connections or genealogy) as valid historical accounts - just as valid as the western knowledge they read in books.

This pedagogical approach also focuses on the inclusion of students in the learning and teaching process as soft reform. Part of this, for PECA, was also to name and discuss the limitations of the western institutions within which they teach. Naming and discussing colonization and racism, issues inherent within the lecture theatres in which these students sit, is an act of including the students in the critique of the institution to decolonize pedagogical practice and focus.

> I am careful to start all my courses with decolonization; it doesn't matter what we are covering we will spend two weeks considering Indigenous thoughts and responses to the subject

matter. We also discuss what the limitations are within the classroom to address Indigenous concerns and ensure that we name racism and colonialism throughout the course

One example from PECA highlighted the need for an intersectional lens in our decolonial pedagogical praxis, where for some Pacific groups the request to be included is seen to be too much by the Pacific. This example pointed to the marginalization faced specifically by queer Pacific identities within the colonial classroom. Even within the politics of inclusion, this example demonstrates a lack of awareness and inclusion within the curriculum and pedagogical practice.

> Being a Pacific queer studies scholar and educator, inclusion optics haunts my every move. Inclusion of queer Pacific identities and experiences into our curriculums and pedagogy is yet to be fully considered in my opinion. Very little has been done to address the ways in which our colonial classrooms reproduce disciplinary technologies on minds and bodies that pathologize queer Pacific people. Even within Pacific communities this is not well understood. Consider a "soft reform" example where I've asked people to include pronouns in their bios as a sign of "inclusion" the response I often get is: that's a bit pālagi (white).

PECA spoke of these soft reforms as spaces of inclusion that allow decolonization driven by personal practice, not through foundational institutional change. These soft reforms are significant acts that validate Pacific knowledges and pedagogies, but as identified by PECA, there is a tension here where we are working within the boundaries of the colonial institution to make changes for ourselves and our students, but there is a limit to what is possible within the parameters set for us by the university – and we know, it is not enough to produce significant, meaningful and transformational change.

Radical-reform

It is clear that PECA engage in forms of radical-reform when practicing decolonizing Pacific pedagogies. However, this appears to be mostly limited to challenging colonial aspects of the overall institution. This challenge comes in the form of taking on the knowledge hierarchies that universities both enforce and benefit from; Eurocentric knowledge systems. As a result, we see Pacific knowledge become 'abyssal knowledge' (Santos 2007, 2018); knowledge that is on the other side of the abyss and therefore, unknowable. However, we see in Pacific decolonial pedagogies by PECA that not only do we bring this abyssal knowledge into the known, but we use this knowledge to not only reframe understandings of what is valid knowledge but also challenge colonial constructions of 'valid' knowledge.

> Through a pedagogy of care centered on relational ethics, I utilize "vā māfana" (inspiring and intimate connections) and loto toka'i (respect, care, generosity), I made a deliberate move to unpack what indigeneity and decolonization meant for my masters students in our supervision meetings at the USP Tonga campus. I chose this pedagogy because my students were female education leaders in Tonga who were older than me and well-versed in the language and culture. Their cultural wisdom surpassed my own, which I respected. They also held esteemed positions within Tongan society.

It is difficult to translate value systems into pedagogical practices within western institutions (Naepi et al. 2017), however, for this particular example, the PECA is not just including cultural practices but using it as a foundation for all pedagogical practices; this is not about creating a moment of 'vā māfana' (inspiring and intimate connections) but actually using 'vā māfana' to frame all things. This example also demonstrates the potential of employing culturally informed relational ethics to challenge and subvert the patriarchal foundations of universities. In particular, the male PECA quoted above, acknowledges the cultural capital that women from outside the academy bring to the teaching relationship and contribute to the teaching environment, which challenges the masculine imprint that is present in universities (Fa'avae, Tecun, and Siu'ulua 2021). This not only embraces the knowledges that Pacific communities have but also shakes up accepted hierarchies within the academy by centering cultural Tongan hierarchies and notions of relational tapu (sacred and/or restricted behaviors) (Mills 2016; Taumoefolau 1991) within the institution, claiming and keeping space distinct from western-centered patriarchal ideals of hierarchy.

> For me, it's important to disrupt some of these taken-for-granted normalities that promote a type of colonial inertia in the way we select our lecturers, the way we teach our students and who gets to be cited in our curriculums. I have instituted a Pacific-first policy in my reading lists. Whereby, wherever I can, I privilege Pacific scholars. Moreover, I choose to embrace Pacific ways of knowing in the classroom; I deliberately choose to bring in members of our communities to tell their stories to students in a panel form.

Again, we see PECA bring community knowledge into the classroom in ways that validate and normalize our communities as the holders of knowledge, thereby inversing the colonial logic of knowledge hierarchies (Santos 2007, 2018). Both prioritizing Pacific thinkers and Pacific knowledge holders outside the university system are acts in radical reform that seek to claim the learning space as a consciously constructed environment that prioritizes Pacific cultural practices and knowledges.

> I use Indigenous resources in a mainstream undergraduate history course as valid primary accounts of history in the Pacific. I set for my students karakia (prayer), songs and dances, motifs on tapa (bark cloth traditional to the Pacific) or kupesi (printed or drawn design on a tapa), and oral accounts as valid ways of telling history, alongside newspaper articles, government documents and other western forms of primary sources. By making Indigenous Pacific ways of telling history central, I am changing the narrative for the Pacific students sitting in front of me and moving away from colonially dominated narratives of Pacific history.

As shown above, PECA challenge colonial knowledge hierarchies by using relational pedagogies that not only acknowledge but actively encourage community knowledge into the classroom and hold Pacific knowledge up as valid with significant learnings (Thomsen et al. 2021a, 2021b). This is an example of pedagogical practice that prioritizes a Pacific worldview and pushes against disciplinary traditions of history to revise expectations of curriculum. This shift of bringing knowledge normally reserved to the abyss challenges colonial construction of knowledge and pushes against the idea that inclusion will solve all things by calling into question the foundations of knowledge itself. Including Pacific ways of knowing as a central tenet and not just a tick-box exercise in inclusivity can be seen as an attempt to move towards decolonization. However, these practices operate as acts of decolonization at the micro level that fundamentally do not shift the colonial foundations of the institution.

Moreover, PECA noted the limitations of the radical within the institutions.

> Even though I'm in a discipline where you think radical and beyond would be embraced, it's not because it threatens the discipline. The only time I have felt able to practice radical

pedagogy was during a global crises - COVID-19 when I was able to take on the structures that bind our pedagogy and really move to a relational space with students - a space that centered their lives and what was happening with them not what the institution wants centered. I was able to say deadlines didn't matter, time is a construct etc.

This example highlights how in spite of Discipline awareness of the radical-reform space it becomes difficult for the individual to engage with radical reform as it often challenges their own scholarship and praxis. This example also highlights how challenging it can be to practice radical pedagogies given that it took a global crisis (COVID-19 pandemic), and an effectual removal from the university environment, to create a space that makes it possible to meaningfully engage in pedagogies that challenge the system overall.

Holding a junior academic position means that I am unable to implement radical reforms even though I undoubtedly believe that radical reforms are needed, even in foundational terms of what universities define and constitute as 'knowledge'. From my vantage point, universities believe that soft reforms are the antidote to structural issues and problems – a simple just add more Pacific academics, resources, artwork, spaces, values to the institutional landscape and design.

This example articulates why it is difficult to engage in radical pedagogies; the universities simply do not envision a need for radical pedagogies. What is hinted at in this example is the precarious position that PECA put themselves in by engaging in radical pedagogies. This is an important commentary on the neo-liberal reward system embedded into our universities (Cupples and Pawson 2012; Curtis 2007; Kidman and Chu 2017, 2019; Kidman 2020; Olssen and Peters 2005); as PECA we exist in a space of tension where we understand reform is necessary but are unable to implement the reform without jeopardizing ourselves. Soft reform impacts the experiences of PECA and Pacific students, which are significant in themselves, but as stated in the above quote, it does not shift the core issues at the heart of the colonially built university system.

Beyond-reform

PECA as a collective expressed a desire in talanoa to engage in the beyond, but felt we were unable to do so because of the university's physical and epistemological limitations. This has caused us to pause and consider what it is about our pedagogical practices that could be considered decolonizing.

I do wish that I could do more to disrupt the classroom further. I find it near impossible to institute full on Pacific-style and informed teaching praxis around creating safe vā (intentional socio-spatial relational space) and spaces when students and I are sharing a lecture theatre with another 100 plus students. The colonial classroom is still cold, lifeless and detached in ways that I do not think promote the types of relational connections that are needed to activate the potentiality of Pacific ways of knowing and learning.

The description of the classroom in this example is a powerful explanation of how physical spaces limit our ability to engage in true Pacific pedagogical practices or the beyond. In particular, the relationality described by this PECA highlights the difficulty in maintaining the vā and creating meaningful connections between students and staff within the university – an aspect of Pacific pedagogies that is frequently depicted as central to Pacific student success (Matapo and Baice 2020; Siilata, Samu, and Siteine 2017; Taufe'ulungaki

2005). It also echoes the work of Smith, Funaki, and MacDonald (2021) who critiqued the public spaces of universities as upholding settler colonialism.

> The pillars of the colonial institution are like a knowledge prison that cannot provide emancipation for those peoples it has trapped inside it being force-fed curated colonial imaginations. The colonial institution has reached its limits –soft reform and institutional reform is not enough. For us to truly liberate our knowledge systems and ways of being we must imagine a different type of learning system that does not reproduce the same hierarchies of knowledge, hierarchies of value, hierarchies of pedagogies – that explores other ways of pedagogical praxis that develops skills that are mana-enhancing, iterative, generative and culturally appropriate.

There is recognition in the above quote that there is a limit to the decolonizing actions PECA can take within the institution; there is a limit to how much the current system can shift its ingrained practices. This particular example speaks to a common thread in higher education research on space invaders (Puwar 2004), where Audre Lorde argued that 'the master's tools will never dismantle the master's house' (2017, 91); this means we cannot use the logic of the institution to remake the institution. This is where the beyond space becomes so urgent; we need to find the space to engage in beyond-reform pedagogical practices or articulate what prevents this in order to remake the institution. Continuing to include Pacific ideas, bodies, and spaces will not change the fundamental reality of institutions of this modernity (Naepi et al. 2017).

> We have significant limitations. Despite our desire to teach Pacific knowledges in Pacific ways, we still have to lecture in a lecture theatre, we still have to set specific types of assignments, we still have to assess learning outcomes in universalized ways, we still have time constraints - we are confined and limited. We are scholars trained in western institutions to teach in western ways - it just so happens we think Pacific Indigenous knowledges need to be prioritized and we want to teach in Pacific ways. We take the small wins but these are not daily realities for us.

The neo-liberalization of higher education that focuses on an input/output model and increased managerialism of the academic (Cupples and Pawson 2012; Curtis 2007; Kidman and Chu 2017, 2019; Kidman 2020; Olssen and Peters 2005) marginalizes Pacific pedagogies and operates as obstacles to engaging in the beyond. The example shared above also points to our own limitations as Pacific scholars trained in western institutions. We are having to resist our own institutional training and assert our culturally and communally informed training. However, the habits formed through, and the expectations associated with, the neo-liberalization of our institutions make this already difficult task impossible.

> I teach in Old Government House - this means that I am asking students to engage in ideas of decolonization in the rooms where the New Zealand government made decisions about which land to steal and how to impose colonial governance on an Indigenous population, not just in Aotearoa but also in the Pacific. Although I acknowledge this in the class; how is it possible to engage in beyond pedagogy when you exist within the very walls that make engaging in the beyond impossible?

Much like Smith, Funaki and Macdonald's (2021) recent analysis of how public spaces in universities operate to reinforce settler colonialism, this example indicates that our teaching spaces operate in similar ways. Practicing decolonial pedagogies within the institution's walls can have serious limitations as PECA and shows us that the very spaces we teach in dictate what is possible and impossible, not just in physical arrangement but also in intellectual engagement. These limitations demonstrate the restrictions within which PECA are attempting to work under to not only excel academically and professionally to secure academic positions, but also to represent their communities, prioritize Pacific knowledges, and serve our Pacific students.

Beyond-reform as it is conceptualized by Andreotti et al.'s (2015) *Cartography of Decolonization* is something that is yet unrealized. PECA as a collective recognized the barriers in realizing this level of decoloniality, confronted simply by the question of whether this is possible within the current structure of the university.

> Is this system beyond salvaging? I think so. Colonial imaginations are being debunked daily, and the Western monopoly on knowledge systems is being challenged not just in syllabi and classrooms, but through the way technology is destabilizing the hegemony and exclusivity held over knowledge colonial institutions once had. Our ideas over whose knowledge is valid and the normative way of delivering it through lectures is being deconstructed and reimagined daily.

There is hope here that some form of decolonization is achievable and determination not to just accept the status quo, although beyond pedagogical practice what that would look like is a wider question; it is after all one aspect of the colonial university. This is a wider question that we hope Indigenous academics across a wider set of disciplines will address in the future, so that we are able to have discussions about what is im/possible across multiple disciplines and how different disciplinary curricula impact what is possible. If we return to the decolonizing arguments of Battiste (2013) and Thaman (2003), PECA are actively working to recognize both visions of decolonization in education at different levels and in different ways. Although PECA are working to debunk colonial Eurocentric assumptions about Pacific peoples and flip learning to center Indigenous Pacific knowledges and worldviews, the impact of this is immediate to the classroom and Pacific students. While the significance of this cannot be denied, there are structural and foundational changes beyond this that are recognized by PECA that must be made in order to decolonize the university.

Conclusion

Our talanoa above highlights the very real tension of attempting to engage in decolonial Pacific pedagogies when we are bound by Eurocentric western institutions. We share a sense of tension when attempting to practice Pacific decolonial pedagogies; we are almost limited to personal acts of decolonization while the wider structural and foundational coloniality of the institution remains intact. Our talanoa contributes to assertions that our universities cannot be changed and transformed through inclusion alone. Instead, what is required is a dramatic foundational shift that shatters the Eurocentric colonial knowledge system that binds our higher learning institutions and destines us to universities and worlds in which our very being is determined by race, capital and the heteropatriarchy.

Disclosure statement

No potential conflict of interest was reported by the author(s).

ORCID

Marcia Leenen-Young ⓘ http://orcid.org/0000-0002-3630-5346
Sereana Naepi ⓘ http://orcid.org/0000-0002-6067-9014
Patrick Saulmatino Thomsen ⓘ http://orcid.org/0000-0001-7498-7192
David Taufui Mikato Fa'avae ⓘ http://orcid.org/0000-0002-6141-961X
Moeata Keil ⓘ http://orcid.org/0000-0002-5870-6124
Jacoba Matapo ⓘ http://orcid.org/0000-0003-4615-0509

References

Ahenakew, Cash, and Sereana Naepi. 2015. "The Difficult Task of Turning Walls Into Tables." In *Sociocultural theory: Implications for curricular across the sector*, edited by Macfarlane A, Webber M, and Macfarlane S, 181–194. Christchurch: University of Canterbury Press.

Ahmed, Sara. 2012. *On Being Included: Racism and Diversity in Institutional Life*. Durham, NC: Duke University Press.

Airini, Deidre Brown, Elana Curtis, Odie Johnson, Fred Luatua, Mona O'Shea, Te Oti Rakena, Gillian Reynolds, et al. 2010. *Success for all: Improving Māori and Pasifika Student Success in Degree-Level Studies*. Wellington: Teaching and Learning Research Initiative. University of Auckland. http://www.tlri.org.nz/tlri-research/.

Alkema, Anne. 2014. *Success for Pasifika in Tertiary Education: Highlights from Ako Aotearoa-Supported Research*. Wellington, NZ: Ako Aotearoa.

Allen, Peter, Leali'ie'e Tufulasi Taleni, and Jane Robertson. 2009. "'In Order to Teach you, I Must Know you.' The Pasifika Initiative: A Professional Development Project for Teachers." *New Zealand Journal of Educational Studies* 44 (2): 47–62.

Anae, Melani, Eve Coxon, Diane Mara, Tanya Wendt Samu, and Christine Finau. 2001. *Pasifika Education Research Guidelines*. Report to the Ministry of Education, Auckland Uniservices. Wellington, New Zealand: Pasifika Education Research Division, Ministry of Education.

Anae, Melani, and Tamasailau Suaalii. 1996. *Pacific Island Student use of Student Services at University of Auckland*. Auckland: PISAAC.

Andreotti, Vanessa de Oliveira, Sharon Stein, Cash Ahenakew, and Hunt. Dallas. 2015. "Mapping Interpretations of Decolonization in the Context of Higher Education." *Decolonization: Indigeneity, Education & Society* 4 (1): 21–40.

Baice, Tim, Betty Lealaiauloto, Selena Meiklejohn-Whiu, Sonia M. Fonua, Jean M. Allen, Jacoba Matapo, Fetaui Iosefo, and David Fa'avae. 2021. "Responding to the Call: Talanoa, va-vā, Early Career Network and Enabling Academic Pathways at a University in New Zealand." *Higher Education Research & Development* 40 (1): 75–89. doi:10.1080/07294360.2020.1852187.

Barber, Simon, and Sereana Naepi. 2020. "Sociology in a Crisis: Covid-19 and the Colonial Politics of Knowledge Production in Aotearoa New Zealand." *Journal of Sociology* 56 (4): 693–703. doi:10.1177%2F1440783320939679.

Battiste, Marie. 2013. *Decolonizing Education: Nourishing the Learning Spirit*. Vancouver: UBC Press.

Benseman, J, Melani A, Helen A, and Eve C. 2002. Pacific peoples and tertiary education: Issues of participation. Final Report. Auckland Uniservices Limited.

Chu, Cherie, Ivy Samala Abella, and Seann Paurini. 2013. *Educational Practices That Benefit Pacific Learners in Tertiary Education*. Wellington, NZ: Ako Aotearoa.

Coxon, Eve, Melani Anae, Diane Mara, Tanya Wendt Samu, and Christine Finau. 2002. *Literature Review on Pacific Education Issues*. Auckland: University of Auckland.

Cupples, Julie, and Eric Pawson. 2012. "Giving an Account of Oneself: The PBRF and the Neoliberal University." *New Zealand Geographer* 68 (1): 14–23.

Curtis, Bruce. 2007. "Academic Life: Commodification, Continuity, Collegiality, Confusion and the Performance Based Research Fund." *New Zealand Journal of Employment Relations* 32 (2): 2–17.

Fa'avae, David. 2019. "Tatala 'ae koloa 'oe to'utangata Tonga: A way to disrupt and decolonise doctoral research." *MAI Journal* 8 (1): 3–15. doi:10.20507/MAIJournal.2019.8.1.1.

Fa'avae, David, Arcia Tecun, and Sione Siu'ulua. 2021. "Talanoa vā moe Veitapui: Wayfinding Higher Education Across the Intersections of Indigeneity, Race, and Gender." *Higher Education Research & Development*. Forthcoming

Fleras, A, and Paul S. 1999. Recalling Aotearoa: Indigenous Politics and Ethnic Relations in New Zealand. Oxford University Press.

Grosfoguel, Ramón. 2012. "The Dilemmas of Ethnic Studies in the United States: Between Liberal Multiculturalism, Identity Politics, Disciplinary Colonization, and Decolonial Epistemologies." *Human Architecture: Journal of the Sociology of Self-Knowledge* 10 (1): 81–89.

Grosfoguel, Ramón. 2013. "The Structure of Knowledge in Westernised Universities: Epistemic Racism/Sexism and the Four Genocides/Epistemicides." *Human Architecture: Journal of the Sociology of Self-Knowledge* 11 (1): 73–90.

Hau'ofa, Epeli. 1993. "Our sea of Islands." In *A New Oceania: Rediscovering our Sea of Islands*, edited by Eric Waddell, Vijay Naidu, and Epeli Hau'ofa, 2–16. Suva: University of the South Pacific.

Hawk, Kay, Esther Tumama Cowley, Jan Hill, and Sue Sutherland. 2002. "The Importance of the Teacher/Learner Relationship for Māori and Pasifika Learners." *Set: Research Information for Teachers* 3: 44–49.

Kidman, Joanna. 2020. "Whither Decolonisation? Indigenous Scholars and the Problem of Inclusion in the Neoliberal University." *Journal of Sociology* 56 (2): 247–262. doi:10.1177% 2F1440783319835958.

Kidman, Joanna, and Cherie Chu. 2017. "Scholar Outsiders in the Neoliberal University: Transgressive Academic Labour in the Whitestream." *New Zealand Journal of Educational Studies* 52 (1): 7–19.

Kidman, Joanna, and Cherie Chu. 2019. "'We're not the Hottest Ethnicity': Pacific Scholars and the Cultural Politics of New Zealand Universities." *Globalisation, Societies and Education* 17 (4): 489–499. doi:10.1080/14767724.2018.1561247.

Koloto, 'Ana Hau'alofa'ia, Alisi N.K, and Lepeka U.T. 2020. Critical success factors for effective use of e-learning by Pacific learners: a report for ITPNZ. Auckland: Koloto & Associates Ltd.

Koya-Vaka'uta, Cresantia Frances. 2017. "Rethinking Research as Relational Space in the Pacific Pedagogy and Praxis." In *Relational Hermeneutics: Decolonising the Mindset and the Pacific Itulagi*, edited by Upolu Lumā Vaai and Aisake Casimira, 65–84. Suva: University of the South Pacific Press.

Leenen-Young, Marcia. 2020. Pasifika Students and Learning to Learn at University. *MAI Journal* 9 (1): 70–80. doi:10.20507/MAIJournal.2020.9.1.8.

Lorde, Audre. 2017. *Your Silence Will not Protect you*. London: Silver Press.

Luafutu-Simpson, Pauline, Elena Moltchanova, Danielle O'Halloran, Lorraine Petelo, John Schischka, and Sam Uta'i. 2015. *Change Strategies to Enhance Pasifika Student Success at Canterbury Tertiary Institutions*. Wellington, NZ: Ako Aotearoa.

Mackley-Crump, Jared. 2011. "Malaga—the Journey: The Performing Arts as Motivational Tool for Pasifika Students in Aotearoa New Zealand." *The Asia Pacific Journal of Anthropology* 12 (3): 255–273.

Macpherson, Cluny, Melani Anae, and Paul Spoonley. 2001. *Tangata O Te Moana Nui: The Evolving Identities of Pacific Peoples in Aotearoa/New Zealand*. Palmerston North, NZ: Dunmore Press.

Manu'atu, Linitā. 2000. "Kātoanga Faiva: A Pedagogical Site for Tongan Students." *Educational Philosophy and Theory* 32 (1): 73–80.

Manuel, Theo, Tainafi Lefono, Wesley Lagolago, and Vedant Zaveri. 2014. "*Peer-Based Pasifika Pedagogies: Gift of knowledge.*" Presented at Samoa Conference III: Opportunities and Challenges for a Sustainable Cultural and Natural Environment. National University of Samoa: Apia, Samoa.

Matapo, Jacoba. 2021. "Mobilising Pacific Indigenous Knowledges to Reconceptualise a Sustainable Future: A Pasifika Early Childhood Education Perspective." *Asia-Pacific*

Journal of Research in Early Childhood Education 15: 119–136. doi:10.17206/apjrece.2021.15.1.119.

Matapo, Jacoba, and Tim Baice. 2020. "The art of Wayfinding Pasifika Success." *MAI Journal* 9 (1): 26–37. doi:10.20507/MAIJournal.2020.9.1.4.

McAllister, Tara, Jesse Kokaua, Sereana Naepi, Joanna Kidman, and Reremoana Theodore. 2020. "Glass Ceilings in New Zealand Universities." *MAI Journal* 9 (3): 272–285. doi:10.20507/MAIJournal.2020.9.3.8.

Mills, Andy. 2016. "Bodies Permeable and Divine: Tapu, Mana and the Embodiment of Hegemony in Pre-Christian Tonga." In *New Mana: Transformations of a Classics Concept in Pacific Languages and Cultures*, edited by Matt Tomlinson and Ty P Kāwika Tengan, 77–105. Monographs in Anthology Series. Canberra: ANU Press. http://press-files.anu.edu.au/downloads/press/p343683/pdf/ch03.pdf.

Ministry of Education. 2001. *Pasifika Education Plan*. Wellington: Ministry of Education.

Naepi, Sereana. 2019. "Why Isn't my Professor Pasifika? A Snapshot of the Academic Workforce in New Zealand Universities." *MAI Journal* 8 (2): 219–234. doi:10.20507/MAIJournal.2019.8.2.9.

Naepi, Sereana. 2020. "'I Didn't Come to Play': Pasifika Women in the Academy." In *Critical Reflections and Politics on Advancing Women in the Academy*, edited by T. Moeke-Pickering, S. Cote-Meek, and A. Pegoraro, 52–69. Hershey, PA: IGI Global. doi:10.4018/978-1-7998-3618-6.ch004.

Naepi, Sereana. 2021. "Pacific Women's Experiences Working in Universities in Aotearoa New Zealand." *Higher Education Research & Development* 40 (1): 63–74. doi:10.1080/07294360.2020.1856792.

Naepi, Sereana, Tara G. McAllister, Patrick Thomsen, Marcia Leenen-Young, Leilani A. Walker, Anna L. McAllister, Reremoana Theodore, Joanna Kidman, and Tamasailau Suaaliia. 2020a. "The Pakaru 'Pipeline': Māori and Pasifika Pathways Within the Academy." *The New Zealand Annual Review of Education* 24: 142–159. doi:10.26686/nzaroe.v24i0.6338.

Naepi, Sereana, Sharon Stein, Cash Ahenakew, and Vanessa de Oliveira Andreotti. 2017. "A Cartography of Higher Education: Attempts at Inclusion and Insights from Pasifika Scholarship in Aotearoa New Zealand." In *Global Teaching: Southern Perspectives on Teachers Working with Diversity*, edited by Carol Reid and Jae Major, 81–99. New York, NY: Palgrave Macmillan.doi:10.1057/978-1-137-52526-0_5

Naepi, Sereana, Reremoana Theodore, Joanna Kidman, Tara McAllister, and Jesse Kokaua. 2020b. *Why Isn't my Professor Māori or Pacific? Data Update*. Auckland: The University of Auckland. Preprint. https://doi.org/10.17608/k6.auckland.13211261.v1.

Naepi, Sereana, Elizabeth Wilson, Samantha Lagos, Sam Manuela, Tara G. McAllister, Joanna Kidman, Reremoana Theodore, and Jesse Kokaua. 2021. "Where are we now? Patterns of Māori and Pasifika Enrolment in the Natural and Physical Science and Society and Culture Fields in Aotearoa New Zealand." *Higher Education Research & Development* 40 (1): 90–103. doi:10.1080/07294360.2020.1857345.

Olssen, Mark, and Michael A. Peters. 2005. "Neoliberalism, Higher Education and the Knowledge Economy: From the Free Market to Knowledge Capitalism." *Journal of Education Policy* 20 (3): 313–345.

Pasikale, Anna, Ta'i George, and Talalo Fiso. 1996. *Seen, but not Heard: Voices of Pacific Islands Learners*. Pacific Islands Education Series: Monograph One. Wellington: Skill New Zealand.

Puwar, Nirmal. 2004. *Space Invaders: Race, Gender and Bodies out of Place*. Oxford: Berg Publishers.

Reynolds, Martyn. 2016. "Relating to va: Re-Viewing the Concept of Relationships in Pasifika Education in Aotearoa New Zealand." *AlterNative: An International Journal of Indigenous Peoples* 12 (2): 190–202.

Salesa, Damon. 2017. *Island Time: New Zealand's Pacific Futures. Vol. 64*. Wellington: Bridget Williams Books.

Samu, Tanya Wendt. 2006. "The 'Pasifika Umbrella' and Quality Teaching: Understanding and Responding to the Diverse Realities Within." *Waikato Journal of Education* 12: 35–49. doi:10.15663/wje.v12i1.297.

Santos, Boaventura de Sousa. 2007. *Another Knowledge is Possible: Beyond Northern Epistemologies*. London: Verso.

Santos, Boaventura de Sousa. 2018. *The end of the Cognitive Empire: The Coming of Age of Epistemologies of the South*. London: Duke University Press.

Siilata, Raewynn. 2014. "Va 'a Tele: Pasifika Learners Riding the Success Wave on Linguistically and Culturally Responsive Pedagogies." PhD diss., University of Auckland.

Siilata, Raewynn, Tanya Wendt Samu, and Alexis Siteine. 2017. "The Va 'Atele Framework: Redefining and Transforming Pasifika Education." In *Handbook of Indigenous Education*, edited by E. McKinley and L. Smith, 1–30. Singapore: Springer.

Smith, Avery (Black American), Hine Funaki (Tongan, Ngāpuhi, Ngāi Tahu, Ngāti Whatua) and Liana MacDonald (Ngāti Kuia, Ngāti Koata, Rangitāne o Wairau). 2021. "Living, Breathing Settler-Colonialism: the Reification of Settler Norms in a Common University Space." Higher Education Research & Development 40 (1): 132-145. doi:10.1080/07294360.2020.1852190

Somerville, Alice Te Punga. 2012. *Once Were Pacific: Māori Connections to Oceania*. Minneapolis: University of Minnesota Press.

Spoonley, Paul, and Cluny Macpherson. 2004. "Transnationalisation of New Zealand's Migrant Populations." In *Tangata, Tangata: The Changing Contours of Ethnicity in Aotearoa New Zealand*, edited by P. Spoonley, C. Macpherson, and D. Pearson, 175–193. Palmerston North: Dunmore Press.

Sterne, Graeme. 2006. "Teaching Students of Pacific Island Descent." *International Journal of Learning* 13 (2): 59–65.

Taufe'ulungaki, 'Ana. 2005. "Classroom Approaches for Optimal Results." In *Polynesian Paradox. Essays in Honour of Futa Helu*, edited by I. Campbell and E. Coxon, 46–57. Suva: Institute of Pacific Studies, University of South Pacific.

Taumoefolau, Melenaite. 1991. ""Is the Father's Sister Really" Black?." *The Journal of the Polynesian Society* 100 (1): 91–98.

Thaman, Konai Helu. 2003. "Decolonizing Pacific Studies: Indigenous Perspectives, Knowledge, and Wisdom in Higher Education." *The Contemporary Pacific* 15 (1): 1–17.

Thaman, Konai Helu. 2009. "Towards Cultural Democracy in Teaching and Learning with Specific References to Pacific Island Nations (PINs)." *International Journal for the Scholarship of Teaching and Learning* 3 (2): 1–11.

Thomsen, Patrick. 2019. "Coming-out in the Intersections: Examining Relationality in how Korean gay men in Seattle Navigate Church, Culture and Family Through a Pacific Lens." *Journal of Homosexuality* 68 (6): 1–22.

Thomsen, Patrick. 2020. "Transnational Interest Convergence and Global Korea at the Edge of Race and Queer Experiences: A Talanoa with gay men in Seoul." *Du Bois Review: Social Science Research on Race*, 1–18.

Thomsen, Patrick, Marcia Leenen-Young, Sereana Naepi, Karamia Müller, Sam Manuela, Sisikula Sisifa, and Tim Baice. 2021a. "In our own Words: Pacific Early Career Academics (PECA) and Pacific Knowledges in Higher Education Pedagogical Praxis." *Higher Education Research & Development* 40 (1): 49–62. doi:10.1080/07294360.2020.1852188.

Thomsen, Patrick, Litia Tuiburelevu, Marcia Leenen-Young, Sereana Naepi, Karamia Müller, Sisikula Sisifa, Moeata Keil, Analosa Veukiso-Ulugia, and Sam Manuela. 2021b. "Practicing Pacific Pedagogies During New Zealand's Level-Four Lockdown: Pacific Early Career Academics and COVID-19." *Waikato Journal of Education*. Forthcoming

Tuagalu, I'uogafa. 2008. "Heuristics of the vā." *AlterNative: An International Journal of Indigenous Peoples* 4 (1): 107–126.

Tuck, Eve, and K. Wayne Yang. 2012. "Decolonization is not a Metaphor." *Decolonization: Indigeneity, Education & Society* 1 (1): 1–40.

Epistemic decolonisation in reconstituting higher education pedagogy in South Africa: the student perspective

Shireen Motala, Yusuf Sayed and Tarryn de Kock

ABSTRACT
This paper seeks to understand how the curriculum is experienced across two higher education institutions to probe students' understandings of epistemic access in the context of decolonisation debates. Three particular aspects of student experience of the decolonised curriculum and pedagogy are scrutinised. First, we look at the kind of sociality encouraged in the pedagogic encounter. Since a core function of education is social and cultural formation, a question arises as to what kind of sociality is possible between students and lecturers in a decolonised education space, including in the context of COVID-19. Second, we explore patterns of participation including, academic activities and support provided. Third, we investigate the knowledge forms and canon to which students are exposed in their respective programmes, with consideration of language issues. Finally, we examine the decolonisation of the curriculum in the context of the Covid-19 pandemic.

Introduction

The decolonisation of the curriculum in South African higher education has generated much debate (Jansen 2017), and arguably raised fundamental questions about the nature of teaching and learning at the micro-level and shone the spotlight on broader political questions about the nature and transformation of the post-apartheid higher education trajectory, more than 26 years on. This has largely been concerned with curriculum, teaching, and learning, in terms of what kind of access to university education disadvantaged learners have, and how subjugated and marginalised ideas are represented, recognised, and affirmed in the pedagogic space. In curriculum terms, questions have been raised about what knowledge and whose knowledge – with only weak answers supplied (De Sousa Santos 2014).

To explore these questions, this paper turns its attention to the processes of pedagogic change and pedagogic encounters, from the perspective of students, as a way of understanding what decolonisation might mean in practice and how it may be realised. Specifically, this paper examines how the curriculum is experienced and transacted across two different institutions – one comprehensive and one a university of technology – to probe students' understandings of epistemic access in the context of decolonisation debates and its application at an institutional level. Particular attention is paid to student views recounting how specific efforts to decolonise and transform the curriculum have allowed them entry into the 'rules of the trade' in academic practice, the space of searching for and working with knowledge.

Framing the paper: decolonising the curriculum in South African higher education

In South Africa, universities have historically formed part of apartheid social engineering in that they were racially segregated, differentially resourced, and invested with institutional orientations aimed at upholding white domination (Rensburg 2020). The post-apartheid higher education system underwent a period of significant reforms, including the merging of some of the higher education institutions, closure of teacher colleges, and their integration into the university sector and establishment of new comprehensive universities (universities that straddle both traditional university offerings as well as technology programmes). There are at present 26 higher education institutions in South Africa with approximately 1,000,000 students across the nine provinces. These 26 institutions are divided into what are classed as traditional universities, comprehensive universities, and universities of technology. Of the 26 universities, 23 provide initial teacher education. This paper is based on two such institutions, one being a comprehensive university and the other a university of technology. Notwithstanding the changes to the university sector and the passing of the Higher Education Act (1996) which sought to transform the university sector, making it more reflective and diverse, responsive to the need of a transforming post-apartheid context, the university sector continued to reflect the racial, and economic inequities of its colonial and apartheid legacy. It is in this context that the #RhodesMustFall movement, which erupted at the University of Cape Town in early 2015 following the defacing of a statue of Cecil John Rhodes (Nyamnjoh 2017) must be understood. It was followed by the The FeesMustFall movement in 2016, which reflected a broad movement of students located across the diverse landscape of public higher education institutions in South Africa taking up and advancing the struggle of other earlier protests. Specifically, the FeesMustFall protests were triggered by an announcement of a 10% fee increase by the University of Witwatersrand, sparking further protests across all universities around the material constraints that made accessing higher education especially challenging, particularly for marginalised black students.

The student protest represented by these two movements in 2015 and 2016 respectively grappled with issues of access, inclusion, curriculum and epistemic erasure, calling for the dismantling of oppressive institutional structures, an overhaul of university curricula, and a reckoning with institutional and social cultures that excluded, invisibilised and subjugated black students in particular (CSVR 2017; Muswede 2017; Sayed, Motala, and De Kock 2019). While the decolonisation agenda came to encompass an extensive array of issues that reflected the heterogeneity of institutions and diversity of student experiences, its core focus was the epistemic and material inequities that characterised university experiences for the majority of black students (Muswede 2017; Cross and Motala 2020; Stroud and Kerfoot 2020).

The decolonisation of the university space and the curriculum was a core and explicit demand of the student movement. Yet what it meant, and what is required, reflect the very diverse voices, movements, and experiences of organisations and individuals making up the student protest movement (Sayed, Motala, and De Kock 2019). However, at its core, was an argument that decolonisation was more than the transformation of the higher education sector that had taken place in South Africa, which has primarily concentrated on demographic representation, inclusivity in teaching culture, expanding access and offering academic support, and thus arguably reflected a politically liberal understanding of what was called for (Joseph 2017; Morreira 2017). In contrast, decolonisation is more radical, concerned with a programme of epistemological, economic and political disruption of forms of coloniality that pervade both higher education and society (Mignolo 2011; Mamdani 2016). Decolonisation as an epistemic struggle is characterised by three sets of issues which this paper examines. The first relates to epistemic questions – what and whose knowledge is affirmed, prioritised, and legitimised (Mignolo 2011; De Sousa Santos 2014). The second relate to material concerns, including issues of resourcing and economic deprivation which frame how teaching and learning is shaped and influence in particular institutional contexts. The third, which is a key focus of this paper, is issues of the pedagogic act and encounter, including the realisation of care and support for enabling epistemic access for students in higher education (Sayed, Motala, and De Kock 2019). Drawing on this understanding of decolonisation, we understand curriculum in its broadest sense as reflecting the institutional context, support and care which characterise and frame the context in which learning takes place, the pedagogic act and the sociality of the teaching and learning encounter including the medium of instruction, and what and whose knowledge, ideas and values are valorised and embedded in the pedagogic encounter. In such an approach, the curriculum is not just about context; it is also about decolonisation as both an epistemic and material movement.

Ndlovu-Gatsheni (2013) and Nyamnjoh (2017) note how universities become sites of the reproduction of coloniality through their endorsement, legitimation and valorisation of particular forms of knowledge, pedagogy and practice. Such scholars (Morreira 2017) argue that coloniality is embedded in the structure of disciplinary knowledge: it animates the boundaries of particular forms, methodologies, and ways of organising knowledge that seal these off from penetration by other epistemologies that are then cast as transgressive, subordinate or inadequate. To effectively decolonise curricula, universities would have to grapple with a foundational dimension of their ontological composition (Ndlovu-Gatsheni 2014). This goes beyond inserting African voices into existing canons or 'Africanising' curricula through a process of reform – it is crucially concerned with reconstituting the institutional landscape itself, a process by which the disciplines, and the very notion of disciplinary knowledge, would require fundamental disruption and reimagining. The student movement tabled these issues to some degree but with differing levels of veracity. As Morreira (2017) argues, the coloniality of knowledge in higher education curricula creates a context in which black students not only do not 'see' themselves reflected in the knowledge they engage with and the pedagogies used to teach them – they are also positioned at a deficit in relation to the institution, where they are unable to access the cultural and social milieu of the space and are systematically excluded from becoming 'ideal knowers' (Morreira 2017, 291).

Decolonising the curriculum also entails unpacking the experiences of alienation and derision of marginalised students as they enter a university space that valorises the cultural and social capital that middle-class, and mostly but not exclusively white students came with (Smit 2012; RMF 2015; Soudien 2020). At historically black institutions, this was manifest as a lack of experience navigating the tertiary space, weak academic literacy, and limited institutional support (Imenda, Kongolo, and Grewal 2004; CSVR 2017; Lekena and Bayaga 2018). While efforts have been made to create inclusive environments and support students in accessing higher education, Cross and Motala (2020) argue that transformation efforts may also be seen as having a placebo effect, papering over a failure to sufficiently transform the essence and structure of the system in ways that continue to perpetuate exclusion and marginalisation. Smit (2012) importantly cautions against perceiving the experiences of black students through a deficit lens when reflecting on issues of university integration and transformation. In her research, she demonstrates that working-class students show remarkable agency and capacity for navigating difficult circumstances, creatively using limited resources, and forming supportive peer groups that are able to circulate academic knowledge, texts, food, and at times, emergency funds (Smit 2012). Cross (2020) refers to these attributes as compensatory capital. Part of thinking about decolonisation in relation to belonging is thus about considering how poverty and social marginality is not an automatic determinant of students' ill-preparation for higher education (Badat 2010).

For the student protest movement decolonising the curriculum is about linking concerns about epistemic access and the pedagogic encounter with concerns about how resources often constrain feasible attempts at substantive transformation. Higher education change in South Africa occurred in a context where large numbers of marginalised students were able to access higher education but with limited state and dwindling institutional resources, they struggle to survive. As such, an expansion of access was not matched by an increase in state funding, and in fact, state funding declined in real terms over time. Students struggle to survive and thus decolonisation becomes a struggle of the material conditions under which they were able to learn meaningfully. This is why scholars such as Jansen (2017) and Motala (2020) have argued that students at historically black institutions were overwhelmingly focused on material issues during FeesMustFall.

It is these concerns which this paper addresses by focusing on the perspectives of those most impacted, students. Much work has been done on the prospects of decolonisation and the impact of decolonising initiatives in universities (Morreira 2017; Sayed, Motala, and De Kock 2019; Cross 2020), but too often the conversation lacks insights about the student experiences of teaching and learning in the aftermath of the reform initiatives triggered by RhodesMustFall and FeesMustFall. This gap is especially glaring in relation to education students, who arguably occupy a critical position between the higher and basic education systems. This paper seeks to respond to this gap by offering emerging insights into how the decolonial imperative has been received and engaged with by students in two education faculties.

Methodology

This research project examines student experiences and pedagogic encounters of the curriculum offered and transacted. In particular, this research reflects on how the ideal of decolonisation as manifest in the student protest is realised in teaching and learning.

This paper forms part of the pilot process for an emerging research project. It is based on interviews conducted with a purposively selected sample of 35 black students enrolled in undergraduate and postgraduate degrees. The paper takes the form of descriptive, exploratory analysis using data collected through semi-structured focus groups and interviews. The aim of the research was to yield initial insights into the problem under investigation, with the view to informing future work in this area. Research questions focused on students' understanding and experience of decolonising curricula, awareness of institutional processes to support decolonisation, issues of belonging, inclusion, and alienation, as well as the impact of the pandemic on their education.

Of the participants, 17 identified as women and 18 as men, in the age range of 20–40. The students were registered in faculties of education in two institutions, one comprehensive and one university of technology, in two provinces, one inland and one coastal, respectively. Both were based in large metropolitan hubs, and the breakdown of students was: 10 B.Ed. and 11 Master's students along with 14 doctoral candidates. The two institutions were selected because they provided institutional variation (one university of technology and the other a comprehensive university), were in different provinces, and had large education programmes in the Faculty of Education. There were two separate focus groups at one institution (Institution A). At Institution B, two focus groups were held with B.Ed. students, with three in each group; one group interview with two doctoral students; seven individual interviews with doctoral students; and one with an M.Ed. student. Institution A is a large university of technology resulting from a merger from two previously racially segregated Technikons in South Africa. It is an institution that has incorporated many teacher training colleges when they amalgamated into the university sector. It is one of the larger providers of teacher education in South Africa. Institution B is a large comprehensive, multi-campus university with 50,000 students, a large faculty of education, a product of a merger, with 92% of the student population defined as 'black African'.

The requisite institutional procedures were followed in getting the sample. It was initially expected for the research to take the form of focus groups at both institutions, but this approach needed to be modified in order to accommodate the limitations of remote access and social distancing, with the result that at Institution A, individual interviews were arranged based on participant availability. Because of COVID-19, all interviews were conducted on Zoom, Skype, or MS Teams and then transcribed. One key reflection of using online data collection methods is that these require attention to who speaks, effective management of virtual interactions, as well as supporting access. Notwithstanding this, a rich body of data was collected and analysed.

Ethical permission for this study was secured through the institutions in which the authors are located. Information sheets and consent forms were shared and discussed with all participants, who were also assured of their and their institutions' anonymity and informed that the data obtained would only be used for research purposes. All participants signed the consent sheet prior to the interviews taking place.

Interview and focus group data were analysed using thematic analysis. The initial selection of themes proceeded from the subheadings used to organise the research questions, with the data analysis supporting the refinement of these into more appropriate analytical categories. Each transcript was analysed before identifying general trends within institutions and among groups, in this case specifically based on education level (i.e. undergraduate, Master's, doctoral). In particular, the analysis sought to understand the limits and constraints of realising a meaningful decolonised curriculum aligned to the conceptual framework of the paper outlined above.

Some limitations of the study should be noted upfront. The data gathered for the research process focused specifically on student experiences and voices, opting to exclude faculty and support staff from the initial research. Participant perspectives should not be taken as generalisable to the entire higher education landscape but viewed within their particular institutional experiences and taken as a flavour of the complexity that currently exists within higher education in South Africa. Moreover, this paper does not attempt to qualify or prove the statements made by participants. Instead, we take the view that their impressions of decolonisation and epistemic access open up pathways for future research by indicating how the policies, processes, and decisions made within higher education institutions are experienced and received by the students they serve. The COVID-19 period meant that body language and verbal cues were not observable, and in the focus groups, the facilitator ensured that participation was maximised, and all voices contributed to the discussion.

The student voice: presentation of findings

The discussion that follows draws on findings from the data collected at two higher education institutions, considering these findings in relation to the literature presented earlier. Institution A is a university of technology that resulted from a series of mergers between technikons and teacher education colleges. It is an important provider of teacher education, and in recent years has been a site of ongoing protest around issues of fees and NSFAS support, accommodation, and epistemic access. Institution B is an urban comprehensive university, situated in one of the commercial hubs in the country, where decolonisation has had a central focus in the re-design and restructuring of knowledge in the aftermath of FeesMustFall. Similar to Institution A, students were asked a series of questions that required them to reflect on the form and content of their course material, seeking to understand whether their experiences of higher education could be considered 'decolonial'. Several themes emerged as significant in Institution A and B: uneven understanding of curriculum decolonisation; decolonisation as language struggles; decolonising the pedagogic act: the affective care and relationships dimension of learning; decolonisation and the material conditions of teaching and learning, and decolonisation in times of disruption and pandemics. These were distilled into the three major foci below.

Uneven understanding of decolonisation

Students at Institution A voiced diverse understandings of how decolonisation is constructed and infused in their programme. In the main, there was some impression that decolonisation was not meaningfully engaged within the curriculum. For example, interviews with B.Ed. Honours students at Institution A demonstrated that decolonisation was not an issue foregrounded in their educational experience. One student described the teaching and learning approach in the programme as highly structured, which had the effect of closing down the space for reflection or critical engagement:

> [F]or us as university students, we don't have a, you know, we get a course guide, and then each subject we will also get like an outline of what is expected for the year. I feel like it's very, it's very rigid. So, there's no part where us as students come in and you know, voice our opinion and ... where our opinions is brought in into, you know the curriculum. [UN_A_HONS_1]

Another doctoral candidate at Institution A, who also initially trained as a teacher, had the following to say about her undergraduate experience:

> I felt like I was learning other people's knowledge, and other people's experiences that were really validated and, in order for me to feel accepted and, to accept the learning, I had to almost assimilate so when it came to like the pedagogies used. It was a pedagogy for a very affluent, middle class individual. [UN_A_DED_4]

These voices speak to pedagogic experiences which are top-down, and in which discursive engagement and disruption are rare. However, there were also emerging insights from participants' responses that demonstrated how they were grappling with these issues:

> In our seminars, there was a wide variety ... we didn't have seminars specifically focusing on decolonization, as a group, when we did our readings together, but there were separate public seminars that dealt with decolonization that we were invited to and there was a lot of student activism as well that was disrupting the normal routine of the day. So, there were different forms of, like, education, taking place so the one level there was activism, from the students and that was a great learning space where students discussed topics, and they read certain literature, but that was only students. [UN_A_DED_5]

> Decolonization for some might mean having food and water and a place to stay while I'm studying, whereas for others, it might be what exactly is in the curriculum, why are you punting this colonial perspective of things, why is my black or Indian or coloured narrative, why is that not coming through the curriculum, so I think that is where a lot of the student groups actually parted ways, because there wasn't a common understanding of [what it means to decolonise]. [UN_A_DED_4]

These responses came from doctoral candidates at Institution A, where it was evident that the FeesMustFall movement had resulted in deep cleavages in institutional memory and understandings of decolonisation.

When probed about what they understood by the term 'decolonisation', undergraduates at Institution B, and postgraduates at both institutions, demonstrated remarkable similarity in what they viewed to be decolonisation in higher education particularly. Below are a few brief, but not exhaustive, extracts from their responses:

> I think is something that has to do with being able to recognise indigenous knowledge, being able to recognise the self within curriculum practices, and that includes content, that includes the mode of operation of the curriculum that is the apparatus of teaching and learning. [UN_B_FG_PHD_2]

it's not about erasing history, or erasing other knowledges, but it's about building a knowledge system that acknowledges global epistemologies you know what is going on around the world, but also legitimising, you know, the local knowledge, contextual knowledge and using that to shape not just the curriculum but the learning environment. [UN_B_FG_B.ED_1]

These views did form part of a spectrum, however, with the perspectives introduced above occupying a middle ground between, on the one hand, students who felt that decolonisation was about improving access and relatability in curriculum content, and on the other, students who took a strongly radical view that decolonising curricula and institutional culture were insufficient, that more needed to be done, and that very little from the current knowledge programme was worth rescuing. While this latter view has salience with the perspectives of a number of scholars (Ndlovu-Gatsheni 2014; Sayed, Motala, and De Kock 2019), in its most extreme form, it also diverges from their work in an important way by making visible the fine line between a form of radicalism that pushes for the disruption and dismantling of archaic practices, institutions and modes of knowing, and radicalism that descends into Afrophobia, essentialism, and primordialism. The latter view emerged in the course of FeesMustFall and bears revisiting in future work for the way it continues to shape how some students and scholars view the decolonial project.

Decolonising the pedagogic act: care and pedagogic interactions with lecturers as a decolonial practice

Well-being concerns significantly shaped whether students felt welcomed and supported in their institutions through services and interventions that mitigated against social and economic alienation. This began with initial experiences of orientation into the institutional culture. At Institution A, it was particularly postgraduate students who reflected on the process of adjusting into the institution, given that they occupied a separate space to undergraduate students and had limited contact with teaching and academic staff outside of supervision. Several students reported feeling quite isolated, but for the research unit, they were located within.

I mean, I can count on my hand how many times I spoke to our director of research on the campus .... That's the level of engagement and we were PhD students, and no one ever came to us to ask how are we doing, or you okay or anything, they did nothing, absolutely nothing. [UN_A_DED_4]

[In our unit] I felt very supported and nurtured ... but I know that it's not the same across the entire institution, and that's the concern, ... to get funding, to get good supervisors, to have the opportunities ... this is not a given for all students at the institution ... I've heard so many complaints from other students about not being supported. [UN_A_DED_5]

Crucially, students' ideas of what constituted support were not only focused on money, but also on regular interaction with academic staff, support in capacity development and finding opportunities for growth, and being equipped to build community with their peers. For postgraduate students, many of them working professionals, more sustained efforts were required to develop a sense of belonging and resonance with the institution, and students generally found the institution to be lacking in this regard. In this respect, students felt unsupported by the institution and resorted to focusing on getting the results needed to pass and move on. This view was supported by a doctoral candidate, who suggested that:

> You have teacher educators when I speak to them and they say 'they are lazy and they expect'; it's that alienation again. I experienced in my ITE program, so that is why a lot of the students, black African specifically are not doing so well in, in ITE programs, because there's ... this feeling of alienation. [UN_A_DED_4]

Smit (2012) argues that one form of deficit thinking towards students involves lowered expectations of student participation, performance, and responsibility. This creates a vicious cycle where lowered standards result in a lower performance which feeds low expectations in the future. This could be one explanation for the sense of malaise expressed by students at Institution A with regards to teaching and learning: not that their experiences were all negative, nor that their education was of absolutely inferior quality, but rather that the institution could be, as one student put it, 'so much more'.

Related to this, a common view that ran through discussions with students at Institution A was that the faculty of education had developed an instrumental approach to teaching and learning, focusing on delivering the content and ensuring students passed, but without deep intellectual engagement occurring between lecturers and students as evidenced in the following quote:

> It's more like a ... business operation ... because it's all about just getting the money in, the lecturer just delivers my lesson, I'm done with you now, kind of thing and up 'til today, you still kind of get that feeling from certain lecturers. [UN_A_HONS_1]

This impression of a transactional relationship between faculty and students was worsened during the COVID-19 pandemic, with students claiming that some lecturers at Institution A were mainly focused on 'ticking off' assessments and activities for the year without focusing on the quality of the emergency online pedagogy.

In contrast, postgraduates at Institution B reported a definite improvement in the services and supports offered to them. One noted that a concerted effort was made to check in with new students from other countries in Africa, finding out how they were settling in after arriving and even providing food and psychosocial support for their transition into the institutional space. There was also an appreciation for the creation of a dedicated space for postgraduate students:

> Before that building that now belongs to postgraduates, you'd just see postgraduate students floating roaming around not really knowing where they belong, but I think having that structure, knowing that belongs to them and giving them a sense of identity and sense of, no matter where you are, and if you feel lost, so long as you get there it feels that there is a community that you belong to. [UN_B_FG_PHD_2]

Feeling welcomed and supported creates a supportive environment that minimises the range of additional pressures and challenges that students must overcome in order to adapt to university life. Respondents were able to identify improvements stemming from FeesMustFall and recognise where steps had been taken to address the alienation the student movement had identified as endemic in the experiences of black and working-class students.

At Institution B, students expressed that there had been consultation around reform processes and that students had been represented in these fora. However, there was concern that this was largely a symbolic representation that did not substantively engage with students' demands, and that effectively froze them out of the 'real' spaces where decision-making and deliberation occurred. One student also argued that exclusion was experienced on different terms for different students, with rural students especially struggling to adjust to a university culture that was still quite urban, cosmopolitan, and expressed through dominant languages and social codes.

> Are you black or white; are you from a rich family, are you from a poor family? So those factors undermine your experience at [Institution B], so you cannot argue that people from Limpopo, from KZN, have the same experience that you know the minorities have at [Institution B], so that culture is very exclusive, it was created for certain people. [UN_B_FG_B.ED_1]

In spite of this, students at Institution B presented as significantly more active and engaged in the debates that circulated on the campus than at Institution A, which functioned almost as a school – students entered, received instruction, and left, without deep engagement or immersion in what space had to offer.

Language struggles as decolonising the pedagogic act

Language and medium of instruction policy is a significant indicator of an institution's progress in transforming the epistemic encounter for students, or at the very least constituting a foundation from which this transformation can proceed. The FeesMustFall protest called for attention to the approach by many universities that learning should take place primarily in English (and Afrikaans in some cases), with African languages not treated seriously as languages of teaching, learning, and research (Sayed, Motala, and De Kock 2019). The medium of instruction can marginalise and exclude, as noted by a student at Institution A.

> I often wonder what is put in place for students that struggle because I know students struggle, because English is my first language but my good Lord, when you learn academic English. I have to Google a word more than five times. [UN_A_MED_1]

Given that it is not only the language but a particular register that universities expect students to conform to, it is reasonable that even English-speaking students may struggle with the transition to higher education. The added complexity and difficulty this adds to the learning experience of students without this linguistic background limits epistemic access, disabling students from meaningfully engaging in the pedagogic act, privileging those schooled in English as their dominant voice.

One approach that a number of institutions have taken, particularly historically white universities, is to institute academic literacy programmes to support black students in the transition to higher education, including adapting to the language level required to participate effectively (Morreira 2017). Other institutions, such as Institution A, offer a compulsory literacy course for first-year teachers, though without the same level of sustained engagement or support.

> I was at one stage teaching reading literacy, which is a compulsory first-year subject and I actually thought there was enormous amounts of inequality in the language … everything was through English … so many students fail and do badly and don't understand what

they need to do and there was just absolutely inadequate provision given to them. [UN_A_DED_6]

This comment, by a doctoral student, demonstrates that linguistic inequality has a major impact on student participation. It also highlights that well-intentioned policies and programmes can have negative effects if their epistemic contribution is not sufficiently scaffolded with the reality of the resources students bring to the educational context.

At Institution B, students were aware that the institution had a more inclusive language policy but were at odds over how effective this was in practice:

I know that one official language of [Institution B] is Sepedi which is a vernac language, and that coming from a previously white dominated university, that shows the form of transformation in a way, so I feel like [Institution B] has made progress. [UN_B_FG_PHD_2]

The language policy of [Institution B] that is relatively inclusive, includes other languages apart from English and Afrikaans, [but] the issue is that it does not get reinforced. [UN_B_FG_PHD_2]

This view was shaped by the sense that the institution had put an inclusive policy in place but still needed to follow through on its progressive intent, something that some students found frustrating, and others had more patience for. Stroud and Kerfoot (2020) argue that language is one of the primary vehicles for students to be able to 'see' themselves in curricula, given that linguistic imperialism under colonialism has enabled languages such as English and Afrikaans to continue to be dominant in educational and social contexts.

Discussion

What the findings presented above show is the complexity of the institutional landscape and the diversity that characterises the higher education system in South Africa which more than 26 years after democracy, still reflects the bitter legacy of colonisation and segregation. The experiences of students in two diverse institutions illustrate how the policy commitment to transform and disrupt the coloniality of South African universities is still an ongoing project. In the discussion below, we reflect and theorise, and further develop the student experiences in relation to unpacking what is at stake for curriculum decolonisation in higher education. In so doing, we extend and develop the insights provided by the students from research conducted.

Decolonising curriculum

Probably the central tenet underpinning decolonisation in higher education is the politics of knowledge (Ndlovu-Gatsheni 2013; Nyamnjoh 2017) and how universities become sites of the reproduction of coloniality through their endorsement, legitimation, and valorisation of particular forms of knowledge, pedagogy, and practice. The findings from both institutions illustrate this to different degrees, and crucially how understandings of students are partial, incomplete, contradictory, and contested. The views of students range from, on the one hand, those perceiving decolonisation of the curricula as opening up the possibilities of radical ways of knowing in which the 'indigenised' and the 'other' is not at the periphery seeking inclusion but is the very core of how the curriculum is constituted. This goes beyond inserting African voices into existing canons or 'indigenising' curricula, and instead challenges the very notion of disciplinary knowledge, and what and whose knowledge is prioritised (Motala 2020). Furthermore, the two institutions reflect very different ways in which this radical call for decolonisation-as-recentring occurs or is likely to occur. In Institution B, embedding a decolonial approach to the curriculum has been an active but not unproblematic process, with participants suggesting that at times these efforts have been formulaic and symbolic, with the effect of diluting the call for decolonisation through a process of co-option and assimilation into the institution's broader developmental vision.

In contrast, in Institution A, participants suggested that getting through the curriculum has become the focus at the expense of challenging dominant knowledge systems. This appears rooted in a deficit view of the students, as well as an instrumental approach to teaching and learning that could perhaps be explained by a misguided institutional understanding of the epistemological foundation of universities of technology. In this way, students are not treated as agents in the learning process but recipients of authorised knowledge for practical application.

The data also demonstrated that decolonisation as filtered through students is a fuzzy, unclear, and somewhat undefined concept. For many, it resonated most with how the pedagogic act is transacted and less with which canons of knowledge are affirmed or subjugated. In this perspective, decolonising the curriculum is about reconstituting the sociality of the pedagogic encounter in various ways, including seeing the students as active partners in the learning act together with the lecturer and, in so doing, (re)affirming what experiences students bring to the pedagogic encounter. Knowledge as such is relationally constructed, a realm in which the encounter between students and lecturers is simultaneously affirming and challenging, conflictual, and nurturing, so that the pedagogic encounter is as much a journey undertaken jointly as one in which a student is led. As Morreira (2017, 291) argues, the coloniality of knowledge in higher education curricula creates a context in which black students not only do not 'see' themselves reflected in the knowledge they engage with and the pedagogies used to teach them – they are also positioned at a deficit in relation to the institution, where they are unable to access the cultural and social milieu of the space and are systematically excluded from becoming 'ideal knowers'.

In the ways in which decolonisation is understood in both institutions, the salience of language is powerful and telling. This issue is not just about what language but also the particular idiom of the language. As such, language, as under apartheid, becomes a site of contestation about what the decolonised curriculum means. Beyond simplistic renditions of English as the global language, curriculum planners and institutions have to navigate how multiple languages are brought to bear in teaching and learning, in which readings are made accessible to whom and how, and in how assessment is conducted. Yet all these issues remain dormant in debates about decolonisation, despite being the very issues that participants at both institutions reported as contributing to feelings of marginalisation and epistemic exclusion, hampering their full participation in the pedagogic encounter.

Decolonising belonging, support and care

The research found that decolonisation is more than material and epistemic. It is also about the struggle to transform the student experience and the ways in which teaching, and learning create conditions of belonging, care, and support for all. As such, the students at both institutions talk back to decolonisation in terms of the teaching and learning programme contexts in which they learn and learn to be-in-the-world. In this respect, they spoke much about access, belonging, care, and relationships as concerns in the interviews. Their views support existing research that suggests that alienation and derision are common experiences for black and working-class students, stemming from not entering the university space with the cultural and social capital that middle-class, and mostly but not exclusively white students enter with (Smit 2012; RMF 2015; Soudien 2020). At both institutions this meant a palpable lack of experience navigating the tertiary space, weak academic literacy and limited institutional support, echoing research findings by other scholars (cf.: Imenda, Kongolo, and Grewal 2004; CSVR 2017; Lekena and Bayaga 2018).

This dimension of student experience also draws out the tension between transformation and decolonisation, as the student interviews indicate. Opening up access to historically excluded students has necessitated the development of programmes for supporting these students through the educational journey lest they be left behind – and indeed, dropout rates among black students indicate that this is a serious concern (Ramrathan 2016; Morreira 2017; Lekena and Bayaga 2018; Soudien 2020). Transformation in higher education has focused on ensuring greater demographic representation of black staff and students, as well as a diversity in programme offerings and orientations, suggesting a notion of institutional reform reflected in numbers and not substantive programmatic or institutional, cultural renewal (Ramrathan 2016). While efforts have been made to create inclusive environments and support students in accessing higher education, Cross and Motala (2020) argue that transformation efforts may also be seen as having a placebo effect, papering over a failure to sufficiently transform the essence and structure of the system which continues to perpetuate exclusion and marginalisation.

In changing institutional cultures and providing a supportive teaching and learning environment, it is important not to, as many support programmes do, perceive black students as deficient and thus establish systems from a deficit perspective (Smit 2012). It is crucial to see students as creative, resilient, and with a remarkable agency, as the student protests illustrate, and more than capable of developing and sustaining supportive peer groups that are able to circulate academic knowledge, texts, food, and at times, emergency funds (Smit 2012; Cross and Atinde 2015). This suggests that it is not the student that is deficient but the institutions which are poorly prepared for the new kinds of students entering their spaces. What is needed is an understanding of the sociality of the pedagogic act and the dialectic relationships that are constituted between students and lecturers, and between students and institutional management.

Decolonising material deprivation

Decolonising knowledge and belonging have to be set against the backdrop of decolonising material deprivation, rooted in a project of belonging and care. The student movement drew together issues of epistemic access with an acknowledgement of the material inequalities that often constrain feasible attempts at substantive transformation, with a view to how this impacts the bid for 'decolonisation'. This is powerfully illustrated in both institutions, but possibly more vividly by Institution A, where a fragile institutional infrastructure focussed on getting students through the system to completion was further set back by the pandemic, with additional demands on its limited resources.

The process of massification of higher education – which received a major boost following the demands of the student movement – formed part of the drive to democratise access and improve equity through delivering on the increase in skilled graduates (Soudien 2020). However, it occurred in a context of significant resource constraints and a higher education funding model torn between the competing demands of equity and efficiency (Badat 2010; Motala 2020).

The student's voice demonstrates powerfully how access to funding, textbooks, accommodation, and even the payment of registration fees affect the ability of students to engage in epistemic decolonisation. The struggle for conducive and equitable teaching and learning environment is part of the struggle for epistemic access – it is not, as many commentators (cf. Jansen 2017) suggest, an either/or proposition. The struggle for decolonisation of the material and structural realities are integrally connected to the struggle to transform the episteme. More importantly, part of the struggle to decolonise the entire education edifice for higher education institutions involves recognising and responding to the inequalities embedded in the basic education system that students emerge from.

Concluding remarks

In this conclusion, we reflect on how calls for epistemic access in higher education of South Africa are mediated and realised in specific programmes and in specific institutional sites.

The first relates to enhancing meaningful epistemic access. The views of the students suggested that epistemic access in education programmes at the university level continues to be a negotiated and mediated practice at both institutions in very different ways. In Institution A, the decolonisation process is implicit and individualised to the level of lecture or programme, contingent on the decision-making of individual lecturers and curriculum designers. At Institution B decolonisation seems to take on a formal institution-wide approach. Yet both approaches reveal glaring weaknesses and challenges which need to be addressed. Where the approach is implicit and individualised, the experience of students of what constitutes decolonisation is uneven and partial. Where it is formalised, the experience is that such a process of decolonisation is symbolic and top-down. In both approaches to decolonising the pedagogic encounter, the key pedagogic question is how students are given access to knowledge and skills that enable them to challenge the lecturers and learning materials and texts they are exposed to in ways that enable them to inscribe their own experiences in the pedagogic act. Further, in both institutions, the imperative is not only to affirm student background and identity but to challenge and confront these in ways that validate experiential understanding. More importantly, what remains a matter of crucial consideration is how student experience relates to the broader academic and institutional experience.

Second, it is very much discernible in both institutions, albeit differently, that decolonisation is more than about content; it is also a struggle for developing what might be termed particular decolonial pedagogies for students who have entered university education programmes from marginal and marginalising positionalities. In this, the students at both institutions called for flexibility, openness, co-construction of meaning, and willingness to incorporate personal narrative into the process of intellectual deliberation. Not only was this an important break with more traditional teaching strategies, but it also represented a deep recognition of students' agency and capacity for intellectual engagement. Further, at both institutions, there was a strident call for the pedagogic moment to be infused with care, empathy, and a recognition of the individual, as well as the collective well-being of students who find themselves materially and socially vulnerable in large, often impersonal university settings. Moreover, the call for a rethink of language policies and the nature of support provided is not simply a call for enhancing academic ability (important as that is), but one of validation. While the implementation was uneven across both institutions, the talk of what a decolonised pedagogy might or might not entail is an important matter for informed deliberation and needs to be harnessed, supported, and built on.

Related to the idea of decolonial pedagogic forms and encounters is a fourth issue of the institutional culture and the nature of teaching and learning programmes. Successful integration is about what Soudien refers to as 'understanding the logic of the space' (2020, 136) and the terms by which knowledge is expressed and validated. While the focus on material conditions is a key enabler, a concurrent focus on institutional culture, as well as the pedagogic and social encounters is critical for a more cohesive approach to curriculum decolonisation.

Finally, no national-level change with respect to decolonising the curriculum is likely to be efficacious without robust policy alignment. A lack of coordination between national and institutional agenda-setting, as well as slow progress in meeting, stated goals for transformation and decolonisation, is most likely to continue to frustrate attempts to oversee effective changes in teaching and learning programmes. As shown in one of the institutions where the research was undertaken, student protest has been a regular feature of the institutional experience both because students' material concerns have not been adequately met, and because the substance of teaching and learning has not drastically changed.

The sociality of the pedagogic encounter as key to curriculum decolonisation in its multiple forms and dimensions is richly described, voiced, and nuanced by South African students studying education in diverse institutional contexts. Their views speak to the complex ways in which they negotiate the teaching and learning space surfacing the idea of pedagogy as relational, as material, as deep engagement, and as care and support (Morreira 2017; Kalantzis and Cope 2020). What this research reveals is that students engage in the pedagogic act and their sense of belonging in higher education deeply infused with rich backgrounds and knowledge challenging the deficit model of student learning, which characterises current teaching approaches. This paper calls for their active and meaningful participation as co-producers of knowledge. As higher education institutions negotiate various epistemic disruptions, care and empathy is required to secure the trust and willingness of students to engage in new and unfamiliar teaching and learning experiences providing real impetus the decolonial turn in South African tertiary education.

Acknowledgement

The work reported in this article was supported by the generous financial assistance of the National Research Foundation (NRF), which funds the South African Research Chair in Teaching & Learning, University of Johannesburg; and the South African Research Chair in Teacher Education, Centre for International Teacher Education (CITE), Cape Peninsula University of Technology (CPUT). Views expressed in this paper are those of the authors and are not to be attributed to the National Research Foundation or UJ or CPUT.

Disclosure statement

No potential conflict of interest was reported by the author(s).

REFERENCES

Badat, S. 2010. "The Challenges of Transformation in Higher Education and Training Institutions in South Africa." *Development Bank of Southern Africa* 8: 1–37.

Cross, M. 2020. *Decolonising Universities in South Africa: Backtracking and Revisiting the Debate. Transforming Universities in South Africa.101-114*. Brill Sense: Leiden.

Cross, M., and V. Atinde. 2015. "The Pedagogy of the Marginalized: Understanding How Historically Disadvantaged Students Negotiate Their Epistemic Access in a Diverse University Environment." *Review of Education, Pedagogy, and Cultural Studies* 37 (4): 308–325.

Cross, M., and S. Motala. 2020. "Introduction." In *Transforming Universities in South Africa: Pathways to Higher Education Reform*, edited by I. Rensburg, S. Motala, and M. Cross, 1–19. Brill Sense: Leiden.

CSVR (Centre for the Study of Violence and Reconciliation) 2017. *#Hashtag: An Analysis of the #FeesMustFall Movement at South African Universities*. Cape Town: CSVR.

De Sousa Santos, B. 2014. *Epistemologies of The South: Justice Against Epistemicide*. Boulder: Paradigm Publishers.

Imenda, S. N., M. Kongolo, and A. S. Grewal. 2004. "Factors Underlying Technikon and University Enrolment Trends in South Africa." *Educational Management Administration & Leadership* 32 (2): 195–215.

Jansen, J. 2017. *As By Fire: The End of the South African University*. Cape Town: NB Publishers.

Joseph, D. T. R. 2017. "Decolonising the Curriculum, Transforming the University: A Discursive Perspective." Paper presented at HELTASA (Higher Education Learning and Teaching Association of Southern Africa) Conference in Durban, South Africa, 21-24 November 2017.

Kalantzis, M., and B. Cope. 2020. "After the COVID-19 Crisis: Why Higher Education may (and Perhaps Should) Never be the Same." In *The Long Read: Reimagining the new Pedagogical Possibilities for Universities Post-Covid-19' in Educational Philosophy and Theory*, edited by M. A. Peters, F. Rizvi, G. McCulloch, P. Gibbs, R. Gorur, M. Hong, Y. Hwang, etal, 24–27. Philosophy of Education Society of Australia, Taylor and Francis. doi:10.1080/00131857.2020. 1777655.

Lekena, L. L., and A. Bayaga. 2018. "Trend Analysis of First Year Student Experience in University." *South African Journal of Higher Education* 32 (2): 157–175.

Mamdani, M. 2016. "Between the Public Intellectual and the Scholar: Decolonization and Some Post-Independence Initiatives in African Higher Education." *Inter-Asia Cultural Studies* 17 (1): 68–83.

Mignolo, W. D. 2011. "Epistemic Disobedience and the Decolonial Option: A Manifesto." *Transmodernity* 1 (2): 3–23.

Morreira, S. 2017. "Steps Towards Decolonial Higher Education in Southern Africa? Epistemic Disobedience in the Humanities." *Journal of Asian and African Studies* 52 (3): 287–301.

Motala, S. 2020. "Key Lessons for South Africa's Curriculum Transformation in the Humanities from Africa and African-American Studies." In *Transforming Ivory Towers to Ebony Towers: Lessons for South Africa's Curriculum Transformation in the Humanities from Africa and African-American Studies*, edited by S. Motala, and O. Tella, 399–408. Johannesburg: Wits University Press.

Muswede, T. 2017. "Colonial Legacies and the Decolonisation Discourse in Post-Apartheid South Africa – A Reflective Analysis of Student Activism in Higher Education." *African Journal of Public Affairs* 9 (5): 200–210.

Ndlovu-Gatsheni, S. 2013. *Coloniality of Power in Postcolonial Africa: Myths of Decolonisation*. Dakar: CODESRIA.

Ndlovu-Gatsheni, S. J. 2014. "What is Beyond Discourses of Alterity? Reflections on the Constitution of the Present and Construction of African Subjectivity." In *The Social Contract in Africa*, edited by S. Osha, 111–130. Pretoria: Africa Institute of South Africa.

Nyamnjoh, A. 2017. "The Phenomenology of Rhodes Must Fall: Student Activism and the Experience of Alienation at the University of Cape Town." *Strategic Review for Southern Africa* 39 (1): 256–277.

Ramrathan, L. 2016. "Beyond Counting the Numbers: Shifting Higher Education Transformation into Curriculum Spaces." *Transformation in Higher Education* 1 (1): 1–8.

Rensburg, I. 2020. "Global Africa: Nelson Mandela and the Meaning of Decolonising Knowledge and Universities – Problems and Opportunities." In *Transforming Universities in South Africa: Pathways to Higher Education Reform*, edited by I. Rensburg, S. Motala, and M. Cross, 74–100. Brill Sense: Leiden.

RhodesMustFall. 2015. Writing and Education Subcommittees, 'RhodesMustFall Statements', The Johannesburg Salon 9, 6.

Rhodes Must Fall. 2015. "Writing and Education Subcommittees." *The Johannesburg Salon* 9: 6.

Sayed, Y., S. Motala, and T. De Kock. 2019. "Between Higher and Basic Education in South Africa: What Does Decolonisation Mean for Teacher Education?" In *Decolonisation in Universities: The Politics of Knowledge*, edited by J. Jansen, 156–180. Stellenbosch: SUN Press.

Smit, R. 2012. "Towards a Clearer Understanding of Student Disadvantage in Higher Education: Problematising Deficit Thinking." *Higher Education Research & Development* 31 (3): 369–380.

Soudien, C. 2020. "The Learning Challenge in South African Higher Education Opportunities." In *Transforming Universities in South Africa: Pathways to Higher Education Reform*, edited by I. Rensburg, S. Motala, and M. Cross, 115–139. Brill Sense: Leiden.

Stroud, C., and C. Kerfoot. 2020. "Decolonising Higher Education: Multilingualism, Linguistic Citizenship & Epistemic Justice.." *Working Papers in Urban Language & Literacies* 265: 1–21.

Disrupting curricula and pedagogies in Latin American universities: six criteria for decolonising the university

Carolina Guzmán Valenzuela 🄳

ABSTRACT
Since the colonial era, Latin American universities have been subjected to narratives about what it means to be a university. Drawing on the concept of coloniality, this paper examines curricular and teaching practices in higher education that aim to decolonise Latin American universities, a particular topic that has been under-investigated. By means of a systematic literature review and a thematic analysis, 40 papers authored by at least one scholar affiliated to a Latin American university were examined. The analysis identified three levels of educational practices (macro, meso and micro) that revolve around the principle of intercultural indigenous education. Further, six essential criteria (cultural, epistemological, relational, ecological, economic, political) in decolonising university education are proposed. The paper concludes by offering insights about decolonising curricula and teaching practices in universities and the ways in which decolonial educational initiatives based on critical border thinking and socialisation of power might transform Latin American universities.

Introduction

Latin America experienced a long history of colonialism exercised by Spain and Portugal between the sixteenth and the nineteenth centuries. Colonialism consisted of the conquest of the lands, their peoples, and resources, and progressively, it also involved a process of cultural domination that has remained until today. This cultural domination has been based on two axes (Quijano 1993, 2000): (i) labour division (between landowners and slaves) and (ii) race (between European white conquers and non-white indigenous peoples). According to Quijano (op.cit.), this domination was exported to the rest of the world so giving way to the modern era in which conquering European white wealthy countries established their supremacy over countries with indigenous populations.

In this paper, coloniality is used to examine imaginaries around universities and the ways in which they have colonised universities in Latin America, with a specific focus on their teaching tasks and curricula. It is argued that colonial ways of thinking and realising universities in Latin America, their curricula and teaching practices were present not only in colonial times but remain now. A western model of university that draws on the competition for prestige and the marketisation of higher education has been dictating contemporary imaginaries about what it means to be a university (Barnett 2013; Marginson and Ordorika 2011; Ordorika and Lloyd 2015). This western model of university has not only been shaping Latin American universities in peripheral countries but most universities around the world (including those located in developed countries in Europe, the USA and Oceania).

As a response to these coloniality processes in higher education, several movements, especially in South Africa, have called for a decolonisation of the curriculum that has been well documented in the media and in the literature (Heleta 2016; Le Grange 2016; Leibowitz 2017a, 2017b). However, little is known about Latin America and its efforts to decolonise its universities, their pedagogies and curricula. A search of the literature on the topic shows that there are several decolonising experiences in universities documented in papers and books but very few have been published in English (David, Melo, and da Silva Malheiro 2013; De Carvalho et al. 2016; Dietz 2012a, 2012b; Guilherme, Morosini and Kohls dos Santos 2018; Mateos Cortés 2017; Mateos Cortés and Dietz 2016; Mato 2011, 2016; Restrepo 2014; Teamey and Mandel 2016; Usma and Ortiz 2018). Further, most of the publications on decolonising universities in Latin America revolve around the so called 'intercultural universities' (Mato 2016), these being universities that recognise the ethnic diversity of their students and academics and that offer a curriculum that is aligned with the cultural specificities of local indigenous groups and their communities (Dietz 2012a, 2012b; Mato 2019, 2016, 2011). However, very few publications address their pedagogies and curricula in detail.

In this paper, the literature about decolonising pedagogies and curricula in Latin American universities is examined. The paper clarifies key concepts regarding colonialism, postcolonialism and decolonialism. Also, some historical notes are offered to contextualise colonialism and coloniality of power (Quijano 2000) and the cultural domination exercised towards indigenous peoples in Latin America. Also, the paper addresses ways through which Latin American universities have been colonised by Western models of universities and briefly describes intercultural universities. Subsequently, so as to examine the production of knowledge about the decolonisation of curricula and pedagogies and to identify key areas of the scholarship about these topics in Latin America – that have been under-explored – both a systematic literature review and a thematic analysis were conducted.

Questions guiding the analysis were: Which are the main practices that universities in Latin America have initiated in an attempt to decolonise their curriculum and pedagogies and that are documented in the literature? What are their main characteristics, who are involved and at what level are these practices led and located (institutional level, academic units, pedagogical practices in the classroom, activities with the wider community)? Which are the main challenges in decolonising the curriculum in Latin American universities as identified in the literature? Which, if any, characteristics do these curricular and pedagogical initiatives have in common? Is there new knowledge that emerges from the analysis of these educational initiatives?

The paper concludes by reflecting on spaces of resistance within and beyond Latin America. In particular, it draws on the concepts of 'critical border thinking' (Mignolo and Tlostanova 2006, 206) and 'socialisation of power' (Quijano 2000, 573) to signify

Postcolonialism, coloniality and decolonialism: terminological clarifications

Throughout history, there have been many colonial stages through which the invasion of territories has been accompanied with the imposition of a culture, language, religion, and a legal system by the settler country. Slavery, devastation and even genocide have been also consequence of colonial processes. Particularly, over centuries, several European countries have maintained colonies in America, Africa, Asia, and Oceania for military, political or economic reasons.

Along with processes of colonisation, school of thoughts have emerged that critically examine such processes, with postcolonialism and decolonialism being two key concepts. Postcolonialism and decolonialism have been sometimes used interchangeably in the literature. Both critically address colonial processes through which a dominant culture imposes its racial, political, religious, financial, and cultural systems on other countries considered as inferior and so neglecting their ways of thinking and being in the world. However, these two concepts have different foci and origins (Bhambra 2014).

Postcolonialism was born as a result of scholars moving from the Middle East and Asia to the UK and the USA mainly in the 1960s and 1970s. It questions the ways in which narratives emanated from imperial European countries – considered to be universal – were imposed upon the ways in which people from former colonised lands see, think about and live in the world (Young 2016). One of its famous exponents, Edward Said (1979), proposed a distinction between the Occident (West) and the Orient (East). As a result of processes of imperialism exercised upon countries in the Orient, western knowledge has been conceived as superior in relation to knowledge produced in the East.

Decolonialism, in turn, has its roots in Latin-American intellectual groups. It examines the imbricated historical and epistemic relationships across modernity (as progress), colonial domination in Latin America, and coloniality (as poverty and inequality) (Grosfoguel 2007, 2011; Mignolo 2003; Quijano 1993, 2000). An important distinction here is that between colonialism and coloniality, coloniality being a fusion of the concepts of colonialism and modernity.

Once the lands in Latin America gained political independence, colonialism gave way to what has been termed 'coloniality' (Quijano 2000). In his work about the coloniality of power, eurocentrism, and America Latina (Quijano 2000), the Peruvian sociologist Anibal Quijano points out that the discovery and colonisation of America constituted the first historical moment and place where modernity emerged as a European colonial project. According to Quijano, modernity is based on two axes of power: first, race as a category of difference between white/superior conquerors and non-white conquered indigenous peoples – perceived as inferior. And second, the control and division of labour around the production, appropriation of and distribution of resources and products into the global market so that the white peoples were entitled to exploit the indigenous peoples' lands, appropriate their resources and trade them to increase their wealthiness. This labour stratification has been helpful in building a world system theory (Prebisch 1962; Wallerstein 1976) that distinguishes between the centre or core countries and peripheral countries.[1]

The binomials dominant-dominated, superior-inferior, white/European-indigenous, centre-periphery have been maintained and reinforced not only in terms of race and economic capital but also in relation to culture, ways of conceiving the world, social relationships, subjectivities, and knowledge (Grosfoguel 2007, 2011; Quijano 1993, 2000). Consequently, indigenous peoples' knowledges, languages, religions, and cultural practices have been conceived as inferior and even supressed (although many of these knowledges, customs and cultural practices have been retained through an informal oral tradition).

The coloniality of power has formed a young region inhabited mainly by mestizos (a mix between Europeans and indigenous peoples) that has experienced a systematic political and financial instability that has increased impoverishment and social inequities (Guzmán-Valenzuela and Bernasconi 2018). Among the major challenges in recent decades have been those of reducing social inequities and poverty (the Latin American region having one of the highest GINI indexes in the world alongside Africa), giving broader access to education and health services and recognising the rights, identities and knowledges of indigenous peoples (UNESCO 2020; World Bank 2015).

Colonialism and neo-colonialism in Latin American universities

The first universities in Latin America, established in the sixteenth century, were attached to both the royal crown and the Catholic church (Arocena and Sutz 2005; Jiménez 2007) so inheriting a model of university inspired by the Universidad de Salamanca in Spain (the oldest university in Spain, founded in the twelfth century). By the end of the colonial era, there were 25 universities that progressively had been initiating a process of secularisation so as to gain autonomy from the church (Levy 1986). By the nineteenth century, many universities in the Latin American region became public universities while some kept their status as Catholic universities.

After the independence from settler countries, most of the countries in the region initiated a process of nation-building, inspired by the French idea of republic (Tunnermann 2003). In this context, a Napoleonic model of university aimed at educating professionals for public administration prevailed. In this model, the teaching task gained traction while research was performed by institutes or academies (Brunner 2008). Public universities were under the tutelage and guidance of the State and their function revolved around national unity and political stability (Tunnermann 2003).

Both the Salamanca and the Napoleonic models of university have been crucial in shaping Latin American universities during and immediately after the colonial period. Historically, these two models of university were created as a space to educate the elite of the region during and after colonial times, that is, the creole elite composed of landowners, the political elite and the nascent commercial bourgeoisie (Tunnermann 2003) while the poorest and usually the less-white were relegated to semi-serfdom and low-paid jobs.

From the second half of the twentieth century onward, many universities in the region have experienced massification processes and an expansion of the private sector in the provision of higher education in which teaching-intensive universities oriented to professional education have prevailed with few research-oriented universities being established. The latter are usually the most prestigious ones and enrol the wealthiest students (Guzmán-Valenzuela 2017; Guzmán-Valenzuela and Bernasconi 2018).

The fact that the research universities in Latin America are the most prestigious and elite universities is not random. A narrative of global higher education dominated by international rankings based on research has been predominant (Dawson 2020; Ordorika and Lloyd 2015; Pusser and Marginson 2013). This research model of university across the world has prompted processes of academic stratification within countries and across regions (Guzmán-Valenzuela and Gómez 2019; Guzmán-Valenzuela 2017; Shahjahan, Blanco Ramirez, and Andreotti 2017). As a result, the most prestigious universities are mainly in core countries (with the USA and the UK leading those rankings) and those with the highest academic and social capital have access to them. In the periphery, in turn, the wealthiest are enrolled in the most prestigious research-oriented universities and then usually seek to obtain a postgraduate degree in the most prestigious universities in core countries (Perez Mejias, Chiappa, and Guzmán-Valenzuela 2018).

Also, an entrepreneurial model of university (Clark 1998; Shattock 2010) that conceives higher education as a private good that can be sold and traded in the market has gained traction as a global model of university. Such a model has prompted the privatisation of higher education institutions across Latin America, the provision of educational programmes at high prices, and low-quality universities that hold out the promise of social mobility alongside the casualisation of academics (Guzmán-Valenzuela and Barnett 2013a, 2013b; Guzmán-Valenzuela, 2016).

Both a research model of university and an entrepreneurial model of university can be conceived as ways of exporting-importing models of universities and, as such, constitute forms of neo-colonialism. Both models have been shaping higher education institutions across the world and especially in Latin America in recent decades.

Decolonising the Latin American universities

In many peripheral countries, the ways of thinking and realising the university have followed a westernised scholarship central to which is the idea of universal knowledge (Mato 2011; de Sousa Santos 2015; Stein et al. 2016). As Dawson notes: 'Still today, knowledge production within the academy relies largely on methodological tools, theoretical premises and styles of writing and argumentation developed and entrenched by European and American scholars' (Dawson 2020, 76).

However, the educational, cultural, historical, language and material conditions of higher education systems in the Latin American region have produced a limited imitation of westernised models of universities. Latin American countries and their universities do not have the monetary and material resources, and specialised educational capacities, to emulate the research capacity of the elite universities in core countries – which in turn reproduces and reinforces a scientific, educational and technological dependency (Alatas 2003; Guzmán-Valenzuela 2019; Obamba and Mwema 2009).

The systematic exportation and importation of models of universities from core (usually English-speaking countries) to peripheral countries, and particularly to Latin American countries, prompts questions about universities as sites of knowledge and intellectual life, and not only regarding the research task. The teaching task, the curricula and the ways in which knowledge, disciplines and pedagogies are conceived and realised (Leibowitz 2017a, 2017b; Manathunga 2018; Shahjahan, Wagner, and Wane 2009) are also issues here. For example, the Bologna process – a process born in Europe to ensure comparability in the standards and quality of higher-education qualifications – has been shaping the ways in which curricula have been organised in Latin American universities with little reflection on the extent to which the Bologna process may constitute a form of colonialism of Latin American universities (Boidin, Cohen, and Grosfoguel 2012).

Also, it is worth mentioning here the so-called intercultural universities. Intercultural universities, conceived as a decolonial project (Mignolo and Walsh 2018; Quijano 2000), explicitly resist the prevailing imaginary of university that revolves around productivity, and progress as economic development (Gudynas 2014). Intercultural universities aim to promote a space in which ethnic diversities and indigenous knowledges and languages are recognised and promoted through teaching, research, and outreach (Mato 2011, 2016). These universities understand themselves as intimately connected with their surrounding communities' ecosystems and seek to promote sustainability. Alongside intercultural universities, other educational initiatives that promote indigenous knowledges have been established, involving universities, programmes and courses in Mexico, Brazil, Chile, Peru, Colombia, Ecuador, and Costa Rica, among other countries.

Although there has been a renewed interest in examining the decolonisation of universities in the wake of student protests in South Africa in 2015 (Le Grange 2016), little is known about corresponding processes in Latin America. Two possible explanations for this latter situation are that (i) only very recently have Latin American universities sought to take on a decolonisation approach (Mato 2011); and (ii) academic work on these projects and disseminated in papers is written mainly in Spanish and Portuguese, which in turn makes them generally inaccessible to English readers and journals. There is a need, therefore, to rehearse in English the scholarship about the curricula and the teaching practices which are taking a decolonial approach in Latin American universities.

Methodology

A systematic literature review was conducted so as to provide an overview of the current state of the art about decolonisation of curricula and pedagogies in higher education in Latin America. A systematic literature review is a 'systematic, explicit, and reproducible method for identifying, evaluating, and synthesising the existing body of completed and recorded work produced by researchers, scholars, and practitioners' (Fink 2019: 6, 3) so as to identify relevant theories, methods and research gaps (Snyder 2019).

Papers authored by at least one academic affiliated to a Latin American university were identified across three well-known journal indexes (Web of Science (WoS) core collection, SCOPUS – these two being the most prestigious indexes and that include the widest collection of papers across the different disciplines – and SciELO – an index created in Brazil in 1987 and well-known and recognised in Latin America and Africa). The time-span for the search in each index was established as the start year of each index (WoS: 1975; SCOPUS: 1960: SciELO: 2002) until 2018.

The main terms and related words (in English, Spanish and Portuguese) included in the search were higher education, colonialism and pedagogy together with specific countries[2]. After a first screening of the papers, the terms 'intercultural universities' and 'intercultural education in higher education' were added. Later, and after a reading of each paper, all those papers documenting initiatives to facilitate access to higher education institutions to indigenous people were discarded since none addressed or documented in detail decolonising pedagogies or curricular practices. A total of 40 papers were identified: 1 WoS, 16 SCOPUS and 23 SciELO.

Once the papers were identified, organised, and read in detail, they were classified according to their empirical or non-empirical nature. Later, a thematic analysis of the empirical papers was conducted (Boyatzis 1998). Through this analysis, different levels of action (national, institutional, meso level and micro practices) were distinguished.

Results

Table 1 shows the main features of the selected papers in terms of type of index (WoS, SCOPUS or SciELO), year, affiliation, language of publication[3], and type (empirical or non-empirical) and methodology:

Table 1 shows that:

- Most papers (30 out of 40) were written in Spanish. This is not surprising since the majority of the selected papers are indexed in SciELO, an index that mainly contains Latin American journals and it is expected that authors use their *lingua franca* (Spanish or Portuguese) to publish their papers.
- Authors from Mexico dominate the landscape (22 papers), followed by Brazil (7), Colombia and Ecuador (2 each). Most of the papers by Mexican authors revolve around the so-called 'intercultural universities.'
- Most of the selected papers (32) are empirical and 8 are non-empirical. Most of the empirical papers are qualitative-oriented (28), 2 use a mixed-method approach and 2 are quantitative.
- Most of the papers (26) were published in the last three years of the time-span of the search (2016–2018). Also, it is important to notice that there were no publications before 2010, which demonstrates that topics related to decolonising the curriculum and teaching practices in Latin American universities are relatively new.

Three levels of action

In identifying the main practices in universities that are aimed at decolonising either curricula and/or their pedagogies, three levels of action of decolonial educational initiatives were identified within the selected papers: an institutional level, a degree programme level and a micro level. All three levels revolve around the idea of interculturality. Interculturality recognises and respects cultural differences between indigenous and non-indigenous peoples, and the richness of their cultures and knowledges, and so attempts to overcome social, cultural, epistemic, and political inequalities (Walsh 2009).

Table 1. Selected papers for the systematic literature review (own source).

	Index	Authors	Title	Year	Type and methodology	Country author' affiliation	Language
1.	WoS	de Carvalho, JJ; Cohen, LB; Correa, AF; Chada, S	The Meeting of Knowledges as a Contribution to Ethnomusicology and Music Education	2016	Empirical – Qualitative	Brazil	English
2.	Scopus	Tavares, M.; Gomes, S.	Epistemological foundations of the institutional matrix for new models of higher education in Brazil: A qualitative approach to institutional documents of Universidade Federal do ABC	2018	Empirical – Qualitative	Brazil	Portuguese
3.	Scopus	Czarny G.; Navia C.; Salinas, G.	Expectativas de estudiantes universitarios indígenas en educación superior [Indigenous uiversity students' expectations on higher education]	2018	Empirical – Qualitative	Mexico	Spanish
4.	Scopus	Carvajal-Jiménez V.; Cubillo-Jiménez K.A.; Vargas-Morales M.	Indigenous populations of Costa Rica and their access to higher education. Rural education Division: A training alternative	2017	Empirical – Qualitative	Costa Rica	Spanish
5.	Scopus	Krainer A.; Aguirre D.; Guerra M.; Meiser A.	Intercultural higher education and knowledge dialogue: The case of Amawtay Wasi University in Ecuador	2017	Empirical – Qualitative	Ecuador	English; Spanish
6.	Scopus	Mateos Cortés, L.S.	Indigenous Youth Graduating from Intercultural Universities: Capability Building Through Intercultural Higher Education in Veracruz, Mexico	2017	Empirical – Qualitative	Mexico	English
7.	Scopus	Olivera Rodríguez, I.	The potential of the Universidad Veracruzana Intercultural educational project: A critical analysis of development viewed through the concept of the good life (Buen vivir)	2017	Empirical – Qualitative	Mexico	English; Spanish
8.	Scopus	Cosme Solano, L.M.; Zevallos Solis, L.C.	Isis kori wayra teaching strategy in the intercultural dialogue	2017	Empirical – Mix-method	Peru	Spanish
9.	Scopus	Mato, D.	Indigenous People in Latin America: Movements and Universities. Achievements, Challenges, and Intercultural Conflicts	2016	Empirical – Qualitative	Argentina	English
10.	Scopus	Teamey, K.; Mandel, U.	A world where all worlds cohabit	2016	Non-Empirical	Costa Rica	English
11.	Scopus	Mateos Cortés L.S.; Dietz, G.	How intercultural is an 'intercultural university'? Some lessons from Veracruz, Mexico	2015	Empirical – Qualitative	Mexico	English
12.	Scopus	Mateos Cortés L.S.; Dietz, G.	New Local Meanings of the Transnational Discourse of	2014	Empirical – Qualitative	Mexico	Spanish

(Continued)

POSSIBILITIES AND COMPLEXITIES OF DECOLONISING HIGHER EDUCATION 141

Table 1. Continued.

Index	Authors	Title	Year	Type and methodology	Country author' affiliation	Language
13. Scopus	Alonso Guzmán, L.; Hernández Alarcón, V.M..; Solis Carmona, E.	Intercultural Higher Education in Veracruz Universidad Intercultural de los Pueblos del Sur: An option in Informal Education for the Indigenous Population in the State of Guerrero, Mexico	2014	Empirical – Qualitative	Mexico	Spanish
14. Scopus	David, M.; Melo, M.L.; Malheiro, J.M.S.	Challenges of multicultural curriculum in higher education for indigenous people	2013	Non-Empirical	Brazil	English
15. Scopus	Dietz, G.	Diversity Regimes Beyond Multiculturalism? A Reflexive Ethnography of Intercultural Higher Education in Veracruz, Mexico	2012	Empirical – Qualitative	Mexico	English
16. Scopus	Dietz, G.	Reflexivity and dialogue in collaborative ethnography: The ethnographic accompaniment of a Mexican 'intercultural' educational institution	2012	Empirical – Qualitative	Mexico	English; Spanish
17. Scopus	Da Silva, R.H.D.; Horta, J.S.B.	Teacher Education Programs for indigenous teachers in public universities in the Brazilian Amazon: Participation and shared protagonism	2010	Empirical – Qualitative	Brazil	Portuguese
18. SciELO	Tamayo Osorio, C.	Degree in pedagogy of Mother Earth, Ethnomathematics and teacher training	2018	Empirical – Qualitative	Brazil	Spanish
19. SciELO	Sena Tomaz, V.; Knijnik, G.	Tensions in the indigenous intercultural teacher education: study of a Xakriabá school	2018	Empirical – Qualitative	Brazil	Portuguese
20. SciELO	Garzón Díaz, K.; Hernández Jaramillo, J.	The imagined Colombia, traces of peace: children's literature as a pedagogic experience in higher education	2018	Empirical – Qualitative	Colombia	Spanish
21. SciELO	Parra, C.	Didactic MediActions, languages and transdisciplinarity: planetary citizenships in higher education	2018	Empirical – Qualitative	Colombia	Spanish
22. SciELO	Navarro-Martínez, S.	Prospects and Scope of the Community Involvement. The Case of the Intercultural University of Chiapas, Oxchuc Campus	2018	Empirical – Qualitative	Mexico	Spanish
23. SciELO	Ramírez Valverde, B.; Bustillos Ibarra, O.; Juárez Sánchez, P.	High Education from the perspective of the students of two intercultural universities	2018	Empirical – Quantitative	Mexico	Spanish
24. SciELO	Hernández Loeza, S.	What distinguishes 'intercultural	2017	Empirical – Qualitative	Mexico	Spanish

(Continued)

Table 1. Continued.

Index	Authors	Title	Year	Type and methodology	Country author' affiliation	Language
		professionals"? The experiences of male and female graduates from the Intercultural University of the State of Puebla				
25. SciELO	Rosado-May, F.	Intercultural higher education for indigenous Yucatec Maya in Mexico	2017	Empirical – Qualitative	Mexico	Spanish
26. SciELO	Peña Piña, J.	La formación de profesionales en desarrollo sustentable en un programa de educación superior intercultural [Professional education in sustainable development in an intercultural higher education programme]	2017	Non-Empirical	Mexico	Spanish
27. SciELO	Albarracín De Alderetes, L.	The higher education certificate in IBE in the Universidad Nacional de Santiago del Estero: challenges of a university course on an indigenous language	2016	Non-Empirical	Argentina	Spanish
28. SciELO	Mora Monroy, Gl.	Two educational and editorial experiences with university indigenous, Afro-Colombian and poor municipalities students from a cultural perspective	2016	Empirical – Qualitative	Colombia	Spanish
29. SciELO	Ávila Romero, L.; Betancourt Posada, A.; Arias Hernández, G.; Ávila Romero, A.	Community Association and Dialogue of Knowledge in Mexico's Intercultural Higher Education	2016	Empirical – Qualitative	México	Spanish
30. SciELO	Bastiani-Gómez, J.; López-García, M.	Production of texts in students from two public universities with intercultural model	2016	Empirical	Mexico	Spanish
31. SciELO	Galán López, F.; Navarro Martínez, S.	Indigenism and Intercultural Education: A Necessary Discussion. Experience in the Intercultural University of the State of Tabasco	2016	Empirical – Qualitative	México	Spanish
32. SciELO	Mateos Cortés, L.; Dietz, G.; Mendoza Zuany, R..	Intercultural Knowledge/ Activities? Professional and Community Experiences of the Graduates of Intercultural Higher Education in Veracruz	2016	Empirical – Qualitative	Mexico	Spanish
33. SciELO	Sartorello, S.	Intercultural Conflict and Interaction: Indigenous and Mestizo University Students at Universidad Intercultural de Chiapas	2016	Empirical – Qualitative	Mexico	Spanish
34. SciELO	Mateos Cortés, L.; Dietz, G.	Just how intercultural is the 'intercultural university"? From the political-	2015	Non-Empirical	Mexico	Spanish

(Continued)

Table 1. Continued.

Index	Authors	Title	Year	Type and methodology	Country author' affiliation	Language
		pedagogical debate to a case study in Veracruz				
35. SciELO	Vargas Moreno, P.	Intercultural Higher Education in dispute. Paths of the Amawtay Wasi Intercultural University	2014	Empirical – Qualitative	Ecuador	Spanish
36. SciELO	Olivera Rodríguez, I.	¿Desarrollo o bien vivir?: rethinking the social role of the Intercultural University from the questioning of the Educational Effect	2014	Non-Empirical	Mexico	Spanish
37. SciELO	Figueroa Saavedra, M.; Alarcón Fuentes, D.; Bernal Lorenzo, D.; Hernández Martínez, J.	The incorporation of national indigenous languages into the academic development of universities: The experience of the Universidad Veracruzana	2014	Empirical – Quantitative	México	Spanish
38. SciELO	Tavares, M.	The University and the epistemological pluri-diversity: the construction of knowledge in terms of other non-western centred epistemological paradigms	2013	Non-Empirical	Brazil	Portuguese
39. SciELO	Arcos Gutiérrez, L.	The Right of Indigenous Peoples to a Higher Education. Reconstruction of Experience: The Case of the 'Jacinto Canek' Indigenous Normal School	2012	Empirical – Qualitative	Mexico	Spanish
40. SciELO	Dietz, G.; Mateos Cortés, L.	La etnografía reflexiva en el acompañamiento de procesos de interculturalidad educativa: un ejemplo veracruzano [Reflevive ethnography in the accompaniment of educational intercultural processes: an example from Veracruz]	2010	Empirical – Qualitative	Mexico	Spani

a) Institutional level: Usually, the papers identified here document the experience and trajectory of a specific case, in which the whole institution (usually created by the central or local government) is devoted to indigenous peoples and their knowledges. Most of the cases are intercultural universities in Mexico (Universidad Veracruzana Intercultural, Universidad del Sur, Universidad Autónoma Intercultural de Sinaloa, Universidad Intercultural Maya, Universidad Intercultural de Chiapas; and Escuela Jacinto Canek (Teacher Training College)). However, a couple of papers are focused on the Universidad Intercultural Amawtay Wasi in Ecuador.

The legal constitutions in both Mexico (Alonso Guzmán, Hernández Alarcón, and Solís Carmona) and Ecuador (Krainer et al.; Vargas Moreno) legally recognise indigenous peoples and their right to access and study a degree programme in a university that includes indigenous knowledges or practices. As a result, in these countries, intercultural universities have been created to address this aim.

144 POSSIBILITIES AND COMPLEXITIES OF DECOLONISING HIGHER EDUCATION

Most of these universities have faced serious challenges in their development related to budgetary restrictions, poor facilities, a shortage of teachers and administrative staff trained to work in intercultural universities and low enrolment and dropout rates. However, there are two extreme cases that stand out: the Universidad Intercultural Amawtay Wasi in Ecuador that was closed in 2013 (since reopened in 2020) for not being able to secure national accreditation and that became a non-formally recognised higher education institution ('Pluriversidad Amawtay Wasi') (Krainer et al.; Mato; Vargas Moreno); and the Universidad del Sur that does not offer certified degrees and whose programmes are oriented towards indigenous needs in agriculture, health, language and culture, law and human rights, environmental management, and local governance (Alonso Guzmán el al.). This challenge shows a divide between traditional and alternatives ways of realising a university. For intercultural universities, it is not easy to be legally recognised in a territory dominated by processes of accreditation that follow the rules of a western model of university (Mato).

b) Degree programmes across different disciplines: These are offered either in traditional or intercultural universities and they are open to both indigenous and non-indigenous peoples. All of them are tightly connected with the indigenous communities' needs and usually include an active involvement of indigenous peoples in the wider community.

Within intercultural universities, these degrees include, for example, intercultural management, alternative tourism, language and culture, sustainable development, intercultural medicine, municipal management and culture, technology of information, art management and development, business development, intercultural education and communication, agro-ecology studies, intercultural law, architecture, teacher education. In traditional universities, new degrees include intercultural management and development (Universidad Nacional Autonoma de México); indigenous education (Universidad Pedagogica Nacional in Mexico and Universidad Nacional in Costa Rica); intercultural management for development with different specialisations (Universidad Veracruzana, Mexico); mother earth and ethnomathematics (Universidad de Antioquia in Colombia); and teacher education for indigenous Mura people in Brazil (Universidade Federale do Amazonas).

The most striking case is, again, the Universidad Intercultural Amawtay Wasi in Ecuador and ways in which it organised engineering, architecture, and educational programmes (Vargas Moreno). All of these programmes worked together in a first semester in which the emphasis was put on the epistemological and political stances of the university. Later, each programme included a first cycle in ancestry sciences, then a second cycle on western knowledges linked to each discipline and finally, a third cycle focused on interculturality. This is a good example of the ways through which a dialogue between knowledges (western and indigenous knowledges) is put into practice.

Some challenges in implementing these degrees in both intercultural and traditional universities have to do with the extent to which these degrees are aligned with the local needs of the community; are recognised as *bona fide* programmes; attracting students and keeping them in the system considering financial restraints or geographic barriers; local job opportunities; an active involvement of the local indigenous community in the development of the degrees; and teacher preparation to offer these degrees (there are few specific degrees in indigenous teacher education). Also, in the case of traditional universities, indigenous students have faced ethnic discrimination.

c) Teaching level: At this level, courses, pedagogical methods, strategies and/or learning assessment methods used in either traditional universities or intercultural universities are included.

For example, this level includes courses of indigenous languages and written language at the traditional Universidad Nacional de Colombia (Mora Monroy); an optional course in which students in the health sciences visit and work closely with the indigenous communities to design and evaluate an experience on indigenous literatures at the traditional Universidad del Rosario also in Colombia (Garzón Díaz and Hernández Jaramillo); the use of a pedagogical indigenous tool to promote intercultural dialogues in the Universidad Nacional Intercultural de la Amazonia in Peru (Solano and Solis); the use of indigenous calendars to teach ethnomathematics in a teacher education degree at the traditional Universidade Federal de Minas Gerais in Brazil (Tomaz and Knijnik); and a project entitled 'Meeting of Knowledges' that is offered in several universities across Brazil and whose aim is to incorporate indigenous musical traditions attached to ancestral knowledges and rituals in the curricular formation of music teachers (De Carvalho et al.).

A striking curricular experience called 'el Receteadero' takes place at the Universidad de Antioquia (Parra) in teacher education. In this course, critical readings around classic and contemporary pedagogical traditions are encouraged. Further, through readings, conversations, and written tasks, environmental problems and their relationship with food, consumption and agricultural practices are addressed.

Challenges at this level have to do with the lack of preparation of teachers so as to teach and evaluate learning in ways that are aligned with indigenous visions rather than western ways of assessing learning. In some indigenous language courses, the assessments were performed in Spanish.

One of the major challenges identified across all three levels has to do with the tension between *top-down educational policies* (usually in the light of a legal framework) and *bottom-up educational initiatives*. There are dozens of indigenous communities across the Latin America region and the teaching practices, pedagogies and curricular projects examined are context-dependent and respond to local indigenous demands. Although some of these initiatives – mainly in Mexico – could be considered as a top-down policy boosted by a legal framework in the constitution, most of them have been progressively built jointly and closely with the local indigenous communities. Also, many are run in partnership between specific departments in the university and formal or informal indigenous groups in the territory where the university is situated. Such partnerships denote a democratisation of the university and the ways in which knowledge is produced and taught.

Six criteria for decolonising curricula and pedagogies

Emerging from the analysis of the selected papers, explicitly or implicitly, six dimensions of the educational practices identified and reviewed are evident:

a) Cultural: all the educational initiatives have in common a will to recognise and preserve the culture of indigenous peoples. This includes indigenous languages, rituals, ancestral practices, knowledges, and historical memories (through music, calendars, and tales, for example). Among the most frequent educational practices at programme level in traditional and indigenous universities, and specific courses and pedagogies, were the promotion and preservation of indigenous languages (see for example, Bastiani-Gómez and López-García; Figueroa Saavedra et al.; Parra; Sartorello, among many others).

b) Epistemological: the educational practices analysed here respect and preserve ancestral visions about the world and alternative knowledges (Mateos Cortés, Dietz, and Mendoza Zuany). Such knowledges are tightly linked to indigenous cultures. Cultivating alternative knowledges contests the supremacy of just one form of knowledge (Western knowledge) (Rosado-May) and also opens spaces to promote a dialogue among all of them.

c) Relational: the initiatives explored here were concerned to develop relationships among all involved – recognising that everyone is different – and based especially on values of care, respect, and solidarity. Supportive relationships within the local community were seen as essential. Also, the importance of wisdom in the elderly and a sense of community in the pedagogical practices – in opposition to an individualised vision of the world – are prevalent (Garzón Díaz and Hernández Jaramillo).

d) Ecological: The ecological dimension turns on a relationship with and respect for the land, Nature and the environment which are conceived as interdependent biodiverse systems (ecosystems) (Teamey and Mandel). The concepts of planetary consciousness and planetary pedagogies (Parra) are good examples. A planetary pedagogy is a type of pedagogy that draws on interculturality and that preserves and educates in ancestral knowledges that interweave human beings in their relationships with the environment (Olivera Rodríguez).

e) Economic: Sustainable development emerges here in opposition to economic progress. In this context, the use of the land and the extraction of natural resources aim at the preservation of the community rather than the accumulation of wealth or transactions in the financial market. All the educational initiatives described here implicitly or explicitly promote an education aiming at a sustainable development focused on the local community (see for example, Avila et al.; Navarro-Martínez; Ramírez Valverde, Bustillos Ibarra, and Juárez Sánchez, among many others).

f) Political: all the practices described may be considered as political projects through which two visions are avoided. On the one hand, a vision that promotes the acculturation of indigenous peoples to the dominant culture so denying their cultures and knowledges. And, on the other hand, a cosmetic vision of indigenism through which indigenous rights are recognised but where economic progress prevails (Hernandez). An educational indigenous project is also political in that (i) it recognises, protects, and preserves the rights, histories, knowledges, and cultures of the indigenous peoples, and (ii) it defies the structures of coloniality by contesting, challenging and transforming them (Tomaz and Knijnik).

POSSIBILITIES AND COMPLEXITIES OF DECOLONISING HIGHER EDUCATION   147

These six dimensions may be seen as *criteria* for guiding decolonial educational projects in Latin America and opening multiple possibilities for imagining ways of decolonising the curricula and teaching and learning processes.

Final remarks

Higher education systems and universities across the world are governed and restrained by colonial and neo-colonial trends that produce and reproduce racism, discrimination, stratification, and social inequalities. In this world order, critical voices against a model of university that reproduces its power on the basis of race, labour division, prestige, language and monocultural ways of knowledge have emerged.

The educational initiatives described in this paper are promising examples of decolonising curricular and teaching practices in universities in Latin America. They open spaces for dialogues between Western and indigenous knowledges and for challenging and transforming coloniality structures (Walsh 2009) through collective actions that involve both the universities and the local indigenous communities. Such decolonial projects are not immune from challenges, budgetary restrictions, accreditation demands and lack of legal or educational recognition, though. Some of these projects have struggled to survive and some have been even terminated since they have not met the accreditation regulations of central governments. However, they represent a hope for the future in Latin America and other peripheral regions.

Following the concepts of 'critical border thinking' (Mignolo and Tlostanova 2006, 206) and 'socialisation of power' (Quijano 2000, 573), the curricular practices and pedagogies examined here can be considered as critical border educational projects. They are concerned with indigenous knowledges and the ways through which they are produced, taught, shared, preserved, and valued in a local community. Further, they seek a transformation of the dominant culture and the democratisation of power through intercultural education. Critical border educational projects are 'critical' since they aim at questioning and transforming the coloniality of power that has produced discrimination and delegitimisation of indigenous peoples and their cultures on the basis of race and labour. They are 'border' since they have been produced from the borders, that is peripheral contexts and institutions in a peripheral region (Latin America). And they promote a socialisation of power since these educational projects empower indigenous communities to act alongside universities to break the coloniality of power.

Drawing on the evidence here, six criteria have been suggested as a means of decolonising curricula and teaching practices (cultural, epistemological, relational, ecological, economic, and political). These six criteria also constitute a space in which further decolonial educational theories can emerge and which can guide educational policies and practices in Latin America and beyond.

Notes

1. The core countries are former coloniser wealthy countries that concentrate a 'high-profit, high-technology, high-wage diversified production ... [and peripheral countries, usually former colonies] in which are concentrated low-profit, low technology, low-wage ... [and]

148 POSSIBILITIES AND COMPLEXITIES OF DECOLONISING HIGHER EDUCATION

less diversified production' (Wallerstein 1976, 462). Semi-peripheral countries, in turn, display features of both core and peripheral countries.

2. The specific terms were: ('higher education' OR 'tertiary education' OR 'college education' OR 'postsecondary education' OR 'post-secondary education' OR 'postsecondary education' OR 'post-compulsory education' OR 'post compulsory education' OR 'post compulsory education' OR 'university education') AND NOT ('secondary education' OR 'primary education' OR 'elementary education' OR 'early childhood education' OR 'preschool education'; decolonial OR 'colonial' OR 'coloniality' OR 'decolonisation' OR 'decolonization' OR 'decolonising' OR 'decolonise' OR 'decolonize' OR 'postcolonial' OR 'indigenous' OR 'epistemic justice' OR 'epistemic injustice' OR 'cognitive justice' OR 'cognitive injustice' OR 'periphery' OR 'global north' OR 'global south' OR 'Western South' OR 'western-south' OR 'Southern theories' OR 'Epistemologies of the south'; 'pedagogy' OR 'pedagogies' OR 'pedagogical' OR 'curriculum' OR 'curricular' OR 'curricula' OR 'teaching' OR 'learning'; Argentina; Bolivia; Brazil; Chile; Colombia; Costa Rica; Cuba; El Salvador; Ecuador; Guatemala; Haiti; Honduras; Mexico; Nicaragua; Panama; Paraguay; Perú; Dominican Republic; Uruguay; Venezuela).

3. A translation of each paper's title is offered where one was not available in English.

Acknowledgements

I greatly appreciate the help provided by Carolina Gómez.

Disclosure statement

No potential conflict of interest was reported by the author(s).

Funding

This work was supported by ANID-FONDECYT Chile: [Grant Number Project number 1200633].

ORCID

Carolina Guzmán Valenzuela http://orcid.org/0000-0002-7974-762X

References

Alatas, Syed Farid. 2003. "Academic Dependency and the Global Division of Labour in the Social Sciences." *Current Sociology* 51 (6): 599–613. doi:10.1177/00113921030516003.
Arocena, Rodrigo, and Judith Sutz. 2005. "Latin American Universities: From an Original Revolution to an Uncertain Transition." *Higher Education* 50 (4): 573–592. doi:10.1007/s10734-004-6367-8.
Barnett, Ronald. 2013. *Imagining the University*. London: Routledge.
Bhambra, Gurminder K. 2014. "Postcolonial and decolonial dialogues." *Postcolonial Studies* 17 (2): 115–121. doi:10.1080/13688790.2014.966414.
Boidin, Capucine, James Cohen, and Ramón Grosfoguel. 2012. "Introduction: From University to Pluriversity: A Decolonial Approach to the Present Crisis of Western Universities." *Human Architecture: Journal of the Sociology of Self-Knowledge* 10 (1): 2.
Boyatzis, Richard E. 1998. *Transforming Qualitative Information: Thematic Analysis and Code Development*. London: Sage.
Brunner, José Joaquín. 2008. "El proceso de Bolonia en el horizonte latinoamericano: límites y posibilidades." *Revista de Educación* 1: 127–128.

Clark, Burton R. 1998. "The Entrepreneurial University: Demand and Response." *Tertiary Education and Management* 4 (1): 5–16. doi:10.1007/BF02679392.

David, Moisés, Maria Lúcia Melo, and João Manoel da Silva Malheiro. 2013. "Challenges of Multicultural Curriculum in Higher Education for Indigenous People." *Educação e Pesquisa* 39 (1): 111–125. 10.1590/S1517-97022013000100008.

Dawson, Marcelle C. 2020. "Rehumanising the University for an Alternative Future: Decolonisation, Alternative Epistemologies and Cognitive Justice." *Identities* 27 (1): 71–90. doi:10.1080/1070289X.2019.1611072.

De Carvalho, José Jorge, Liliam Barros Cohen, Antenor Ferreira Corrêa, Sonia Chada, and Paula Nakayama. 2016. "The Meeting of Knowledges as a Contribution to Ethnomusicology and Music Education." *The World of Music, New Series* 5 (1): 111–133. Accessed November 11, 2020. http://www.jstor.org/stable/44652698.

de SousaSantos, Boaventura. 2015. *Epistemologies of the South: Justice against epistemicide.* London: Routledge.

Dietz, Gunther. 2012a. "Reflexividad y diálogo en etnografía colaborativa: el acompañamiento etnográfico de una institución educativa" intercultural" mexicana." *Revista de Antropología Social* 21: 63–91. 10.5209/rev_RASO.2012.v21.40050.

Dietz, Gunther. 2012b. "Diversity Regimes Beyond Multiculturalism? A Reflexive Ethnography of Intercultural Higher Education in Veracruz, Mexico." *Latin American and Caribbean Ethnic Studies* 7 (2): 173–200. doi:10.1080/17442222.2012.686334.

Fink, Arlene. 2019. *Conducting Research Literature Reviews: From the Internet to Paper.* London: Sage.

Grosfoguel, R. 2007. "The Epistemic Decolonial Turn: Beyond Political-Economy Paradigms." *Cultural Studies* 21 (2–3): 211–223. doi:10.1080/09502380601162514.

Grosfoguel, Ramón. 2011. "Decolonizing Post-Colonial Studies and Paradigms of Political-Economy: Transmodernity, Decolonial Thinking, and Global Coloniality." *Transmodernity: Journal of Peripheral Cultural Production of the Luso-Hispanic World* 1: 1. https://escholarship.org/uc/item/21k6t3fq.

Gudynas, Eduardo. 2014. "Conflictos y extractivismos: conceptos, contenidos y dinámicas." *Decursos. Revista en Ciencias Sociales,* 27 (2): 79–115.

Guilherme, Alexandre, Marilia Morosini, and Pricila Kohls dos Santos. 2018. "The Process of Internationalisation of Higher Education in Brazil: the Impact of Colonisation on South-South Relations." *Globalisation, Societies and Education* 16 (4): 409–421.

Guzmán-Valenzuela, Carolina. 2016. "Unfolding the Meaning of Public (s) in Universities: Toward the Transformative University." *Higher Education* 71 (5): 667–679. doi:10.1007/s10734-015-9929-z.

Guzmán-Valenzuela, Carolina. 2017. "Tendencias globales en Educación Superior y su impacto en América Latina: desafíos pendientes." *Lenguas Modernas* 50: 15–32.

Guzmán-Valenzuela, Carolina. 2019. "Values and the International Collaborative Research in Higher Education: Negotiating Epistemic Power between the Global South and the Global North." In *Values of the University in a Time of Uncertainty,* edited by L. Gormall, L. Sweetman, and B. Thomas, 137–153. Cham: Springer.

Guzmán-Valenzuela, Carolina, and Ronald Barnett. 2013a. "Academic Fragilities in a Marketised age: The Case of Chile." *British Journal of Educational Studies* 61 (2): 203–220. doi:10.1080/00071005.2013.776006.

Guzmán-Valenzuela, Carolina, and Ronald Barnett. 2013b. "Marketing Time: Evolving Timescapes in Academia." *Studies in Higher Education* 38 (8): 1120–1134. doi:10.1080/03075079.2013.833032.

Guzmán-Valenzuela, Carolina, and Andrés Bernasconi. 2018. "The Latin-American University: Past, Present and Future." in *The Idea of the University: Contemporary Perspectives Volume 2,* edited by R. Barnett, and M. Peters, 776–294. New York: Peter Lang.

Guzmán-Valenzuela, Carolina, and Carolina Gómez. 2019. "Advancing a Knowledge Ecology: Changing Patterns of Higher Education Studies in Latin America." *Higher Education* 77 (1): 115–133. doi:10.1007/s10734-018-0264-z.

Heleta, Savo. 2016. "Decolonisation of Higher Education: Dismantling Epistemic Violence and Eurocentrism in South Africa." *Transformation in Higher Education* 1 (1): 1–8. 10.4102/the.v1i1.9.

Jiménez, Elsi. 2007. "La Historia de la Universidad en América Latina." *Revista de la Educación Superior*, XXXVI(1) 141: 169–178.

Le Grange, Lesley. 2016. "Decolonising the University Curriculum: Leading Article." *South African Journal of Higher Education* 30 (2): 1–12. doi:10.20853/30-2-709.

Leibowitz, Brenda. 2017a. "Cognitive Justice and Higher Education." *Journal of Education* 68 (2017): 93–112.

Leibowitz, Brenda. 2017b. "Power, Knowledge and Learning: Dehegomonising Colonial Knowledge." *Alternation Journal* 24 (2): 99–119. doi:10.29086/2519-5476/2017/v24n2a6.

Levy, Daniel C. 1986. *Higher Education and the State in Latin America: Private Challenges to Public Dominance.* Chicago: University of Chicago Press.

Manathunga, Catherine. 2018. "Decolonising the Curriculum: Southern Interrogations of Time, Place and Knowledge." *SOTL in the South* 2 (1): 95–111. 10.36615/sotls.v2i1.23.

Marginson, Simon, and Imanol Ordorika. 2011. ""El central volumen de la fuerza." *Global Hegemony in Higher Education and Research.*" In *Knowledge Matters: The Public Mission of the Research University*, edited by D. Rhoten, and C. Calhoun, 67–129. New York: Columbia University Press.

Mateos Cortés, Laura. 2017. "Indigenous Youth Graduating from Intercultural Universities: Capability Building Through Intercultural Higher Education in Veracruz, Mexico." *Journal of Intercultural Studies* 38 (2): 155–169. doi:10.1080/07256868.2017.1291496.

Mateos Cortés, Laura, and Gunther Dietz. 2016. "How Intercultural is An"Intercultural University"? Some Lessons from Veracruz, Mexico." *Revista Lusófona de Educação* 31: 125–143.

Mato, Daniel. 2011. "There is No 'Universal' Knowledge, Intercultural Collaboration is Indispensable." *Social Identities* 17 (3): 409–421. doi:10.1080/13504630.2011.570978.

Mato, Daniel. 2016. "Indigenous People in Latin America: Movements and Universities. Achievements, Challenges, and Intercultural Conflicts." *Journal of Intercultural Studies* 37 (3): 211–233. doi:10.1080/07256868.2016.1163536.

Mato, Daniel. 2019. "Educación Superior y Pueblos Indígenas: Experiencias, estudios y debates en América Latina y otras regiones del mundo." *Revista del Cisen Tramas/Maepova* 6 (2): 41–65.

Mignolo, Walter D. 2003. *Historias locales/diseños globales: colonialidad, conocimientos subalternos y pensamiento fronterizo. Vol. 18.* Madrid: Ediciones Akal.

Mignolo, Walter D., and Madina V. Tlostanova. 2006. "Theorizing from the Borders: Shifting to Geo-and Body-Politics of Knowledge." *European Journal of Social Theory* 9 (2): 205–221. doi:10.1177/1368431006063333.

Mignolo, Walter D., and Catherine E. Walsh. 2018. *On Decoloniality: Concepts, Analytics, Praxis.* Durham: Duke University Press.

Obamba, Milton Odhiambo, and Jane Kimbwarata Mwema. 2009. "Symmetry and Asymmetry: New Contours, Paradigms, and Politics in African Academic Partnerships." *Higher Education Policy* 22 (3): 349–371. doi:10.1057/hep.2009.12.

Ordorika, Imanol, and Marion Lloyd. 2015. "International Rankings and the Contest for University Hegemony." *Journal of Education Policy* 30 (3): 385–405. doi:10.1080/02680939.2014.979247.

Perez Mejias, Paulina, Roxana Chiappa, and Carolina Guzmán-Valenzuela. 2018. "Privileging the Privileged: The Effects of International University Rankings on a Chilean Fellowship Program for Graduate Studies Abroad." *Social Sciences* 7 (12): 243. doi:10.3390/socsci7120243.

Prebisch, Raul. 1962. "The Economic Development of Latin America and its Principal Problems." *Economic Bulletin for Latin America* 7: 1–12.

Pusser, B., and S. Marginson. 2013. "University Rankings in Critical Perspective." *The Journal of Higher Education* 84 (4): 544–568. doi:10.1080/00221546.2013.11777301.

Quijano, Aníbal. 1993. "Modernity, Identity, and Utopia in Latin America." *Boundary 2* 20 (3): 140–155.

Quijano, Anibal. 2000. "Coloniality of Power and Eurocentrism in Latin America." *International Sociology* 15 (2): 215–232. doi:10.1177/0268580900015002005.

Restrepo, Paula. 2014. "Legitimation of Knowledge, Epistemic Justice and the Intercultural University: Towards an Epistemology of 'Living Well'." *Postcolonial Studies* 17 (2): 140–154. doi:10.1080/13688790.2014.966416.

Said, Edward W. 1979. *Orientalism.* New York: Vintage.

Shahjahan, Riyad, Gerardo Blanco Ramirez, and Vanessa De Oliveira Andreotti. 2017. "Attempting to Imagine the Unimaginable: A Decolonial Reading of Global University Rankings." *Comparative Education Review* 61 (S1): S51–S73. doi:10.1086/690457.

Shahjahan, Riyad, Anne Wagner, and Njoki Nathani Wane. 2009. "Rekindling the Sacred: Toward a Decolonizing Pedagogy in Higher Education." *Journal of Thought* 44 (1–2): 59–75. doi:10.2307/jthought.44.1-2.59.

Shattock, Michael. 2010. "The Entrepreneurial University: An Idea for its Time." *London Review of Education* 8 (3): 263–271. doi:10.1080/14748460.2010.515125.

Snyder, Hannah. 2019. "Literature Review as a Research Methodology: An Overview and Guidelines." *Journal of Business Research* 104: 333–339.

Stein, Sharon, Vanessa Andreotti, Judy Bruce, and Rene Suša. 2016. "Towards Different Conversations About the Internationalization of Higher Education." *Comparative and International Education/Éducation Comparée et Internationale* 45 (1): 2. doi:10.5206/cie-eci.v45i1.9281.

Teamey, Kelly, and Udi Mandel. 2016. "A World Where all Worlds Cohabit." *The Journal of Environmental Education* 47 (2): 151–162. doi:10.1080/00958964.2015.1099512.

Tunnermann, Carlos. 2003. *La universidad latinoamericana ante los retos.* Ciudad de México: Unión de Universidades de América Latina.

UNESCO. 2020. Education in the time of COVID-19. Accessed November 3, 2020. https://www.cepal.org/en/publications/45905-education-time-covid-19.

Usma Wilches, Jaime A., Janeth M. Ortiz Medina, and Claudia Gutiérrez. 2018. "Indigenous Students Learning English in Higher Education: What Are the Challenges?." *Íkala, Revista de Lenguaje y Cultura* 23 (2): 229–254. doi:10.17533/udea.ikala.v23n02a03.

Wallerstein, Immanuel. 1976. "Semi-Peripheral Countries and the Contemporary World Crisis." *Theory and Society* 3 (4): 461–483. doi:10.1007/BF00161293.

Walsh, Catherine. 2009. "The Plurinational and Intercultural State: Decolonization and State Re-Founding in Ecuador." *Rudn Journal of Philosophy* 1: 103–115.

World Bank. 2015. Indigenous Latin America in the Twenty-First Century. Accessed November 3, 2020. http://documents1.worldbank.org/curated/en/145891467991974540/pdf/Indigenous-Latin-America-in-the-twenty-first-century-the-first-decade.pdf.

Young, Robert J. C. 2016. *Postcolonialism: An Historical Introduction.* Oxford: John Wiley & Sons.

🔓 OPEN ACCESS

Indigenizing Engineering education in Canada: critically considered

Jillian Seniuk Cicek 🆔, Alan Steele, Sarah Gauthier, Afua Adobea Mante, Pamela Wolf, Mary Robinson and Stephen Mattucci

ABSTRACT

This article critically considers the work being done to bring Indigenous Peoples, Knowledges, and perspectives into the dominant structures of engineering education in Canada. We use Gaudry and Lorenz's (2018. "Indigenization as Inclusion, Reconciliation, and Decolonization: Navigating the Different Visions for Indigenizing the Canadian Academy." *AlterNative: An International Journal of Indigenous PeoplesAlterNative* 14 (3): 218–227. doi:10.1177/1177180118785382) spectrum of Indigenization to evaluate self-reported contributions from 25 engineering programs and four engineering organizations. Findings show much of the work being done in Canada is in Indigenous Inclusion and Reconciliation Indigenization, with some Decolonial Indigenization. Efforts in reconciliation and decolonization are seen predominantly in integrated, grassroots initiatives, with institutional initiatives found largely in inclusion. We submit that a diversified strategy and decolonized policies are needed to achieve Decolonial Indigenization. The intention of this work is to create an ethical space where Indigenous and non-Indigenous engineering educators can listen to and learn from one another. Guided by *Etuaptmumk* (*Two-Eyed Seeing*), we can advance Indigenous ways of knowing, being, and doing in engineering education in Canada and around the world.

Introduction

Indigenous Peoples in North America were engineering their world long before settlers arrived (Keoke and Porterfield 2003; Pierotti 2011; Weatherford 2010). Indigenous science and innovation led to the development of technologies that were used for transportation, housing, clothing, hunting, farming, and aquaculture. Many of these

This is an Open Access article distributed under the terms of the Creative Commons Attribution-NonCommercial-NoDerivatives License (http://creativecommons.org/licenses/by-nc-nd/4.0/), which permits non-commercial re-use, distribution, and reproduction in any medium, provided the original work is properly cited, and is not altered, transformed, or built upon in any way.

technologies are still or were precursors to technologies that are currently in use today. Despite this, engineering practices that surged in Canada in the mid-1800s were settler-driven, purposed to design and develop a 'modern' Canada (Gareau et al. 2021). At the time when engineering schools became increasingly prevalent, and engineering curricula emerged, the voices of Indigenous Peoples were ignored (Pierotti 2011). Knowledges held by Indigenous Peoples, including of land, climate, and natural environment, holistic focus on observation, experiential learning, and oral storytelling as central ways of knowing, were excluded (Indigenous Canada 2021). The prevailing Western knowledge system dominated the modern basis of engineering across Canada.

Residential Schools were one mechanism by which this Western knowledge domination was imposed (Kilada et al. 2021). They were implemented in Canada in the 1800s and in operation for over 160 years (Canadian Geographic 2020). The system attempted to eradicate pre-existing Indigenous culture from over 150,000 First Nations, Inuit, and Metis children (Government of Canada 2019). Indigenous children were forcibly removed from their homes, stripped of their native languages, indoctrinated in Euro-Canadian ways of living through Christian religious affiliation, and abused (Truth and Reconciliation Commission [TRC] of Canada 2015a). Six thousand Indigenous children are estimated to have died in this system (Puxley 2015), countless of whom are still unnamed (APTN 2020). Residential Schools were a 'tool in a broader plan of "aggressive assimilation" and colonization of Indigenous Peoples and territories in Canada' (Canadian Geographic 2020). This truth challenges the narrative that Canada is a country 'which has long prided itself on being a bastion of democracy, peace, and kindness throughout the world' (TRC 2015a).

Canada's dark history was publicly acknowledged and apologized for by the Federal Government in 2008 (The Canadian Encyclopedia 2021). The Truth and Reconciliation Commission (TRC) of Canada led by three Indigenous commissioners was formed. Their mandate was to document the experiences of the systematic genocide and inter-generational trauma that Indigenous children, families, and communities experienced through Residential Schools. They travelled from coast to coast to coast with a sacred fire to collect the stories of survivors, families, and communities, and in 2015, made 94 Calls to Action to 'advance the progress of Canadian reconciliation' (TRC 2015b). Specific to this work on the state of Indigenizing engineering education in Canada are the Calls for Education, and for Business and Reconciliation. Indigenous Peoples and ways of knowing, being, and doing must have equitable space in postsecondary education.

Despite the hope incurred by the TRC's work, the explicit steps outlined in the Calls have yet to materialize, with some progress even declining. 15 December 2020, marked the Calls to Action five-year anniversary. The three TRC Commissioners reconvened to bring attention to the 'slow and uneven pace of implementation of the Calls to Action' and to call for a renewal of the 'sense of urgency, purpose and unity' that originally drove the work (National Centre for Truth & Reconciliation 2020). They shared that 'Essential foundations for reconciliation have yet to be implemented, despite government commitments. In some jurisdictions, there is danger of losing gains that have been made'. They state, 'Reconciliation requires all Canadians to come together with resolution and common purpose.'

It has taken the TRC to bring national attention to the crisis in Canada wrought by the inhumane treatment of Indigenous Peoples. Notwithstanding the dire five-year anniversary announcement, there has been some movement in the incorporation of Indigenous Knowledges and perspectives into engineering curricula in Canada, but much more needs to be done. In addition to our responsibility to learn the truth about our colonial history in Canada and seek reconciliation by making 'ethical space' (Ermine, Sinclair, and Jeffery 2004) for Indigenous Peoples in Canada's educational systems, engineering educators have a professional obligation to integrate Indigenous knowledges and build capacity for intercultural understandings. Future engineers must be positioned to engage in 'meaningful consultation, building respectful relationships, and obtaining the free, prior, and informed consent of Indigenous Peoples before proceeding with economic development projects' (TRC 2015b).

Further to the mandate of the TRC, the authors of this paper argue that Western knowledge systems are not the only knowledge systems existing, and it is time to learn about and be open to other ways of knowing, being, and doing in engineering education. In Euro-colonialized nations such as Canada, we specifically have a responsibility to engage with First Peoples and their knowledge systems. We are facing tremendous challenges in today's world driven by the social inequities and human and environmental crises, and through partnership with Indigenous Peoples and their diverse knowledge systems, engineers will be better equipped to address them (Bowra 2018). Fundamentally, dominant perspectives across the world need to hear and make space for silenced perspectives, as it will be through the interaction of diverse perspectives that we will achieve better, healthier futures for subsequent generations of all living beings.

The purpose of this article is to critically consider the work being done to bring Indigenous Peoples, Knowledges, and perspectives into the dominant structures of engineering education. We employ Gaudry and Lorenz's (2018) spectrum of Indigenization as the conceptual framework to critically assess whether the work is inclusion, reconciliation, or decolonization. Then we offer our perspectives on, *To what extent should decolonizing policies be imposed across engineering education institutions?* We are guided by *Etuaptmumk*, 'Two-Eyed Seeing', and the teachings of Mi'kmaw Elder Albert Marshall.

Indigenous ways of knowing and engineering education

There are over 1.67 million Indigenous Peoples in Canada who identify as First Nations Peoples, Métis, or Inuit, the three groups of Aboriginal Peoples recognized by the Canadian Constitution (Statistics Canada 2021). There are more than 50 First Nations, each with their own language, culture, social structure, legal and political systems (Indigenous Corporate Training 2019), 400,000 Métis, and 53 Inuit communities (Government of Canada 2017). In acknowledging this, Indigenous Peoples share some common core principles, valuing relationships and qualitative and subjective understandings and experiences.

Indigenous Knowledges are characterized as participatory, experiential, and process-oriented, and do not separate science, art, and philosophy but rather embrace a holistic worldview (Mejia and de Paula 2019). Indigenous Traditional Knowledge (TK) is the collective knowledges of Indigenous cultures 'resulting from the group's use and occupation of a specific region over many generations' (as quoted in Pierotti 2011, 9). It 'encompasses practical, empirical, and ideological aspects of understanding and is both the information itself and a way of knowing' (Pierotti 2011, 9). It 'draws upon the community of elders and other knowledge holders, as well as the collective consciousness of the people, and is 'living knowledge' (Bartlett, Marshall, and Marshall 2012, 336–337), continually evolving from centuries of living respectfully and in harmony alongside nature (Grommes and Riley 2004; O'Sullivan 2019). It centres on management of renewable resources, considering environmental, social, cultural, economic, and spiritual elements ... holistically, underscoring how all aspects of life are interconnected (Indigenous Corporate Training 2018). It shares philosophical similarities with current-day sustainable design (Martin et al. 2010) and is fundamental to addressing today's global challenges (Reconciling Ways of Knowing 2020).

Comparatively, Western scientific and engineering knowledge can be classified as objective and quantitative, dependent on experiences supported by Western research (Mazzocchi 2006) and tending to compartmentalize knowledge and experience (Suzuki 2020). Across engineering disciplines, the approach has gravitated toward specific tasks and services determined by the Western worldview (Droz 2014). Engineering solutions are technologically focused, judged with respect to the optimization of resources and predetermined criteria and constraints (Foster and Jordan 2014). As such, many engineering practices and sustainability worldviews conflict (Hess and Strobel 2013). The standardization of the engineering process has resulted in 'closed system engineering', where the influence of a solution or design on the surrounding environment is not always considered, and the environment is treated as constant (Droz 2014). Lucena and Downey (1999) suggest that a conventional engineering curriculum with its uni-dimensional approach to problem solving might not adequately prepare engineering students for real-world engineering work. Further, Catalano (2016) argues that conventional engineering paradigms lack a well-defined value system that incorporates personal values alongside professional values. Overall, there are negative environmental, social, and economic consequences to engineering solutions that do not factor in the complexities of the natural world (Halbe, Adamowski, and Pahl-Wostl 2015).

Considering the need for an engineering system that takes personal values into account, and the importance of multiple perspectives in enriching problem solving (Murray et al. 2019; Wang, Dogan, and Lin 2006), the inclusion of additional perspectives, philosophies, and knowledge bases could improve engineering (Forrest and Seniuk Cicek 2021). We argue that Indigenous worldviews, more likely to consider environmental and social ramifications, are vital to engineering education, as Western knowledges and sciences have largely left 'a destructive wake' and alone, are not enough to ensure the healing and survival of the environment (Suzuki 2020). Engineering is a pragmatic discipline, embedded in problem solving (Foster and Jordan 2014). The inclusion of Indigenous perspectives, philosophies, and knowledges will enhance engineering problem solving, and benefit engineering education and practice (O'Sullivan 2019) by steering engineering in a more holistic direction (Forrest and Seniuk Cicek 2021). Together, Indigenous Knowledges and Western knowledge should reside alongside engineering knowledge; all have a place in engineering education (Kennedy et al. 2016).

Constructing a 'new' engineering education in Canada that includes Indigenous Peoples and Knowledges is a large undertaking that requires learning, understanding, and the building of relationships. There is a movement in engineering education in Canada to increase Indigenous representation and belonging, reconcile relations, and to decolonize and Indigenize engineering curricula (Engineers Canada 2021b). Initiatives have started in diverse ways and are at different stages of development in engineering institutions across the country (Seniuk Cicek et al. 2020). However, much of this work is being undertaken by individuals or small groups within institutions, with few connections to others doing similar work. To support and advance this work it is vital to share and examine the initiatives that are taking root nationally. We need to critically understand where we are in decolonizing and Indigenizing engineering curricula, and where we still need to go. This work will inform engineering education in Canada and will help us engage in dialogue with other Euro-colonial nations on this journey (e.g. Goldfinch et al. 2016; Indigenous Engineering 2020; Jordan et al. 2019; Leigh et al. 2014).

Participatory action and the positionality of authors

This work began in November 2019 with a team of six Indigenous (five from Turtle Island and one from Ghana) and five non-Indigenous engineering educators from across Canada. The purpose was to share the national Indigenous initiatives in CEAB (Canadian Engineering Accreditation Board) accredited engineering programs with the broader community as a catalyst for advancement. We engaged in Participatory Action Research (PAR) to gather collective voices in the engineering education national community, an approach chosen to honour Indigenous relational worldviews and approaches to evaluation (Morelli and Mataira 2010; Scott 2010). We invited engineering educators as contributors from across Canada to share the Indigenous initiatives in which they are involved. This initial work was intended as an inclusive collection of information, not a critique. The findings were reported in Seniuk Cicek et al. (2020).

This author team of one Indigenous, two mixed settler and Indigenous, and four white settler individuals extend the work here by analyzing the findings using Gaudry and Lorenz's (2018) three-stage spectrum of Indigenization. One author, white settler, mother, wife, sister, daughter, educator and learner, will 'serve as narrator' 'for stylistic purposes' (Goodchild 2021, 79) and weave our voices together. As another author, Indigenous woman, mother, wife, daughter, sister, engineer, explains, *We do not speak for all engineering educators; only our perspectives are reported here. We acknowledge that this article documents where we are now, in time and space. Our individual journeys are at different places and are dynamic; they will and are changing and growing as we do this work.*

In critically considering the work and efforts to make space for Indigenous Peoples and Knowledges in engineering education we criticize engineering, which can be difficult to accept by engineering educators, and could result in building barriers rather than bridges. We are also limited by our Western training. For example, as one author, male, husband, father, engineer, settler of European origin expresses, *As educators of engineers, supporters of Indigenization and often initiators of the reported schemes, we could be seen as risking* – or undermining – the *objectivity* of engineering. In challenging the status quo, we risk unsettling relationships with our colleagues. As articulated by another author, woman, daughter, sister, and engineer of mixed settler and Métis decent, *It is emotionally challenging for me to apply a critical academic lens to what has gone beyond professional collaborations and exchanging of dry knowledge to deep friendships and shared embodied ways of knowing. Neither friendship nor gifts are suited to critique.*

Those of us – all of us – educated by Western knowledge systems have much to learn from Indigenous and non-dominant Knowledge paradigms; and engaging in this work is daunting. As another team member, partner, father, white, male, engineer, shares, *Personally, I find it challenging to engage in spaces related to equity, diversity, and inclusion because of my privilege. I worry how I will be perceived, as I embody the physical characteristics of the traditional oppressor.* However, as the author, woman, mother, wife, engineer, descendent of the original peoples of Ghana understands, we must embrace this journey: *The journey to decolonize engineering is not for only Indigenous Peoples to travel. Everyone is part of that journey. And being present on this land is enough justification to get aboard. It is also clear that there is a lot of learning to do and a lot of evaluation of existing structures to make sure we intentionally create the space for decolonization.*

We must work to deconstruct our colonial lens and see this space as is seen from marginalized perspectives. But as we are working within 'the system' of engineering education, can we know and understand 'the system'? Engineering positivistic mindset is very 'outcome' driven, focusing on frameworks such as schedules and systematic approaches. Whereas constructivist mindsets are more characteristic of Indigenous ways of knowing and being and are more focused on 'process' with an understanding of and respect for diversities in perspectives. How do we reconcile these ways of knowing? *What do we let go and what do we bring in to advance decolonization of engineering education?* We try to strike a balance between sharing truths, honouring friendships, facing our privilege status, and avoiding the polarization of Western and Indigenous and engineering knowledge systems and their villainization.

Guiding principle: etuaptmumk, two-eyed seeing

Etuaptmumk is

> learning to see from one eye with the strengths of Indigenous Knowledges and ways of knowing, and from the other eye with the strengths of Western knowledges and ways of knowing ... and learning to use both these eyes together, for the benefit of all. (Cape Breton University 2020a)

This Mi'kmaw worldview, coined as 'Two-Eyed Seeing' by Elder Marshall (Bartlett, Marshall, and Marshall 2012), was first introduced to us by Leah Fontaine, an Anishinaabe-Métis-Dakota Indigenous Initiatives Educator (Fontaine and Chen 2018). It has been applied to medical research (McKivett et al. 2020), care of the aged (Sivertsen, Harrington, and Hamiduzzaman 2020), oral healthcare (Shrivastava et al. 2020), and science education (Gilbert, Onwu, and Mufundirwa 2020; Michie, Hogue, and Rioux 2018). It is shared here with the permission of Elder Marshall, who explains, 'Two-Eyed Seeing adamantly, respectfully, and passionately asks that we bring together our different ways of knowing to motivate people, Aboriginal and non-Aboriginal alike, to use all our understandings so we can leave the world a better place' (336).

Elder Marshall teaches us, 'When you force people to abandon their ways of knowing, their ways of seeing the world, you literally destroy their spirit' (Bartlett, Marshall, and Marshall 2012). Dr Cheryl Bartlett explains that if an education system ignores who one is, or who one thinks they are, and the curriculum does not include one's understandings, we deny students' ability to form 'a well-balanced and deep understanding' of themselves (Cape Breton University 2020b). Fundamentally, a dominant colonial education system does not teach us to embrace knowledge from diverse, non-dominant worldviews and perspectives, inhibiting diverse Peoples' ability to thrive, and diverse worldviews from creating a better world for all.

Bartlett 'acknowledge[d] the need for … an "ethical space" within the precarious relationship between Indigenous Peoples and the Western world' (Cape Breton University 2020a). In this work, we are committed to creating an 'ethical space' (Ermine, Sinclair, and Jeffery 2004) where Indigenous Peoples and ways of knowing, being, and doing are visible, respected, taught, and celebrated in engineering education.

Spectrum of indigenization

Gaudry and Lorenz (2018) found 'Indigenization' 'varie[s] significantly' across Canadian universities and colleges (218) in a three-stage spectrum of *Indigenous Inclusion, Reconciliation Indigenization,* and *Decolonial Indigenization* moving from the least to the most significant path. They define *Indigenous Inclusion* as attempts to increase the number of Indigenous faculty, staff, and students in engineering institutions. This includes outreach attempts to create pathways to postsecondary programs and professional careers, and camps for children/students. *Reconciliation Indigenization* includes Indigenous Knowledges to educate faculty, staff, and students via courses and training. At the far end of the spectrum, they locate *Decolonial Indigenization,* described as decentring hierarchical Western Eurocentric postsecondary structures and 'empower[ing] Indigenous communities to regain educational sovereignty' (223). This looks like Knowledge Keepers and Elders in postsecondary spaces, exclusive Indigenous spaces, and Indigenous Knowledges centred in curricula.

Gaudry and Lorenz's (2018) three-stage spectrum provides a framework to critically assess the Indigenous initiatives in engineering education in Canada. Once understood, we can have the larger discussion on what engineering education communities should be aiming for. Are we ultimately aiming for solely decolonization, or is a spectrum of Indigenization needed/beneficial? Should Indigenization institutional policies be characterized along this spectrum, and to what proportion should efforts be directed? What roles do/should institutions play in achieving inclusion, reconciliation, and decolonization? The findings will enable us to be realistic about how our efforts are impacting Indigenization and think critically about how we should advance this work.

Methodology

We used a participatory action research (PAR) methodology to learn about Indigenous initiatives in engineering education across Canada, which has been used with *Etuaptmumk* (Peltier 2018). PAR finds its roots in action research (MacDonald 2012), where data is collected and analyzed to generate practical knowledge to make change (Gillis and Jackson 2002). PAR enables the co-creation of meaning with participants 'to bring about social justice and change' (Castleden, Garvin, and First Nation 2008, 1394). PAR aligns with Indigenous values and approaches to evaluation (Morelli and Mataira 2010; Scott 2010), enabling 'participatory and empowerment models that allow meaningful impact from the community' (Grover 2010, 36). It honours the epistemology of 'collective interdependence' held by many Indigenous cultures (Cram 2016, 300). It reflects Indigenous circular worldviews of interconnectedness through its iterative cycle of planning, implementing, observing, and critically reflecting (MacColl et al. 2005; Minkler 2000). It is a suitable approach as it supports the participation of a community – in this case, engineering educators – and makes space for the interaction of Indigenous, Western/dominant, and engineering worldviews.

We invited engineering educators in CEAB-accredited programs and engineering organizations across Canada to participate by sharing the Indigenous initiatives in which they are involved. Recruitment methods included two consecutive calls via the Canadian Engineering Education Association-Association canadienne de l'éducation en génie (CEEA-ACEG) monthly newsletter in February and March 2020, and personal email invitations to participate. We identified all institutions with accredited engineering programs and reached out to most of these institutions via our networks.

When asked to review their institutional data once it was analyzed, contributors were exposed to the categories that emerged from the complete data set. Subsequently, contributors were able to enhance their contributions. Thus, data were collected using snowball sampling (Creswell 2013, 158) generated by member-checking cycles and broadened understandings. Data were collected between February and June 2020.

Limitations

The work represented here is explicitly focusing on efforts in engineering education in CEAB accredited programs and national engineering organizations in Canada. The perspectives shared herein are positioned within the viewpoints of the authors, characterized by the dominant, colonial perspective. This is because over half of the authors are white settlers, and they and the mixed settler and Indigenous authors have been educated in the dominant colonial systems in Canada. As a team, we are limited by our own experiences and perspectives within the dominant perspective. We lean heavily on our Indigenous team members to critically assess this narrative and guide our voices to be mindful, respectful, and truthful. We work together to negotiate our biases and fears and our varied stances on how these initiatives should be imposed. We range from advocates for encouragement to advocates for complete disruption. Our intentions are to offer critically informed ways forward, while avoiding alienating the community of engineering educators, as we want engineering educators to engage in this work.

The information presented here is not exclusive: we were unable to gather information on all initiatives or from all institutions in this scope. Further, limiting the scope to accredited programs does not negate the Indigenous initiatives in engineering education in diploma or technology programs, or in professional associations. There is important work in diverse contexts to advance Indigenous engagement and achievement in engineering education not represented here.

Findings

There are 44 higher education institutions with accredited engineering programs across Canada (Engineers Canada 2021a). We received contributions from 25 (Table 1).

Table 1. Data Contributions from Institutions across Canada ($n = 25$).[a]

West	Central	East
University of Victoria	Western University of Ontario	University of New Brunswick
University of British Columbia[b]	University of Waterloo[b]	Université de Moncton
UBC–Okanagan[c]	McMaster University[b]	Dalhousie University
Simon Fraser University	Ryerson University	University of Prince Edward Island
University of Alberta	University of Toronto[b]	Memorial University of Newfoundland
University of Calgary[b]	Conestoga College	
University of Saskatchewan[b]	Queen's University	
University of Regina	Carleton University[b]	
University of Manitoba[b]	Université d'Ottawa/University of Ottawa	
	Université Concordia	
	McGill University	

[a]There are no accredited engineering programs in the North of Canada.
[b]Team members' institutions (i.e. authors of Seniuk Cicek et al. 2020).
[c]University of British Columbia–Okanagan

Table 2. Data Contributions from Organizations across Canada ($n = 4$).

1. Decolonizing and Indigenizing Engineering Education Network (DIEEN) – Engineers Canada working group
2. Canadian Indigenous Advisory Council (CIAC) to AISES (American Indian Science & Engineering Society)
3. Canadian Engineering Education Challenge (CEEC) – initiative supported by the Engineering Change Lab and Engineering Deans across Canada
4. Canadian Federation of Engineering Students (CFES)

We also received contributions from four engineering organizations (Table 2).

All contributions except one were via personal and professional networks; none came via the CEEA-ACEG monthly newsletter. A collaborative approach was taken by contributors; therefore, this information represents collective understandings.

From the 29 contributing institutions and organizations, 11 categories characterizing Indigenous initiatives in progress or planned in engineering education emerged (Table 3).

The 11 categories were then analyzed using Gaudry and Lorenz's (2018) three-stage spectrum of Indigenization (Table 4). Categories were classified by where most of the initiatives within them were positioned on the spectrum (i.e. not all initiatives in each category were in the same place on the spectrum).

Out of the 11 categories of initiatives, three can be interpreted as Indigenous Inclusion, five as Reconciliation Indigenization, and three as Decolonial Indigenization.

Inclusion

Three of 11 categories of Indigenous initiatives in engineering education in Canada were analysed as Inclusion: *Outreach, Faculty and Institutional Positions,* and *Access and Bridging Programs or Mechanisms.*

Nineteen institutions and one organization are/will engage in engineering outreach. Activities include:

- Indigenous community and school visits
- Workshops and science/summer camps delivered in Indigenous communities

Table 3. Ranked (from most to least) categories of Indigenous initiatives in engineering education across Canadian institutions ($n = 25$) (plus organizations [$n = 4$]).

Categories (numbered high to low by institutional representation)	# Institutions ($n = 25$) (+ # organizations [$n = 4$])		
	In progress	Planned	Total
1. Outreach	17 (+ 1)	2	19 (+ 1)
2. Provincial & National Collaborations/Research	17 (+ 3)	0 (+ 1)	17 (+ 4)
3. Curricula	15	2	17
4. Committees/Councils/Strategies	15 (+ 4)	2	17 (+ 4)
5. Access & Bridging Programs/Mechanisms	8 (+ 1)	6	14 (+ 1)
6. Faculty Training/ Workshops	12	2	14
7. Faculty/Institution/Organization Positions	11 (+ 4)	2	13 (+ 4)
8. Elders/Knowledge Keepers/ Community Members	10	2	12
9. Student Training	8	3	11
10. Indigenous Student Organizations	8	1 (+ 1)	9 (+ 1)
11. Indigenous Cultures	6 (+1)	1	7 (+ 1)

Table 4. Categories of Indigenous initiatives in engineering education across Canadian institutions and organizations analyzed via Gaudry and Lorenz's (2018) three-stage spectrum of Indigenization.

Categories of Indigenous initiatives in engineering education in CEAB accredited engineering programs & organizations	Stage of Indigenization (Gaudry and Lorenz 2018)	Number of Institutions ($n = 25$)in progress & planned initiatives	Number of Organizations ($n = 4$)	Examples
1 Outreach	Inclusion	19	1	Outreach to schools. Camps. Tours. Land-based learning.
7 Faculty & Institutional Positions	Inclusion	13	4	Indigenous representation in faculty. Positions dedicated whole/part to Indigenous initiatives.
6 Access & Bridging Programs or Mechanisms	Inclusion	13	1	Transitioning and support help. Awards. Entrance conditions.
2 Provincial/National Collaborations/ Presence/Research	Reconciliation	17	4	Collaborations through networks or existing councils or Indigenous communities.
4 Committees/Councils/ Strategies	Reconciliation	17	4	Indigenous strategic plans or institutional councils.
3 Curricula	Reconciliation	17	0	Integrated and/or standalone course content.
5 Faculty Training/ Workshops	Reconciliation	14	0	Training for faculty. Indigenous history/ Knowledges/perspectives/ pedagogies.
9 Student Training	Reconciliation	11	0	Training for students. Indigenous history/ Knowledges/perspectives.
8 Elders/Knowledge Keepers/Indigenous Community Member	Decolonization	12	0	Engaging Elders or Knowledge keepers or community members in curricula and programs. Elders-in-residence.
10 Indigenous Student Organizations	Decolonization	9	1	Indigenous student organizations or chapters of larger organizations.
11 Indigenous Cultures	Decolonization	7	1	Land Acknowledgements/ Events/Smudging/ Indigenous Space/ Indigenous artifacts.

- Programs delivered in city schools (e.g. Indigenized STEM curricula, activities related to Ancestral (Indigenous) Engineering Design)
- Programs offered at postsecondary institutions (Summer Engineering Academy and camps)
- Engineering challenges, robotics competitions (with engineering student mentors), and science fairs
- Tribal Council tours of engineering buildings
- Recruitment/promotion events

Thirteen institutions currently/will advance Indigenous representation, engagement, and achievement in engineering education via 29 *Faculty and Institutional Positions*. Positions are/will be held by Indigenous Peoples and non-Indigenous people, organized into 12 categories:

- Staff (Assistant Director Indigenous Office) ($n = 1$)
- Faculty (Tenure Track, research and teaching stream) ($n = 5$)
- Indigenous Faculty (Industry Professor Contract Position) ($n = 1$)
- Engineer- and in-Residence positions ($n = 6$)
- Teaching Chairs ($n = 2$)
- Research Chairs (Indigenous Reconciliation in Engineering; Integrated Knowledge, Engineering & Sustainable Communities; Centennial Enhancement in Water Stewardship for Indigenous Communities) ($n = 3$)
- Coordinators (Outreach and Student) ($n = 3$)
- Directors (Engineering Access Program; Engineering Pathways & Indigenous Partnership; Decolonizing Curriculum & Pedagogy) ($n = 3$)
- Advisors (Equity, Diversity & Inclusion (EDI); to the Dean on Indigenous Initiatives) ($n = 2$)
- Associate/Assistant Dean with Indigenous Initiatives Portfolios ($n = 3$)

All four engineering organizations have positions dedicated to advancing Indigenous representation, engagement, and achievement in engineering education.

Twelve institutions and one organization have/are planning engineering access/bridging programs/mechanisms. These are wholly within engineering or combined with institution-wide supports like Indigenous student centres. They function to support students' academic, social, personal, emotional, professional and/or financial needs and include:

- Admission structure modification (e.g. requiring two of three high school sciences for entry instead of physics)
- Transitioning/bridging programs
- Program/Academic supports
- Awards, scholarships, or financial support
- Dedicated housing options
- Institutional Student Services/Resource Centres
- Emotional/Personal/Social support
- Professional development

Reconciliation

Reconciliation work is being done in five of the 11 categories: *Provincial/National Collaborations/Presence/Research; Committees/Councils/ Strategies; Curricula; Faculty Training/ Workshops;* and *Student Training.*

Seventeen institutions and three organizations (and one planning) are involved in provincial or national collaborations and/or research connected to Indigenous initiatives in engineering education.

Fifteen institutions (and two planning) and all four organizations have committees/councils/strategic plans/initiatives/blueprints/Calls to Action for Indigenous engagement and advancement in, and/or decolonizing and Indigenizing engineering education. Ten are connected to or supported by university-wide strategic plans.

Fifteen institutions (and two planning) are engaged with integrating Indigenous Knowledges, perspectives, values, and principles into engineering curricula. Integration includes:

- Course content (e.g. modules, 'learning bundles', assessment, reflections, projects, presentations, Traditional Knowledge (TK), local history/examples, research/projects)
- Indigenous/Elder guest speakers
- Case studies
- Design teams
- Ceremonies/Protocols (Treaty Acknowledgement, sharing circles)
- Retreats
- Open office hours/ mentoring/guidance/role-modeling
- Indigenous activities
- Indigenous Industry Advisors and clients for assignments/design projects
- Events (e.g. 'ChangeMakers'; Film Festival; Storytelling project)

Stand-alone initiatives include courses like *Infrastructure Engineering in Indigenous Communities, Pursuit of Reconciliation,* and *Shoal Lake 40 First Nation Design and Build* (see Seniuk Cicek, Friesen, and Bailey 2019a) offered at three institutions respectively, with technical and complementary studies courses in development at three institutions. One institution is planning to implement an electronic credentialing (i.e. 'badging') system to ensure foundational levels of competence on Indigenous history for all students, staff, and faculty.

Twelve institutions (and two planning) have engineering-specific or institution-wide access to training that faculty are encouraged to take. Opportunities range from learning about consulting with Indigenous communities; history and Truth and Reconciliation; Indigenous rights, terminology, cultural technologies, arts, practices, principles, values, ways of knowing and being; cultural practices and events; and decolonizing and Indigenizing the curriculum.

Eight institutions (and three planning) offer student training via courses, modules, or a certificate program, broadly characterized as encompassing knowledge (Indigenous history, colonialism), skills (Indigenous approaches to decision-making, mentorship, leadership, maker skills) and Indigenous principles/values (cultural awareness, including the KAIROS Blanket Exercise (2020), and participatory approaches).

Decolonization

Decolonizing efforts in Canadian postsecondary engineering education are found in three of the 11 categories, including *Elders/Knowledge Keepers/Indigenous Community Members; Indigenous Student Organization;* and *Indigenous Cultures.*

Ten institutions (with two planning) engage Elders, Knowledge Keepers and/or Indigenous Community members in engineering education for:

- Cultural Activities Leadership/Participation
- Curriculum Co-Development
- Research/Project Partnerships/ Industry Advisors/Clients for Design Projects
- Elder Guidance/Support /Role Models for students and faculty
- Course Teachers/Guest Speakers
- Elder-in-Residence
- Consultation/Collaboration/Advisory Committees

There are eight institutions (and one planning) that have student organizations that are either dedicated Indigenous Engineering Student Organizations, engineering student groups with dedicated Indigenous foci, or chapters of AISES (American Indian Science & Engineering Society) in Canada.

Six institutions (with one planning) and one organization have explicit examples or made specific reference to Indigenous culture in engineering. Examples include:

- Events (e.g. Orange Shirt Day)
- Having/creating dedicated spaces for Indigenous students
- Smudging/purification ceremonies and Indigenous protocols
- Land Acknowledgements
- Artifacts recognizing Indigenous students/Peoples and their accomplishments
- Explicit work with Indigenous community partners and in engineering education to understand culture, trust, relationships

Of note: Decolonizing work is also found in *Outreach, Faculty Training/Workshops* (which is categorized as Inclusion) where Land-based learning is integrated, and in *Curricula* (categorized as Reconciliation) via 'living bundles of knowledge' that include recordings of Indigenous Elders or Knowledge Keepers (Stranger and Pashagumskum 2020).

Discussion

The team involved in communicating this work has come to realize it takes time and the building of relationships to uncover this knowledge. This is a collaborative space, which resonates with Indigenous epistemologies regarding interconnectedness and the importance of relationships (Corntassel 2012; Grover 2010; LaFrance, Nichols, and Kirkhart 2012; Morelli and Mataira 2010). It calls attention to the principles regarding how knowledge is shared, communicated, and acknowledged, which is perceived and respected differently in Indigenous and Western cultures (Cram 2016; Scott 2010; Smith 2006).

So too are interpersonal skills. As our author of mixed Indigenous and settler ancestry shares, *When I was an undergraduate student… I observed that the communication skills that were valued were limited to communicating hard facts, just as design work was limited to objective materialism. This was, perhaps, vocationally suited to engineering industry that was judged on whether a design had sufficient physical strength to hold up to its task. I assert that engineering projects are now judged by the public on whether they are good for the public… this requires socio-constructivist communication skills such as dialogue. The nascent inclusion of these skills in Engineering is, at present, too little too late to a profession that is actively engaging with Indigenous communities.*

Overall, most of the work reported on is in Reconciliation Indigenization, followed by Indigenous Inclusion and Decolonial Indigenization. There is a broad range of initiatives within the 11 categories, and across the Indigenization spectrum. Activities are integrated into existing engineering education environments, as well as stand-alone initiatives via courses, activities, events, protocols, and culture. Some institutions are at planning stages, and others have distinct initiatives underway. Some initiatives are grassroots, with individuals and small groups of faculty members and/or students taking the lead, and others are top–down initiatives, implemented by the administration.

Forms of Inclusion are numerous, perhaps to be expected if viewed as the first stage of Indigenization. They also inherently top-down, as *Outreach, Faculty and Institutional Positions,* and *Access and Bridging Programs or Mechanisms* require structural change and support. The most significant activity is in Indigenous outreach, which is hopeful for the future of engineering where Indigenous Peoples are underrepresented (Ricci 2016) and could lay a foundation for the development of relationships with Indigenous communities.

Reconciliation Indigenization is underway, particularly in research and engineering curricula. Here we see more grassroots initiatives, especially in *Provincial/National Collaborations/Presence/Research; Curricula; Faculty Training/Workshops;* and *Student Training,* with many of the relationships required in these collaborations advanced by faculty and students, albeit supported by the administration. These initiatives are impactful for valuing Indigenous Peoples and Knowledges, and for educating faculty and students. Worrisome is that these initiatives require collaborations between Indigenous and non-Indigenous Peoples, and there are relatively few Indigenous Peoples working in or connected to institutional spaces. The degree of activity in curricular work for example is not matched with Indigenous faculty positions. Many Indigenous faculty are stretched in accommodating requests to support Indigenous initiatives. Thus, to do the work of Reconciliation, we need more Inclusion: more positions for Indigenous Peoples and with portfolios exclusively Indigenous. However, we must be cognizant that postsecondary institutions are built on Western structures. We must consider how to decolonize these structures to support Indigenous colleagues. Thus, Reconciliation requires Inclusion and Decolonization. For example, in one university, the administration and Faculty Association signed a memorandum of understanding 'to look at equivalency so that we can bring knowledge-keepers and elders into the community to teach' (Di Donato 2019). This is a recommended decolonizing approach for hiring Indigenous faculty.

There is less work in Decolonizing Indigenization engineering education, and much of this work begins with grassroots initiatives, although requires support by administration. *Elders/Knowledge Keepers/Indigenous Community Members; Indigenous Student Organization;* and *Indigenous Cultures* are taking root in the work of faculty and students. What is being done is making space for Indigenous Peoples and Indigenous cultures *within* the colonial system. This is one approach to decolonization. We argue that to advance ethical space for Indigenous Peoples in engineering education, larger decolonization efforts requiring systems changes are needed. Examples include Indigenous institutions that function independently but in parallel to colonial institutions, like Turtle Island Institute (2021), 'an Indigenous social innovation think and do tank – a teaching lodge – enabling transformative change' that draws on Indigenous ways of knowing 'to support the application of decolonized systems thinking concepts and processes ... to shift systems and to support the sovereignty and self-determination of Indigenous communities across Turtle Island'. Another is land-based education, of which we see a few examples, for 'if colonization is fundamentally about dispossessing Indigenous peoples from land, decolonization must involve forms of education that reconnect Indigenous peoples to land and the social relations, knowledges and languages that arise from the land' (Wildcat et al. 2014, I).

There are arguments against stand-alone Indigenous initiatives when interpreting the TRC Calls for Action, believing reconciliation in this spirit is best demonstrated through immersion in, not separation from, the present system. This view holds concern that stand-alone initiatives may 'check boxes' in the process of reconciliation but not achieve it. Then arguments are made for intensive, concentrated, specialized initiatives in engineering focusing exclusively on Indigenous ways of knowing, being, and doing, to provide some balance to the dominant curriculum.

We offer that it is not one way that is best, but rather a diversified approach will strengthen the work to explore the truth, seek reconciliation, and achieve Decolonial Indigenization in engineering education. This is what we are seeing take root. As we have argued, multiple perspectives enrich problem solving (Murray et al. 2019). It stands to reason that diverse approaches support diverse perspectives. Constructing a 'new' engineering education in Canada with Indigenous Peoples is a large undertaking that requires learning, understanding, and the building of relationships. As we have experienced, trying to navigate colonial academic structures yet pay respect to Indigenous approaches has proven difficult. Working from within the colonial system makes it challenging to see the dominant structure. If we are to create an ethical space in engineering education, we must embrace diversified approaches that support diversified perspectives, and have integrated initiatives as well as exclusive Indigenous initiatives to balance the dominant curriculum. This will encourage vertical – within courses – and horizontal – across curricula, programs and the educative environment – integration, which is required for *Etuaptmumk,* and to achieve genuine decolonialization.

This leads us to consider *To what extent should decolonizing policies be imposed across an institution/ the disciplines / professional education?* For engineering education, this question can be contemplated at both institutional and national levels. Institutionally, there is a range of voluntary Indigenous curricula and training offered to students and faculty, and in conception, a few mandatory initiatives (generally for students). In these mandatory initiatives, we see a commitment to our legal, moral, social, and cultural responsibility to learn the truth about our Canadian history and the impact of colonization on Indigenous Peoples, and engage respectfully, reciprocally, and relationally in reconciliation (Kirkness and Barnhardt 1991). We argue that as engineering educators we have a professional, legal, ethical, and social responsibility to train our faculty and future engineers in truth and reconciliation to practice culturally safe engineering (Morelli and Mataira 2010) and demonstrate cultural humility (Chávez 2012) and leadership in reconciliation (Castleden, Garvin, and First Nation 2008). This work should not be a choice. Thereby, we support decolonizing strategies should be imposed in engineering education in Canada.

Yet, there are challenges. At an administrative level, the pressure to implement policy risks a superficial approach. As one author comments, *administrative leaders don't always fully understand what it means to address 'Indigenization', so it becomes a box-checking exercise, resulting in under-resourced initiatives.* Gaudry and Lorenz (2018) agree, and warn, 'in this policy framework ... indigenization is conceived of primarily a matter of inclusion and access, and by merely including more Indigenous peoples, it is believed that universities can indigenize without substantial structural change' (219). The author who comments on box-checking deliberates, *To what extent should decolonizing policies be imposed across engineering education institutions? is a tricky question based on the meaning of 'imposed'. The types of policies that I see being most effective are those that empower individuals to make change to the system – institutional roles dedicated to driving decolonization from within. People in this space can make change in more meaningful and sustained ways. Not only are we seeing this within institutions with dedicated champions and Indigenous Peoples in Faculty roles, but we are also seeing this in the network that is growing and strengthening across institutions.*

Further, the question to what extent decolonizing policies should be imposed requires a critical look at engineering accreditation policies. These policies lay the foundation for engineering education and training. There have been top-level and grassroots discussions about explicit Indigenous inclusion in the CEAB graduate attributes, for example. These are 12 competencies all graduating engineering students are required to demonstrate for program accreditation (for an interpretation of the CEAB graduate attributes through an Indigenous lens, see Seniuk Cicek et al. 2019b). However, there are mixed responses to this approach. When considering this question, box-checking is again the concern: *Many see accreditation of engineering programs as an opportunity to drive educational improvement, while others see it as a measure that limits change and creativity. Over time, these imposed criteria tend to drift to 'check boxing', and away from what they are truly trying to achieve. I worry the same might happen by attempting to 'impose' decolonizing policies.* Another team member, a white settler woman, mother, wife, engineer, is more adamant: *Indigenization cannot and should not be treated as only a legislated requirement; if an institution is creating a hostile environment and Indigenous students do not come, stay, or feel safe, then trying to achieve these goals is applying colonial ways on yet another system. Instead, institutions should be encouraged to work together to learn from one another and connect with their local communities to heal past harms, and remove barriers (rewrite rules, change degree requirements, adjust funding models), so we encourage and motivate each other forward.* Although creating a hostile environment via imposed structures is not the desired outcome, creating space for Indigenous Peoples and their ways of knowing, being, and doing is not a choice. We must educate all stakeholders to value this work, to ask and answer the tough questions. Everyone is at different stages in decolonizing engineering education, and not everyone is on board. This work requires continuous awareness and capacity building that must be enacted by institutional and governing bodies' policies and strategies with Indigenous Peoples at the table.

Still, arguing compulsory top-down requirements does not negate, nor should it discourage the grassroots initiatives that are predominant across Canadian institutions and organizations as demonstrated in the data contributed here, and that Bartlett, Marshall, and Marshall (2012) argue are integral to this work. Therefore, we make the case for institutions to implement inclusion, reconciliation, and decolonialization via structures and practices while encouraging and supporting grassroots reconciliation and decolonization initiatives. Indigenous inclusion initiatives are easily assigned to an administrative staff portfolio, whereas to decolonize university structures and processes, significant capacity is often required at levels of influence within organizational hierarchy. Further, initiatives by engineering deans and program directors can help with kick-starting not just change, but with educating faculty on the broader need and responsibility for Indigenizing the curriculum. Grassroots initiatives can gain momentum to drive change, but they require administrative support and typically take longer to establish institutional alteration. There are some superficial changes that can be made quickly, but true decolonization is an intentional process requiring 'deep', 'profound', 'radical', 'disruptive,' 'transformative change' (Cote-Meek 2020, xvi–ii). Engineering is a self-regulated profession, which adds to the challenge. If the community is willing, change can happen quickly, but if not (or legislative inertia exists) change from within can be a struggle. This work requires what we are seeing, just more of it especially in terms of top-down initiatives. Bottom-up *and* top-down initiatives will build horizonal and vertical integration to create the disruptive, revolutionary change needed to achieve Decolonial engineering education on Turtle Island, in Canada.

Concluding remarks

The story told here can help build the narrative of how engineering postsecondary institutions rise to the TRC Calls to Action and take steps in Indigenizing and decolonizing curricula. It is a call to action, for more work is needed. Gaudry and Lorenz's (2018) three-stage spectrum is one mechanism by which to think about the work we are doing to share space with Indigenous Peoples in engineering education, and the impact of this work on achieving meaningful change. Reconciliation is an iterative, dynamic, living process. It is dependent on place, on the connection to the land, to the people who are part of the land, and those settled on the land. There is not a 'one size fits all' solution, but institutional pressure and encouragement should be applied, as what is happening in engineering education in Canada is largely proliferated by small, grassroots factions.

Of the work being done in Canada, much is Indigenous Inclusion and Reconciliation Indigenization, with some efforts in Decolonial Indigenization. We acknowledge that to reach Decolonial Indigenization work must be done in partnership with Indigenous Peoples and non-Indigenous people, and in recognition of the rights of Indigenous Peoples to self-determination. This requires making space for more Indigenous Peoples in the academy. It must be done along the spectrum of Indigenization in both grassroots and institutionally imposed initiatives, in integrated and stand-alone capacities. Bottom-up and top-down, and horizontal and vertical approaches will provide the diversified strategy needed to achieve Decolonial Indigenization. Having national and global dialogues on decolonizing engineering education will benefit all societies. We must learn from one another as we look to build a critical mass to disrupt the dominant status quo and ultimately achieve *Etuaptmumk*, where Indigenous Peoples and their ways of knowing, being, and doing are recognized, respected, and taught ethically and equitably in a decolonized academy.

Acknowledgements

The authors are thankful for the wisdom and guidance of Elder Albert Marshall. The authors are also grateful to their contributors, team members, and journal reviewers, and value the relationships and understandings that have grown through this work.

Disclosure statement

No potential conflict of interest was reported by the author(s).

ORCID

Jillian Seniuk Cicek ⓘ http://orcid.org/0000-0002-3349-9704

References

APTN National News. InFocus. 2020. *Truth and Reconciliation, Five Years Later.* https://www.aptnnews.ca/national-news/survivors-commissioners-come-together-to-talk-about-reconciliation-five-years-after-final-report/. Statement by Marie Wilson. https://www.facebook.com/APTNNews/videos/218112723100358/.

Bartlett, Cheryl, Murdena Marshall, and Albert Marshall. 2012. "Two-eyed Seeing and Other Lessons Learned Within a Co-learning Journey of Bringing Together Indigenous and Mainstream Knowledges and Ways of Knowing." *Journal of Environmental Studies and Sciences* 2: 331–340.

Bowra, Matilda. 2018. "Dr. Tom Goldfinch: Stories of Indigenous Engineers." Engineers Without Borders Australia. https://ewb.org.au/stories-of-indigenous-engineering/tom-goldfinch/.

The Canadian Encyclopedia. 2021. "Government Apology to Former Students of Indian Residential Schools." https://www.thecanadianencyclopedia.ca/en/article/government-apology-to-former-students-of-indian-residential-schools.

Canadian Geographic. 2020. "Indigenous Peoples Atlas of Canada. Truth and Reconciliation: 1. History of Residential Schools." https://indigenouspeoplesatlasofcanada.ca/article/history-of-residential-schools/.

Cape Breton University. 2020a. "Guiding Principles (Two Eyed Seeing) | Integrative Science." Accessed May 15, 2020. http://www.integrativescience.ca/Principles/TwoEyedSeeing/.

Cape Breton University. 2020b. Institute for Integrative Science and Health. "Videos | Integrative Science." Accessed May 15, 2020. http://www.integrativescience.ca/Media/Video/.

Castleden, Heather, Theresa Garvin, and Huu-ayaht First Nation. 2008. "Modifying Photovoice for Community-based Participatory Indigenous Research." *Social Science & Medicine* 66 (6): 1393–1405. doi:10.1016/j.socscimed.2007.11.030.

Catalano, George D. 2016. "Learning about Design from the Lakota Nation." In *Proceedings American Society for Engineering Education (ASEE) Annual Conference and Exposition.* Washington DC: ASEE. https://doi.org/10.18260/p.25533.

Chávez, Vivian. 2012. "Cultural Humility." YouTube video. https://www.youtube.com/watch?v=SaSHLbS1V4w.

Corntassel, Jeff. 2012. "Re-Envisioning Resurgence: Indigenous Pathways to Decolonization and Sustainable Self-determination." *Decolonization: Indigeneity, Education & Society* 1 (1): 86–101. https://jps.library.utoronto.ca/index.php/des/article/view/18627.

Cote-Meek, Sheila. 2020. "Introduction: From Colonized Classrooms to Transformative Change in the Academy: We Can and We Must Do Better!." In *Decolonizing and Indigenizing Education in Canada*, edited by Sheila Cote-Meek and Taima Moeke-Pickering, xi–xxiii. Toronto: Canadian Scholars.

Cram, Fiona. 2016. "Lessons on Decolonizing Evaluation from Kaupapa Māori Evaluation." *Canadian Journal of Program Evaluation* 30 (3): 296–312. doi:10.3138/cjpe.30.3.04.

Creswell, John W. 2013. *Qualitative Inquiry and Research Design: Choosing Among Five Approaches. 3rd ed.* Thousand Oaks, CA: SAGE.

Di Donato, Nicole. 2019. "Greater representation of Indigenous staff and faculty comes one year after Ryerson's TRC report." *Ryersonian*, February 18. https://ryersonian.ca/greater-representation-of-indigenous-staff-and-faculty-comes-one-year-after-ryersons-trc-report/.

Droz, P. E. 2014. "Biocultural Engineering Design: An Anishinaabe Analysis for Building Sustainable Nations." *American Indian Culture and Research Journal* 38 (4): 105–126. doi:10.17953/aicr.38.4.w1g6521017726785.

Engineers Canada. 2021a. "Accreditation: Accredited Engineering Programs in Canada by Program." Accessed January 11, 2021. https://engineerscanada.ca/accreditation/accredited-programs.

Engineers Canada. 2021b. "Indigenous Peoples in Engineering." Accessed January 11, 2021. https://engineerscanada.ca/diversity/indigenous-peoples-in-engineering.

Ermine, Willie, Raven Sinclair, and Bonnie Jeffery. 2004. *The Ethics of Research Involving Indigenous Peoples*. Regina, SK: Indigenous Peoples' Health Research Centre, 272 pp. http://drc.usask.ca/projects/legal_aid/file/resource385-2c4c0417.pdf.

Fontaine, Leah, and Yunyi Chen. 2018. *Wiingashk: Sweet Grass – Braiding Ways into Inclusive Education*. Workshop. Centre for the Advancement of Teaching and Learning. University of Manitoba, November 13.

Forrest, Reed, and Jillian Seniuk Cicek. 2021. "Rethinking the Engineering Design Process: Advantages of Incorporating Indigenous Knowledges, Perspectives, and Methodologies." In *Proceedings Canadian Engineering Education Association (CEEA-ACEG) Annual Conference.* OJS: PKP. https://ojs.library.queensu.ca/index.php/PCEEA/index.

Foster, Chrissy H., and Shawn S. Jordan. 2014. "A Philosophy of Learning Engineering and a Native American Philosophy of Learning; An Analysis for Congruency." In *Proceedings American Society for Engineering Education (ASEE) Annual Conference and Exposition.* Washington DC: ASEE. doi:10.18260/1-2—19976.

Gareau, Paul, Tracy Bear, Alannah Mandamin-Shawanda, and Isaac Twinn. 2021. "*Indigenous Canada* [MOOC]." University of Alberta, Faculty of Native Studies. Accessed 2020. https://www.ualberta.ca/admissions-programs/online-courses/indigenous-canada/index.html.

Gaudry, Adam, and Danielle Lorenz. 2018. "Indigenization as Inclusion, Reconciliation, and Decolonization: Navigating the Different Visions for Indigenizing the Canadian Academy." *AlterNative: An International Journal of Indigenous Peoples* 14 (3): 218–227. doi:10.1177/1177180118785382.

Gilbert, O., M. Onwu, and Charles Mufundirwa. 2020. "A Two-eyed Seeing Context-based Approach for Incorporating Indigenous Knowledge Into School Science Teaching." *African Journal of Research in Mathematics, Science and Technology Education* 24 (2): 229–240. doi:10.1080/18117295.2020.1816700.

Gillis, Angela, and Winston Jackson. 2002. *Research for Nurses: Methods and Interpretation.* Philadelphia, PA: F.A. Davis Co.

Goldfinch, Tom, Jade Kennedy, Elyssebeth Leigh, Les Dawes, Juliana Prpic, and Timothy Mccarthy. 2016. "Embedding Indigenous Perspectives into Engineering Education." Australian Government, Department of Education, 48 pp. https://ltr.edu.au/resources/ID13-2899_FinalReportrevisedv4.pdf.

Goodchild, Melanie. 2021. "Relational Systems Thinking: That's How Change is Going to Come, from Our Earth Mother." *Journal of Awareness-Based Systems Change* 1 (1): 75–103. https://doi.org/10.47061/jabsc.v1i1.577.

Government of Canada. 2017. "Indigenous Peoples and Communities." https://www.rcaanc-cirnac.gc.ca/eng/1100100013785/1529102490303.

Government of Canada. 2019. "Crown Indigenous Relations and Northern Affairs Canada. Reconciliation. Indian Residential Schools." https://www.rcaanc-cirnac.gc.ca/eng/1100100015576/1571581687074.

Grommes, Amy V., and David R. Riley. 2004. "Learning from Native Cultures: Educational Opportunities in Sustainability, Cultural Sensitivity and Global Awareness." *ASEE Annual Conference Proceedings*, 8849–8861.

Grover, Jane G. 2010. "Challenges in Applying Indigenous Evaluation Practices in Mainstream Grant Programs to Indigenous Communities." *Canadian Journal of Program Evaluation* 23 (2): 22–50.

Halbe, Johannes, Jan Adamowski, and Claudia Pahl-Wostl. 2015. "The Role of Paradigms in Engineering Practice and Education for Sustainable Development." *Journal of Cleaner Production* 106: 272–282. doi:10.1016/j.jclepro.2015.01.093.

Hess, Justin L., and Johannes Strobel. 2013. "Sustainability and the Engineering Worldview." In *2013 IEEE Frontiers in Education Conference (FIE)*, Oklahoma City, OK, USA, 2013, pp. 644–648, doi: 10.1109/FIE.2013.6684905.

Indigenous Canada Massive Open Online Course. 2021. *Killing the Indian In the Child: Module 5.* Accessed 21 November 2020. https://www.ualberta.ca/admissions-programs/online-courses/indigenous-canada/glossary/lesson-5-killing-the-indian-in-the-child.html.

Indigenous Corporate Training Inc. 2018. *What Does Indigenous Knowledge Mean? A Compilation of Attributes.* https://www.ictinc.ca/blog/what-does-indigenous-knowledge-mean.

Indigenous Corporate Training Inc. 2019. *Indigenous Peoples Are All the Same, Right?* https://www.ictinc.ca/blog/indigenous-peoples-are-all-the-same.

Indigenous Engineering. 2020. *Indigenous Engineering – Designing Across Cultures.* https://indigenousengineering.org.au/.

Jordan, Shawn S., Chrissy H. Foster, Ieshya K. Anderson, Courtney A. Betoney, and Tyrine J.D. Pangan. 2019. "Learning from the Experiences of Navajo Engineers: Looking Toward the Development of a Culturally Responsive Engineering Curriculum." *Journal of Engineering Education* 108 (3): 355–376. doi:10.1002/jee.20287.

KAIROS Blanket Exercise Community. 2020. https://www.kairosblanketexercise.org/.

Kennedy, J., T. Goldfinch, E. Leigh, J. Kaya Prpic, T. McCarthy, and L. Dawes. 2016. *A Beginner's Guide to Incorporating Aboriginal Perspectives into Engineering Curricula.* https://issuu.com/uoweis/docs/eac_v4.

Keoke, Emory Dean, and Kay Marie Porterfield. 2003. *Encyclopedia of American Indian Contributions to the World: 15,000 Years of Inventions and Innovations.* New York: Checkmark Books.

Kilada, George, Jillian Seniuk Cicek, Victoria Thomsen, Afua Adobea Mante, and Randy Herrmann. 2021. "The Impact of Indigenous Knowledges and Perspectives in Engineering Education: One Student's Story." In *Proceedings Canadian Engineering Education Association (CEEA-ACEG) Annual Conference.* OJS: PKP. https://ojs.library.queensu.ca/index.php/PCEEA/index.

Kirkness, Verna J., and Ray Barnhardt. 1991. "First Nations and Higher Education: The Four R's– Respect, Relevance, Reciprocity, Responsibility." *Journal of American Indian Education* 30 (3): 1–15.

LaFrance, Joan, Richard Nichols, and Karen E. Kirkhart. 2012. "Culture Writes the Script: On the Centrality of Context in Indigenous Evaluation." *New Directions for Evaluation* 2012 (135): 59–74. doi:10.1002/ev.20027.

Leigh, Elyssebeth, Thomas Goldfinch, Juliana Kaya Prpic, Les Dawes, Jade Kennedy, and Tim McCarthy. 2014. "Shared Values: Diverse Perspectives - Engaging Engineering Educators in Integrating Indigenous Engineering Knowledge into Current Curricula." In *Proceedings of* the 2014 Annual Conference of the Australasian Association for Engineering Education (AAEE2014), Edited by T. Qi and A. Bainbridge-Smith, 1–10. Massey University.

Lucena, Juan, and Gary Lee Downey. 1999. "Engineering Cultures: Better Problem Solving Through Human and Global Perspectives?" In *Proceedings American Society for Engineering Education (ASEE) Annual Conference and Exposition*. Washington, DC: ASEE. https://peer.asee.org/7632.

MacColl, Ian, Roslyn Cooper, Markus Rittenbruch, and Stephen Viller. 2005. "Watching Ourselves Watching: Ethical Issues in Ethnographic Action Research." In *Proceedings of OZCHI 2005*, Canberra, Australia, November 23–25. Narrabundah, AU: Computer-Human Interaction Special Interest Group (CHISIG) of Australia. http://eprints.qut.edu.au/90140/1/p28-maccoll.pdf.

MacDonald, Cathy. 2012. "Understanding Participatory Action Research: A Qualitative Research Methodology Option." *The Canadian Journal of Action Research* 13 (2): 34–50.

Martin, Jay F., Eric D. Roy, Stewart A.W. Diemont, and Bruce G. Ferguson. 2010. "Traditional Ecological Knowledge (TEK): Ideas, Inspiration, and Designs for Ecological Engineering." *Ecological Engineering* 36: 839–849. doi:10.1016/j.ecoleng.2010.04.001.

Mazzocchi, Fulvio. 2006. "Western Science and Traditional Knowledge: Despite Their Variations, Different Forms of Knowledge Can Learn from Each Other." *EMBO Reports* 7 (5): 463–466. https://www.embopress.org/doi/full/10.1038/sj.embor.7400693.

McKivett, Andrea, Judith N. Hudson, Dennis McDermott, and David Paul. 2020. "Two-eyed Seeing: A Useful Gaze in Indigenous Medical Education Research." *Medical Education* 54 (3): 217–224. doi:10.1111/medu.14026.

Mejia, Joel. A., and Matias N. de Paula. 2019. "'Ingeniero como vos': An analysis of the Mbya-Guarani Practices Associated with Engineering Design." In *Proceedings American Society for Engineering Education (ASEE) Annual Conference and Exposition*. Washington DC: ASEE. https://doi.org/10.18260/1-2-31921.

Michie, Michael, Michelle Hogue, and Joel Rioux. 2018. "The Application of Both-ways and Two-eyed Seeing Pedagogy: Reflections on Engaging and Teaching Science to Post-secondary Indigenous Students." *Research in Science Education* 48: 1205–1220. doi:10.1007/s11165-018-9775-y.

Minkler, M. 2000. "Assessment/Evaluation. Using Participatory Action Research to Build Healthy Communities." *Public Health Reports* 115 (2-3): 191–198. doi:10.1093/phr/115.2.191.

Morelli, Paula T., and Peter J. Mataira. 2010. "Indigenizing Evaluation Research: A Long-awaited Paradigm Shift." *Journal of Indigenous Voices in Social Work* 1 (2): 1–12. http://scholarspace.manoa.hawaii.edu/handle/10125/18773.

Murray, Jaclyn K., Jaryn A. Studer, Shanna R. Daly, Seda McKilligan, and Colleen M. Seifert. 2019. "Design by Taking Perspectives: How Engineers Explore Problems." *Journal of Engineering Education* 108 (2): 248–275. doi:10.1002/jee.20263.

National Centre for Truth & Reconciliation. 2020. "TRC Commissioners Statement." University of Manitoba. https://news.nctr.ca/articles/trc-commissioners-statement.

O'Sullivan, Nan. 2019. "Walking Backwards Into the Future: Indigenous Wisdom Within Design Education." *Educational Philosophy and Theory* 51 (4): 424–433. doi:10.1080/00131857.2018.1476236.

Peltier, Cindy. 2018. "An Application of Two-eyed Seeing: Indigenous Research Methods with Participatory Action Research." *International Journal of Qualitative Methods* 17: 1-12. 10.1177/1609406918812346.

Pierotti, Raymond. 2011. *Indigenous Knowledge, Ecology, and Evolutionary Biology*. New York: Routledge.

Puxley, Chinta. 2015. "Up to 6,000 Children Died at Canada's Residential Schools, Report Finds." *Global News*, May 31. https://globalnews.ca/news/2027587/deaths-at-canadas-indian-residential-schools-need-more-study-commission/.

Reconciling Ways of Knowing. 2020. *Reconciling Ways of Knowing Forum*. Online Dialogues 2020–2021. https://www.waysofknowingforum.ca/.

Ricci, Jamie. 2016. "Indigenous' Peoples Access to Postsecondary Engineering Programs: A Review of Practice Consensus." *Engineers Canada*. Accessed January 9, 2021. https://engineerscanada.ca/reports/research/review-practice-consensus-indigenous-peoples-access-post-secondary-engineering-programs.

Scott, Sheryl. 2010. "Drawing on Indigenous Ways of Knowing: Reflections from a Community Evaluator." *Canadian Journal of Program Evaluation* 23 (2): 73–92.

Seniuk Cicek, Jillian, Marcia Friesen, and Shawn Bailey. 2019a. "Transdisciplinary Design and Build Studio Course in Collaboration with the Shoal Lake 40 First Nation: Development and Assessment." In 2019 *IEEE Frontiers in Education Conference (FIE)*, Covington, KY, USA, 2019, pp. 1–7. doi: 10.1109/FIE43999.2019.9028515.

Seniuk Cicek, Jillian, Afua Mante, Carolyn Geddert, and Leah Fontaine. 2019b. "Engineering Education Re-Interpreted Using the Indigenous Sacred Hoop Framework." In *Proceedings of the 8th Research in Engineering Education Symposium: Making Connections (REES)*, edited by Bruce Kloot, 510–519. Red Hook, NY: Curran Associates. http://www.proceedings.com/49995.html.

Seniuk Cicek, Jillian, Alan L. Steele, Deanna Burgart, Pamela Rogalski, Sarah Gauthier, Stephen Mattucci, Jason Bazylak, et al. 2020. "Indigenous Initiatives in Engineering Education in Canada: Collective Contributions." In *CEEA-ACEG 2020 Proceedings of the Canadian Engineering Education Association Conference*. doi:10.24908/pceea.vi0.14162.

Shrivastava, Richa, Yves Couturier, Felix Girard, Lucie Papineau, and Elham Emami. 2020. "Two-eyed Seeing of the Integration of Oral Health in Primary Health Care in Indigenous Populations: A Scoping Review." *International Journal for Equity in Health* 19 (107): 1–18.

Sivertsen, Nina, Ann Harrington, and Mohammad Hamiduzzaman. 2020. "'Two-eyed Seeing': The Integration of Spiritual Care in Aboriginal Residential Aged Care in South Australia." *Journal of Religion, Spirituality & Aging* 32 (2): 149–171. doi:10.1080/15528030.2019.1669515.

Smith, Linda T. 2006. "Researching in the Margins Issues for Māori Researchers: A Discussion Paper." *AlterNative: An International Journal of Indigenous Peoples* 2 (1): 4–27. doi:10.1177/117718010600200101.

Statistics Canada. 2021. *Statistics on Indigenous Peoples*. https://www.statcan.gc.ca/eng/subjects-start/indigenous_peoples.

Stranger, Darrell, and Jamie Pashagumskum. 2020. "Survivors, Commissioners Come Together to Talk About Reconciliation Five Years After Final Report." *APTN*, January 15.

Suzuki, David. 2020. *Reconciling Ways of Knowing Forum*. Online Dialogues 2020–2021. https://www.waysofknowingforum.ca/.

Truth and Reconciliation Commission (TRC) of Canada. 2015a. *Honouring the Truth, Reconciling for the Future: Summary of the Final Report of the Truth and Reconciliation Commission of Canada*. Ottawa, ON: Truth and Reconciliation Commission of Canada. http://publications.gc.ca/pub?id=9.800288&sl=0.

Truth and Reconciliation Commission (TRC) of Canada. 2015b. *Truth and Reconciliation Commission of Canada: Calls to Action*. Winnipeg, MB: Truth and Reconciliation Commission of Canada. https://nctr.ca/assets/reports/Calls_to_Action_English2.pdf.

Turtle Island Institute. 2021. https://turtleislandinstitute.ca/.

Wang, Yan, Enis Dogan, and Xiaodong Lin. 2006. "The Effect of Multiple-Perspective Thinking on Problem Solving." In *Proceedings of the 7th International Conference of the Learning Sciences*, 2, 812–817.

Weatherford, Jack. 2010. *Indian Givers: How Native Americans Transformed the World*. New York: Three Rivers Press.

Wildcat, Matthew, Mandee McDonald, Stephanie Irlbacher-Fox, and Glen Coulthard. 2014. "Learning from the Land: Indigenous Land Based Pedagogy and Decolonization." *Decolonization: Indigeneity, Education & Society* 3 (3): I–XV. https://jps.library.utoronto.ca/index.php/des/issue/view/1584.

Holding space for an Aboriginal approach towards Curriculum Reconciliation in an Australian university

Jade Kennedy 📵, Alisa Percy 📵, Lisa Thomas 📵, Catherine Moyle and Janine Delahunty 📵

ABSTRACT

Since Universities Australia's Indigenous Strategy recommended a sector-wide approach to 'closing the gap' between Indigenous and non-Indigenous Australians, universities have grappled with how to do this. Resisting mainstream approaches to curriculum development that eschew any kind of relational accountability (Wilson, Shawn. 2008. *Research is Ceremony: Indigenous Research Methods*. Manitoba: Fernwood Publishing) requires entering difficult relations of power and occupying space to transform the act of curriculum development itself. This paper is the second in a series understanding *Jindaola*, a programme led by a Local Aboriginal Knowledge Holder within one Australian university. It 'hacks' the curriculum development space with staff through Aboriginal *way* towards Curriculum Reconciliation, building knowledge-based relationships between disciplinary and relevant Aboriginal Knowledge. We deliberately and controversially enact this type of relationship, by temporarily bringing the Foucauldian lens of 'heterotopia', and interview data from 30 participants, to describe how *Jindaola* usurps the neocolonial remit to embed Indigenous Knowledge, and creates and holds a counter-hegemonic space to decolonise curriculum development.

Before embarking on this Journey together, it is important that the authors stop and take a moment to be aware of our surroundings and to appreciate that everything they know has been gifted to them from Country. The authors Acknowledge that all things come from the Country, and specifically that the knowledge and perspectives they shared all come from Yuin Country. The authors acknowledge the Yuin people, their ancient and sacred knowledge and stories, and their ever-present Dreaming. Most significantly, and with much respect and thanks, the authors acknowledge the elders and local knowledge holders across Yuin Country who contributed and consulted with the mob around the appropriate knowledge embedded within Jindaola and, in doing so, informed the article the readers are about to read.

Introduction

A protector of Knowledge, the goanna *Jindaola* [*Jinda-ole-la*] walks from place-to-place helping people know '*proper way*'. He speaks of protocol, the sacred and the special, and the appropriate practices we must perform to maintain the continuation of these

---

ⓑ Supplemental data for this article can be accessed at https://doi.org/10.1080/13562517.2021.1953979.

(Kennedy et al. 2018, 5). At the University of Wollongong, *Jindaola* is represented in a unique programme that takes its participants on a sustained reflective journey towards Curriculum Reconciliation, a process of knowledge reconciliation situated on Country that leads to a greater appreciation for epistemological equivalence, ontological plurality, and relational accountability.

This paper represents the second in a series of explorations of the *Jindaola* programme and the emerging concept of Curriculum Reconciliation. The first introduced the concept of Curriculum Reconciliation as an aim and outcome of the *Jindaola* programme, explained the programme's positionality within an integrated set of landscapes, and described its principles and protocols. This second`paper draws on the Foucauldian concept of heterotopia (Foucault 1986) to describe nested contestations. Admittedly a non-Indigenous theoretical perspective, heterotopia is nevertheless productive in explaining how Jindaola creates and holds for its participants a counter-hegemonic site of resistance within these landscapes, where the dominant social order can be found to be wanting, norms transgressed, and new subjectivities emerge (Topinka 2010; Beckett, Bagguley, and Campbell 2017). Heterotopia is best explained, less in clarity of definition and more in terms of the work it can do (Haghighi 2020). We, therefore, use this concept to show how *Jindaola*: directly resists the pressure to take a western transactional approach to curriculum development; deliberately usurps the resources of the academy to this end; and provides a sustained, embodied, relational, and affective experience to enable its participants to navigate their own personal and shared journey towards Curriculum Reconciliation between two bounded systems of knowledge: Country and the academy.

This particular story cannot be explained through a generalisation of Indigenous literature, as this journey is grounded in and of this place. We, therefore, adopt a lens and theory that is of nowhere and, therefore, everywhere, to walk the reader through *Jindaola* and the way it contributes to the emerging understanding of Curriculum Reconciliation from afar

Australian higher education context

As Australia continues its unstable and highly problematic process of reconciliation to 'strengthen relationships between Aboriginal and Torres Strait Islander and non-Indigenous peoples' (Reconciliation Australia 2020), education has a critical role to play. Within the Australian higher education context, the peak sector body, Universities Australia, recently developed its *Indigenous Strategy* (2017) to provide a cohesive sector-wide approach to 'closing the gap' between Indigenous and non-Indigenous Australians. This strategy extends the long-standing commitment of Australian universities to improve the participation and success of Indigenous students and furthers the development of intercultural capability through curriculum reform that 'ensure[s] all students will encounter and engage with Aboriginal and Torres Strait Islander cultural content as integral parts of their course of study' (Universities Australia 2017, 14). And while this national strategy is a welcomed and positive move towards reconciliation, the more promising possibilities of decolonisation tend to be subsumed by an emphasis on 'practical reconciliation'; that is, a process of 'closing the gap' in educational outcomes for Indigenous peoples, but in the settlers' ways (Burridge 2009; McKnight 2016). We argue that such approaches are underpinned by a deficit view of first nations' peoples and make a case for 'substantive reconciliation' as a respectful and reciprocal approach to what we term, Curriculum Reconciliation (Kennedy et al. 2019).

In our work, we describe Curriculum Reconciliation as 'a process of knowledge reconciliation within Country, where participants are invited and supported to reflectively reconcile their own disciplinary knowledge with Aboriginal Knowledge that are situated in the Country on which they teach' (Kennedy et al. 2019, 149). From a post-colonial perspective, and drawing on the social cartography of reform described by Andreotti et al. (2015), we would argue that the Universities Australia *Indigenous Strategy* (2017) seeks compliance to 'soft reform' measures, such as its targets to increase the access, retention, and completion of Aboriginal and Torres Strait Islander people in university education. It also contains a commitment to 'radical reform' approaches, such as taking a whole-of-institution approach, sharing the responsibility for Indigenous education with non-Indigenous staff, building effective community partnerships, and increasing the cultural capability of graduates (Universities Australia 2017). However, the Strategy falls short of advocating for decolonising processes that could foster a more substantive approach to reconciliation in Australia (Burridge 2009). While soft reform approaches that promote inclusion and access are important, they also tend to reproduce the marginal and deficit-based view of Indigenous people as a problem to be managed through the educational tactics of assimilation (e.g. pathway programmes, peer mentoring, and learning support). And while the 'radical reform' approaches are critical in that they address epistemological domination within the academy (Nakata et al. 2012) through greater Indigenous representation and recognition (e.g. the Indigenisation of the workforce and curricula) (Darlaston-Jones et al. 2014), they also tend to lead to tokenism and superficial and decontextualised approaches to embedding Indigenous content (Tuck and Wade Yang 2012; Synot et al. 2019). Both the soft and radical reform approaches to reconciliation fail to recognise and challenge the ontological and metaphysical dominance of the neocolonial university itself and, as such, tend to contribute to the expansion rather than the overhaul of dominant neocolonial processes and agendas (Andreotti et al. 2015; Bawaka Country et al. 2016).

This is particularly evident in the approach to curriculum reform promoted by the Universities Australia *Indigenous Strategy* (2017), which requires universities to utilise frameworks, graduate attributes, and changes to teaching practices that reflect Indigenous Knowledge (Behrendt et al. 2012, xiv). Within a colonial and neoliberal institution, the concepts of curriculum reform, cultural content, graduate attributes, and teaching practices are all Western concepts. These concepts are deeply embedded within intellectual and regulatory frameworks that deal in the commodification of universal decontextualised knowledge (Gonzales and Núñez 2014), take a compliance-focussed approach to quality assurance (Harvey and Newton 2004), insist on accountability through rigid key performance indicators (Bullen and Flavell 2017), and tend to value the measurability of tangible outcomes against pre-specified standards (Bradley et al. 2008; Commonwealth of Australia 2009). This is precisely what Bullen and Flavell (2017, 592) warn us about; they suggest that the 'embedding of Indigenous knowledge' utilising a Western approach to curriculum development leads to a 'transactional' or 'capitalist exchange' approach to including Indigenous content in curricula. This kind of superficial 'Indigenisation' of the curricula tends to bypass the work required for both students and staff: to first recognise and then 'unlearn' colonial privilege; to experience and develop a deep respect for other ways of being in and of the world; and to 'become critically self-reflexive and develop capacity for ontological pluralism (essential for … intercultural capability)'

(Bullen and Flavell 2017, 583). This begs the question of how we might decolonise, not just the disciplinary curriculum but the very act of curriculum development itself.

Operating within this highly compromised policy and practice landscape, *Jindaola* is a whole-of-institution Aboriginal educational development grants programme in one Australian university. The programme is attempting to decolonise the university's more transactional approach to curriculum development by making subversive use of the mainstream academic development space to take the university's approach to reconciliation 'beyond reform'. For Andreotti et al. (2015), moving 'beyond reform' involves more than just acknowledging different ways of knowing, such as retrofitting cultural content into curricula (radical/epistemological reform); it involves drawing attention to the oppressive nature of the system itself and creating and holding a space within these power relations.

Of the various 'beyond reform' tactics suggested by Andreotti et al. (2015), in this paper, we explain how *Jindaola* engages its participants in the tactic of 'system-hacking', where the places, spaces, and resources of the system are utilised to highlight its systemic continuing violence and orient their desires away from it. *Jindaola* deliberately decentres curriculum development, achieving its remit to embed Aboriginal knowledge and perspectives through an enactment of relational accountability (Wilson 2008) achieved with practices of relational, affective, and embodied pedagogy. By carving out and holding an alternative space in a sustained way within the academy, participants experience and develop a deep respect for an Aboriginal way as they are guided towards developing knowledge-based relationships and reconciling their experiences of the intersection between multiple worldviews.

Taking a strengths-based approach, we articulate how the tactic of system-hacking is displayed through the building of knowledge-based relationships between the practices, protocols, principles, and philosophies of *Jindaola* and the Foucauldian concept of heterotopia. *Jindaola* operates in a complex space where many worldviews meet. Therefore this paper aims to demonstrate how *Jindaola* functions as a counter-hegemonic and decolonising space within the institution while continuing to close the gap between Aboriginal and non-Indigenous knowledge; resisting colonial approaches to curriculum development, working at the level of personal transformation, and producing new subjectivities (authentic advocates and allies) who come to recognise themselves as lifelong agents of Curriculum Reconciliation (Atchison and Kennedy 2020; Fildes et al. 2021).

Jindaola

Jindaola is an Aboriginal educational development grants programme modelled on traditional Aboriginal systems for maintaining knowledge integrity, grounded in the principles of respect, responsibility, and reciprocity and governed by the protocols of regularity, routine, and relevance. Led by a Local Aboriginal Knowledge holder and supported by an academic development team, it takes interdisciplinary teams on an 18-month journey across Country to support them as they decolonise and deconstruct their approaches to knowledge, learning, and teaching while engaging them in the process of negotiating and establishing authentic knowledge-based relationships between Aboriginal Knowledge and their disciplinary knowledge. The teams engage a series of five full-day Formal Gatherings that take place off campus and on Country.

These full-days [Joining the Journey, Sharing your Landscape, Sharing your Way, Sharing your Walking, Sharing you Story] are representative of 'passing through knowledge' ceremonies, and are staged appropriately across the programme. Formal Gatherings are interspersed with fortnightly informal gatherings for consistent coaching and mentoring from a lecturer in Indigenous Knowledge with support of Aboriginal community Elders and Knowledge holders.[1]

Importantly, *Jindaola* furthers the concept of 'Curriculum Reconciliation' as an approach that takes a horizontal rather than vertical approach to 'closing the gap', where the 'gap' is defined not by the deficit-based assumption of the cultural, social, and educational disadvantages of Indigenous people, but by the strengths-based assumption of epistemological equivalence (Darlaston-Jones et al. 2014; Zubrzycki et al. 2014) and the deep respect for ontological plurality (Bullen and Flavell 2017).

What is curious about *Jindaola*, however, is that while the programme owes its very existence to the remit of the Universities Australia *Indigenous Strategy* (2017), particularly in terms of embedding of Indigenous Knowledge and perspectives into the curriculum; rather than simply being 'radical' in its approach, *Jindaola* focuses effort not on the transaction of cultural content, but on creating and holding space in sustained ways for the participants to experience and generate new ways of being in relationship with knowledge and knowing. Drawing on interview data from programme participants (see Supplementary Material for participant and ethics approval details), we explore how *Jindaola* is able to maintain this counter-hegemonic space through the lens of a Foucauldian heterotopia.

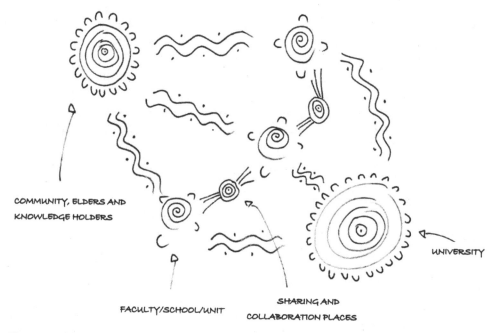

Figure 1. Aboriginal iconographic representation of the *Jindaola* program methodology (For a deeper articulation of the methodology please refer to Kennedy et al. 2018).

Jindaola as a heterotopia

We describe the space that *Jindaola* creates and holds for its participants as a heterotopia because it resides in a very tangible way between two bounded knowledge systems: Country and the institution, as shown in Figure 1.

Where Bhaba (cited in Dudgeon and Fielder 2006) and Nakata (2007) both describe the interface of cultures as generative spaces of counter-hegemonic potential, we propose that *Jindaola* can be regarded as heterotopic for the insight such a lens provides into how *Jindaola* disturbs norms, order, language, time and space, and invites participants to experience themselves, knowledge and knowing in new ways as shown in Figure 2.

Despite being nested within the academy, *Jindaola* operates as a generative site of resistance and transformation by deliberately attending to policy imperatives in the 'wrong' way (Beckett, Bagguley, and Campbell 2017), that is, through an Aboriginal way rather than a colonial way. Refusing the expectation that it will enact a kind of 'practical' (hierarchical) reconciliation as defined by the Universities Australia *Indigenous Strategy* (2017) by embedding Indigenous content into curricula as its first priority, *Jindaola* deliberately decentres the curriculum development demands for superficial, transactional or capitalist exchange approaches to Indigenous education (Bullen and Flavell 2017; Castell et al. 2018; Synot et al. 2019).

Instead, *Jindaola* works towards 'substantive' (horizontal) reconciliation by inviting participants on a sustained journey to come into a relationship with themselves, each other, with Country, and with knowing and learning on Country. It is in this safe container and on this journey that 'Curriculum Reconciliation' as a space, a journey, and a

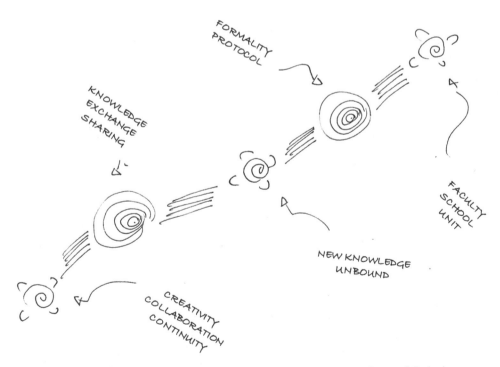

Figure 2. Aboriginal iconographic representation of the participant experience of *Jindaola*.

lifelong process of coming into relationship functions as an enacted utopia (Charteris et al. 2017, 340). To illustrate how *Jindaola* operates as a heterotopia, we explore it through the six principles identified by Foucault (1986): regulated entry, a space of deviation, juxtaposition of the incompatible, disturbing spatio-temporal arrangements, transforming over time, and intersecting with the spaces that remain.

Regulated entry – creating an exclusive pathway

It can be initially stated that *Jindaola* is a university-funded educational development grants programme, and as such, like other grants programmes, access is limited by the financial support available. In this instance, at UOW, the activity of embedding Indigenous Knowledge and perspectives into ones' curriculum is positioned and understood as a privilege to be earned. A basic principle across the Aboriginal Countries and communities of Australia is the appreciation that knowledge is an earnt right, and it is in this knowing that one may enter into the dialogue and undertake the knowledge journey.

Because *Jindaola* functions as the legitimate institutional gateway to Aboriginal knowledge and community, entry is regulated to ensure adherence to the philosophies, protocols and rites of passage embedded within the programme. Entry is considered through a comprehensive process of expressions of interest, interviews, and consultation. Teams are selected based on criteria that include aspects of their disposition towards the programme, including openness, passion, interest, orientation towards collaboration, and a commitment to be involved in the programme.

These points are communicated to applicants to assist them in preparing written expressions of interest and for the interview stage of the selection process. However, from the interviewers' perspectives, nuances exist. For example, while an articulate plan is requested, it is important that teams are very willing to adapt and change their plans as the journey unfolds. A participant from the first cohort at the end of their journey reflects upon their experience of the application process:

> I had no idea what I was in for. I just knew that it was something we needed to do for our students and for the world ... and for our country. But I had no idea what we were going to do ... the thing about the grant is that you have to put a proposal forward on how you were going to spend $50,000 on embedding Aboriginal knowledges and ways and you have no idea what they are ... we tackled it like a typical grant process ... we went to the grant panel with a very linear, structured diagram saying, "We're going to put it in first year, second year, third year, post grad ... and we're going to do all of that in 18 months ... " And I think, yeah, again, that was so silly of us. But that's all we knew at the time. That's where we were at 18 months ago. (P18)

Jindaola seeks teams whose members are genuine in their pursuit to learn more and see their involvement as a key driver for enacting change. When asked about their motivations to engage in *Jindaola*, some of our participants demonstrated clear gestures of such intent. These included:

> I don't know, it hit something pretty strong and personal in me. I wanted to stand up and start dismantling some of the crap that is being set up around the place ... I don't understand how it works in my area yet. But as part of an institution, I know I can make a

difference and once something goes off in me then that is it. It is what I need to do. It is like a calling. It is something I need to be part of. (P24)

For me, personally, I like the idea of changing the university from within ... This program's about looking in and it's about looking into the individual. What I liked about it was the opportunity to change within myself ... I like the idea that it's not just about curriculum transformation, it's not a cultural awareness program, it's about personal transformation. That's basically what it was. I wanted to be transformed to think and do differently in a way that is privileging Indigenous knowledge that have been actively erased. (P4)

Once an entry has been gained into the *Jindaola* journey, the teams progress through informal and formal gatherings akin to rites of passage that take place on Country over the course of the programme. As initiation points, participants come together collectively to share the continuous unfolding and embodiment of their learning as they experience a permanent shift in their own *way*. As is often the case with engagement in a rite of passage, individuals undergo significant personal change as they are pushed out of their comfort zone. This is evident throughout the *Jindaola* gatherings, with insights from two participants:

I can remember the various [workshops] ... the most meaningful so far was a big one that we had at the Aboriginal centre in town ... I was quite tired, I really broke down into tears and I sort of blamed it a bit on the flight but it wasn't. Just the whole thing was so personal and ever since then at all of these workshops there have been so many tears. I'll probably start crying now ... I think it's been very valuable. One of the things that I want to highlight [is that] there has been no other course at university or no other program I've been involved in that would have ever moved me to tears or would move anyone else, and I cry quite easily, perhaps I am not the best indicator, but a number of people have been in tears I think and we have talked about that. (P1)

I found the first workshop very tiring, mentally and emotionally very tiring. It was really challenging and confronting and I think that's because I understood for the first time how entrenched we are, and the enormity of trying to shift some of that even a little way, it's like pushing against a tall story building, the enormity of the whole project really overwhelmed me to begin with ... This is not just about learning. This is about exploring who you are, what you think and what your biases are, how you see the world, how you can challenge that view. And that's what I want to do. (P13)

Throughout the journey, participants are drawn to the philosophy of *Jindaola*. This includes the principles of *Respect, Responsibility, and Reciprocity* for each other, for the group, for the *Jindaola* community, and for all communities with which they engage. The programme also requires the protocols of *Regularity, Routine and Relevance* around contact and communication. One of the key outcomes emerging from adherence to the principles and protocols is that every individual is responsible for all other individuals, their tribe; no one gets left behind. This is an introduction to custodianship and fosters a sense of community that becomes self-sustaining. While entry into the journey of *Jindaola* is regulated, the ongoing journey is a lifelong process. It is akin to being adopted into Aboriginal *ways* of being, and also a gateway, as the journey itself provides entry into a growing community of university staff who are committed to incorporating Aboriginal Knowledge, perspectives, and relationships in authentic ways while following the appropriate protocols,

[*Jindaola*] is bringing us together and we all had that feeling of we're bringing everyone together ... It's a lifelong learning journey. It's not going to stop. So, we're all there, no matter where you think you sit on the Indigenous engagement scale ... we're all at the same place. We've all got the same objective. (P4)

A space of deviation – tearing at the fabric of the western academy

Restricted access and rites of passage are part of the way *Jindaola* deliberately makes subversive use of the mainstream academic development space to function as a heterotopia of deviation or counter-hegemonic space within the academy. In contrast to the 'heterotopia of crisis', which Foucault defines as 'elsewhere' or 'nowhere' spaces with no geographical markers reserved for the conduct of abnormal occurrences (Foucault 1986; Topinka 2010), *Jindaola* is deeply grounded in Country. As such, it tears at the fabric of the western academy, providing an 'alternative space' within an existing social order where norms are suspended, neutralised or inverted (Haghighi 2020), that is, where behaviour outside the norm can be exercised.

Within the space created and held for participants in the programme, *Jindaola* deliberately subjugates western ways of doing, being, and knowing to an Aboriginal *way*, which for participants, is experienced as an unsettling, sometimes disturbing, sometimes emancipatory, 'rule-breaking and norm-refusing' space (Beckett, Bagguley, and Campbell 2017, 169). The first Formal gathering, 'Joining the Journey', marks the opening initiation point where participants are inducted into a way of being and given the protocols governing their journey. This first gathering is run as a yarning (talking) circle based on the Aboriginal traditions of learning from a collective group and building respectful relationships. From the moment they arrive, participants recognise that they have entered an alternative space to what they are used to operating in. As busy university teachers and professionals, genuinely interested in learning, their socialisation includes certain norms and rules, particularly within the curriculum development space that values agendas, checklists, efficiency, and outcomes-based processes, as the following comments reveal,

> I probably thought I'd have had a checklist of what I wanted to achieve, and we'd just achieve that in a year, and that'd be it. Yeah, that's what I thought. (P19)

> We went into this [with] the attitude, here is a box we need to tick it. We do that a lot when we have to do something on [curriculum reform]; we don't feel it at a deep level. It's more often that 'we just have to do this'. When you talk about curriculum transformation, sometimes its tongue in cheek. (P1)

Participants often arrive on their first day, keen, but also unsure. As the day progresses, many experience discomfort because the process is so unfamiliar, although this can quickly abate to unexpected freedom, as P1 describes,

> I went into the first Workshop, totally naïve, unprepared, not knowing what to expect ... going into it very much how I would go into any workshop ... looking at the agenda, looking at the time, working out what would be of interest for me and what I could miss, what other work I could get done on the same day. That would be my normal attitude of trying to fit a whole lot of things into the workshop. I sent an email saying 'What's the agenda, what are the times?' ... And there was no agenda! That already got my back up because I thought 'What?' It's not what I'm used to, so I went in

there thinking, 'This going to be different', and probably a little bit with a negative feeling 'How is this going to work?' But within 5 minutes within that workshop, or maybe an hour in that space, I just realised that it is totally different and the journey began from that time on, and it's been fantastic, it's been a real learning experience and now I would not go into any of the Workshops expecting that there'll be an agenda, expecting not to be engaged, expecting to try to get anything else done. I would just give my total undivided attention. And that's all been about learning to do it the Aboriginal way and the whole experience has been very personal, really valuable, really emotional and stuff like that. It has been great. (P1)

The act of bringing together the personal and professional, sitting in a circle, taking turns speaking, listening deeply to each other all day, talking about themselves personally, and witnessing their own and other's vulnerability, for example, breaks all the rules of how curriculum development actually 'gets done' currently in a university setting.

Juxtaposition of the incompatible – appreciating ontological plurality

A key aspect of the counter-hegemonic space that *Jindaola* creates and holds for participants is the journey into an experience of ontological plurality which is enabled by the juxtaposition 'in a single real place several spaces, several sites that are in themselves incompatible' (Foucault 1986, 25). During the *Jindaola* journey, participants experience the tensions between intersecting and incompatible ways of being, doing, knowing, and relating, such as juxtaposing the colonial, transactional, and performative regime of western approaches to curriculum development with an Aboriginal *way* of coming to know.

One of the first challenges of the *Jindaola* program is simply learning how to listen, 'listening is so important' (P5). The experience of yarning circles highlighted some of the incompatibilities with academic culture through the communal and relational aspect. As people were supported to share openly, this became 'very powerful' (P11) as 'everyone gave a bit of themselves' (P4). This was a place where comfort was experienced alongside discomfort, in fact, 'you *had* to be uncomfortable' (P4). Others expanded on this notion in terms of self-exposure and working in opposition to normal practices,

I guess what would seem an unusually long period of time for us in a standard sort of meeting … taking that time to actually allow people to say a little bit about themselves. I think people probably said more about themselves than they would normally. (P2)

I loved the gentle progression of those workshops … you are not on a deadline, 'We need to get all of this information in under an hour'. You take whatever time you need and … it's just a very gentle process. That's such an antithesis of what we have to do on a daily basis. I find that really nice. More of that please! [laugh]. (P13)

As the programme unfolds, participants engage with multiple ways, places, and knowledge that sit alongside, rather than in opposition to, each other. Experience of this multiplicity, and frequent incompatibility, becomes a generative site of struggle over the production of knowledge, 'a productive clash of spaces as one system of order challenges another' (Topinka 2010, 63). It is in this space and on this journey that the rules of knowledge production become visible, and the participants begin to see firsthand the operation of power in colonial and disciplinary regimes – and to see their own positionality within that, often for the first time. One such significant struggle is captured in the following admission, in which privilege is recognised as complicit in perpetuating disadvantage,

> I'm a product of a racist Australia. I'm a product of being able to benefit from systems and structures that actively disadvantage other peoples, peoples of colour, first nations peoples and I am a product by my education, within the university system that … perpetuates that disadvantage of certain groups, to my advantage and to other people in my position's advantage. (P4)

This tension is a critical aspect of *Jindaola*; occurring at multiple levels within the institution, within the disciplines, and within the individual. The process of reconciling or coming into a relationship with themselves and their knowledge can be a particular source of disquiet, as this participant highlights,

> I like learning about the yarning circles … and I'd like to incorporate some of those … but I'm still really nervous about appropriation … at the same time I feel like we need to start using those kind of tools because otherwise this kind of dominant culture is never going to change. (P6)

Incompatibility also comes into view when Aboriginal knowledge systems present a challenge to 'unlearn' some of the socialized values of the discipline or academic culture, which sometimes is difficult to reconcile, as P3 explains,

> Coming from a very well-defined set of "this is what we take to be evidence … the kind of knowledge that has this particular kind of status" so … we can adjudicate between ideas, theories, outcomes, based upon that particular status. (P3)

But *Jindaola* also offers participants a safe space, a community, a set of protocols, to begin to reconcile themselves with Australia's history, to recognise how unconscious bias plays out in their everyday actions, to begin to come into a relationship with Country, and to learn to sit comfortably with the uncomfortable. A Formal gathering on a particularly cold day provided a situated experience of the comfort-discomfort juxtaposition. Sitting around a fire on Country provided physical protection from the bitterness of the weather while emotional comfort was situated in the haven of the yarning circle, through listening and building relationships. The experience was often evoked as significant,

> The thing that stood out for me was the fact that I felt really at home. In that group of people and really home on the mountain and I left just feeling such a sense of peace. (P16)

The bitterness of the weather inadvertently became metaphoric for the bitterness of a 'giant shitstorm' that awaited some on their return to campus,

> Yeah … I walked into a giant mess when I got back … just a giant shitstorm. And if I hadn't have had that day, it would have been a lot harder to deal with all of that bureaucratic mess that we came back to. (P16)

It is only in this space that Curriculum Reconciliation, as the authentic formation of knowledge-based relationships, can begin to emerge. In this sense, *Jindaola* can be described as providing a safe container for participants to begin to 'refuse who [they] are' in the present (Foucault 1982, 785), enabling new knowledge and subjectivities to emerge. For example, one of the teams used Kintsugi, the Japanese art of repairing

POSSIBILITIES AND COMPLEXITIES OF DECOLONISING HIGHER EDUCATION   185

broken pottery with gold, as a metaphor for brokenness-healing, embracing the beauty of flaws and imperfections. While the truth of history can be devastating, P16 reflects,

> in the places that have been shattered … the healing is kind of like the gold coming through and you have something that's beautiful despite all of their pain. (P16)

Disturbing spatio-temporal arrangements

An important element of *Jindaola* as a counter-hegemonic space relates to the radical disruption it poses to the spatio-temporal arrangements of the western academy. Foucault (1986, 26) suggests that heterotopias can be thought to be fully functioning when participants experience an absolute break with their traditional sense of time. This may be experienced as an intensification of chronological time, linked to slices of time, or the 'creative reorganisation of the effects of time and place' (Dumm 1996, 40). At 18-months, the calendaring of the programme sits outside all of the institution's timeframes and neoliberal expectations. *Jindaola* moves in its own way and its own time,

> Oh, it was not what I expected. But it was much more enriching than I expected … We've come around at the end of the program to where I thought we were going to start! (P10)

Jindaola also disrupts spatio-temporal normalcy as participants are introduced to an Aboriginal perspective of time as circular, a cycle in which the past, present, and future are continually and simultaneously happening all the time. Within this system, the yarning circles of *Jindaola* can travel backward and forwards through time depending on what participants share. Participants also learn that they walk forward along with their storyline with the responsibility of looking back to where they have come from,

> [I keep asking] where can (we) get to at the end?' and [he's] been like 'no, take your eyes off the horizon. Put them down at your feet and watch where you go. (P10)

Culturally, 'walking forward, looking back' requires us to travel back through the story that preceded us because it is part of our story. Academically, it necessitates understanding the storyline of the discipline within which participants find themselves walking so that they understand their disciplinary grounding, and in doing so develop a more intimate relationship with themselves and their knowledge. This process of always looking at where they stand in their landscape and what they stand for is unanimously embraced as participants realise that they have embarked on a 'lifelong learning journey' (P4) in direct contrast to the discrete training packages and competencies that are commonplace in the university sector.

> I don't ever think we will ever learn these ways. They're so beautiful but they're endless … I don't know … in 18 months, we've probably learned two percent of everything we should be aware of. (P18)

Jindaola further shifts participants' perspectives of time as they are taught to slow things down and value time for deep listening and reflection. This validation is contrary to the neoliberal worldview of the institution and the high achieving participants who often report an appreciation of the opportunity to slow pace for reflection, learning to value just 'sitting in the moment' (P14). As another participant explains 'you've got to stop talking to get to a point where you can start to crystallize some information to go, "this is the direction we need to be heading in"' (P26), and can be powerful,

> This idea of slowing down and rethinking how you do things and not coming in with the traditional academic way of doing things has been really powerful. One of the best things about it is just the hope that the university and the infrastructure around the project recognizes that. That this isn't going to be done in the same way and it might be a slow process. (P11)

Jindaola also provides a spatial disruption, ironically by reconnecting participants to place and, more specifically, Country. It brings the relationship back to the original knowledge base grounded in place rather than being scaffolded and articulated through a system and disciplines that are created from everywhere yet nowhere. Gatherings off campus, in culturally significant local places, are a staple of *Jindaola* as participants learn to come back into relationships with Country and themselves within these contexts,

> So being in place and kind of out of this place and in another place, always makes such a big difference to the conversations that we have as colleagues. (P14)

> I think the fire, and the scout camp music is a beautiful idea. It was really lovely. It was freezing up there, but it was lovely … that just made it all very authentic, and very real. And … I just took away a greater understanding of different ways of knowing, and being, and living in a place. (P18)

> Most meetings are held on campus and most work is done on campus, so to get away from all of that really helps you to think outside the box and just relax a little bit more. (P13)

Transforming over time

Because *Jindaola* essentially creates and holds a space of emergence for its participants, its internal workings and experiences change over time. Inherent in the way of *Jindaola* is that participants are always walking across a landscape that may seem familiar to them, but the work that they do requires them to look at that landscape through a different lens, a cultural lens that is grounded in relationality and reflexivity. Through the work of *Jindaola*, participants build a new and ever-deepening intimacy with themselves, the landscape and their storyline or journey within, upon and with it,

> It's like putting a puzzle together, after some time you say, 'Oh, I can see the pattern now. I can see the key pieces. Now I can start to build.' So it definitely didn't happen in the first three months. It would have taken me nearly a year to understand. (P17)

Knowledge moves through these relationships, which in turn is then embodied and enacted. The perpetual emergence of these relationships mean that no person can ever actually walk the same landscape, as the landscape for each individual emerges out of the intra-action of all the relationships within it; equally, no two people or groups will ever have the same journey. This holds true for the individual, the interdisciplinary teams, the cohort, and the broader *Jindaola* community. Similarly, each individual and group walks a practice of contribution as they move through the space *Jindaola* creates. Knowledge flows between individuals and groups, always building and deepening; there is no stasis. Nothing ever stays the same if you are moving or learning. And as Yunkaporta reminds us, 'If you don't move with the land, the land will move you' (2019, 3).

Intersecting with the spaces that remain

Finally, *Jindaola* is unique in terms of its placement and enactment within the university, which relates to the principle that heterotopias have 'a function in relation to all the space that remains' (Foucault 1986, 24). According to this principle, *Jindaola* creates a space of illusion in that it exposes every real space as even more illusory (Foucault 1986, 26). By this, we mean that from within the experience of the space of *Jindaola*, it is possible to call all the values, power arrangements, and unconscious activities of other spaces into question – professional and personal spaces, all aspects of a life worth living.

While *Jindaola* responds to institutional policy calls for Aboriginal knowledge to be embedded, it has its own entity and its own way that transcends tokenistic approaches to embedding Aboriginal content, a superficiality which participants feel increasingly confident to point out,

> My big concern is I don't want to do things in a superficial way. I don't want to go in, and say, 'Oh, well, okay, here's something … Let's just go, and co-opt an Indigenous practice, and let's shoe-horn it into this without really any understanding of what the broader principles are of it in an Indigenous population, and also without taking those, and making those work'. (P3)

Jindaola invites participants to walk in a grounded way; operating from a relational perspective through the facilitation of meaningful relationships with Country, knowledge and all other things. *Jindaola* elicits the reconciliation of knowledge and in doing so, curriculum and the reconciliation of self. Walking with *Jindaola* affords participants the knowledge and the time to be able to reconcile their own identities that are compartmentalized through the dominant system. Individuals move beyond what they do, to who they are as they move to reintegrate these disparate dimensions into a holistic and decolonised self, articulated in various ways such as,

> I feel like what *Jindaola* has given me personally is … an experience that I've felt kind of in a bodily way. That I would want to then bring into the classroom which is about each person being respected and having a chance to speak. (P16)

> I think it's important. I think for me, I guess, personally … you evaluate the way you do everything. Like, everything. And you think about things very, very, differently. (P18)

> This is now a very long-term sort of journey we are on, how we can do this, how we can bring more people in to do it properly and effectively? So we don't do it in 6 months ticking boxes, write a report and move onto the next project. This is really a lifelong journey now. (P1)

Conclusion

In this paper, we have presented the idea of 'system-hacking' and the principles of a Foucauldian heterotopia to describe how a programme, whose institutional remit to embed Indigenous Knowledge and perspectives into the curriculum, takes the university beyond the soft and radical reform approaches to reconciliation in Australia. The programme focuses instead on actively and subversively using the space and resources of the neocolonial university to create the conditions for new subjectivities to emerge. These subjectivities, authentic advocates and allies, are empowered to: call the violences of the neocolonial university to account; resist colonial imperatives for curriculum development, and focus on the creation of authentic knowledge-based relationships that operate at the intersection between Aboriginal and other worldviews. We have described the way the *Jindaola* programme engages 'system-hacking' to work toward Curriculum Reconciliation within the academy through creating and holding a counter-hegemonic space for participants to make sense of their own decolonial work in the curriculum development space.

It is worth noting here, however, that it is rare for Indigenous education to have a place within a mainstream academic development unit. Functioning as a heterotopia of deviation from within this highly colonised space, which generally has the remit of meeting quality targets, means that toleration of *Jindaola* as a site of resistance is always tenuous. *Jindaola's* very existence as a formal programme promoting a form of substantive reconciliation within the academy depends largely upon the political will of the Executive, and their perception of its value. As Dumm suggests,

> the connections made through a heterotopia are not determined by the heterotopia itself but by the contents a heterotopia's placement bring into play. Its position is crucial to the experiences that people have, the ways in which they will understand themselves and the importance (or lack of importance) of what they do (1996, 40).

Despite its overt resistance to the more practical tendencies of the Universities Australia Indigenous Strategy, it is important that *Jindaola* is able to speak 'both ways' to find ways to do its work and also demonstrate its value to the social order in which it exists: while the programme deliberately decentres curriculum development, development of the curriculum remains a strong but indirect outcome of the programme (see Fildes et al. 2021; Atchison and Kennedy 2020 as examples).

Note

1. See Kennedy et al. (2019) for a full description of the programme structure.

Disclosure statement

No potential conflict of interest was reported by the author(s).

ORCID

Jade Kennedy ⓘ http://orcid.org/0000-0001-8233-5944
Alisa Percy ⓘ http://orcid.org/0000-0001-7212-9194
Lisa Thomas ⓘ http://orcid.org/0000-0003-2764-0836
Janine Delahunty ⓘ http://orcid.org/0000-0001-5620-1352

References

Andreotti, Vanessa, Sharon Stein, Cash Ahenakew, and Dallas Hunt. 2015. "Mapping Interpretations of Decolonization in the Context of Higher Education." *Decolonization: Indigeneity, Education & Society* 4 (1): 21–40.

Atchison, Jennifer, and Jade Kennedy. 2020. "Being on Country as Protest: Designing a Virtual Geography Fieldtrip Being on Country as Protest: Designing a Virtual Geography Fieldtrip

Guided by Jindaola Guided by Jindaola." *Journal of University Teaching & Learning Practice* 17 (4): 1–9. https://ro.uow.edu.au/jutlp/vol17/iss4/8/.

Beckett, Angharad E., Paul Bagguley, and Tom Campbell. 2017. "Foucault, Social Movements and Heterotopic Horizons: Rupturing the Order of Things." *Social Movement Studies* 16 (2): 169–181. doi:10.1080/14742837.2016.1252666

Behrendt, Larissa, Steven Larkin, Robert Griew, and Patricia Kelly. 2012. *Review of Higher Education Access and Outcomes for Aboriginal and Torres Strait Islander People – Final Report*. Canberra: Commonwealth of Australia.

Bradley, Denise, Peter Noonan, Helen Nugent, and Bill Scales. 2008. "Review of Australian Higher Education." *Final Report*. Canberra, Australian Capital Territory: DEEWR.

Bullen, Jonathan, and Helen Flavell. 2017. "Measuring the 'Gift': Epistemological and Ontological Differences Between the Academy and Indigenous Australia." *Higher Education Research and Development* 36 (3): 583–596. doi:10.1080/07294360.2017.1290588

Burridge, Nina. 2009. "Perspectives on Reconciliation & Indigenous Rights." *Cosmopolitan Civil Societies: An Interdisciplinary Journal* 1 (2): 111–128. doi:10.5130/ccs.v1i2.1046

Castell, Emily, Jonathan Bullen, Darren Garvey, and Nicola Jones. 2018. "Critical Reflexivity in Indigenous and Cross-cultural Psychology: A Decolonial Approach to Curriculum?" *American Journal of Community Psychology* 62: 261–271. doi:10.1002/ajcp.12291

Charteris, Jennifer, Marguerite Jones, Adele Nye, and Vicente Reyes. 2017. "A Heterotopology of the Academy: Mapping Assemblages as Possibilised Heterotopias." *International Journal of Qualitative Studies in Education* 30 (4): 340–353. doi:10.1080/09518398.2016.1250178

Commonwealth of Australia. 2009. *Transforming Australia's Higher Education System*. Canberra, Australia: Attorney General's Department. https://www.voced.edu.au/content/ngv%3A14895.

Darlaston-Jones, D., J. Herbert, Kelleigh Ryan, Whitney Darlaston-Jones, J. Harris, and P. Dudgeon. 2014. "Are We Asking the Right Questions? Why We Should Have a Decolonising Discourse Based on Conscientisation Rather Than Indigenising the Curriculum." *Canadian Journal of Native Education* 37 (1): 86–104.

Dudgeon, Pat, and John Fielder. 2006. "Third Spaces Within Tertiary Places: IndigenousAustralian Studies." *Journal of Community and Applied Social Psychology* 16: 396–409. doi:10.1002/casp.883

Dumm, Thomas. 1996. *Michel Foucault and the Politics of Freedom*. Thousand Oaks, Cal: Sage Publications.

Fildes, Karen J., Eleanor Beck, Tatiana Bur, Pippa Burns, Laurie A. Chisholm, Carolyn T. Dillon, Tracey A. Kuit, et al. 2021. "The First Steps on the Journey Towards Curriculum Reconciliation in Science, Medicine and Health Education." *Higher Education Research & Development* 40 (1): 194–206. doi:10.1080/07294360.2020.1852393

Foucault, Michel. 1982. "The Subject and Power." *Critical Inquiry* 8 (4): 777–795. doi:10.1086/448181

Foucault, Michel. 1986. "Of Other Spaces." *Diacritics* 16 (1): 22–27.

Gonzales, Leslie, and Anne-Marie Núñez. 2014. "The Ranking Regime and the Production of Knowledge: Implications for Academia." *Education Policy Analysis Archives* 22 (31): 1–24. doi:10.14507/epaa.v22n31.2014

Haghighi, Farzaneh. 2020. "Heterotopic Sites of Knowledge Production: Notes on an Architectural Analysis of Lecture Halls." *Cultural Dynamics* 32 (4), https://doi.org/10.1177/0921374020907111

Harvey, Lee, and Jethro Newton. 2004. "Transforming Quality Evaluation." *International Journal of Phytoremediation* 10 (2): 149–165. doi:10.1080/1353832042000230635

Kennedy, Jade, Lisa Thomas, Alisa Percy, Bonnie Dean, Janine Delahunty, Kathryn Harden-Thew, and Maarten de Laat. 2019. "An Aboriginal Way Towards Curriculum Reconciliation." *International Journal for Academic Development* 24 (2): 148–162. doi:10.1080/1360144X.2019.1593172

Kennedy, Jade, Lisa Thomas, Alisa Percy, Janine Delahunty, Kathryn Harden-Thew, Brondalie Martin, Maarten de Laat, and Bonnie Dean. 2018. *Jindaola: An Aboriginal Way of Embedding Knowledges and Perspectives*. 4th Ed. [ebook] Wollongong: University of Wollongong. https://www.uow.edu.au/dvca/ltc/teachdev/jindaola/index.html.

McKnight, Anthony. 2016. "Meeting Country and Self to Initiate an Embodiment of Knowledge: Embedding a Process for Aboriginal Perspectives." *The Australian Journal of Indigenous Education* 45 (1): 11–22. doi:10.1017/jie.2016.10

Nakata, Martin. 2007. "The Cultural Interface." *The Australian Journal of Indigenous Education* 36 (S1), Cambridge University Press: 7–14. doi:10.1017/S1326011100004646

Nakata, Martin, Victoria Nakata, Sarah Keech, and Reuben Bolt. 2012. "Decolonial Goals and Pedagogies for Indigenous Studies." *Decolonization: Indigeneity, Education & Society* 1 (1): 120–140.

Reconciliation Australia. 2020. "What Is Reconciliation." *Reconciliation Australia Website.* https://www.reconciliation.org.au/what-is-reconciliation/.

Synot, Edward, Mary Graham, John Graham, Faith Valencia-Forrester, Catherine Longworth, and Bridget Backhaus. 2019. "Weaving First Peoples' Knowledge Into a University Course." *Australian Journal of Indigenous Education*, 1–7. doi:10.1017/jie.2019.29

Topinka, Robert J. 2010. "Foucault, Borges, Heterotopia: Producing Knowledge in Other Spaces." *Foucault Studies* 9: 54–70. doi:10.22439/fs.v0i9.3059

Tuck, Eve, and K. Wade Yang. 2012. "Decolonization Is Not a Metaphor." *Decolonization: Indigeneity, Education and Society* 1 (1): 1–40.

Universities Australia. 2017. *Indigenous Strategy 2017–2020.* Canberra. http://hdl.voced.edu.au/10707/428054.

Wilson, Shawn. 2008. *Research is Ceremony: Indigenous Research Methods.* Manitoba: Fernwood Publishing.

Bawaka Country including Wright, Sarah, Sandie Suchet-Pearson, Kate Lloyd, Laklak Burarrwanga, Ritjilili Ganambarr, Merrkiyawuy Ganambarr-Stubbs, Banbapuy Ganambarr, and Djawundil Maymuru. 2016. "The Politics of Ontology and Ontological Politics." *Dialogues in Human Geography* 6 (1): 23–27. doi:10.1177/2043820615624053

Yunkaporta, Tyson. 2019. *Sand Talk: How Indigenous Thinking Can Save The World.* Melbourne: Text Publishing.

Zubrzycki, Joanna, Sue Green, Victoria Jones, Katrina Stratton, Susan Young, and Dawn Bessarab. 2014. *Getting It Right: Creating Partnerships for Change. Integrating Aboriginal and Torres Strait Islander Knowledges in Social Work Education and Practice.* Sydney: Australian Government Office for Learning and Teaching.

A *Calle* decolonial hack: Afro-Latin theorizing of Philadelphia's spaces of learning and resistance

Amalia Dache, Jasmine Blue, Devaun Bovell, Deja Miguest, Sydney Osifeso and Fabiola Tucux

ABSTRACT

Rarely are Latinx and African-American spatial narratives read alongside each other, let alone as sites of pedagogy and learning. In the City of Philadelphia, we interpreted this racial grammar as spatial dimensions of our classroom learning through decolonial praxis. During the spring of 2020, a professor of education and 14 of her students explored three sites of resistance across Philadelphia: The MOVE Bombing site (1985), Girard College (racially desegregated in 1968), and El Centro de Oro (founded 1970s). The course, Urban Geography and Critical Higher Education framed the university and broadly modernity and its impact on our consciousness and imagination, as part of both domination and resistance, and we as scyborgs.

Introduction

In the field of Afro-Latin American Studies there are two main branches of inquiry, the first is the study of African descended people of Latin America, and the second is inquiry into the geographies these populations occupy. Topics related to 'Black histories, cultures, strategies and struggles' (de la Fuente and Andrews 2018, 1) draw from the first area of inquiry, which focuses on people. Whereas topics related to 'Blackness and race more generally as a category of difference (de la Fuente and Andrews 2018, 1)' as a mechanism for division, and inequity and its relationship to how space and place evolves given processes of racialization, draws from the second body of scholarship. Across the United States, where Blackness with and without ethnicity meet (Sansone 2003), rarely are African-American, Afro-Latinx, and Latinx spatial narratives read alongside each other, let alone as sites of pedagogy and learning. In the City of Philadelphia, we interpreted this racial grammar as spatial dimensions of our classroom learning through decolonial praxis.

As such, the purpose of this study is to explore how teaching and learning in Philadelphia, through a combination of field research, photographs and observations, employed decolonial forms of education within an urban university. Philadelphia has been the location where the Arturo Schomburg symposium has taken place in the last 24 years

(Laurent-Perrault 2010). This annual event brings scholars, activists and community members from across the country together to discuss the intersections of race and ethnicity as hybrid results of modernity. The symposium anchors the cultural strengths of the commonalities and differences Philadelphia's Brown to Black resident's encounter. Although this community cultural event may be analyzed as a 'soft-reform' (de Oliveira Andreotti et al. 2015), it has served as a site of learning and education for and by the Philadelphia community. When these spaces emerge as collective and nurturing, they contribute to community strength and consciousness.

Literature review

Afro-Latinx, Black, and Latinx communities across the United States enhance collective learning through their forms of resistance and knowledge production. Black and Brown neighborhoods have used their ingenuity and cultural consciousness to create a street pedagogy or *Calle* that relies on community spaces (like recreational facilities, bodegas, and churches) to employ activist strategies, identity formation, resistance to white supremacy, and more (Dache 2019b). This pedagogy challenges the notion of the streets solely as a place of oppression or violence and schools as the only place for learning (Dache 2019). By identifying other places of knowledge and other ways of learning, they gain visibility within the long history of discriminatory practices in the American education system.

While Afro-Latinx populations are understudied in education (Dache 2019), the 'triple-consciousness' that these students navigate as inhabitants of Black, Latinx, and American identities serves as an example of overlooked knowledge (Flores and Román 2009, 327). Despite shared characteristics, little research has explored the educational experiences and environments of students with cultural ties to both Blackness and Latinidad and the associated implications for teaching and learning (García-Louis 2018). In fact, it was not until 2016 that a U.S. nationally representative survey asked Latinx populations whether they considered themselves Afro-Latinx (López and Gonzalez-Barrera 2016). This is reflective of the complex intersections of identity that are omitted by monoracial methodologies (Haywood 2017). Perhaps because of the limited efforts in capturing Afro-Latinx identity and demographical intricacies, academic literature on Afro-Latinx populations has also been scant, leading to yet another invisibility – institutional invisibility. However, despite the lack of contributions on Afro-Latinx research, scholars like Dache and others (see García-Louis 2016, 2018; Haywood 2017) offer a new body of research with innovative methodologies such as *Calle*, that pave the way for visibility of the Afro-Latinx population within higher education and urban communities.

Following Yosso's (2005) trends of scholarship, we challenge deficit approaches to Black, Latinx, and Afro-Latinx students by recognizing systemic inequities in educational opportunity and exploring the cultural wealth within these communities. In order to fully understand the value of spaces of learning (informal/formal, external/internal) for students of color in Philadelphia, we must explore their local histories and legacies.

At the margins: communities of color and education access

In *The Philadelphia Negro*, Du Bois (1899) rejected the prevailing idea that Black communities were responsible for their social conditions, arguing that white Philadelphians actively participated in their subjugation through racial discrimination in employment and educational opportunity. Black Philadelphians were forced to accept lower wages, work in lower status positions, and pay higher rents for lower quality housing than whites (Du Bois 1899). Du Bois' other written works have connected the struggles of Afro-Latin American, African-Americans to racial oppression and resistance on a global scale. He wrote about the influence of the Haitian Revolution in the emancipation of slaves in northwestern U. S. states and the abolition of the African Slave Trade as a North Star for Latin American countries with enslaved Africans (Du Bois 1896; Du Bois 1939; Hooker 2017). As a prominent intellectual within the Pan-African movement, Du Bois advocated for a world without colonial rule, using aspirational capital to 'dream of possibilities beyond present circumstances' (Yosso 2005, 78).

This form of capital extends to Philadelphians of color, who have persisted despite barriers to resources based on race and ethnicity. The first school for Black children in Philadelphia was established in 1770, though public school options were not provided until 1822 (Du Bois 1899). These developments offered new educational opportunities for Black community members, however, governmental law and policies prohibited Black students from attending the same schools as white students. Due to funding disparity, Black school houses were structurally inferior to white school houses and lacked books, blackboards, and educators of basic subjects (Ansalone 2006). Claiming separate but equal, *Plessy v. Ferguson* (1896) justified Jim Crow and further cemented the hierarchy between Whites and minoritized groups (Harper, Patton, and Wooden 2009). Though the Supreme Court overturned this ruling in *Brown v. Board of Education* (1954) and public schools were legally required to desegregate, unequal access to education was already embedded in the system and sustained through the 'racialization of place' (Inwood and Yarbrough 2010, 299).

Neighborhoods with high concentrations of people of color are more likely to have under-resourced public schools and limited access to selective higher education institutions (Orfield 2013; Dache-Gerbino 2017). This trend occurs in many urban cities and as the fifth largest metropolitan area for self-identifying single-race Black or Black Hispanics, Philadelphia is no exception (Tamir 2021). The No Child Left Behind Act of 2001 gave the city local governance of K-12 schools (Jack and Sludden 2013), which led to the closure of thirty secondary schools. Because cuts were based on performance evaluations that were largely tied to funding and resources, school closures were concentrated in low-income communities of color (Jack and Sludden 2013). Additionally, between 1990 and 2010, Northeast Philadelphia experienced over a 50% decrease in its white population (Philadelphia Research and Policy Initiative 2011, 5). This process of white flight signaled the ghettoization of Philadelphia's Latinx community.

The School District of Philadelphia now serves a student population that is 52% Black and 21% Hispanic/Latino (District Performance Office 2020). These students share educational characteristics and outcomes, such as overrepresentation in lower-performing schools, lower rates of 'on-track' status, and higher rates of summer melt (Tanz and Erdem-Akcay 2020; Tanz and Park 2020; Tanz, Schlesinger, and Smith 2020). U.S. college enrollment has increased overall for Black and Hispanic groups (Krogstad 2016); however, single-race Black adults and Black Hispanic adults have the lowest shares of bachelor's and advanced degrees among all subgroups of the Black population (Tamir 2021). Afro-Latinos are also less likely than other Latinos to have some college education, as they encounter cultural barriers that complicate their in-group acceptance and academic persistence (García-Louis 2016; López and Gonzalez-Barrera 2016).

An untold history of racial segregation in Philadelphia community and schooling

In our study, the following three field sites were carefully chosen because of the history of resistance that Black, Latinx, and Afro-Latinx communities physically and spiritually imprinted. We centered the MOVE Bombing site, the site of Freedom Fighter's desegregation of Girard College, and *El Centro De Oro*, to acknowledge and recognize the seeds of wisdom that have been planted, but academically overlooked. Although all three sites that we explored were sites of resistance among Black and Latinx communities, the MOVE bombing site was located in West Philadelphia, the same neighborhood as our institution. We thus sought to learn from the site itself as our first point of reference in challenging the discourse surrounding the history of MOVE and its invisibility as a topic of local educational awareness within our graduate school curriculum.

Founded by John Africa, the origins of MOVE as a spiritual organization align with the historical relationship between religion and activism in the Black community. Franklin (2002) highlights that many early Black social and cultural institutions were the result of community interest and investment from religious denominations and organizations. Employing *community cultural wealth*, groups tapped into their own knowledge and resources to benefit their community (Yosso 2005). MOVE sought to do something similar.

Africa's philosophy sought to disrupt the social norms of an individualistic culture and assert a collectivist community that had power, resources and the capability to reimagine their current system (Floyd-Thomas 2002; de Oliveira Andreotti et al. 2015). John Africa started MOVE as a way to harness the skills, ideas, and abilities of his local community to resist oppression and colonial practices of modernity which seek to dismantle other ways of living and being (Floyd-Thomas 2002; Yosso 2005; de Oliveira Andreotti et al. 2015). Their alternate form of communing and active protesting garnered attention from police. In 1978, after a 50-day siege on MOVE's Powelton Village properties, officers used multiple weapons to forcefully remove MOVE residents (Harry 1987; Sanders and Jeffries 2013). The events in Powelton forced MOVE members to a new residence on Osage Avenue in the early 1980s. They were then bombed by officials in 1985 (Harry 1987). MOVE was framed in the media as cultural deviants and the acts of brutality against them were normalized as maintaining order and control (Sanders and Jeffries 2013).

Though Girard College was established with the intention of expanding secondary educational opportunities in Philadelphia to orphans, the same year as the landmark *Brown v. Board* decision, six Black children were rejected from the school solely on the basis of their race. Integration at Girard College was not achieved until 1968, after a decade of community demonstrations coordinated by notable NAACP leader and activist Cecil B. Moore (Phillips 2005). Their efforts highlight a confluence of social, navigational, and resistant capital, which served as resources for Black students as they were integrated and expected to assimilate into a white school culture (Yosso 2005). At the building ceremony of Girard College, the President of the Board of Trustees proclaimed, 'there shall be collected within these walls all that the knowledge and research of men have accumulated to enlighten and improve the minds of Youth' (Biddle 1833, 229). This assumes students are containers in which teachers must deposit knowledge, known as the banking model of education (Freire 1973). In reality, Black youth have already accumulated a wealth of knowledge through surviving and resisting oppressive social structures (Yosso 2005), yet these repertoires go unvalued by educational systems.

Similarly, Puerto Rican communities hold a wealth of knowledge in their language, culture, and migration histories for the island commonwealth to the mainland. However, in the late 1950s, Puerto Rican students at a school in the Spring Gardens area had to learn English, despite being 45% of that school's population, because only three of the teachers could speak Spanish. Therefore, in order to properly assimilate into K-12 U.S. schooling, Puerto Rican students had to disconnect from their native language (Arnau 2012). This process still continues for students classified as 'English Learners.'

Colonial practices have racialized forms of speaking, and those with bilingual vocabularies are viewed as lacking the academic language [English] that 'allows' for complex ways of thinking (Rosa and Flores 2017). The linguistic and cultural diversity of communities of color are rarely understood as a source of capital that can empower Black, Latinx, and Afro-Latinx communities and engage them as learners. Students who do not belong to the dominant culture face pressure to abandon their traditional values in order to succeed academically, affecting their speech, dress, and friendships (Montoya 1994). Although policy changes and code switching have allowed non-white groups to gain access to education, minoritized racial groups are still at a disservice. Yet, to this day, Puerto Ricans and other Latinx populations claim their language and heritage in the rich and colorful streets of *El Centro De Oro*, an ethnic enclave in North Philadelphia. They resist assimilation to white Western culture by counteracting mainstream practices through opening businesses such as *botanicas* and *bodegas* (Otero 2007).

Reclaiming space through spirituality and creative expression

The intersection of race, ethnicity, and space can be seen through the social and political acts of Black, Latinx, and Afro-Latinx peoples in Philadelphia against the forces of racism, segregation, and educational inequalities. Specifically, art and creative expression serve as an act of resistance by Latinx and Afro-Latinx communities. Dache (2019) reminds us that the history of bondage and freedom of Afro Latin Americans is evident through spirituality as a tool of resistance, which is often seen through creative expression. When exploring art and spirituality as resistance, we rely on the scholarly literature of *conocimiento* (Anzaldúa 2002), which poses a self-knowledge and deconstruction and reconstruction of the self and the social world. This allows oppressed groups to dismantle power binaries and connect with their spiritual selves in order to break free from the status quo. This is evident in *botanicas* – as a spiritual resource and a conceptual sacred space for Latinx communities. Otero (2007) refers to *botanicas* as a 'form of expression for constructing, negotiating, and ritualizing diasporic identity and memory in music, art, writing, and ritual practice' (175). Through these *botanicas*, the notion of home for Latinx communities is recreated and re-imagined. The transcendence of spiritual identity into place through migration is an act of resistance for the northeast Puerto Rican community and leads Latinx communities to recognize their *conocimiento*.

Historical socio-political acts of Latinx populations in the northeast are also seen in the grassroots community activism of the Young Lords in New York and Philadelphia in 1970. Otero (2007) highlights the diasporic context of the Young Lords as a 'Nuyorican nostalgia [and] sense of diaspora as community' (184). This group, founded by Puerto Ricans who identify as Afro-Puerto Rican, organized around issues that impacted lower-income communities of color. They partnered with associations like the Taller Puertorriqueño (in North Philadelphia) to provide cultural training and arts workshops for cultural preservation. Today, the Taller preserves Puerto Rican culture, 'grounded in the conviction that embracing one's cultural heritage is central to community empowerment' (Taller Puertorriqueño 2021). Indeed, community-based organizations have served as sites of social and political education among Black, Latinx, and Afro-Latinx urban youth, strengthening their cultural identities and promoting critical civic engagement (Ginwright 2007; Moya 2017). The postcolonial urban landscape embodies these legacies, where communities of color direct resistant capital toward the transformation of unequal conditions within and beyond schooling environments (Yosso 2005).

Epistemology: postcolonial geographies and decolonial hacking through a pedagogical theory of *Calle*

In our course, *Urban Geography and Critical Higher Education* we framed the university and broadly modernity and its impact on our postcolonial consciousness and imagination, as part of both domination and resistance, and we as scyborgs (la paperson 2017; Dache 2019). Through a Postcolonial Geographic Epistemology (Dache-Gerbino 2017) we mapped quantitative/demographic data collected from the U.S. Census 2015–2019 American Community Survey estimates. We illustrate the locations of where the Philadelphia Hispanic population who also identify as Black reside across the county (Figure 1). These data frame the results of domination, while the sites of resistance were mapped and geocoded as spaces of resistance within the Philadelphia landscape. Our research design is informed by a Postcolonial Geographic Epistemology (Dache-Gerbino 2017), that focuses on the binaries of dominant and subaltern educational experiences/data. The qualitative data in this study are 70 student observations collected through three field research sites and public transit riding from these sites to colleges and universities across the county that took place over four weeks. We used a theory of *Calle* and saw our field exploration as a decolonial pedagogical approach to geographic research.

As scyborgs, we recognize that we were part of the colonial machine and also its malfunction (Dache 2019a). The class consisted of an AfroLatina professor and 14 undergraduate and graduate students (Table 1), of which 76% of students were of color. In addition, the course was based on a previous course that explored Ferguson, Missouri as a site of resistance and the discourses of college accessibility in greater St. Louis (Dache-Gerbino et al. 2019). Using geography courses as sites for both teaching and research inform the foundation of this study (Melik and Ernste 2019). Throughout the semester, students in the course engaged in field site observations, traveling to and from Black and Latinx neighborhoods to learn of the college access discourses of Black and Latinx residents. Central to study were the three historical and contemporary sites of resistance in Philadelphia: The MOVE Bombing Historical Marker (West

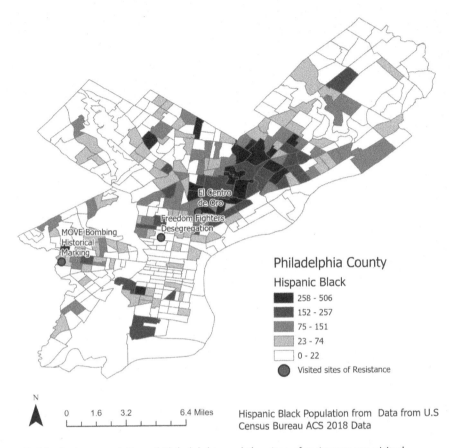

Figure 1. Afro-Latinx population of Philadelphia and the sites of resistance we visited.

Table 1. Student demographics of the *Urban Geography and Critical Higher Education* course.

Student name	Race/Ethnic identification	Gender	Student classification
Serena	Black/African American	F	Graduate student
Darien	Black/African American	M	Graduate student
Jennifer	Asian American	F	Graduate student
Yolanda	Black	F	Undergraduate student
Annette	Black	F	Graduate student
Danielle	Black	F	Graduate student
Rosie	White & Asian	F	Graduate student
Sasha	Black	F	Graduate student
Carlos	Black	M	Graduate student
Mitch	White/Caucasian	M	Graduate student
Marcia	White/Caucasian	F	Graduate student
Melissa	White/Caucasian	F	Undergraduate student
Itiotia	American Indian or Alaska Native	F	Graduate student

Philadelphia), El Centro de Oro (North Philadelphia), and Freedom Fighters Desegregation Site at Girard College (North Philadelphia). We read and engaged postcolonial scholarship and research within and outside the field of education (e.g. Dache-Gerbino et al. 2019) as entry points during the first four weeks of the semester prior to engaging in 4 weeks of field research.

Conceptual framework

With the sites in mind, we use Dache's (2019) theoretical framework within broader understandings of modernity and university classroom teaching as areas that can function as 'beyond-reform' spaces (de Oliveira Andreotti et al. 2015, 25). "*Calle* is a working-class Afro-Latinx form of capital that emerges from residing in urban areas that are sites for both resistance and domination. Areas that – while suffering from urban decline, segregation, underfunded education systems, and neoliberal municipal policy failures … are predominantly working-class with high concentrations of Black, Latinx, or immigrant people of Caribbean or Latin American descent" (Dache 2019, 1096). *Calle* acknowledges racial and spatial oppression, while honoring the steps Black and Latinx residential communities take to resist forms of domination. Through strategic pedagogical choices, such as learning resistant local histories by being physically present in these spaces, we reject that *higher* learning in college and universities are the only way forward.

Through a theory of *Calle*, which translates closely to 'street,' Dache (2019) gained the resilience necessary to resist 'a cultural supremacy of whiteness' (1094) cultivated in urban areas. This sense of resistance transcends place because it recognizes the connectedness and variety of Black diaspora experiences throughout the trans-Atlantic world (1094). Afro&/-Latinx people learn how to navigate systems of oppression and blend life in multiple geographies, embodying resistance and perseverance. Dache (2019) acknowledges the realities of urban decline and underfunded education systems, but, through a decolonial lens, affirms the value of *Calle*.

In this regard, decoloniality is 'neither a "field of study" nor a "discipline" but a way of being in the world, interrogating the structures of knowledge and knowing that have thrown us … .' (Mignolo 2018, 381). Decoloniality goes beyond decolonizing space – decoloniality is not about eradicating settlers so 'natives might build their own nation-state but, rather … to change the terms (assumptions and rules) of the conversation' (Mignolo 2018, 380). As a decolonial theory, *Calle* does this by emphasizing the community's cultural capital, and, therefore, challenging the 'assumptions and rules' of Western society and education (Mignolo 2018, 380). Communities leverage aspirational, linguistic, familial, navigational, and resistant capital to form community cultural wealth (Yosso 2005). Black, Latinx, and Afro-Latinx communities maintain hope for a reimagined future within a system that actively disregards their presence.

Studying sites of resistance in Philadelphia, we engaged in decolonial 'system hacking,' 'creating spaces within the system, using its resources, where people can be educated about the violences of the system and have their desires re-oriented away from it' (de Oliveira Andreotti et al. 2015, 27). System hacking involves '"playing the game" of institutions at the same time that rules are bent to generate alternative outcomes' (de Oliveira Andreotti et al. 2015, 27). Studying sites of resistance in Philadelphia was a form of decolonial hacking since we learned of the violence of modernity in Philadelphia through being present in the spaces where the violence took place. By studying these sites, we understood learning and knowledge as both sensorial and cognitive (Flockemann 2020) – a link between what was taught and what individual students experienced during their observations as collective responses to 'modernity's myriad oppression … as interlinked' (27).

Through course design, Philadelphia's Black, Latinx, and Afro-Latinx history and environments were centered, turning the city into a classroom. This allowed us to philosophize as we walked the streets of Philadelphia, rejecting the four walls of the classroom space as static in our learning toward decolonial imaginaries. University resources funded student travel for observational data collection, while postcolonial thought and course readings were used to interrogate the invisibility of urban community spaces within higher education curriculum and scholarship.

Findings and interpretations

Sensorial and cognitive experiences

Exiting the classroom enabled us to experience 'affective' encounters with the research sites–our bodies were able to precede our minds in reacting to the environment (Flockemann 2020). This led to sensorial responses followed by cognitive ones. The power of affective environments in decolonial pedagogy is the shifting of power in university classrooms from solely cognitive to sensorial *and* cognitive. Through reflection and observation, affective environments give 'voice' to the bodily reactions people experience in response to particular people, places, and moments (Flockemann 2020, 293). In the context of our course, these reactions helped capture not only what we thought about the visits to the MOVE Bombing Historical Marker site, the Freedom Fighters Desegregation Site, and El Centro de Oro from a critical, cognitive lens, but also how we *experienced* the site visits from a sensorial perspective. Our findings from each site reflect this common weave between sensorial and cognitive learning that is important to reimagining classrooms and decolonial learning.

MOVE bombing historical marker

On the surface, Osage Avenue, located in the heart of West Philadelphia, is an unassuming street. Our class walked several blocks, passing dozens of homes, to get there. Unlike other blocks, there were construction bins lining the street and contractors fixing homes. An unaware visitor might assume this block was undergoing renovations, but with the context we gained from course materials, we were aware of the real reason construction bins lined a block that used to look like the ones surrounding it. On Osage Avenue in1985, a Pennsylvania State Police helicopter bombed the house of MOVE activists, destroying 61 homes and killing eleven MOVE members and five children. Neighbors complained over an extended period of time about MOVE's actions, which included cursing over loudspeakers, leaving raw and rotting meat outside, placing trash on others' property, and threatening violence (Massiah 1986). When police entered the space, they horrifically escalated the conflict, demonstrating their disregard for Black life. One of the only public signs of the MOVE Bombing today is a historical marker removed from the block, which is now hard to access due to the lack of a crosswalk (Figure 2).

One student commented:

> Busy street on the other end of the block and no crosswalks, hard to cross to the memorial plaque (Melissa).

The marker is not only physically distant from the block, but its language is distant from the bombing itself. While reflecting on the marker, another stated:

> To say that an 'uncontrolled fire' killed MOVE members seems to elide state responsibility, suggesting happenstance without perpetrators, when indeed, it was the state that committed an act of violence against its own residents (Jennifer).

Still, it is worth noting that the marker would not exist in the first place without the tireless efforts of a group of 5th and 6th grade Jubilee School students in Philadelphia who researched the MOVE bombing and advocated for its proper recognition in the city (Malek 2017).

Figure 2. The MOVE Bombing Marker, across the street from where the bombing occured in West Philadelphia.

Not only was historical violence considered by our class, but also modern violence. Using a decolonial framework in our course, our reflections questioned, what de Oliveira Andreotti et al. (2015) call, 'modernity.' 'Modernity's "shine" is articulated in ways that hide its shadow, or the fact that the very existence of the shiny side requires the imposition of systematic violence on others' (de Oliveira Andreotti et al. 2015, 23). In the case of Osage Avenue, someone visiting the block today, completely unfamiliar with the state sanctioned violence that happened there in 1985, could believe the new townhomes were a sign of 'progress' instead of a sign of violence and the city's negligence to heal the violent wounds it opened.

Coming from University City, we could see gentrification further west, but on Osage Avenue, most signs of University City seemed far away. Even still, we knew Osage Avenue was threatened by modernity. When we arrived, students reflected on modernity's violence:

> The street near MOVE seems to be renovated by realtors. The closer we got to the street; I noticed more real estate posters advertising purchasing homes for cash. The renovated homes and older non-renovated homes had a clear divide in physical space (Mitch).

While walking down the street, we talked to a doctoral candidate who lives in one of the newly renovated homes. Our conversation with him brought to the forefront some of our thoughts on 'modernity' and gentrification in the neighborhood, as one student said:

> Mr. A discussed beautification versus gentrification, which really stuck with me. He lives in a nice home a few steps from the MOVE house, and in the same neighborhood. Hearing him discuss the prices of housing and pushing out those originating from that area is obviously upsetting. As he stated, there must be more effort to provide nicer quality of housing to black people without it carrying a financial burden (Annette).

Reflecting on what happened on Osage Avenue, by learning about it in class and visiting the site, helped us bridge the past and present while expanding our understanding of resistance and the power of decolonial learning.

Freedom fighters desegregation site

A 10-foot stone wall, equipped with a gated entrance and security office, wraps around Girard College in North Philadelphia. After exiting a Philadelphia bus a few blocks from the school, our class turned a corner and the wall loomed in front of us. (Figure 3) After seeing the wall and gate, one student wrote:

> The gate still separates Girard College from the surrounding community, though it is no longer legally segregated it still feels like it is keeping its students in and keeping the surrounding area out (Danielle).

Girard College was founded by Stephen Girard, a nineteenth century millionaire who amassed his wealth through the slave trade and by stealing from enslaved Africans (Millies 2018). He was a shipowner and banker who exploited Haiti en route to becoming the richest man in the United States until his death in 1831 (Millies 2018). He used money, acquired from the work of enslaved people in Haiti and on his own plantation in Louisiana, to establish Girard College upon bequest (Canton 2020). Girard College,

Figure 3. The wall surrounding Girard College.

founded exclusively for white male orphans, will forever be connected to the Civil Rights Movement's school desegregation efforts. In 1965, a lawyer named Cecil B. Moore began organizing protests with local students and youth activists, known as Freedom Fighters, to desegregate Girard College (Kativa 2021). While Moore fought inside and outside court, the Freedom Fighters endured police brutality on the sidewalks to force the school to desegregate. In spite of the embattled and triumphant struggles of the youth activists and Cecil, the school honors Stephen Girard through statues, instead of them.

For example, outside Girard College's Founders Hall, a statue of Stephen Girard entitled, 'The Spirit of Girard,' features Girard with smiling students of color (Figure 4). Meanwhile, the Freedom Fighters who actually desegregated Girard College, are not memorialized in perpetuity through statue, stone, or mural. When our class visited the school, we spoke with two of the Black women who were 1960s Freedom Fighters, Bernyce and Karen (the latter was only 15 years old when their protest began) (Rybak 2016). They were a part of the 'Young Militants,' also known as 'Cecil's Army,' a group of teenagers who marched for 'seven months and 17 days' in order to desegregate Girard College (Rybak 2016). After our conversation with them, two students reflected:

> Bernyce and Karen mentioned that they are only invited to speak during Black History Month or other special occasions, which indicates to me that the institution is very much concerned with having control over the narrative, even if it means embellishment and erasure (Sasha).

> What if they replaced Stephen Girard with Cecil B. Moore in the front statue? What would it look like if Girard added the names of the freedom fighters to the walls? Or quotes from

Figure 4. 'The Spirit of Girard' statues depicting Stephen Girard with smiling students of color.

leaders? Or a memorial or mural dedicated to them in the stones, so the walls could 'speak' of the struggle and triumph? What would it look like? What would it mean for the City of Philadelphia? And how would the freedom fighters and non-white students at Girard feel because of it? (Serena).

Statues, building names, and other physical memorials highlight pieces of history. When a person like Stephen Girard, who built his legacy on the backs of enslaved people, is memorialized on campus, it can be seen as a colonial relic. A major movement to decolonize higher education has included the removal of statues, which should extend to primary and secondary schools like Girard College. The removal of Cecil Rhodes' statue at the University of Capetown as a result of the Rhodes Must Fall movement (Chaudhuri 2016) shows the impact decolonizing education can have. It allows for further reflection on institutional racism and demonstrates how 'beyond-reform' practices such as system hacking (de Oliveira Andreotti et al. 2015, 34) can truly transform educational spaces by educating others on the 'violences of the system' and having 'their desires reoriented from it' (27). As the student reflected, replacing Stephen Girard with a Cecil B. Moore statue, adding the names of freedom fighters to the wall, or highlighting quotes from leaders of the Civil Rights Movement could positively alter the relationship between the school, its students, and the surrounding community.

The students in our class were able to reflect and pose questions that push back on the demonstrated historical narrative because of system hacking, the direct actions of our class using university resources to learn from the community. We had sensorial experiences and formulated cognitive interpretations of the Freedom Fighters Desegregation site and its historical context within Philadelphia by being in the space, instead of solely relying on readings and lectures. During our visit, we envisioned transformations of the school that represent a more accurate telling of its history and the *Calle* Moore and the Freedom Fighters relied on.

El Centro De Oro

Vibrant murals, beautifully painted flags, and tall palm trees line the streets of El Centro de Oro, a predominantly Latinx neighborhood in North Philadelphia. It is known as The Golden Block [English translation] because of the rich Latinx history and culture connected to the block and its residents. Our class visited this neighborhood to learn more about its history and how it functions as a site of Latinx resistance in Philadelphia (Figure 5). When we first arrived, students quickly noted the environment from a sensorial perspective and through a *Calle* framework:

> We couldn't have visited El Centro de Oro on a more perfect day. Although it was extremely windy and cold, the sun was out and blue skies followed us the entire trip. We took the Market Frankford Line and then took the bus the rest of the way. When we arrived, I immediately noticed the beautiful mural of Latin American flags, the palm trees, and the golden roads. The HACE center was right across the street, and we met Harry Tapia who shared valuable information with us (Itiotia).

Figure 5. West Lehigh Avenue, main street of the El Centro de Oro neighborhood.

Harry Tapia, Director of Operations at the Hispanic Association of Contractors and Enterprises (HACE), (HACE 2020) gave us a tour of the organization's office, spoke about El Centro de Oro's history, and explained the purpose of HACE. The community struggled during the 1980s economic recession resulting in business closures, housing issues, and a drug epidemic (Mandell 2020). Latinx residents formed local grassroots organizations, including HACE, to combat the social and economic inequities they faced (Mandell 2020). At times of greatest need in the community, residents assist each other and make themselves heard amongst city government agencies and politicians who can support their efforts. Harry mentioned to the group that:

> Residents protest through HACE to keep the city accountable about crime, lack of resources and affordable housing, and drug problems in the neighborhood. The Conrail Line, used for moving hazardous materials, crossed through this neighborhood for many years and created spaces for buying and using drugs. HACE worked with the city to get the line shut down (Darien).

The community, in partnership with HACE, pushes back against the 'neoliberal municipal policy failures', and the exploitative and racist systems that significantly harm their neighborhood (Dache 2019, 1096). We were able to draw on our knowledge from class readings and connect them with our 'new' or experiential knowledge (Flockemann 2020) by visiting the neighborhood and learning from the HACE staff.

In addition to researching the three sites of resistance, our class navigated public transportation from the three sites to different universities around the city. After completing our trip to El Centro de Oro, one student traveled to a private university in Philadelphia via public transportation. She commuted for two hours from El Centro de Oro to the university located north of Fairmount Park. During her commute, she noticed 'brick bridges, a river, so many trees' and businesses, such as Saks Fifth Avenue and Hilton Hotels. Once she arrived, she noted the 'beautiful campus [which included] ample space, a huge tennis court, brick entrances, quiet, calm, and lots of grass space.' As the student made her way back home, she wrote the following observation:

> I stayed on the 60 to Kensington so that I could catch the MFL back to University City. I was heartbroken by what I saw there. I was still on observation mode and my mind was racing, looking for answers and thinking about what I could do to help. There wasn't a single sober person in sight and those who weren't blatantly high, were anxious and irritable. I had heard of the opioid epidemic, but seeing it first-hand was something else. A man got high on the seat right behind me and I saw him trip out until I made it to 40th street station. I got home and researched the epidemic for hours (Itiotia).

Notably, this is in stark contrast to the student's observation en route to the university. Following the visit, the student spent hours researching the epidemic, a learning moment that might not have occurred if the course remained inside the classroom.

Discussion and conclusion

In this study we applied *Calle* in an urban university classroom in Philadelphia, and used it as a tool to hack the university and modernity (Dache 2019; de Oliveira Andreotti et al. 2015), by centering the diasporic, the external and the racially marginal. Data revealed how our sensorial and cognitive experiences from being in the three sites, allowed us to forge deeper connections with past and present forms of resistance. *Calle* rejects the notion that Western ways of knowing are the most valuable, and changes the terms of colonial learning assumptions that center an authority figure as teacher (Mignolo 2018). The racial and social transformation process that happens in residential communities that are rich in neighborhood histories and educational institutions make them resistant and locally sustainable. de Oliveira Andreotti et al. (2015) caution against the ways system hacking can lead to 'vanguardist heroism that inadvertently recenters individuals' (28) and through collective observational data, our bodies and minds were at once a challenge to traditional higher learning. Western education assumes individual knowledge gain and 'bureaucratic' structures of learning and credentialing legitimize learning (Woolsey Des Jarlais 2009, 9–10), yet it was the learning outside of the university that pushed us to ask questions that while may not have answers, reverberate beyond the echo chambers of the academy.

Teaching and learning from our immediate environment provided a **reality** to the articles and books that we read inside the classroom. The data reveal sensorial and cognitive experiences that embody the different ways that history can be told (Flockemann 2020), allowing us to contextualize our academic coursework, adding value to the historical knowledge of Philadelphia's communities of color. Seen in the observation below, this reality fueled an energy for social justice and motivated students to work towards change.

> Being new to the city, I heard plenty of things. Taking your class and piecing things together, hearing Harry Tapia (HACE Director of Operations) talk about safe injection sites, and reading articles about this epidemic, I think is a part of everything we are talking about in class and social justice … It was a part of my personal observation and I thank you for teaching a class that goes extremely beyond the classroom walls and pushes us to question our environment and our positionality.
>
> Yesterday turned out to be eye-opening and important to me and I know I am going to continue growing from here. (Itiotia)

By incorporating an epistemology that recognizes the results of domination through quantitative data (Figure 1), while using qualitative data from field observations to photos, Black and Latinx external environments/spaces were explored as sites of knowledge. Our course created space for a new body of academic research that is racially and culturally inclusive evidence of our sensorial and cognitive reflections. We used the theoretical framework of *Calle* as a decolonial hacking tool in order to acknowledge and center the cultural capital and histories of the communities we visited. Residential communities surrounding universities are often older than the universities themselves, and as such, the communities inhabiting said lands contain the primordial knowledge of the land.

Concluding and continuing

Our commitment to decolonial hacking involved disrupting the university's logics, which constrain learning to classroom walls, while ignoring structural power relations. Being physically present at the MOVE bombing historical marker site allowed us to see and feel the consequences of racial and spatial oppression. This same feeling led Jubilee school students to pay respect to a community and organization's legacy that might have been lost (Owens 2017). The Jubilee school applied *Calle* to transpose their classroom teaching into a form of liberation that evoked community activism, centering their identities and the lived experience of Black residents (Dache 2019) in the Cobbs Creek region. Though Jubilee students learned about MOVE in the classroom, their work within the community positions the MOVE historical marker as an active space of engagement – memorializing the lives and legacies lost. Traveling outside the academy allowed university students to experience and feel how the memorialization of MOVE has residues of coloniality.

Curricular structures in the U.S. education system do not traditionally highlight *Calle* as a form of capital for Black, Latinx, and Afro-Latinx communities, neglecting this valuable source of knowledge. Our class learned about the Freedom Fighters Desegregation site at Girard College as a site of resistance through literature and visited to learn from voices at the school. We saw Girard College's present statues and relics, but more importantly reflected on what was absent from campus. Modernity (de Oliveira Andreotti et al. 2015) promotes 'progress' at the expense of marginalized communities. We noticed how modernity functions at Girard College to diminish the impact of neighborhood activists, like Bernyce and Karen. As educators employ decolonial hacking in teaching and learning practices, centering community-based efforts allows students to connect the impact of *Calle* on a community's past and present.

North of the Freedom Fighters Desegregation Site, El Centro De Oro served as a site of resistance and a site of cultural growth for Latinx residents. It is also the city geography with the highest concentration of Latinxs who also identify as Black (see Figure 1). Decades later, the Taller Puertorriqueño within El Centro remains a prominent space of Afro-Latinx education (read: Arturo Schomburg Symposium), and organizations like HACE have become invaluable sites for learning and teaching. HACE works with Latinx residents to navigate racial and economic oppression in the community, such as gentrification and housing discrimination. Through creative expression and community organizations, Afro-Latinx communities in *El Centro* exert their cultural capital to create a *home*[1] space that is tasted, felt, heard, and smelled in this North Philadelphia neighborhood. Dache is continuing this study and is focused on North Philadelphia. By continuing to work with HACE as a community partner – she is engaging affordable housing residents in research exploring their educational experiences across the Philadelphia landscape.

As our course dove into informal and non-traditional methods of learning from Philadelphia's residents and neighborhoods, we centered and valued different mediums of creative expression, while using *Calle* to resist whiteness embedded in normative pedagogical practices. Working together as undergraduate students, graduate students, and faculty in different university programs allowed us to bring different perspectives to the course, but our knowledge was only amplified once we hit the streets.

Note

1. Home is used here to refer to Latin American countries of origin.

Disclosure statement

No potential conflict of interest was reported by the author(s).

References

Ansalone, George. 2006. "Tracking: A Return to Jim Crow." *Race, Gender & Class* 13 (1/2): 144–153. https://www.jstor.org/stable/41675228.

Anzaldúa, Gloria E. 2002. "Now Let us Shift … the Path of Conocimiento … Inner Work, Public Acts." In *This Bridge we Call Home: Radical Visions for Transformation*, edited by Gloria E. Anzaldúa, and AnaLouise Keating, 540–579. New York: Routledge.

Arnau, Ariel. 2012. "The Evolution of Leadership Within the Puerto Rican Community of Philadelphia, 1950–1970s." *The Pennsylvania Magazine of History and Biography* 136 (1): 53–81. doi:10.5215/pennmaghistbio.136.1.0053.

Biddle, Nicholas. 1833. "The Girard College Address." *Journal of the Franklin Institute* 16 (4): 228–232. doi:10.1016/S0016-0032(33)90251-3.

Canton, David A. 2020. "Girard College." *The Encyclopedia of Greater Philadelphia*. Accessed May 5, 2020. https://philadelphiaencyclopedia.org/archive/girard-college/#:~:text=Opened%20in%201848%2C%20Girard%20College,but%20only%20for%20white%20boys.

Chaudhuri, Amit. 2016. "The Real Meaning of Rhodes Must Fall." *The Guardian*, March 16. Accessed December 21, 2020. https://www.theguardian.com/uk-news/2016/mar/16/the-real-meaning-of-rhodes-must-fall.

Dache-Gerbino, A. 2017. "Mapping the Postcolonial Across Urban and Suburban College Access Geographies." *Equity & Excellence in Education* 50 (4): 368–386. doi:10.1080/10665684.2017.1393639.

Dache-Gerbino, A., D. Aguayo, M. Griffin, S. L. Hairston, C. Hamilton, C. Krause, and H. Sweeney. 2019. "Re-imagined Post-Colonial Geographies: Graduate Students Explore Spaces of Resistance in the Wake of Ferguson." *Research in Education* 104 (1): 3–23.

Dache, A. 2019a. "Ferguson's Black Radical Imagination and the Scyborgs of Community-Student Resistance." *The Review of Higher Education* 42: 63–84.

Dache, A. 2019b. "Teaching a Transnational Ethic of Black Lives Matter: An AfroCuban Americana's Theory of Calle." *International Journal of Qualitative Studies in Education* 32 (9): 1094–1107. doi:10.1080/09518398.2019.1645906.

de la Fuente, Alejandro, and George R. Andrews. 2018. "The Making of a Field: Afro-Latin American Studies." In *Afro-Latin American Studies: An Introduction*, edited by Alejandro de la Fuente, and George R. Andrews. Cambridge: Cambridge University Press. doi:10.1017/9781316822883.

de Oliveira Andreotti, Vanessa, Sharon Stein, Cash Ahenakew, and Dallas Hunt. 2015. "Mapping Interpretations of Decolonization in the Context of Higher Education." *Decolonization: Indigeneity, Education & Society* 4 (1): 21–40.

District Performance Office. 2020. "District Enrollment & Demographics." https://www.philasd.org/performance/programsservices/open-data/school-information/#district_enrollment.

Du Bois, W. E. B. 1896. *The Suppression of the African Slave Trade to the United States of America, 1638–1870.* New York: Kraus-Thomas.

Du Bois, W. E. B. 1899. *The Philadelphia Negro: A Social Study.* Philadelphia: Ginn.

Du Bois, W. E. B. 1939. *Black Folk, Then and Now: An Essay in the History and Sociology of the Negro Race.* New York: Henry Holt.

Flockemann, Miki. 2020. "'Connecting Mind to Pen, to Eyes, to Face, to Arms and Legs': Toward a Performative and Decolonial Teaching Practice." *Cambridge Journal of Postcolonial Literary Inquiry* 7 (3): 286–296. doi:10.1017/pli.2020.8.

Flores, Juan, and Miriam Jiménez Román. 2009. "Triple-consciousness? Approaches to Afro-Latino Culture in the United States." *Latin American and Caribbean Ethnic Studies* 4 (3): 319–328. doi:10.1080/17442220903331662.

Floyd-Thomas, J. M. 2002. "The Burning of Rebellious Thoughts: MOVE as Revolutionary Black Humanism." *The Black Scholar* 32 (1): 11–21. http://www.jstor.org/stable/41068961.

Franklin, V. P. 2002. "Introduction: Cultural Capital and African American Education." *The Journal of African American History* 87: 175–181. http://www.jstor.org/stable/1562461.

Freire, Paulo. 1973. *Education for Critical Consciousness.* New York: Seabury Press.

García-Louis, Claudia. 2016. "Beyond Multiracialism: Acknowledging AfroLatina/o Students." *Journal of Student Affairs in Higher Education* 25: 21–27.

García-Louis, Claudia. 2018. "Ni Latino, Ni Negro: The (In) Visibility of Afro Latino Males in Higher Education Research." *Journal Committed to Social Change on Race and Ethnicity* 4 (1): 97–122.

Ginwright, Shawn A. 2007. "Black Youth Activism and the Role of Critical Social Capital in Black Community Organizations." *American Behavioral Scientist* 51 (3): 403–418. doi:10.1177/0002764207306068.

HACE. 2020. "HACE CDC." Accessed May 5, 2020. https://www.hacecdc.org/.

Harper, Shaun R., Lori D. Patton, and Ontario S. Wooden. 2009. "Access and Equity for African American Students in Higher Education: A Critical Race Historical Analysis of Policy Efforts." *The Journal of Higher Education* 80 (4): 389–414. http://www.jstor.org/stable/25511120.

Harry, Margot. 1987. "Attention MOVE! This is America!" *Race & Class* 28 (4): 5–28. doi:10.1177/030639688702800402.

Haywood, Jasmine M. 2017. "'Latino Spaces Have Always Been the Most Violent': Afro-Latino Collegians' Perceptions of Colorism and Latino Intragroup Marginalization." *International Journal of Qualitative Studies in Education* 30 (8): 759–782. doi:10.1080/09518398.2017.1350298.

Hooker, Juliet. 2017. *Theorizing Race in the Americas: Douglass, Sarmiento, Du Bois, and Vasconcelos.* New York: Oxford University Press. doi:10.1093/acprof:oso/9780190633691.003.0004.

Inwood, Joshua F., and Robert A. Yarbrough. 2010. "Racialized Places, Racialized Bodies: The Impact of Racialization on Individual and Place Identities." *GeoJournal* 75 (3): 299–301. doi:10.1007/s10708-009-9308-3.

Jack, James, and John Sludden. 2013. "School Closings in Philadelphia." *Penn GSE Perspectives on Urban Education* 10 (1): 1–7. https://eric.ed.gov/?id=EJ1015745.

Kativa, Hillary S. 2021. "What: The Desegregation of Girard College." *Temple University Libraries.* Accessed January 12, 2021. http://northerncity.library.temple.edu/exhibits/show/civil-rights-in-a-northern-cit/collections/desegregation-of-girard-colleg/what-interpretative-essay.

Krogstad, Jens Manuel. 2016. "5 Facts About Latinos and Education." *Pew Research Center*, July 28. Accessed March 23, 2021. https://www.pewresearch.org/fact-tank/2016/07/28/5-facts-about-latinos-and-education/.

la paperson. 2017. *A Third University is Possible.* Minneapolis: University of Minnesota Press. doi:10.5749/9781452958460.

Laurent-Perrault, Evelyn. 2010. "Invoking Arturo Schomburg's Legacy in Philadelphia." In *The AfroLatin@ Reader: History and Culture in the United States*, edited by Miriam Jimenez, and Juan Flores, 92–99. Durham: Duke University Press.

López, Gustavo, and Ana Gonzalez-Barrera. 2016. "Afro-Latino: A Deeply Rooted Identity among U.S. Hispanics." *Pew Research Center*, March 1. Accessed March 23, 2021. https://www.pewresearch.org/fact-tank/2016/03/01/afro-latino-a-deeply-rooted-identity-among-u-s-hispanics/.

Malek, Paulina. 2017. "Historical Marker Unveiled at MOVE Bombing Headquarters." *University City Review*, July 5. http://ucreview.com/historical-marker-unveiled-at-move-bombing-headquarters-p7382-1.htm.

Mandell, Melissa. 2020. "El Centro de Oro - The 'Golden Block'." *PhilaPlace.* Accessed April 26, 2020. http://www.philaplace.org/story/329/.

Massiah, Louis. 1986. *The Bombing of Osage Avenue.* Philadelphia, PA: Scribe Video Center. https://www.pbs.org/video/whyy-specials-bombing-osage-avenue-1986/.

Melik, Rianne Van, and Huib Ernste. 2019. "'Looking with Intention': Using Photographic Essays as Didactical Tool to Explore Berlin." *Journal of Geography in Higher Education* 43 (4): 431–451. doi:10.1080/03098265.2019.1660864.

Mignolo, Walter D. 2018. "Decoloniality and Phenomenology: The Geopolitics of Knowing and Epistemic/Ontological Colonial Differences." *The Journal of Speculative Philosophy* 32 (3): 360–387. doi:10.5325/jspecphil.32.3.0360.

Millies, Stephen. 2018. "How Haiti Helped Build Philadelphia." *Workers World*, January 21. https://www.workers.org/2018/01/35178/#:~:text=Haiti%20also%20helped%20build%20Phila delphia,countries%20while%20exploiting%20sailors%20mercilessly.

Montoya, Margaret E. 1994. "Mascaras, trenzas, y grenas: Un/Masking the Self While un/Braiding Latina Stories and Legal Discourse." *Chicano-Latino Law Review* 15 (1): 185–220.

Moya, Jesse. 2017. "Examining How Youth Take on Critical Civic Identities Across Classroom and Youth Organizing Spaces." *Critical Questions in Education* 8 (4): 457–475. https://eric.ed.gov/?id=EJ1159309.

Orfield, Gary. 2013. "Housing Segregation Produces Unequal Schools." In *Closing the Opportunity Gap: What America Must do to Give Every Child an Even Chance*, edited by Prudence L. Carter, and Kevin G. Welner, 40–61. Oxford: Oxford University Press.

Otero, Solimar. 2007. "BARRIO, BODEGA, AND BOTANICA AESTHETICS: The Layered Traditions of the Latino Imaginary." *Atlantic Studies* 4 (2): 173–194. doi:10.1080/14788810701510894.

Owens, Cassie. 2017. "Why Philly's MOVE Bombing Historical Marker is Only Temporary." *Billy Penn*, June 23. Accessed December 30, 2020. https://billypenn.com/2017/06/23/why-phillys-move-bombing-historical-marker-is-only-temporary/.

Philadelphia Research and Policy Initiative. 2011. "A City Transformed: The Racial and Ethnic Changes in Philadelphia Over the last 20 Years." *Pew Charitable Trusts*. https://www.pewtrusts.org/~/media/legacy/uploadedfiles/wwwpewtrustsorg/reports/philadelphia_research_initiative/PhiladelphiaPopulationEthnicChangespdf.pdf.

Phillips, Anne E. 2005. "A History of the Struggle for School Desegregation in Philadelphia, 1955–1967." *Pennsylvania History: A Journal of Mid-Atlantic Studies* 72 (1): 49–76. http://www.jstor.org/stable/27778658.

Rosa, Jonathan, and Nelson Flores. 2017. "Unsettling Race and Language: Toward a Raciolinguistic Perspective." *Language in Society* 46 (5): 621–647. doi:10.1017/S0047404517000562.

Rybak, Sue. 2016. "Women Recall 1960s Protests to Desegregate Girard College." *Chestnut Hill Local*, February 10. https://www.chestnuthilllocal.com/stories/women-recall-1960s-protests-to-desegregate-girard-college,8038.

Sanders, Kimberly, and Judson L. Jeffries. 2013. "'Framing MOVE: A Press' Complicity in the Murder of Women and Children in the City of (un) Brotherly Love." *Journal of African American Studies* 17 (4): 566–586. http://www.jstor.org/stable/43525528.

Sansone, L. 2003. *Blackness Without Ethnicity: Constructing Race in Brazil*. New York: Palgrave MacMillan.

Taller Puertorriqueño. 2021. "About us (Sobre nosotros)." Accessed May 5, 2020. https://tallerpr.org/about/.

Tamir, Christine. 2021. "The Growing Diversity of Black America." *Pew Research Center*, March 25. Accessed March 23, 2021. https://www.pewresearch.org/social-trends/2021/03/25/the-growing-diversity-of-black-america/.

Tanz, Ashley, and Ebru Erdem-Akcay. 2020. "From Ninth Grade on-Track to College Matriculation: The Path of the 2015-16 SDP Ninth-Grade Cohort." *School District of Philadelphia, Office of Research and Evaluation*. https://www.philasd.org/research/2020/06/04/from-ninth-grade-on-track-to-college-matriculation-the-path-of-the-2015-16-sdp-ninth-grade-cohort/.

Tanz, Ashley, and Ji Eun Park. 2020. "Summer Melt: College Intentions vs. College Enrollment of SDP Seniors (2016-17 through 2018-19)." School District of Philadelphia, Office of Research and Evaluation. https://www.philasd.org/research/2020/10/21/summer-melt-college-intentions-vs-college-enrollment-of-sdp-seniors-2016-17-through-2018-19/.

Tanz, Ashley, Molly Schlesinger, and Allison Smith. 2020. "Demographic Enrollment Trends and School Progress Report (SPR) Performance from 2014-15 to 2018-19." *School District of Philadelphia, Office of Research and Evaluation*. https://www.philasd.org/research/wp-content/uploads/sites/90/2020/09/SPR_Demographic_Enrollment_Trends_Report_September_2020.pdf.

Woolsey Des Jarlais, Cheryl L. 2009. "Cultural Characteristics of Western Educational Structures and Their Effects on Local Ways of Knowing." *Graduate Student Theses, Dissertations, & Professional Papers.* https://scholarworks.umt.edu/etd/1301.

Yosso, Tara J. 2005. "Whose Culture has Capital? A Critical Race Theory Discussion of Community Cultural Wealth." *Race Ethnicity and Education* 8 (1): 69–91. doi:10.1080/1361332052000341006.

Distilling pedagogies of critical water studies

Sheeva Sabati 🆔, Linnea Beckett 🆔, Kira Cragun-Rehders, Alyssa Najera, Katerina Hise and Anna Geiger

ABSTRACT
Writing as both instructors and students who worked together in the undergraduate course *Water Justice*, we reflect on the limits and possibilities of engaging in anticolonial teaching-learning practices within the ongoing contexts of settler colonialism and racial violence that shapes universities. We describe how we designed *Water Justice* as a place-based, anticolonial research collaboration, and focus on how students grappled with the substantive and affective dimensions of their (un)learning process. Together, we illustrate the tensions and possibilities of anticolonial approaches to undergraduate education.

Introduction

What is water? This seemingly simple question, which opened the undergraduate course, *Water Justice: Global Insights for a Critical Resource*, was a lot easier to answer at the start of the class, according to one student. Rather than providing a singular response, we engaged this question as an entry point to surface a broader constellation of often implicit assumptions about research and water itself. For example, how do our disciplinary perspectives and epistemological frameworks inform how we come to know water? How might our positionalities figure into these processes of meaning making?

Water Justice operated from the premise that in order to study water injustice, we had to complicate our assumptions about Western knowledge production and how we 'know' water itself. Our class centered decolonial feminist critiques of the over-representation of Western science as universal truth (Tuhiwai Smith 2012; Watts 2013), making connections to how these epistemologies narrowly frame water as merely a molecule or a resource (Linton 2010; Linton and Budds 2014). We considered histories of irrigation and agricultural development in the western U.S. as tools of settler colonialism and empire (Worster 1985). Learning from Indigenous scholars' framings of the colonial climate crisis (Estes 2017; Sherwood 2019; Todd 2017; Whyte 2017), we also critically interrogated contemporary policy initiatives in California that aim to manage severely depleted groundwater aquifers through data collection and monitoring.[1]

This paper is an invitation to think with and beyond the substantive interventions of the *Water Justice* class towards the role of pedagogy within anticolonial educational praxis. Following the important insight that decolonization must always be connected to material practices of land rematriation to Indigenous Nations (Patel 2016; Tuck and Yang 2012), we frame *Water Justice* as an example of an anticolonial (not decolonial) teaching-learning space.[2] We argue that anticolonial curricular interventions are not merely intellectual exercises, but are also fundamentally relational, affective, and situated processes. That is, our pedagogies – how we enact the values that we teach and facilitate sense-making in relation to our own identities and lives – are essential to anticolonial praxis. Challenging the supremacy of coloniality/modernity requires that we not only deeply re-envision our curriculum (Luckett, Hayes, and Stein, forthcoming) but also our engagements as learners and educators through concrete connections to our lives.

The discussion we develop in this paper is two-fold. First, we describe the design of *Water Justice*, which was developed to articulate with the methodology of the campus-based Apprenticeship in Community Engaged Research or (H)ACER program, and in support of an international research collaboration, Transformations to Groundwater Sustainability (T2GS).[3] We explain how the class supported students to think and engage as researchers, including as co-authors of this paper.

Second, we uplift students' characterizations of their experiences in the class, providing texture to the salient analytical shifts and affective dimensions they described when reflecting on their learning process.[4] We focus on three themes that emerged from students' reflections, including: (1) the process of unsettling Western epistemologies as universal ways of knowing, (2) how questions of positionality and place shaped students' learning experiences, and (3) the types of emotional labor and relationships that supported students to *unlearn.* We conclude by highlighting the ongoing tensions of engaging in anticolonial praxis within racial-colonial institutions (Wilder 2013), including public land 'grant' universities (Stein 2017). This contradiction was punctuated during the winter course in which students witnessed the campus administration's militarized response to a graduate student wildcat strike (Karlis 2020).

Our discussion centers students' reflections to show how unsettling coloniality requires reflexivity – an engagement not solely focused on abstracted content, but connected to our own lives. Even while Western universities are invested in upholding the architecture of coloniality/modernity, we believe it is important to uplift the mundane, yet important possibilities of collective processes of study through 'third spaces' (la paperson 2017). The fraught contexts of the colonial institutions within which we work do not diminish the internal and relational resistances that allow us to express ourselves beyond the hegemon (Beckett 2020; Lugones 2003). Our intention is to add texture to anticolonial praxis and share insights with undergraduate educators.

Developing a place-based anticolonial research collaborative in the undergraduate classroom

Research as pedagogy: our methodology for the course

As instructors, we developed *Water Justice* to substantively focus on emergent strands of our Transformations to Groundwater Sustainability (T2GS) research project, while also utilizing the methodology of the (H)ACER Program. (H)ACER trains and supports undergraduates to participate in hands-on research opportunities at the University of California, Santa Cruz, a large public research university.[5] The (H)ACER Program is also the institutional node for the California T2GS research team, an international collaboration which emphasizes the role of grassroots knowledges in practices of groundwater governance, use, and sustainability. As such, instructors connected the undergraduates with T2GS as collaborators and researchers through the class. Students interviewed T2GS scholars to learn more about the distinct interdisciplinary approaches of different team members and to make connections across our research sites, globally.

The design and pedagogy of *Water Justice* mirrored (H)ACER's methodology of research as pedagogy with a focus on student inquiry, collective study and hands-on research training. We recognize undergraduates rarely have opportunities to engage as active knowledge producers in research endeavors, even at public research universities. *Water Justice* was designed to scaffold this possibility, while also supporting students to think critically about research processes and knowledge itself. All students in the class learned about developing semi-structured interview protocols, conducting interviews, and interviewed water scholars from the T2GS international collaboration. They also completed our institutional research ethics compliance training, which was supplemented with discussions about the ethics of research from decolonial feminist frameworks to push beyond the limited notions of research ethics that are codified through the IRB (Sabati 2018). Students in the class also transcribed portions of the interviews that they conducted with the T2GS scholars and conducted analytic summaries, drawing from their engagement with the course readings and the scholars' research.[6]

Developing anticolonial dispositions: an overview of the class

Water Justice examined environmental damage, drought, and inequity by unpacking the relationship between settler colonialism, racial capitalism, sustainability, and unequal access to water. The class was built upon the thesis that environmental issues generally, and water scarcity specifically, cannot be studied, managed, or addressed as merely abstract 'scientific' problems (Linton 2010), nor can they be solved by techno-fixes. The class was also designed to reflect the importance of the specificity of the knowledges we utilize to ask research questions, and how we are located in relation to the places and issues we study. Drawing from Tuck and McKenzie (2014), we considered place-based inquiry as a method to 'understand places as themselves mobile, shifting over time and space and through interactions with flows of people, other species, social practice' (19). We enacted this method, foregrounding Indigenous and decolonial frameworks to render the contemporary California water crisis as one that is upheld through settler colonial institutions, knowledge systems, and practices.[7]

Firstly, our class focused on California as the geographic context where we live, study, and where many of us have spent the majority of our lives. Importantly, California is also a national agricultural hub, one that has gained global economic status through the capacity to make land 'productive' through engineering feats and hydraulic maneuvers (Arax 2020; Reisner 2017). At the same time, vast economic and environmental inequities are particularly concentrated in low-income, unincorporated, migrant, communities of color across the state who lack access to safe, affordable drinking water and whose labor often underwrites these lucrative agro-economic exports (Pannu 2012). California's model of intensive water extraction has also traveled to places such as the Ica Valley, a desert region turned agro-economic hub or the 'California of Peru' (Oré et al. 2013) as well as regions in Morocco (Swearingen 1987). In short, studying the development of California's hydraulic infrastructure allowed us to track the weaponization of water as a tool of settlement and imperialism, and offered compelling insights for untangling the co-constitutive forces of racial capitalism and Western knowledges within the architecture of coloniality/modernity (Underhill, Beckett, and Sabati, forthcoming).

Secondly, we arranged texts, discussion forums, and assignments for students to layer their existing understandings of California history, natural resources, and their identities into our studies as a class. At the outset of our discussions, instructors asked students to reflect on their upbringing and places that evoked a sense of home to consider how this had shaped their relationships to water and their conceptions of water injustice. Students also reflected on how their understanding of their experiences and the places they called home may have been socially constructed through their schooling or through the assumptions they had acquired over time.

Thirdly, the course was designed to be research-based. Drawing from decolonial methodologies (Tuhiwai Smith 2012), the course readings challenged dominant Western conceptions of research and knowledge production, asking questions such as: What is research? What aspects of the research process are impacted by researchers? How do disciplines *discipline* what counts as knowledge? Who should research benefit? How are the epistemologies that shape research reflective of place and relationships of power? Students grappled with these questions through their written reading reflections and class discussions.

As instructors, we designed assignments to capture students' experiences in the course through weekly synthesis reflections that asked them to make explicit connections across the course texts, discussions, lectures, and learning activities. We encouraged students to pay attention to the affective dimensions of their learning process – how were they reacting to the material? What might these embodied responses teach them? The midterm 'Positionality and Place' essay assignment was both analytical and reflexive. Students engaged the overarching course questions, such as, 'what are the worldviews that emerge from Western epistemologies?' and 'how do these worldviews shape our relationships to water?' They also reflected on their personal connections to water, or what an absence of a relationship to water might mean. The midterm was not solely an academic exercise, but instead asked students to situate themselves in relationship to questions of power and place that threaded across our studies of unequal access to water in the class.

Class composition and dynamics

Students identified California as their primary place of home; 9 out of 11 had lived in California for all of their lives, 1 student moved to California before the age of 6 from Mexico and 1 moved as a teenager from Virginia. As a result, they had been exposed to dominant narratives of water in the settler state, from droughts to floods, or calls for conservation that framed water scarcity as individual rather than structural issues. Despite their distinct social locations, including cultural backgrounds, racialization, and socioeconomic status, students did not need to be convinced that environmental racism factored into questions of water justice.[8] Students in the fall course had training in a variety of majors, including one student each in the following: Electrical Engineering; Environmental Studies, with an emphasis in Agroecology and Sustainable Food Systems; Environmental Studies and Earth Sciences (double major); Psychology; and Literature and Critical Race and Ethnic Studies or CRES (double major). In the winter course, students were CRES and Feminist Studies double majors (two students); CRES and Sociology, CRES and Environmental Studies, Linguistics, and Environmental Studies majors (one student each).[9] As a result, a majority of the winter students had familiarity with anticolonial frameworks, a core feature of CRES classes on our campus. Overall, students' disciplinary training shaped their perceptions of the course and offered differing points of emphasis in each focus group debriefing the class.

The classes foregrounded seminar-style discussions. Student enrollment consisted of only five students in fall quarter and six in winter, a radical shift from the norm for undergraduates at a large, public university.[10] A strong theme in the students' reflections was the impact of class size on the classroom culture that was fostered in support of their learning. This included the absence of a rigid hierarchical structure and instead, a classroom culture that encouraged exploratory thought, raising and engaging questions. As educators, we know that smaller class sizes and active learning spaces offer more robust and meaningful learning experiences for all. The conditions of the learning environment, as well as the relationships they developed with each other, encouraged students to value and investigate the knowledges of other students, the instructor, the texts, and themselves without the hierarchy of 'one truth' that is perpetuated in other classroom contexts.

Methods: situating our collaboration

As co-authors, we write from our distinct vantage points as educators and undergraduate student researchers and draw insights from our positioned perspectives within the teaching-learning process. Sheeva and Linnea are instructors who co-designed and taught the course in fall 2019 and winter 2020 quarters, respectively, while Kira, Anna, Alyssa, and Katerina are undergraduates who were students in the class in one of these two quarters. Students from both quarters were invited to participate in a paid opportunity to work as research assistants with the California T2GS research team since *Water Justice* provided social science research training generally and on decolonial approaches to groundwater sustainability, specifically. Thus, after taking the class, Kira, Anna, Alyssa, and Katerina supported multiple components of the T2GS California research and international collaboration as undergraduate research assistants. Our exploratory study of the *Water Justice* classes is one component of our broader collaboration as the California T2GS research team.

We engaged students' written course assignments as an incomplete archive of their learning process. In order to study the class, we submitted our project to and received approval from our campus Institutional Review Board (IRB) ethics process. Students who consented to the research did so via an opt-in process at the end of the course, selecting the assignments they wanted included in the study after grades had been provided by the instructors. Ten of the total 11 students across both classes submitted all of their assignments to be included in the research and all 11 students consented to participate in the focus groups scheduled at the end of each course.

After the completion of both courses, the instructors anonymized all assignments before we engaged them as a team for our study. The undergraduate research assistants transcribed the focus groups and anonymized the transcripts.[11] We all met on a bi-weekly basis and began our research process by collaboratively selecting and discussing readings on California groundwater governance, indigenous knowledge production, and decolonial perspectives that might complement our T2GS research and our analysis of students' experiences in the class. We then read the students' course papers and the focus group transcripts. Through the process of closely reading students' written materials, and using the selected literature as a guide, we co-developed, revised, and utilized a system of coding based on common themes we identified throughout the student material (Saldaña 2013).

As we moved through the process of analyzing students' experiences, we discussed the tensions involved in coding. This included the potential colonial nature of coding as a method of decontextualizing data through desires to obtain objectivity. This led us to articulate how all research is positioned, and to clarify that our process – first as students and instructors, then as co-researchers – had been guided by decolonial frameworks. Inarguably, this shaped not only the data we analyzed, but also our engagement with it. Informed by feminist frameworks (Harding 1991), we agreed that our task was to make explicit our process, including the frameworks that guided our analysis. Furthermore, we discussed how our goal was not to make causal claims about the course; as an exploratory study, we instead aimed to highlight students' reflections about their learning process. We came to understand coding as an important process and a heuristic for facilitating our engagement with the data and with each other, to discuss our different interpretations and tensions, and to develop overarching, emergent themes.

While we read and analyzed all of the students' assignments that were part of our study, this paper draws solely from the focus groups conducted at the culmination of each class. The quotes that we analyze come out of this coding process and our collaboration to highlight some of the salient themes of the course. Given our involvement with the two courses, both as students and instructors, and our work as collaborators on the T2GS project, we write from a unified voice and analytic framework that is the result of our collective research process. Overall, we aimed to gain more insight into how students made sense of their own learning through their reflections, with the goal of learning from students' descriptions of their own engagement with an anticolonial curriculum.

Engaging anticolonial pedagogies: students making-sense of processes of (un)learning

In this section, we uplift students' reflections about the class, focusing on the salient analytical shifts they highlighted as well as the affective dimensions of these (un)learnings. We surface three emergent themes that came forward in our analysis of the focus group transcripts across both classes, including the challenge and significance of unsettling Western epistemologies as universal; how considerations of positionality supported students' engagement with the course content; and the role of relationships and the intimate classroom culture that created a container for the types of emotional labor – and trust – that was required of students to (un)learn. We also highlight the interconnections of these themes.

Complicating Western science as universal knowledge

> I think a major thing that I can see myself doing is following how we've been analyzing what the dominant thought patterns are with[in] Western scientific knowledge and how that has been created and it's not ... the *only* knowledge and the *only* truth as it's been displayed to me for my whole life. So I've found that in some of my classes my teachers will be like 'Okay, this is what cognition is' and I think to myself that there are more definitions to it and I think that I'm analyzing things [that I learn] more than I had before instead of just accepting that that is what it is ... Like being condensed within this certain framework that, I don't know, basically how settler colonialism involves being shown [an understanding of the world] through just this one view.[12] (Melissa, Fall 2019)

As Melissa highlights, *Water Justice* supported her to trouble the overrepresentation of Western epistemologies and worldviews as universal perspectives through which we understand being and the world (Quijano 2007; Wynter 2003). Melissa seems to use the reflexive praxis of the class to think through how positivism had been central to her learning experiences in formal educational spaces. She also considers how settler colonialism has erased Indigenous and alternative histories. Melissa acknowledges that settler myths had been 'displayed to [her] for [her] whole life,' not only shaping discrete ways of understanding science or history, but cohering a broader worldview.

The intimate design of the class and the significance of the positionality and place essay brought the experiences and knowledges of each student to the forefront as something to be studied and critically examined. In-class discussion questions included, for example, 'how have we learned about science – and thus about research – through solely a Western, positivist framework?' and 'How does this way of thinking about research also produce our subjectivities?' As we studied the role of irrigation in securing white settlement in California, students reflected on how the multi-layered histories of colonialism and anti-Indigenous violence had been erased in their standard California K-12 education, most notably through the mission curriculum.[13] In this way, assignments, such as the positionality and place essay, as well as our ongoing discussions, supported students to ask: how do our framings of what counts as knowledge not only shape what counts as research, but also shape our cosmologies – the ways we make sense of ourselves in the world, our relationship to each other, to systems of power, and to more-than-human beings (Lugones 2015)?

This praxis of engaging students as researchers supported Melissa to critically engage beyond the class and in her primary major, Psychology. By asking what other definitions of 'cognition' exist and 'analyzing things [she learns] more,' Melissa describes a shift from being a passive recipient of knowledge to being actively engaged in the process. Melissa describes a process of looking for more onto-epistemological complexity by way of her experience utilizing anticolonial frameworks to reframe research.

These anticolonial sensibilities towards knowledge production offered some students, such as Sara, tools to speak back on how framings of neutrality within research can actually uphold systematic violence. The course supported Sara in understanding:

> how you can reorient science to challenge colonial narratives and white supremacy. STEM [science, technology, engineering, and math] is able to be very ... it's de-politicizing and STEM is often able to try to remove itself from social consequences of the science and technology [it studies or produces]. This class really made me think about a responsible way to look at these questions [of] these very scientific aspects of groundwater and groundwater management. (Sara, Winter 2020)

Here, Sara recognizes that she has a responsibility beyond what she is taught through traditional Western science. She articulates how understanding research through anticolonial frameworks provides her tools to argue for a decolonial ethics of responsibility. This kind of interdisciplinary thinking had meaningful resonances for Sara to think about connectivity in and beyond the context of the university, and to question how science could possibly 'challenge colonial narratives and white supremacy.'

In order to reflect on the dominance of Western epistemologies, students explored the contours of their own experiences in their respective fields, thinking about the culture of conducting science as one dominated by Western frameworks. Melissa reflected on how she learned Western science as the only science and, as such, developed a narrow view of the possibilities, peoples, histories, worldviews and epistemologies that can comprise science. The anticolonial interdisciplinary approach of the class sought to 'desettle expectations' of Western science (Bang et al. 2012; Medin and Bang 2014) and, through this process, students worked through their own conditioning as Western scientific thinkers. This critical reflexive praxis, where students reflected upon their learning, opened space for students to think beyond the confines of Western sciences and imagine a more expansive view of what counts as science, research, and knowledge.

Connecting positionality and place in praxis

> It's like questioning how we learn what we've learned. I think something I struggled with was trying to explain how I was understanding water, and I noticed that in the [positionality] essay, it took me a while to finish that because I think it becomes a personal issue. A personal identity politics, like it's impossible to leave that out. (Nina, Winter 2020)

When we asked students to reflect on the class concepts that were most challenging, Nina reflected on the difficulty of questioning 'how [she] learned what [she] learned' before the class. She found it challenging to position herself in relation to the water story she wanted to tell, which she realized was one about herself, her history, and her identity. Nina struggled to find the words to describe the story, yet she knew the story she wanted to tell centered on water as an important aspect of her life.

Our framing of positionality in the class drew from the (H)ACER Program's approach, which supports students to unpack their identities and to consider how they are situated in relation with the topics of research themselves. As Arthur reflected,

> I was trying really hard to think about what my perspectives of water were before this class and it was really hard for me because I really wasn't thinking about it that much. I think it's really amazing how easy it is to like drink water from your tap and never think about where your water comes from or hear your whole life that we're in a drought and just understand from what people tell you that it's just because of the environment, not because of how we're using that water ... this class made me realize more than anything that I wasn't considering my relationship to water very deeply but now I feel like every interaction I have with water is ... I just think more deeply about it than I think I did before. (Arthur, Fall 2019)

Arthur describes how difficult it was for him to recall what his perspectives on water were before the class, because he 'wasn't thinking about it that much.' In this excerpt, he shows surprise at his ability to go through life drinking water without actually knowing where the water comes from and how that water relates to the overall sociopolitical ecology of the region where he grew up. He then explains that now he thinks more about water, although he doesn't extrapolate on how his relationship to water has shifted. This shows the significance of supporting students to think about how the absence of a relationship to water and place were not mere absences, but were products of settler colonial ways of being in relation to land and water.

Writing about their relationship to water proved to be a personal and exploratory process for both Nina and Arthur. What is not reflected in their quotes is how they searched to express their experiences. Through a desire to convey the process, both stumbled over words and struggled to find a way to describe how the process of understanding their relationship with water to be so personal, as in Nina's case, and also how hard it was to articulate what water means now, which was the case with Arthur. It was clear that they felt a new relationship but they stopped short of being able to express how they understand and relate to water thoroughly. This moment is a reflection of their becoming, a liminal moment in consciousness where the individual moves away from 'common sense' and into differential consciousness (Freire 1998; Sandoval 2000). The fact that they have yet to articulate their new-found relationships with water is not of import here. Instead, through their reflections on their relationship with water, they are learning to build different relationships with water that are personal and indescribable, but still notably different from what they were.

Affective and relational dimensions of the class

> In the beginning it felt … like fumbling in darkness and it takes a lot of trust to learn … to be guided through that I guess? Trust maybe not in the literal sense like a trust fall but it's something that's more … trust in the sense 'Am I actually going to open myself up to this? Or am I going to stay rooted in my positionality to a certain degree?' Which isn't necessarily something you publicly submit to like, 'I am going to be open to what you teach me, Professor.' … I guess that's where a lot of change occurred because if you do hold on to your positionality, I could totally see this material easily … going in and out, sort of. (Rae, Fall 2019)

Rae describes the affective dimensions of rethinking research and water from anticolonial perspectives as a process of 'fumbling in darkness,' something that required 'a lot of trust' in order to be guided through unlearning their existing ways of knowing and their worldviews. They elaborate how engaging in anticolonial thought required a sense of openness or perhaps vulnerability – would they be willing to be moved and changed by the process of learning, or would they stay rooted in their worldviews? Beyond a conceptual exercise, the class challenged Rae to not stay fixed in their perspectives. They had to actively engage with the material and be willing to be reshaped by their learning, rather than staying 'rooted in [their] positionality'. As Rae notes, this level of engagement required them to trust the process of (un)learning, which involved a type of disorientation that they experienced on an affective level.

In contrast, Sam, a student in the same class reflected,

> I really enjoyed that feeling of being like 'Wow, I feel like I'm such an active learner in my own being at the moment' and I really enjoyed that feeling so I feel like I came into this class like, 'Yeah, mess me up.'

As Sam voices, this course not only asked students to complicate notions of water justice, but also to rethink their place in the world and to become, for Sam, an 'active learner in

[her] own being.' Rather than experiencing distress, as Rae articulated, Sam's process of rethinking her positionality and worldviews was one that was exciting and sparked enjoyment.

Of course, students' distinct positionalities and prior experiences shaped their affective responses to the substantive content. Sky entered the class fully engaging in critical race and feminist lexicons. At the end of the quarter, they explained how their notion of positionality changed. While they had initially understood the importance of an intersectional analysis of the world and ourselves as historical subjects and believed deeply in movement work, Sky had yet to situate themselves in this process. They explain,

> Positionality was something that I talked about a lot in the different pieces that I wrote, but I tended to set myself apart every time I talked about positionality when I shouldn't have been. Because all of the readings with the Indigenous practices, it kept on reminding me that yeah, everything is interconnected, but when it came to me and actually debriefing and talking about how water is affecting my life, I started breaking it down into different structures that have been set up around me and why those structures are affecting me in the way that water is entering my life. (Sky, Winter 2020)

Sky describes how the process of thinking about Indigenous knowledges and practices supported them to realize that they could develop an even more nuanced understanding of positionality; one that helped them see the way water was 'entering [their] life.' Although they are not focused on their affect, they allude to a kind of openness to deepening their criticality and exploring what water can teach them about their own positionality. The way they describe how water 'affect[s their] life' and the way they let water into their analysis is both poetic and metaphorically profound. They describe how their understanding of positionality allowed them to 'set [themselves] apart,' or distanced from the phenomena or peoples. When they describe water, it seems to flow through the structures that shape their life, creating a connection and integration, supporting a more interconnected worldview. It is as if water facilitated Sky's reorientation and integration of their understanding of positionality and possibly their own positionality itself.

Surely, the context of the class – in addition to the culture of student activism on our campus, the students in the room, the instructors, and the structure of the class – supported the possibility for students to feel comfortable enough to engage in these processes of (un)learning. In both focus-groups, students spoke to the importance of the small class size to facilitate these intellectually and personally challenging forms of learning:

> I think another factor that has really stood out for me in this class is just the structure of the class itself. The format is so small and so intimate that we're able to all be on the same-level of discussion as opposed to a large scale lecture hall where the teacher is this removed entity and the class is operating kind of like sheep and is like, doing the thing, being herded around ... We're all kind of talking together every single time and you [the professor] can suggest things to us to think about, and yet we also all bring in so much in terms of considering the topics that it's kind of ... a re-imagination of how education could be if things weren't so focused on research production and faculty performance and separating from undergraduate education. (Corey, Winter 2020)

Corey's analysis of the conditions that shape his learning – and what sorts of spaces of possibility open up – remind us how institutional contexts that shape our teaching-learning environments are intimately connected to the types of anticolonial interventions we may hope to inspire with our students. He identifies the benefits of a small class size, specifically regarding the relationships between students and instructors. In explaining how everyone is 'able to all be on the same-level of discussion,' Corey highlights a shift from hierarchies, where professors may seem to hold the sole source of knowledge in the classroom, to a space for discussion where each person's contributions are valued.

Corey signals the importance of class size while providing an anti-capitalist critique of education as a call to re-imagine what universities could look like. He also identifies that these classroom dynamics allowed for everyone to bring their experiences, expertise, and perspectives to the table. He alludes to this structure and praxis as a possibility to re-imagine universities from his status-quo experiences; classrooms that are more intimate, that draw on the students as active participants and experts, and that are not focused on research production and performance at the expense of undergraduate learning. Corey seems to highlight the incentivized prioritization of research over teaching, especially as a student at a large public research university like our campus, suggesting that care be taken to engage with students and to value the contributions they offer in courses.[14] Corey identifies and seemingly calls for a paradigm shift of what we imagine education to be, leaving us as educators at a large public research university asking, what could higher education look like if our institutions weren't organized to reward research production or by separating research from undergraduate education?

Anticolonial pedagogies in a settler colonial institution: grappling with the contradictions and considerations for educators

Winter quarter was marked by a massive graduate student wildcat strike[15] for a cost of living adjustment, contesting the ways in which graduate students are underpaid, pushed into debt, and, ultimately, take on a major portion of the teaching load to support undergraduate education on our campus. This effort, which began with a grade strike that was met with increasingly punitive responses by the campus administration, escalated in the winter quarter as graduate students fully withheld their labor and successfully shut down campus on multiple days. Rather than engaging in good faith bargaining, the administration met the coalition of graduate students, undergraduates, faculty, and staff with increasingly excessive and costly policing and militarized surveillance (wildcats, n.d.).

During the strike, the winter *Water Justice* class met at various off-campus locations, including a student's home, a park, and the picket line itself. A few of the students in the class dedicated ample time to this organizing, one of whom was a striking graduate student herself. Because of this, discussions about the strike became integrated into the class. The significance of the strike and its connection to course materials had a subsequent impact on the frameworks through which students were thinking about the course and articulating their learning during the winter focus group. On the last day of the quarter, the class met on a park bench close to the picket line and Nayla, a student who had been involved in an undergraduate group supporting the strike, shared her reflections on how her organizing experience connected with questions about the politics of knowledge production in the class:

> I was thinking about this in terms of the strike ... look at how much we've been learning together and look at how much knowledge we've been producing here at this picket line.

We don't necessarily need the university-sanctioned knowledge, or just I guess questioning that. And personally, just in terms of the strike, I feel like I have learned so much in the past four weeks even though I have missed so many classes. So, I think that's interesting to think about what knowledge is validated. Like, the kind that you're learning in a classroom setting, but all the experiences that are brought to these collective groups and in this collective action and solidarity. (Nayla, Winter 2020)

We see Nayla's reflections as surfacing both the affordances and limitations of anticolonial classes like *Water Justice*. Nayla's ability to make connections between class concepts and experiences of 'collective action and solidarity' emphasizes the broad scope of students' learning. For the two of us co-authors who were also students in the winter *Water Justice* class, learning outside of the classroom heightened our way of thinking about the meaning of studying at a research-based university. Lessons we learned at the picket line directly challenged ongoing racial-colonial logics of the accumulation of universities. Similarly, Nayla's movement work supported her to grapple with the tensions and contradictions of being a student within the university, an institution whose role is to sanction 'what forms of knowledge are validated.' Another student, Lucca, grappled with the irony of paying for tuition and going into debt in order to learn knowledges that 'perpetuate industry and capitalism and colonialism,' and how the strike had brought these tensions to the fore.

These are the contradictions that we continue to stay with as both students and instructors as we write this paper and think through possibilities for decolonizing practices within racial-colonial institutions of higher education. We do this while acknowledging that settler colonialism is not a totalizing system; that counter spaces have, and always will, exist (la paperson 2017), whether at the scale of the *Water Justice* classes or in the movement context of the strike. We believe this tension is one that we should not seek to easily resolve, but to instead actively engage. That is, engaging these contradictions is precisely what anticolonial praxis can support – to stay with the messy, incomplete, and necessary ongoing work towards decolonization.

We hope this paper offers educators a window into our own anticolonial praxis, and we conclude by distilling a set of considerations that might continue to inform your own teaching contexts. First, we encourage educators to support students to unsettle the universality of Western knowledges and to center reflexivity as part of the substantive content. In *Water Justice*, it became telling for students to consider how Western ways of knowing not only narrowly define research, but also shaped their ways of making sense of their lives and the world around them. Second, we find that anticolonial sensibilities are enlivened when we design curricula that are critically grounded in interrogating conceptions of place and the coloniality of present-day issues. Students reflected that they were able to best understand decolonial theoretical critiques by applying them to unsettle the idea of the California water crisis as an apolitical environmental problem.

Finally, we urge educators to engage their classroom pedagogy as central as the content itself. This requires us to think through: How do we support students to build meaningful relationships, with each other and with instructors, regardless of class size? How do we create community in the classroom so students feel open to move more deeply in the ways that anticolonial curricula ask of them? How do we model this openness as instructors? We believe that this means rethinking how we show up in the classroom, centering practices of community-building and relationality. If we are serious about engaging our students through an anticolonial praxis, this requires that we inhabit ways of being that do not reproduce the forms of colonial separability that are cultivated through dominant Western educational systems (Andreotti et al. 2019; Lugones 2003). It requires that we begin this work in our daily classroom practice.

Notes

1. The citations here and throughout this paper come from the course syllabus. This tracks the intellectual arch of the course readings, the scholarship that informed the course design as well as our team's research process.
2. As Patel (2016) explains, the term anticolonial brings 'into relief the ways in which coloniality must be known to be countered, and decolonial should always address material changes' (7).
3. The T2GS project, funded by the Belmont NORFACE international Transformations to Sustainability grant and the National Science Foundation (NSF), is a three-year grant which brings together an interdisciplinary and international team of scholars, engineers, and water justice advocates to engage in feminist analyses of how people share, care for and manage groundwater through grassroots practices. Research sites included India, Tanzania, Morocco, Peru, Algeria, Zimbabwe, Chile and the USA (California): https://www.t2sgroundwater.org.
4. The courses had an uncharacteristically small enrollment for our campus, with five students in the fall term and six in the winter term.
5. The (H)ACER Program at UCSC's Colleges Nine and Ten emerged to address the campus's history as a predominantly white institution by creating spaces that allow students from Black, Indigenous, and People of Color (BIPOC), first-generation, and other systematically excluded communities to critically situate and engage questions around 'sense of belonging' and to leverage their education towards community-based efforts for social justice (Beckett, Sabati, and Lu, forthcoming).
6. The students' analytical summaries are published on our project website: https://www.t2sgroundwater.org/undergraduate-student-learning.
7. In addition to the settler colonial context of the U.S., coloniality/modernity structures violent relationships across geopolitical contexts (Quijano 2007; Lugones 2010).
8. We did not ask students how they self-identify in terms of cultural background or racial identity for this study. Based on the ways that students discussed their positionality in the midterm essay, and accounting for those of us who are former students, three students situated their identity as Latinx, five students as white, and the remaining three students did not specify.
9. In winter, the course was cross-listed with and attracted CRES majors.
10. It is very unusual to have courses with this small of a class size on our campus.
11. The student names we use throughout this paper are pseudonyms.
12. Italics reflect Melissa's spoken emphasis.
13. During the period of Spanish colonial rule, the missions were constructed as a site to maintain, control, and violently exploit Indigenous peoples in the place that today we call California (Madley 2016; Rizzo-Martinez 2021). In many schools, the history of the Mission System continues to be taught in ways that not only erase the violences enacted upon Indigenous peoples, but also situate them as benevolent institutions that sought to evangelize so-called 'less modern' peoples.
14. It should be noted that both of the instructors were contingent faculty (i.e. adjunct or lecturer).
15. A wildcat strike is when unionized workers strike without the support or authorization of the union's leadership.

Disclosure statement

No potential conflict of interest was reported by the author(s).

Funding

This work was supported by National Science Foundation [grant number ICER-1912361].

ORCID

Sheeva Sabati http://orcid.org/0000-0003-2565-760X
Linnea Beckett http://orcid.org/0000-0002-2174-6763

References

Andreotti, V. de O., S. Stein, R. Susa, C. Ahenakew, E. Jimmy, D. D'Emilia, T. Cajkova, et al. 2019. "Pedagogical Experiments." Gesturing Towards Decolonial Futures, June 21. https://decolonialfutures.net/experiments-2/.

Arax, M. 2020. *The Dreamt Land: Chasing Water and Dust Across California*. New York, NY: Alfred A. Knopf.

Bang, M., B. Warren, A. S. Rosebery, and D. Medin. 2012. "Desettling Expectations in Science Education." *Human Development* 55 (5–6): 302–318. doi:10.1159/000345322.

Beckett, L. 2020. "Tantear Practices in Popular Education: Reaching for Each Other in the Dark." *Frontiers: A Journal of Women Studies* 41 (1): 120–140. doi:10.5250/fronjwomestud.41.1.0120.

Beckett, L., S. Sabati, and F. Lu. Forthcoming. "Reflections in Praxis: Developing Sense of Belonging through an Apprenticeship in Community-Engaged Research." *Social Sciences Journal*.

Estes, N. 2017. "Fighting for Our Lives: #NoDAPL in Historical Context." *Wicazo Sa Review* 32 (2): 115–122. doi:10.5749/wicazosareview.32.2.0115.

Freire, P. 1998. *Pedagogy of Freedom: Ethics, Democracy, and Civic Courage*. Lanham: Rowman & Littlefield.

Harding, S. 1991. "'Strong Objectivity' and Socially Situated Knowledge." In *Whose Science? Whose Knowledge?: Thinking from Women's Lives*, edited by S. G. Harding, 138–163. Cornell University Press.

Karlis, N. 2020. "Emails Show UC Santa Cruz Police Used Military Surveillance to Suppress Grad Student Strike." *Salon*, May 18. https://www.salon.com/2020/05/18/emails-show-uc-santa-cruz-police-used-military-surveillance-to-suppress-grad-student-strike/.

la paperson. 2017. *A Third University is Possible*. Minneapolis, MN: University of Minnesota Press.

Linton, J. 2010. *What Is Water?: The History of a Modern Abstraction*. Vancouver, Canada: UBC Press.

Linton, J., and J. Budds. 2014. "The Hydrosocial Cycle: Defining and Mobilizing a Relational-Dialectical Approach to Water." *Geoforum; Journal of Physical, Human, and Regional Geosciences* 57: 170–180. doi:10.1016/j.geoforum.2013.10.008.

Luckett, K., A. Hayes, and S. Stein. Forthcoming. "Introduction to Special Issue: Possibilities and Complexities of Decolonising Higher Education: Critical Perspectives on Praxis." *Teaching in Higher Education* 26 (7–8): 887–900.

Lugones, M. 2003. *Pilgrimages = Peregrinajes: Theorizing Coalition Against Multiple Oppressions*. Lanham, MD: Rowman & Littlefield.

Lugones, M. 2010. "Toward a Decolonial Feminism." *Hypatia* 25 (4): 742–759. doi:10.1111/j.1527-2001.2010.01137.x.

Lugones, M. 2015. *Mestizaje and the Communal. Feminist Architecture of Gloria Anzaldúa: New Translations, Crossings and Pedagogies in Anzaldúan Thought*. Santa Cruz: University of California.

Madley, B. 2016. *An American Genocide: The United States and the California Indian Catastrophe, 1846–1873*. New Haven: Yale University Press.

Medin, D. L., and M. Bang. 2014. "12. Culturally Based Science Education: Navigating Multiple Epistemologies." In *Who's Asking?: Native Science, Western Science, and Science Education*, 179–192. Cambridge, MA: MIT Press.

Oré, M.-T., D. Bayer, J. Chiong, and E. Rendon. 2013. "Water Emergency in Oasis of the Peruvian Coast: The Effects of the Agro-Export Boom in the Ica Valley."

Pannu, C. 2012. "Drinking Water and Exclusion: A Case Study from California's Central Valley." *California Law Review* 100 (1): 223–268.

Patel, L. 2016. *Decolonizing Educational Research: From Ownership to Answerability*. New York: Routledge.

Quijano, A. 2007. "Coloniality and Modernity/Rationality." *Cultural Studies* 21 (2–3): 168–178. doi:10.1080/09502380601164353.

Reisner, M. 2017. *Cadillac Desert: The American West and Its Disappearing Water*. Westminster: Penguin Books.

Rizzo-Martinez, M. A. 2021. *We Are Not Animals: Indigenous Politics of Survival, Resistance, and Reconstitution in 19th Century California*. Lincoln: University of Nebraska Press.

Sabati, S. 2018. "Upholding 'Colonial Unknowing' Through the IRB: Reframing Institutional Research Ethics." *Qualitative Inquiry* 25 (9–10): 1056–1064. doi:10.1177/1077800418787214.

Saldaña, J. 2013. *The Coding Manual for Qualitative Researchers*. Los Angeles: Sage.

Sandoval, C. 2000. *Methodology of the Oppressed*. Minneapolis: University of Minnesota Press.

Sherwood, Y. P. 2019. "The Political Binds of Oil Versus Tribes." *Open Rivers: Rethinking Water, Place & Community* 13. https://editions.lib.umn.edu/openrivers/article/the-political-binds-of-oil-versus-tribes/.

Stein, S. 2017. "A Colonial History of Higher Education Present: Rethinking Land-Grant Institutions Through Processes of Accumulation and Relations of Conquest." *Critical Studies in Education* 61 (2): 212–228. doi:10.1080/17508487.2017.1409646.

Swearingen, W. D. 1987. *Moroccan Mirages: Agrarian Dreams and Deceptions, 1912–1986*. Princeton: Princeton Univ Press.

Todd, Z. 2017. "Fish, Kin and Hope: Tending to Water Violations in Amiskwaciwâskahikan and Treaty Six Territory." *Afterall: A Journal of Art, Context and Enquiry* 43: 102–107. doi:10.1086/692559.

Tuck, E., and M. McKenzie. 2014. *Place in Research: Theory, Methodology, and Methods*. New York: Routledge.

Tuck, E., and K. W. Yang. 2012. "Decolonization Is Not a Metaphor." *Decolonization: Indigeneity, Education & Society* 1: 1–40.

Tuhiwai Smith, L. 2012. *Decolonizing Methodologies: Research and Indigenous Peoples*. London: Zed Books.

Underhill, V., L. Beckett, and S. Sabati. Forthcoming. "Colonial Circularities of California's Hydraulic Frontiers: A Beacon and a Warning." *EPE: Nature and Space*.

Watts, V. 2013. "Indigenous Place-Thought and Agency Amongst Humans and Non Humans (First Woman and Sky Woman Go On a European World Tour!)." *Decolonization: Indigeneity, Education & Society* 2 (1). https://jps.library.utoronto.ca/index.php/des/article/view/19145.

Whyte, K. 2017. "Indigenous Climate Change Studies: Indigenizing Futures, Decolonizing the Anthropocene." *English Language Notes* 55 (1): 153–162. doi:10.1215/00138282-55.1-2.153.

wildcats. n.d. "Pay Us More: UC Grad Student Workers Fighting for a Cost of Living Adjustment." Accessed January 15, 2021. https://payusmoreucsc.com/.

Wilder, C. S. 2013. *Ebony & Ivy: Race, Slavery, and the Troubled History of America's Universities*. New York: Bloomsbury Press.

Worster, D. 1985. *Rivers of Empire: Water, Aridity, and the Growth of the American West*. New York: Pantheon Books.

Wynter, S. 2003. "Unsettling the Coloniality of Being/Power/Truth/Freedom: Towards the Human, After Man, Its Overrepresentation – An Argument." *CR: The New Centennial Review* 3 (3): 257–337. doi:10.1353/ncr.2004.0015.

Decolonising while white: confronting race in a South African classroom

Sally Matthews

ABSTRACT
In this paper, I explore whether and how white people can make a meaningful contribution to decolonising university curricula. Drawing on my experiences as a white academic teaching at a South African university, I argue that identity matters when talking about decoloniality and that whites need to think carefully about the effects of their whiteness on their attempts to contribute to decolonial scholarship. I also suggest that white contributions to attempts to decolonise university curricula involve a kind of ambivalence that needs to be recognised and worked with, rather than denied and obscured. Without such recognition, white participation in decolonial struggles may ultimately do more to alleviate the guilt of white academics than it does to dismantle the hierarchies that decolonial struggles ostensibly oppose.

Introduction

The #RhodesMustFall protests drew heightened attention to long-standing concerns about the need for the decolonisation of university curricula. Since then, much ink has been spilt on the topic. Indeed, Behari-Leak (2019, 58) suggests that there is something of a 'decolonization hype' at present and Moosavi (2020) warns that there are several dangers that need to be addressed by those clambering on the 'decolonial bandwagon' or else they may actually end up reinscribing coloniality (see also Vandeyar 2020). Voicing considerable scepticism about current enthusiasm for decolonisation, Tuck and Yang (2012, 3) argue that a 'too-easy adoption of decolonizing discourse' can play out in a way that ultimately serves to 'reconcile settler guilt and complicity, and rescue settler futurity'. There is a danger that writing on the topic of decolonisation may do more to help alleviate the guilt of white academics and to ensure their[1] continued prominence in academia than it does to meaningfully contribute to decolonial struggles.

In this short discussion piece, I reflect on the uneasy question of white involvement in decolonial struggles, using my positionality as a starting point. I am a white university lecturer teaching at a South African university. Over the last few years, I have been thinking about how to decolonise the curriculum in my disciplinary areas (Political Studies and African Studies). While the paper takes my context and disciplinary background

Setting the scene

It is 2016 – a time of heightened student protests here in South Africa. In response to these protests, my academic department has invited our senior students to give us some honest advice about how we might go about decolonising our curriculum. The students welcome the opportunity and we have a robust but mostly cordial discussion. As the discussion is ending, a student seated next to me, who took an African Studies course with me the previous year, turns to me and says, with quite some anger, that I should not be teaching the African Studies course. 'I need a black body in front of me!' she says and points to one of my black colleagues saying something like 'Why doesn't she teach the course rather than you?' I was quite shaken by her comments and by the visible anger behind them and I cannot remember exactly what I mumbled in reply (probably something rather defensive). This was not the first time (nor the last) when a student has said (or implied) that my whiteness makes me an unsuitable teacher at this time (and, particularly, an unsuitable teacher of a course focused on Africa), but I am yet to work out exactly how to respond. This article is an attempt to grapple further with the questions the arise in encounters like this one.

I have some ambivalence about starting the discussion with this incident. I fear that doing so invites some degree of sympathy towards me – 'poor me, I'm doing my best to decolonise my teaching but some nasty students just refuse to see past my skin colour and say hurtful things'. My seeking such sympathy is a form of what DiAngelo (2018) and others call 'white fragility'. However, I include a description of this incident as it usefully highlights the questions informing this article and may resonate with the experiences of others – both those who have come to feel like this student did and those who have been confronted like I was. Can white people play a genuine role in decolonising university curricula? If so, is their role different to that of black scholars? Are there particular issues that arise when white people try to embark on the decolonisation of university curricula? I cannot do justice to these complex questions in this short article, but I would like to share a few preliminary thoughts. In doing so, I must emphasise that I remain very unsure about the answers to these questions. For this reason, this article is not some kind of manual for white people who want to get decolonising right and is also not meant as a defensive response to black people who are sceptical of white people's commitment to decolonisation. I am not qualified to write such a manual and I think such scepticism is for the most part justified. All I would like to do is to share some readings and throw out some tentative thoughts in the hope that they might be helpful to someone as we fumble our way towards more 'decolonised', curricula.

On bodies in the classroom

University curricula are communicated to students by human beings who are embodied in particular ways and who have particular identities and histories. Yet, some commentators note that we spend comparatively little time thinking about the body and embodied experiences of scholars in the classroom. bell hooks (1994, 191) argues that academics are so well-schooled in Western metaphysical dualism that we have accepted the idea that the mind and the body are separate and believe that it is minds not bodies that should enter the classroom. From this perspective, the lecturer stands in front of the class as a disembodied mind interacting with other minds. But of course, this is not true. Each of us is embodied in a particular way and the bodies in which we dwell affect how others respond to us and interpret what we say.

When I stand in front of a class, I stand there embodied as a white woman. In my context – that of a university whose student body is now mostly black but was previously exclusively white – my presence may remind black students of the history of their exclusion from this place of learning. It might call to mind negative experiences they have had in previous classrooms where the instructor was white. Regardless of what I might say, the very fact that it is me – a white person – who has the authority to stand in front of the classroom and decide what will be in the curriculum is a reminder of the long history of white dominance in educational spaces in South Africa and of the fact that whites are still very much over-represented as academics, authors and educational authorities.

To say that identity matters in the classroom is not to say that the meaning that attaches to a person's race (or other identitying characteristics) is fixed and unchanging – not all white bodies will be interpreted in the same way, for example. As Cooks and LeBesco (2006, 235) explain: 'the teacher's body is slippery; privilege or oppression does not attach itself forever to a body but varies in interaction'. However, as Brisett (2020) observes, although our identities do not determine what we teach and how we teach it, our teaching is influenced by the identities we assume and which others attribute to us. Therefore, it is important to reflect on how our identities might influence what happens in the classroom.

There is now a considerable body of literature in which black instructors reflected on their experiences of teaching at predominantly white institutions in the West – just a few examples of this kind of writing are those by Brisett (2020), Dlamini (2002), Hartlep and Ball (2020), Tuitt et al. (2009) and Turner, González, and Wood (2008). In a useful summary of the experiences of black scholars at predominantly white institutions, Trower (2003, 3, 6) says that such scholars experience both overt and covert racism; feel isolated, excluded and marginalised; bear the burden of tokenism and feel that they have to 'represent' their race; experience the negative consequences of being perceived as being 'affirmative action' appointments; feel that they have to work harder to achieve tenure and promotion; and, finally, are generally less happy as academics and more likely to leave academia than their white counterparts. The above summary relates to the experiences of black scholars in the West, but there is a smaller body of literature focusing on the experiences of black scholars in the South African context – see for example Dass (2015), Hlatshwayo (2020), Hlengwa (2015), Khunou et al. (2019), Mahabeer, Nzimande, and Shoba (2018), Njovane (2015) and Potgieter (2002). While these scholars are teaching at South African universities, their experiences in many ways mirror those of their colleagues in the West as South African universities have also historically been dominated by white people.

While there is thus existing rich debate about what it means to be teaching while embodied as a black person, there is relatively little literature in which white academics reflect on how their race affects their experience of the classroom (some exceptions are Behm Cross 2017; Davis, Mirick, and McQueen 2015; Jawitz 2016; Routley 2016). This lack of scholarship is itself reflective of the very problem that those calling for the decolonisation of universities are raising: there is something so apparently 'natural' about white people being positioned as scholars and teachers that it seems unnecessary to comment on what it is like to teach as a white person. While black university instructors often find the experience so uncomfortable and difficult that they are driven to write about it, white instructors seem to less often experience significant discomfort when positioned as teachers, regardless of the race of their students, and therefore are seldom compelled to write on this topic. Indeed, it was only once my own authority had been unsettled by incidents like the one described earlier that I was pushed to think more both about my privilege as a white educator and about my (un)suitability for the project of decolonisation.

The ambivalent position of white scholars in a decolonising classroom

The experience of having some students and colleagues show scepticism about my ability to understand and teach a decolonised curriculum, has pushed me to ask the question: Can white people make any meaningful contribution at all to decolonising university curricula? So far, my tentative response to this question is 'Whites should try to do so, but not assume their ability to do so or their right to participate in decolonial projects'. They should try to do so because to withdraw completely from all attempts at decolonising the curriculum is to leave the burden of decolonising on the shoulders of those who already bear the burden of racism and other forms of discrimination. Also, given how over-represented whites are in educational institutions around the world, any decolonised curriculum will have to be taught, at least in part, by white scholars (unless, of course, white scholars are to be driven out of the academy altogether, which is not something likely to be seriously recommended).

But do white scholars have to engage *differently* to black scholars? I suspect so. For the most part, any scholar committed to decolonising university curricula, has to follow a similar programme of reading, listening, reflecting and interrogating. I hope other contributions to this special issue will lay out some of the general work to be done. The focus of this paper is narrower: I ask what white scholars who wish to contribute to decolonial scholarship might need to do that other scholars do not need to do. As I have emphasised before, I remain very unsure about the answer to this question, but I have come to think that there is something ambivalent about white people's involvement in decolonial struggles and that whites need to recognise and work with this ambivalence rather than to try to obscure or deny it. There may be some ambivalence in other scholars' engagement with decolonisation too, but white participation in decolonial initiatives is *unavoidably* ambivalent and this has a range of implications.

What do I mean when I say that white involvement is unavoidably ambivalent? Acknowledging and addressing the wrongfulness of colonialism entails recognition of white complicity with colonialism. But there is something awkward about being complicit with colonialism *and* being an avowed advocate of decolonisation. Decolonisation must necessarily dismantle some of the benefits whites have come to enjoy. Whites might recognise the rightfulness of decolonisation, but surely cannot unambivalently celebrate their loss of comfort, centrality and privilege. Critical commentators on this issue point out that white scholars often attempt to escape this awkward position by recentering themselves through vociferous participation in debates on decolonisation. Moosavi (2020, 343–345) warns that in so doing scholars from the Global North sometimes appropriate the ideas of those from the Global South and, in their eagerness to remain relevant, may displace such scholars. He asks scholars from the Global North to 'step aside rather than taking up more space than [they] deserve' (Moosavi 2020, 345). While he refers to Northern scholars rather than white scholars, the point applies in a similar way to white scholars. The implication of this is that whites need to work harder to demonstrate their commitment to decolonisation (because there are good reasons to doubt this commitment) and that they need to do so in a way that does not involve taking up too much space.

White people's involvement in decolonial struggles is also ambivalent because this involvement almost inevitably functions as an example of what Tuck and Yang (2012) call 'settler moves to innocence'. They define such moves as 'strategies or positionings that attempt to relieve the settler of feelings of guilt or responsibility without giving up land or power or privilege' (Tuck and Yang 2012, 10). By inserting themselves into attempts to bring about a decolonised university, whites are trying to find a way to remain relevant and important and are, at least partly, acting out of a fear that decolonisation might render them irrelevant and unwanted. White participation in decolonial initiatives involves a kind of trade off: whites hope that their participation will enable them to claim the position of a 'redeemed subject' (Hook 2011, 28). Even if this is not their conscious or stated intention, white contributors to projects aiming to dismantle racism are likely to receive what Hook (2011, 29) calls 'narcissistic gains' linked to their involvement. By being involved in attempts to decolonise university curricula, white academics are able to distance themselves from racism and to present themselves as non-racist subjects whose presence ought to be welcomed and affirmed. In this way, they protect themselves from the possible loss of privilege and prestige that decolonisation may bring. Perhaps the real test for white contributors is whether they are willing to commit to decolonisation even when it seems that such commitment does not lead to any affirmation of their continued relevance.

White contributions to decolonising the curriculum are undermined by the ambivalence discussed above. Whites who are doing this work are both part of the problem *and* trying to be part of the solution. Occupying this ambivalent position does not mean that whites cannot make any meaningful contributions to decolonial initiatives, but in attempting to do so whites need to be aware of this ambivalence rather than trying to move too quickly beyond it. I am reminded here of Sara Ahmed's comment that whites need to 'inhabit the critique [of white racism], with its lengthy duration' (2004) and of Samantha Vice's (2010) call for white South Africans to recognise themselves 'as a problem' and to learn to live with this awareness. Both authors insist that the problem of white racism (and of colonialism) is a persistent one and that whites need to recognise its tenacity and their entanglement with it, rather than trying to 'rush too quickly past the exposure of racism' (Ahmed 2004) in order to present themselves as innocent, as on the 'right side', as 'good whites' who are contributing to decolonisation. Also useful here is Tuck and Fine's (2007) discussion of their frustration with white people who, when presented with a critique of colonialism, ask 'What can I possibly

What does this look like in the classroom?

do?' This question, they argue, is an attempt to escape being an object of scrutiny and bearer of guilt by moving quickly to a position of action and innocence. Whites are so eager to be 'part of the solution' that they do not stop for long enough to reflect on the ways in which they might be part of the problem.

What does this look like in the classroom?

I began this piece by telling of an incident in which a black student suggested that my whiteness makes me an unsuitable person for teaching about Africa (or, perhaps, even for teaching at this juncture in South Africa at all). It seems fair to end the article by detailing where interactions like this one have led me since. I still teach African politics and, in so doing, clearly do not think that my whiteness makes it completely impossible for me to understand or teach about Africa. I do, however, recognise that white, non-African scholars have dominated, and still dominate, the study of Africa and I encourage students to recognise and respond critically to this continued dominance.[2] As part of eroding this dominance, my course on African politics is based principally, but not exclusively, on the work of African authors. But, of course, there is the irony of my own positionality – while I am South African by birth and upbringing,[3] I am white and therefore there is a tension between my insistence that we ought to address the continued dominance of white scholars in African Studies and my own authority and influence as the lecturer of the course. When teaching the course, I comment briefly on this irony and respond to questions about it, without spending too much time focusing on my own positionality (partly due to my own discomfort, but also out of a desire not to make the question of my identity take up too much space). A few years ago, I introduced another change to the presentation of the course, by replacing some lectures with small group discussions, facilitated by a black postgraduate student. One of several motivations for this change was to de-centre my presence as a white person in the classroom. I attend these group discussions, but only to listen.

Do these changes mean that my course can be considered to be 'decolonised'? I do not believe so. In a recent discussion of decoloniality, Lewis Gordon (2021, 16) suggests that we should not think of decolonisation as an objective and try to demonstrate that we have achieved decolonisation. He says that rather than focusing on 'decolonisation *from*', we should adopt a more forward-looking and open-ended orientation – a 'decoloniality *for*'. This approach reminds us that the aim of any scholar participating in decoloniality ought not to be the demonstration that they have 'arrived' and are able to produce decolonised knowledge. But this insight is particularly important for white scholars whose attempts to produce 'decolonised' knowledge can function as attempts to present themselves as 'redeemed', non-racist subjects. Rather than this moralistic and potentially narcissistic response, perhaps it is better to acknowledge that struggles against coloniality are ongoing and that the contribution any of us can make is a partial, incomplete one which ought to be transcended and improved upon in the future. This is certainly the case with my course on African politics, which no doubt remains entangled in coloniality, but which will I hope will continue to change in response to the engagements I have every year with thoughtful, critical student participants in the course.

Conclusion

In concluding, I would like to acknowledge that my general experience of participating in initiatives to decolonise the curriculum has been that students and colleagues have been supportive of my efforts and have graciously welcomed my attempts to contribute.[4] I am very grateful for that openness and trust. But the occasional more hostile response (such as the one I describe at the beginning of this article), has been helpful in preventing complacency and improving understanding. In my context, and so many others, there are several sticky, recalcitrant layers of racism and colonial oppression that cannot easily be understood and eliminated. The very brief foregoing discussion highlights some of the reasons why black scepticism of white involvement in curriculum decolonisation may be justified. Rather than insisting on their right to involvement in struggles for curriculum decolonisation, I suggest that white contributors need to be a bit more hesitant and vigilant about any implicit expectation that their apparent commitment to curriculum decolonisation earns them the right to be seen as redeemed subjects. But, ironically, the writing of this article is undoubtedly not the muting of my voice and my contribution to this special issue cannot escape the accusation that it is written in order to secure exactly the narcissistic gains I suggest whites forego.[5] Avoiding engagement is not the right thing to do, but engaging can also not be the right thing to do. Curriculum decolonisation is a fraught and treacherous topic and the best way to contribute is difficult to discern. But this does not mean that we should not continue to try to move forward, however tentatively.

Notes

1. I struggled to decide which pronouns to use in this piece when referring to white people. As I am white, it makes sense for me to use 'we', 'our' and 'us' in reference to white people. However, doing so might make the article read like a discussion between 'us white people' and that is not my intention. For this reason, I use 'they', 'their' and 'them' when referring only to white people and reserve 'we', 'our' and 'us' for general comments that are aimed at all possible readers of this text.
2. For evidence of the continued dominance of non-African authors in African Studies, see Basedau (2020) and Briggs and Weathers (2016). For discussion of the implications of this continued dominance of non-African authors, see Adomako Ampofo (2016), Hountondji (2009) and Olukoshi (2006).
3. Some might say that my place of birth means that I can legitimately claim the identity 'African' and therefore that my contribution to scholarly writing on Africa can be considered to be an African contribution. For a range of reasons which I have laid out elsewhere (Matthews 2011, 2015), I do not think I can so easily assume the identity 'African'.
4. I am fortunate to work in a department and a faculty in which I feel generally supported by my colleagues and students. I would like to recognise and express gratitude for this support.
5. Derek Hook (2011) has some helpful thoughts about this kind of problem – see especially his comments on 'guilt superiority'.

Disclosure statement

No potential conflict of interest was reported by the author(s).

ORCID

Sally Matthews ⓘ http://orcid.org/0000-0002-7635-3908

References

Adomako Ampofo, A. 2016. "Re-viewing Studies on Africa, #Black Lives Matter, and Envisioning the Future of African Studies." *African Studies Review* 59 (2): 7–29.

Ahmed, S. 2004. "Declarations of Whiteness: The Non-Performativity of Anti-Racism." *Borderlands e-Journal* 3 (2).

Basedau, M. 2020. "Rethinking African Studies: Four Challenges and the Case for Comparative African Studies." *Africa Spectrum* 55 (2): 194–206.

Behari-Leak, K. 2019. "Decolonial Turns, Postcolonial Shifts, and Cultural Connections: Are We There Yet?" *English Academy Review* 36 (1): 58–68. doi:10.1080/10131752.2019. 1579881.

Behm Cross, S. 2017. "Whiteness in the Academy: Using Vignettes to Move Beyond Safe Silences." *Teaching in Higher Education* 22 (7): 879–887. doi:10.1080/13562517.2017.1340266.

Briggs, R. C., and S. Weathers. 2016. "Gender and Location in African Politics Scholarship: The Other White Man's Burden?" *African Affairs* 115 (460): 466–489.

Brisett, N. O. M. 2020. "Teaching Like a Subaltern: Postcoloniality, Positionality, and Pedagogy in International Development and Education." *Comparative Education Review* 64 (4): 577–597.

Cooks, L. M., and K. LeBesco. 2006. "Introduction: The Pedagogy of the Teacher's Body." *Review of Education, Pedagogy, and Cultural Studies* 28 (3-4): 233–238. doi:10.1080/ 10714410600873159.

Dass, M. 2015. "Making Room for the Unexpected: The University and the Ethical Imperative of Unconditional Hospitality." In *Being at Home: Race, Institutional Culture and Transformation at South African Higher Education Institutions*, edited by P. Tabensky, and S. Matthews, 99–115. Pietermaritzburg: University of KwaZulu-Natal Press.

Davis, A., R. Mirick, and B. McQueen. 2015. "Teaching from Privilege: Reflections from White Female Instructors." *Affilia: Journal of Women and Social Work* 30 (3): 302–313.

DiAngelo, R. 2018. *White Fragility: Why It's So Hard for White People to Talk about Racism*. Boston: Beacon Press.

Dlamini, S. N. 2002. "From the Other Side of the Desk: Notes on Teaching about Race when Racialised." *Race, Ethnicity and Education* 5 (1): 51–66. doi:10.1080/13613320120117199.

Gordon, L. 2021. *Freedom, Justice and Decolonization*. New York: Routledge.

Hartlep, N. D., and D. Ball, eds. 2020. *Racial Battle Fatigue in Faculty: Perspective and Lessons from Higher Education*. New York: Routledge.

Hlatshwayo, M. 2020. "Being Black in South African Higher Education: An Intersectional Insight." *Acta Academica* 52 (2): 163–180.

Hlengwa, A. 2015. "Employing Safe Bets: Reflections on Attracting, Developing and Retaining the Next Generation of Academics." In *Being at Home: Race, Institutional Culture and Transformation at South African Higher Education Institutions*, edited by P. Tabensky, and S. Matthews, 99–115. Pietermaritzburg: University of KwaZulu-Natal Press.

Hook, D. 2011. "Retrieving Biko: A Black Consciousness Critique of Whiteness." *African Identities* 9 (01): 19–32. doi:10.1080/14725843.2011.530442.

hooks, b. 1994. *Teaching to Transgress: Education as the Practice of Freedom*. New York: Routledge.

Hountondji, P. 2009. "Knowledge of Africa, Knowledge by Africans: Two Perspectives on African Studies." *RCCS Annual Review* 1: 121–131.

Jawitz, J. 2016. "Unearthing White Academics' Experience of Teaching in Higher Education in South Africa." *Teaching in Higher Education* 21 (8): 948–961. doi:10.1080/13562517.2016. 1198760.

Khunou, G., E. D. Phaswana, K. Khoza-Shangase, and H. Canham. 2019. *Black Academic Voices: the South African Experience*. Cape Town: HSRC Press.

Mahabeer, P., N. Nzimande, and M. Shoba. 2018. "Academics of Colour: Experiences of Emerging Black Women Academics in Curriculum Studies at a University in South Africa." *Agenda* 32 (2): 28–42. doi:10.1080/10130950.2018.1460139.

Matthews, Sally. 2011. "Becoming African: Debating Post-Apartheid White South African Identities." *African Identities* 9 (1): 1–17.

Matthews, Sally. 2015. "Shifting White Identities in South Africa: White Africanness and the Struggle for Racial Justice." *Phronimon* 16 (2): 112–129.

Moosavi, L. 2020. "The Decolonial Bandwagon and the Dangers of Intellectual Decolonisation." *International Review of Sociology* 30 (2): 332–354. doi:10.1080/03906701.2020.1776919.

Njovane, T. 2015. "The Violence Beneath the Veil of Politeness: Reflections on Race and Power in the Academy." In *Being at Home: Race, Institutional Culture and Transformation at South African Higher Education Institutions*, edited by P. Tabensky, and S. Matthews, 99–115. Pietermaritzburg: University of KwaZulu-Natal Press.

Olukoshi, A. 2006. "African Scholars and African Studies." *Development in Practice* 16 (6): 533–544.

Potgieter, C. 2002. *Black Academics on the Move. How Black South African Academics Account for Moving Between Institutions or Leaving the Academic Profession*. Johannesburg: ComPress.

Routley, L. 2016. "Teaching Africa, Presenting, Representing and the Importance of Who Is in the Classroom." *Politics* 36 (4): 482–494.

Trower, C. 2003. "Leveling the Field." *The Academic Workplace* 14 (2): 1, 3, 6–7; 14–15.

Tuck, E., and M. Fine. 2007. "Inner Angles: A Range of Ethical Responses to/with Indigenous and Decolonial Theories." In *Ethical Futures in Qualitative Research: Decolonizing the Politics of Knowledge*, edited by N. K. Denzin, and M. D. Giardina, 145–168. New York: Routledge.

Tuck, E., and K. W. Yang. 2012. "Decolonization Is Not a Metaphor." *Decolonization: Indigeneity, Education & Society* 1 (1): 1–40.

Tuitt, F., M. Hanna, L. M. Martine, M. Salaar, and R. Griffin. 2009. "Teaching in the Line of Fire: Faculty of Color in the Academy." *Thought & Action*, Fall: 65–74.

Turner, C. S. V., J. C. González, and J. L. Wood. 2008. "Faculty of Color in Academe: What 20 Years of Literature Tells us." *Journal of Diversity in Higher Education* 1 (3): 139–168. doi:10.1037/a0012837.

Vandeyar, S. 2020. "Why Decolonising the South African University Curriculum Will Fail." *Teaching in Higher Education* 25 (7): 783–796. doi:10.1080/13562517.2019.1592149.

Vice, S. 2010. "How Do I Live in this Strange Place?" *Journal of Social Philosophy* 41 (3): 323–342.

Navigating student resistance towards decolonizing curriculum and pedagogy (DCP): a temporal proposal

Kirsten T. Edwards and Riyad A. Shahjahan 🆔

ABSTRACT

A concerted attempt to offer a temporal lens (the way we make sense of and relate to time changes) underlying decolonizing pedagogy and curriculum (DCP) remains absent. Drawing on student resistance as an entry point, we offer a temporal account of DCP by unearthing the entanglements between past, present, and future underlying DCP enactments. We explore timescapes shaping DCP from three specific temporal perspectives on student resistance: a) student orientations to the past, b) student perspectives on present allocations of time and c) student orientations to the future. We argue that to deliver DCP effectively, educators need to engage the temporal aspects of DCP, particularly students' temporal assemblages receiving and engaging with DCP. We suggest that future DCP research and enactments require probing the entangled timescapes underlying HE institutions, disciplines, classrooms, students' lives, and past/future aspirations.

Introduction

In the recent decade, we see a growing emphasis on decolonizing curriculum and pedagogy (DCP), sparked by student movements, academics collectively, and national policy initiatives. In response, a body of DCP literature emerged.[1] Two years ago, we embarked on critically examining this growing body of literature. Based on our analysis, across disciplines and global contexts, we realized that actualizing DCP encompasses probing the positionality of knowledge, constructing an inclusive curriculum, fostering relational teaching and learning, and/or partnering between higher education (HE) institutions and entities outside of the institution (Shahjahan et al, forthcoming).[2] While the insights we gained were informative, we felt something was missing in the above literature. Specifically, a concerted attempt to offer a temporal lens underlying such pedagogical and curricular phenomena remains absent (Burke and Manathunga 2020). The present point of departure is our attempt to offer a temporal account of the complexities, paradoxes, and tensions of enacting DCP in HE.

However, both DCP[3] and temporality are huge concepts; the intersections of which are too complex to explore in a brief essay. We needed a useful pathway to explore this vast forest of knowledge. As Black and Brown faculty, who have experimented with and enacted DCP in classroom settings, we decided to focus on a pathway relevant to our own positionalities. Localizing our attention within the classroom necessarily implicated our interactions with students. As racially minoritized faculty (and former students), we have found student resistance particularly salient in our experiences as well as a larger area of consideration in the literature. Hence, we decided to explore the relationship between DCP and time, focusing on student resistance.

We provide a temporal account of DCP to help unearth the entanglements between past-present-future underlying DCP. By temporal, we are going beyond clock-time to include any phenomenon tied to making meaning and related to time-related changes (e.g. physical, biological, psychological, social, spiritual, aesthetic) (Alhadeff-Jones 2017). We critically examine how student resistance to DCP can be understood from a temporal lens, arguing that while many discuss decolonizing ways of knowing (i.e. mind, knowledge, etc.), scholars rarely engage with temporality in DCP (a recent exception is Shahjahan 2015). Given DCP is about change, 'and the study of changes involves time, time appears as an unavoidable issue to consider' (Alhadeff-Jones 2017, 33). Therefore, engaging in DCP requires unpacking timescapes underlying DCP practices.

A timescape denotes an assemblage of temporal categories implicating each other but may not be equally salient in a given context (Adam 1998, 2004). Second, timescapes signify 'complex maps of time', informing 'what we do and how we decide to do it' (Burke et al. 2017, 5) and manifesting across various social settings, such as work, domestic/family life, and/or learning. Third, a timescape encompasses social difference, given one experiences time differently based on their social positionality (Streamas 2020). Timescapes offer us a temporal heuristic to tease out the temporal landscapes upon which DCP occur. We explore timescapes shaping DCP from three temporal perspectives on student resistance: a) orientations to the past, b) perspectives on allocations of time in the present, and c) orientations to the future. We argue that to deliver DCP effectively, educators need to engage the temporal aspects of DCP, particularly students' temporal assemblages. We end by considering what it would take to forward DCP in HE given varying timescapes.

Past orientations

The past plays an important role in how majoritized[4] students in the Global North orient themselves to DCP (Iseke-Barnes 2008). Students bring into the classroom individual and collective orientations to the past. Both orientations influence how students respond to DCP.

If prior curriculum and pedagogy introduced students in the Global North to aspects of non-dominant cultures, such allocations limited the amount of time for dialogue and/or presented minoritized communities in a compressed and/or exoticized manner. For example, when discussing Canadian students' prior exposure to indigenized curriculum, Pete (2018), a 'First Nations professor' (100), noted students' comments such as, 'we made dream catchers, heard a storyteller, or saw that movie' (104). Other students remarked that they 'didn't take Native Studies in high school and so I didn't know anything about Aboriginal people until now' (Pete 2018, 107–108). Student comments reveal how past educational experiences shape students' responses to DCP. Contemporary encounters with difference reflect the temporal assemblages students inherited from their academic pasts. Literature on student resistance to DCP reveals not only the curricular and pedagogical '[h]istorical demarcation' (Davis 2010, 141) that shields majoritized students from substantively addressing oppression, but also a failure on the part of DCP to account for majoritized students' temporal assemblages.

When confronted with a curriculum that acknowledges the history and ongoing manifestations of racial hierarchies produced by European colonization, students reject a systemic problem and attempt to (re)contain racism in the past. Dutta's (2018) experience, as an 'Indian, non-American woman of Color from the [Global South]' (275) applying a decolonial lens to a 'critical social justice agenda of community psychology' (272), exemplified how majoritized students use the past. Remarks such as, 'How can we have an African American president then?' and 'An actual caste system would prevent all African Americans from achieving higher office' (Dutta 2018, 277) expose a temporal orientation that situates the past as a container for oppression. When the evidence for contemporary injustice exceeds dismissal, majoritized students universalize or de-historicize racial hierarchies to alleviate white responsibility for present racist conditions: 'Are not caste systems universal?' (Dutta 2018, 277). When students (re)contain or de-historicize colonization, the defensive impulses reveal attempts to protect a white temporal assemblage.

Past educational experiences also shape how students deal with national histories. Majoritized students in the Global North often detach national 'achievements' in the past from European colonization. They resist tethering dominant models, theories, and methodologies to the oppressive contexts which produced them. For example, when Dutta (2018) critiqued traditional methodologies in an effort to decolonize the research process, students responded, 'Are we not throwing the proverbial baby out with the bath water' (276)? 'How can we use our centuries of scientific knowledge and well-developed methodologies to engage with communities and their perspectives' (276)? Dutta's (2018) students' responses to decolonizing methodologies reflect an attempt to protect the history of 'dominant knowledge structures' (Dutta 2018, 277). By viewing dominant methodologies as essentially helpful, students neutralize the past violence against minoritized communities that made research in the West possible (e.g. Tuskegee Experiment, tuberculosis experiments on Native children in Canada, pain experiments on Aboriginal Australians, sterilization of Puerto Rican women, etc.), projecting a net positive onto the present of Western science. Similarly, when she reflected on DCP in women and gender studies, Davis (2010) noted that her white middle-class heterosexual women students often resisted transnational perspectives to feminism and, in particular, critiques of past U.S. policies and practices, as these perspectives displaced the U.S. from the center of a progressive historical narrative. Her students commented that they 'did not think the [U.S.] should be 'put down'' believing that 'our country was the best in the world' (Davis 2010, 138). White women students' 'resistance … alerted [her] to just how significantly intersectional and transnational methods critically unsettle perceptions and assumptions inherited through cultural legacies of the "imperialist centuries"' (Davis 2010, 141). Student responses suggest that white orientations to the past work as a temporal gaze stifling DCP.

Majoritized students' past educational experiences and their desires to keep racism in the past, universalize racial hierarchies, and valorize white histories, reflect how the 'past' works as a container for white temporal assemblages. Engaging decolonized accounts of time via class dialogue about white violence throughout history and its nonlinear, recursive presence across time disrupts how they perceive the world and themselves. Majoritized student resistance to DCP surfaces the complex raced power relations embedded in educational contexts, revealing how traditional HE practice works as a temporal compass orienting students towards whiteness (Shahjahan & Edwards 2021). A more rigorous temporal analysis creates conditions for transformational possibilities across timescapes. In light of time's role in knowing and being, we suggest that DCP attend to different cultural orientations to time, and account for the temporal assemblages students bring to curricula and pedagogies.

Present allocations of time

Student resistance to disruptive past orientations often takes the form of demanding certain temporal parameters in the present. While some students embrace the decolonial shift, others react in ways that privilege existing temporal assemblages refusing to cede the present to DCP. Pete (2018) noted that majoritized students responded to indigenized education by writing in teaching evaluations that she 'talk[s] too much about Indians' (110) and that she is 'biased towards First Nations' (110). Students' perceptions of 'bias' and quantity of time allocated to First Nations people directly correlate with the lack of time spent on non-Western perspectives in their past coursework. Temporal comparisons serve as justification for resistance by providing rationale for appropriate time allocations in the present. Student resistance also exposes how time allocations indicate priority and importance. Like physical landscapes, density and occupation mark timescapes. The amount of time a particular idea occupies denotes its importance to the larger timescape. Student assessments of time allocations are assessments of priority. Therefore, students' resistance to increases in time allocations is a refusal to engage temporal assemblages that prioritize non-dominant perspectives.

Students' affective responses to DCP also shape the temporal atmosphere of learning. Fellner (2018), who is 'Cree/Metis from central Alberta' (283), teaching in the Canadian context, noted: 'Perhaps the greatest challenge in this work has come through students' reactions to embodying decolonial education in the academy … [such as] anger, frustration, and other intense emotions' (292). Similarly, Davis (2010) noted, 'Students were demonstrably angry when they were unable to locate their own subject positions reflected or "mirrored" in the center of course materials' (139). Student resistance to negative feelings and/or decentering produces a variety of temporal effects. Challenges to DCP lead to learning delays (Zinga and Styers 2018). Faculty must allocate more time to content and critical ideas when students' resistances impede learning. Also, faculty designing curriculum from a decolonial perspective (who are often people of color) must spend more time aligning course objectives with institutional mandates in an effort to circumvent negative student evaluations and administrative censure. Delays compound with structural challenges such as being 'limited by lecture times' (Fellner 2018, 291). Temporal conditions that arise from resistance to DCP reveal that students not only experience discomfort with shifting temporal assemblages, but they also resist discomfort through temporal modes. Said differently, majoritized students

Future self and global subjectivity

So far, we have discussed the past and present timescapes underlying majoritized students' resistance to DCP within the Global North. However, some have observed student resistance to DCP in the Global South context tied to their future global subjectivity aspirations (Fomunyan 2017; Winberg and Winberg 2017). Here we demonstrate how DCP operates beyond a nationally bounded temporal field, but a global timescape – entangling individual aspirations, global labor market, and academic mobility. In short, DCP operates within the temporal constraints of 'future self' tied to the global market.

Here, we briefly refer to two empirical studies in the South African context to illustrate our argument. Both studies focus on decolonizing the engineering curriculum and student responses (Fomunyan 2017; Winberg and Winberg 2017), highlighting the temporal constraints tied to global timescapes. Winberg and Winberg (2017) sought to identify elements of a decolonized computer engineering curriculum through interviews with academic and practicing engineers, as well as a student survey. For their participants, the decolonized curriculum had to both meet local needs and emphasize globally transferable skills. Some students expressed uneasiness about 'Africanizing' the curriculum, as they wanted to study overseas. For instance, one student noted: 'I am planning to work or study overseas for some years to gain specialized skills ... ' (251). While many invited a more inclusive African Engineering curriculum, some were anxious about the loss of transferable skills, across disciplines and national scales. Similarly, Fomunyan (2017) conducted a qualitative case study on the decolonization of the engineering curriculum at a South African university of technology. Using questionnaires completed by 116 students and lecturers, this study sought to articulate 'what needs to be decolonised in engineering education, how this should be decolonised, what can enhance the decolonisation process' (Fomunyan 2017, 6800). Many of Fomunyan's participants favored DCP in bridging theory with practice in local contexts, using more 'home' languages in the curriculum, and improving Black faculty's representation in their programs. However, for some, a decolonizing curriculum stifled 'mobility of labour since most graduates would simply possess contextual knowledge which cannot be used elsewhere in the globe' (Fomunyan 2017, 6802). As one student put it: 'why would anyone want to do this? Engineering and Science is a field of study which is a universally agreed upon set of rules. Decolonizing it would be a waste of time and make it much more difficult for people to leave this country and work elsewhere' (Fomunyan 2017, 6802). Another participant added that 'it will be difficult to find work overseas' (Fomunyan 2017, 6802). To these students, a future decolonized Engineering curriculum has numerous career implications.

As these studies highlight, DCP, in particular disciplinary and Global South contexts, operate within temporal constraints. Given the geopolitics of knowledge (Mignolo 2011), a globally-oriented labor market and credentials validate particular 'transferrable' and 'mobile' knowledge systems that a decolonizing curriculum might thwart. Student resistance reveals that educational desires are dictated by 'ideal *future selves*' (Shahjahan 2020, 793). Such students are concerned about attaining their *future selves* (i.e. working or studying overseas), thus hampering their willingness to participate in DCP. Given the unknowns of a decolonizing curriculum in terms of international qualifications, credential mobility, and career trajectories, students are also concerned about the 'precarity' introduced by DCP. To put it simply, while DCP may introduce temporal continuity with local contexts, for some Global South students, it also introduces precarity to future aspirations and career mobility.

Conclusion

Using students' resistance as an entry point, our temporal account of DCP helps unearth the entanglements between past-present-future underlying DCP enactments. First, a temporal lens illuminates how majoritized students' 'past orientations' either to past histories or lack of experience with certain knowledge systems (e.g. indigenous knowledge) can disrupt DCP. More specifically, students' affective attachments to previous temporal accounts of a national imaginary impede partaking in new temporal accounts of the nation-state evoked by DCP. Second, a temporal lens highlights the contestation of temporal allocations with certain knowledges (e.g. 'talks too much') and classroom temporal rhythms. Finally, a temporal gaze helps illuminate the underlying geopolitics of knowledge informing students' future aspirations, and, thus, acts as a barrier to DCP.

So far, the DCP literature has paid little attention to the temporal challenges of engaging DCP in HE. Several conditions contribute to this absence: a) temporality is often taken for granted in the HE literature (Burke and Manathunga 2020), particularly in DCP, b) temporality is invisible because it's so abstract to begin with (Shahjahan 2018), and c) temporality is usually associated with linear clock-time, and therefore undertheorized, rather than approached from a broader sense of temporality encompassing various temporal categories and timescapes (Burke et al. 2017). As a result, DCP often assumes that everyone possesses the same temporal orientations and resources to engage in decolonization.

However, our temporal account of student resistance suggests otherwise and raises further questions. What are the differences between decolonizing pedagogies and decolonizing curriculum and how does that shape student resistances differently across different timescapes? How are resistances (re)produced in institutional timescapes and in relation to raced/gendered/classed/sexualized/linguistic/religious inequalities and differences (Streamas 2020)? What are the intersections of student resistances at the micro-level with wider systems, discourses and structures of oppression (e.g. geopolitics of knowledge)? How are the wider institutional structures positioning students differently across time and space and how might this inter-relation between structures, power and the micro-level of perspectives towards DCP shape (im)possibilities (Burke and Manathunga 2020)?

A temporal gaze also raises many questions about DCP beyond simply student resistance: How does one's (instructor, student, or administrator's) past orientations and one's notion of temporality serve or disrupt engagement with DCP? Similarly, how does institutional or disciplinary temporal rhythms (like classroom time, academic calendar, clock-time, or future aspirations) facilitate or disrupt DCP? We challenge pedagogues to attend more intentionally to the temporal conditions of decolonization. Since decolonizing is deeply contextual, historical, and political, educators attempting to decolonize

Notes

1. See for example, Attas 2019; Adefarakan 2018; Diab et al. 2020; Dutta 2018; Knight 2018; Schultz et al. 2018; Sian 2019; Walsh 2015.
2. It is beyond the scope of this short piece to unpack the contextual meaning of 'decolonizing' across and within different timescapes. Elsewhere (Shahjahan et al forthcoming) we provided a comprehensive review of debate about 'decolonizing' pedagogy and curriculum across disciplines and global HE contexts, illuminating what decolonizing means and how to decolonize are deeply contextual, historical and political. However, one area lacking in this debate were temporal perspectives, hence why we focus on temporality here.
3. We acknowledge the complexities and nuances surrounding concepts of curriculum and pedagogy, but driven by what predominantly emerged in the DCP literature, we view a) pedagogy as detailing instructional and relational learning practices, and b) curriculum as material content and purpose, manifesting inside/outside of classrooms, such as in a course, program, discipline/profession, institution, and/or minoritized community setting (Shahjahan et al forthcoming).
4. By 'majoritized' we are signifying students who are part of social majority groups, not simply numerically, but receive privilege due to their racial, gender, class, and linguistic asymmetries tied to socio-politico-cultural and temporal landscapes. As such students often shift in and out of these categories, while the majoritized identity is revealed in the ontological moment of 'being,' when the student is occupying the privileges of asymmetry. It is the moments (or times) when DCP and majoritization intersect for which we are concerned.

Disclosure statement

No potential conflict of interest was reported by the author(s).

ORCID

Riyad A. Shahjahan (iD) http://orcid.org/0000-0002-3244-3215

References

Adam, B. 1998. *Timescapes of Modernity: The Environment and Invisible Hazards.* London: Routledge.
Adam, B. 2004. *Time.* Cambridge and Malden: Polity Press.
Adefarakan, T. 2018. "Integrating Body, Mind, and Spirit Through the Yoruba Ori: Critical Contributions to a Decolonizing Pedagogy." In *Wong, Sharing Breath: Embodied Learning and Decolonization*, edited by Sheila Batacharya and Yuk-Lin Renita Wong, 229–252. Athabasca, Canada: Athabasca University Press.
Alhadeff-Jones, M. 2017. *Time and the Rhythms of Emancipatory Education: Rethinking the Temporal Complexity of Self and Society.* United Kingdom: Taylor & Francis.
Attas, R. 2019. "Strategies for Settler Decolonization: Decolonial Pedagogies in a Popular Music Analysis Course." *Canadian Journal of Higher Education* 49 (1): 125–139. doi:10.47678/cjhe.v49i1.188281
Burke, P. J., A. Bennett, M. Bunn, J. Stevenson, and S. Clegg. 2017. "It's About Time: Working Towards More Equitable Understandings of the Impact of Time for Students in Higher

Education." Sheffield Hallam University Research Archive, Australia, Curtin University. http://shura.shu.ac.uk/15364/

Burke, P. J., and C. Manathunga. 2020. "The Timescapes of Teaching in Higher Education." *Teaching in Higher Education* 25 (6): 663–668. doi:10.1080/13562517.2020.1784618.

Davis, D. R. 2010. "Unmirroring Pedagogies: Teaching with Intersectional and Transnational Methods in the Women and Gender Studies Classroom." *Feminist Formations* 22 (1): 136–162. doi:10.1353/nwsa.0.0120

Diab, M., G. Veronese, Y. A. Jamei, and A. Kagee. 2020. "The Interplay of Paradigms: Decolonizing a Psychology Curriculum in the Context of the Siege of Gaza." *Nordic Psychology* 72: 183–198.

Dutta, U. 2018. "Decolonizing 'Community' in Community Psychology." *American Journal of Community Psychology* 62: 272–282. doi:10.1002/ajcp.12281

Fellner, K. D. 2018. "Embodying Decoloniality: Indigenizing Curriculum and Pedagogy." *American Journal of Community Psychology* 62: 283–293. doi:10.1002/ajcp.12286

Fomunyan, K. G. 2017. "Decolonising the Engineering Curriculum in a South African University of Technology." *International Journal of Applied Engineering Research* 12 (7): 6797–6805.

Iseke-Barnes, J. M. 2008. "Pedagogies for Decolonizing." *Canadian Journal of Native Education* 31 (1): 123–148.

Knight, J. 2018. "Decolonizing and Transforming the Geography Undergraduate Curriculum in South Africa." *South African Geographical Journal* 100 (3): 271–290. doi:10.1080/03736245.2018.1449009

Mignolo, W. 2011. *The Darker Side of Western Modernity: Global Futures, Decolonial Options.* Durham: Duke University Press.

Pete, S. 2018. "Meschachakins, a Coyote Narrative: Decolonising Higher Education." In *Decolonising the University*, edited by Gurminder K. Bhambra, Karem Nişancıoğlu, and Dalia Gebrial, 173–189. London: Pluto Press.

Schultz, T., D. Abdulla, A. Ansari, E. Canlı, M. Keshavarz, M. Kiem, L. Prado de O. Martins, and P. J. S. Vieira de Oliveira. 2018. "What is at Stake with Decolonizing Design? A Roundtable." *Design and Culture* 10 (1): 81–101. doi:10.1080/17547075.2018.1434368

Shahjahan, R. A. 2015. "Being 'Lazy' and Slowing Down: Toward Decolonizing Time, our Body, and Pedagogy." *Educational Philosophy and Theory* 47 (5): 488–501. doi:10.1080/00131857.2014.880645

Shahjahan, R. A. 2020. "On 'Being for Others': Time and Shame in the Neoliberal Academy." *Journal of Education Policy* 35 (6): 785–811. doi:10.1080/02680939.2019.1629027

Shahjahan R.A. (2018). "Re/conceptualizing time in higher education." *Discourse: Studies in the Cultural Politics of Education.* doi:10.1080/01596306.2018.1550041

Shahjahan, R., & Edwards, K. T. . 2021. "Whiteness as futurity and globalization of higher education." *Higher Education.* doi:10.1007/s10734-021-00702-x

Shahjahan, R., Estera, A., Surla, K., & Edwards, K. T. . (forthcoming). "Towards 'Decolonizing' Curriculum and Pedagogy (DCP) across Disciplines and Global Higher Education Contexts: A Critical Synthesis".

Sian, K. P. 2019. *Navigating Institutional Racism in British Universities.* New York University: Springer International Publishing.

Streamas, J. (2020). "The war Between 'School Time' and 'Colored People's Time'." *Teaching in Higher Education* 25 (6): 709–721. doi:10.1080/13562517.2020.1782882

Walsh, C. E. 2015. "Decolonial Pedagogies Walking and Asking. Notes to Paulo Freire from AbyaYala." *International Journal of Lifelong Education* 34 (1): 9–21. doi:10.1080/02601370.2014.991522

Winberg, S., and C. Winberg. 2017. "Using a Social Justice Approach to Decolonize an Engineering Curriculum." In *2017 IEEE Global Engineering Education Conference (EDUCON)*, 248–254. New York City: IEEE.

Zinga, D., and S. Styers. 2018. "Decolonizing Curriculum: Student Resistances to Anti-Oppressive Pedagogy." *Power and Education* 11 (1): 30–50.

Four 'moments' of intercultural encountering

Meike Wernicke

ABSTRACT
Teaching a graduate course focused on critical understandings of interculturality offers an opportune space in which to explore decolonizing pedagogical practices. In this short paper, I examine my own attempts at decolonizing students' experiences of intercultural learning by incorporating non-Western knowledge systems to draw attention to dominant cultural perceptions, authority structures, and power relations. Using extracts of students' texts and multimodal representations of cultural discourses, I focus on four 'moments' of intercultural learning: (1) the importance of connecting to history on one's own terms; (2) how knowledge and experience shape our relationship to the land; (3) the need for uncomfortable and vulnerable spaces as potentially facilitating anti-racist/decolonial pedagogy; (4) the tensions around cultural appropriation in relation to teaching resources. In sharing these practical realizations of teaching in higher education I hope to contribute to the larger discussion of the possibilities and challenges of a decolonizing praxis.

Introduction

The increasing emphasis on Indigenous priorities, anti-racism and decolonizing approaches in Canadian higher education (Gaudry and Lorenz 2018; Motha 2020) has prompted me to explore how I might incorporate decolonizing learning experiences in my own teaching as a multilingual settler educator of European heritage. Through these intentional, often complicated and messy attempts I have sought to make space for non-Western knowledge systems and languages other than English to highlight and shift authority positions, cultural perceptions, and power relations in meaningful ways within classroom interactions. In this contribution, I take stock of some of the tensions that have emerged during my teaching of a graduate-level course, which explores conceptual and pedagogical aspects of interculturality in language education. I focus on four 'moments' of intercultural learning that have occurred in the English and French iterations I have taught over the past five years. The course is primarily taken by practicing teachers or post-secondary instructors pursuing further studies in language education at the master's and doctoral level. The English course generally comprises a majority of multilingual students from abroad, in addition to recently arrived immigrants or long-established settlers like myself, and local students from across Canada and the province. Most teach in English-medium educational settings and speak English as a second language in addition to one or several other languages. The French course is offered within an online master's cohort program for in-service teachers in French-as-a-second-language programs across Canada who are mostly Canadian-born francophone or second language users of French. The course thus addresses a wide range of students who have varying levels of familiarity with Canada's colonial history, and who differ greatly in how the course content connects to their teaching. For me as instructor, the four encounters are instances of reflection and professional learning as I seek to disrupt the learned, deeply-embedded White Eurocentric perspectives and practices I have internalized and to better understand my role and responsibilities as an educator. In addition to describing the actions and thinking that underpin the intercultural encounters, I make use of multimodal texts that feature various languages, yet without offering a direct translation. By only paraphrasing the general meaning conveyed in these artefacts, I aim to highlight the (typically invisiblized) multilingual resources we rely on to makes sense of our worlds, and to purposefully invoke a 'disorientation outside of English' as eloquently noted by one reviewer of this article.

Moment one: reconciling relationship to land

A first step is to conceptualize the central topic of the course in light of emerging alternative understandings of interculturality. Historically grounded in Western models of cross-cultural communication, intercultural competence is viewed as developing individuals' ethnorelative perspectives and capacity for openness (e.g. Deardorff 2009). The celebratory promotion of intercultural dialogue in Europe (e.g. Byram 1997) generally assumes mutual empathy and coherent cultural equality among nations and citizens (Aman 2018). This notion of a stable cultural identity is most often associated with a touristic view of difference, as something that exists outside one's local sphere (Byrd Clark, Haque, and Lamoureux 2012). To challenge this Eurocentric view, I decided to have students engage directly with Canada's own colonial history by framing the course within the local context of reconciliation, conceptualized by Regan 'as an intercultural encounter [that] involves creating a space for critical dialogue' (2010, 41). The concept of 'reconciliation' is associated with the Truth and Reconciliation Commission of Canada (2015) which documented the historical violence perpetrated by the Canadian government against Indigenous people through the residential school system. Despite critique, reconciliation highlights the current impetus to examine these histories and confront past and ongoing colonial dominance, and is seen as an important means for non-Indigenous people in Canada to acknowledge 'their role in keeping Aboriginal peoples on the social, economic, and educational margins of the places where we live and learn' (Hare and Davidson 2016, 261). Within the context of the course, it means moving away from Eurocentric conceptions of interculturality toward *interculturalidad*, which refers to Indigenous peoples' role in furthering intercultural understanding in the Global South, emphasizing multilingualism and decolonization as principal objectives in reclaiming their identities and cultures. It provides 'a view from the underside of the colonial difference' (Aman 2018, 15) which draws attention to the forms of knowledge privileged in intercultural education and foregrounds epistemic diversity in understanding interculturality in not only cultural but also colonial terms.

An initial encounter in exploring reconciliation with the students, inspired by Celia Haig-Brown (2009), is to have them reflect on their relationship to the land they are on. Drawing on class readings and discussions about Canada's history, current socio-political issues, and the concept of reconciliation within education, students are encouraged to write a brief reflection about how they have come to be on this land, whose land it is, and how their knowledge and experiences shape that relationship. Generally, the assignment shows students articulating a positioning as outsider and acknowledging some apprehension with this unfamiliar history. At the same time, the reflections also demonstrate a thoughtful and serious effort to arrive at a better understanding of what it means to be a student on traditional xʷməθkʷəy̓əm territory at this Canadian university. Some students make connections to childhood experiences or the histories of their home countries, whereas others recount first impressions upon arriving in Canada or first learning about the devastating multi-generational impact of Indian residential schooling on Indigenous communities. For the most part, there is evident hesitancy or perhaps inability to grasp at a more tangible exploration of a relationship to land, one that explicitly reflects on the perplexity, contradictions, disappointment, and questions of identity that such a self-inquiry might provoke, as for example in the excerpt presented in Figure 1.

For me, as course instructor, this assignment provides a constant reminder to consider my own relationship to the land on which I teach, and the ways I have sought to navigate privilege, guilt, the need for knowledge, and a desire for reparation, among other responses. It recently occurred to me that part of the answer may lie in the task's question itself, in the prepositional distinction between 'in' and 'on.' While many of us talk about being *in* a particular *place*, we are perhaps less prone to consider this particular place as a material entity and what it means to be *on* the *land*. From this perspective, 'the word *place* always includes an explicit awareness of *Land* on which place exists' (Styres, Haig-Brown, and Blimkie 2013, 39).

Moment two: *Das Brot*

For many language teachers, integrating cultural learning into the curriculum remains a key challenge in their teaching practice. This is due in part to prevailing grammar-based

Since I received the first email from UBC, I am informed by the signature template that we are now on "Traditional Territory," and later on when I read more about it, it is the land that used to belong to Indigenous people like Sandra Styres (2019), and this is the land they have built a deeply "intimate and sacred" relationship with. I felt quite surprised and also disappointed that this group of people is almost invisible in that little Canadian educational community, yet here, they originally owned this land and were deeply bonded with the land.

Figure 1. Excerpt from a student's reflection (reproduced with permission of the student).

approaches that rely on static conceptions of language as merely a communicative tool that allows for the straight-forward transmission of information. A main objective of the course is to familiarize students with a more critical, social practice-based perspective, which views language use as 'a creative, cultural act in its own right' (Liddicoat and Scarino 2013, 13). Intercultural learning thus becomes a performance of identity, a situated process of meaning-making that requires decentering from pre-existing assumptions and practices as one confronts 'multiple, changing and conflicting discourse worlds' (Kramsch 2011, 356). In class, I encourage students to attend to the way language produces culturally situated meaning through a short story activity. Students read a translation of *Das Brot* by German author Wolfgang Borchert (1949/2007) and then, in groups of three or four, write 200-word summaries of the story which are subsequently compared and discussed in class. The story explores a number of themes related to poverty, food rationing, gender roles, societal and cultural values within the context of post-war Germany (Figure 2). The story is about ….

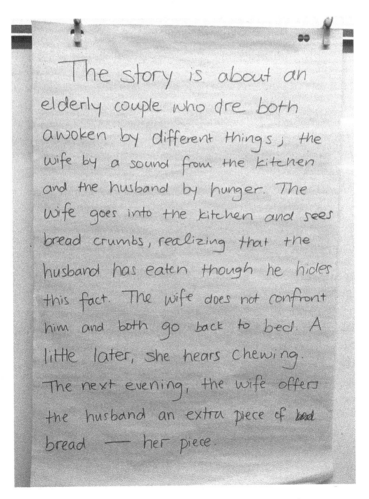

Figure 2. An example of a collaboratively-produced story summary by one group of students (January, 2017, reproduced with permission of the students).

During the post-task discussion we collectively examine the meaning-making process on several levels: how students have understood the story; what knowledges, experiences, and resources they used to arrive at their interpretations; the content and discursive choices they made in summarizing the story; the ways in which the collaborative aspect of the task facilitated or constrained the meaning-making process. In past discussions, the role of identity has emerged as a salient resource for meaning-making, especially for students trying to make sense of the story. An important lesson I have learned from this activity is to not overestimate students' familiarity with the story's historical context, to be mindful of how my own taken-for-granted understandings – which draw on post-war memories I myself have encountered through family stories, my childhood upbringing and subsequent study – may get in the way of students connecting to the story on their own terms. This was the case during one particular class in which a student was visibly struggling to grasp the symbolic meaning attributed to the slice of bread in the story, despite her (from my perspective) evident knowledge about the conditions of post-war Europe, given her heritage and the past experiences and reflections she had shared in previous classes. However, it was only when another student related how the war's circumstances of poverty had impacted her family and others in her country that the first student was able to establish a meaningful personal connection, first to the second student's experiences and then extending this to the short story. For me, this interaction demonstrated that the process of decentering should not only involve a means of questioning preconceptions but must also provide a means of restructuring new knowledge within existing understanding. To echo scholar and teacher educator, Ann Lopez: 'We are good at deconstructing the world for our students, but then we have to help them put it back together somehow' (Lopez 2016). In other words, this intercultural 'moment' highlights the need for deep or active listening (Hart 2010) as part of a decolonial pedagogy, one which allows us 'to enter the world with another' to learn *from* and not *about* the Other and potentially arrive at transformed understandings (LeBaron 2002, 237).

Moment three: countering the 'Wuhan-Virus'

The third 'moment' of intercultural learning occurred in early 2020, a few weeks before coronavirus restrictions were imposed in various parts of the world, including Canada. At the time, media news were increasingly reporting explicit instances of anti-Asian racism in the community. While waiting in a healthcare laboratory room, I was reminded of how even unintentional, careless language on a sign was visibly contributing to the shaping of these racializing discourses (Figure 3). I decided that an opinion piece in the New York Times, titled 'I'm Chinese. That doesn't mean I have Coronavirus' (Tien, March 2020), would offer one means of attending to the topic in class. The article described how a client in a nail salon in the United States had confronted the racism directed at her with a public counter narrative. To my pleasant surprise, upon reading the students' class reflections that week, one of the students who was originally from Wuhan had already done exactly that – she had offered her own counter narrative to the 'groundless and ridiculous' misconceptions being constructed about people from China in association with the coronavirus. Although acknowledging that she and fellow Chinese international students at the university were 'impressed by the kindness and

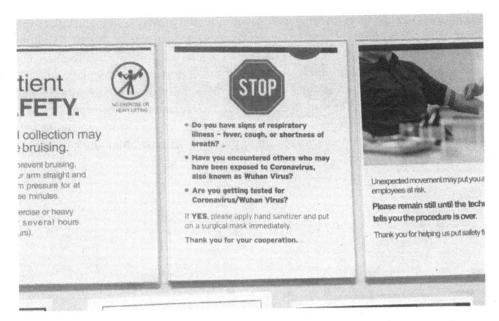

Figure 3. Healthcare laboratory room instructions for patients who may have been exposed to or are getting tested for COVID19, characterized here twice as the 'Wuhan Virus' (author's photo).

support of people around [them],' her post clearly articulated that they were 'also fearful and sad.' To counter the 'rumour, gossip, bias, and discriminations' she included a link in her post to a promotional video, 'Wuhan: The rise of a city | 武汉大城崛起 (2016), using this visual representation unconnected to the pandemic to create a space for us in which 'to uncover the 'invisible parts' of the city Wuhan' and thereby 'alter our ways of knowing [her] world.' She compellingly reinforced the countering function of the video with references to the cherry trees that were coming into bloom in our city, noting 'the same as Vancouver, Wuhan is also famous for its cherry blossoms.'

Despite framing this part of her reflection as 'off-topic' and taking pains to acknowledge support within the university community, the student demonstrated enormous courage. I am immensely grateful for this 'moment' and yet, I am also left wondering what emboldened her to embrace our classroom as a 'brave space' (Arao and Clemens 2013). In articulating the visibly devastating experiences with anti-Chinese racism she was encountering at the time and confronting us with alternative perspectives to these prevailing discourses, she was risking potential discomfort among her classmates and instructor. And yet, explicitly addressing local instances of racism as a form of critical inquiry are a necessary component of recognizing uncomfortable, vulnerable spaces of 'not knowing' as potentially anti-racist/decolonizing moves.

A fourth and final moment: confronting cultural appropriation

The final 'intercultural moment' occurred with the cohort of French-as-a-second-language teachers. The teachers took advantage of the decolonial framing of the course to integrate Indigenous perspectives and knowledges into their existing lesson plans in order to align their teaching with newly designed provincial curricula that explicitly prioritize Indigenous education across all subject matters (e.g. British Columbia Ministry of Education 2021; Wernicke 2019). As a final assignment, two teachers presented a mini-science-lesson on ecosystems that incorporated a representation of 'The Cycle of Life' (Figure 4) created by Cree Elder Manchus S'Kwao Amy Eustergerling based on the Medicine Wheel to symbolize the interrelationships of organisms with their natural environment (Pevec 2002). In an attempt to have students connect the Medicine Wheel with the Western concept of the food chain pyramid, the two teachers

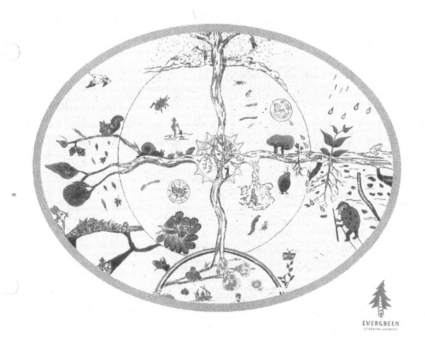

Figure 4. Book cover with 'The Cycle of Life' created by Cree Elder Manchus S'Kwao Amy Eustergerling; Source: https://www.evergreen.ca/downloads/pdfs/Patterns-Relationships-Ethnobotany.pdf.

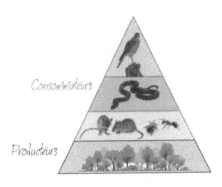

Figure 5. Presentation slide illustrating the parallel between the Western concept of the food chain and Indigenous teachings of the cycle of life (Mini-lesson, 2020; reproduced with permission of the two presenters).

created a circular visual to illustrate this parallel (Figure 5), in essence 'grafting' (Ahenakew 2016) the Indigenous teaching onto a Western epistemological framework. I decided to seize this unanticipated teaching moment to discuss cultural appropriation, a matter of importance for teachers developing and using Indigenous educational resources (see for example FNESC and FNSA 2016). I approached the topic by acknowledging my own lack of certainty as to whether the representation on the slide constituted an example of cultural appropriation, hoping to minimize any potential negative reactions on the part of the teachers for being called out during a graded class presentation. Despite further framing the conversation as a valuable learning experience for the entire class and thanking the two presenters for their openness in discussing how they had arrived at the visual, I received an email from one of the teachers a week later (Figure 6). In it the teacher related her mortification about having produced a lesson that was not authentic, accurate or respectful of Indigenous knowledge and the steps she had taken to learn from the incident.

While initially preparing the mini-lesson, the teacher had consulted with the district Aboriginal teacher about the 'Cycle of Life' poster, and had received approval to use it in the assignment. After the presentation in class, the teacher took the initiative to consult with the district Aboriginal lead teacher a second time to seek clarification as to why the 'food chain circle' might constitute cultural appropriation and was provided with alternative options of how to approach the lesson more respectfully. This demonstration of professional learning, sought by the teacher herself, and her sharing of it with me and the class, led me to integrate the consultation as a component of the assignment to underscore the importance of taken a 'listening stance' as non-Indigenous educators. Grappling with the tensions of creating culturally appropriate teaching materials raises important questions such about 'whose knowledge' is being presented and the need for awareness about what that knowledge means. In this case, it exemplified moving away from a position of 'perfect stranger' – the desire to protect oneself from having to recognize one's role in the history of the relationship between Indigenous people and Canadians (Dion 2007) toward a position of the 'Not-so-perfect-stranger' (Dion

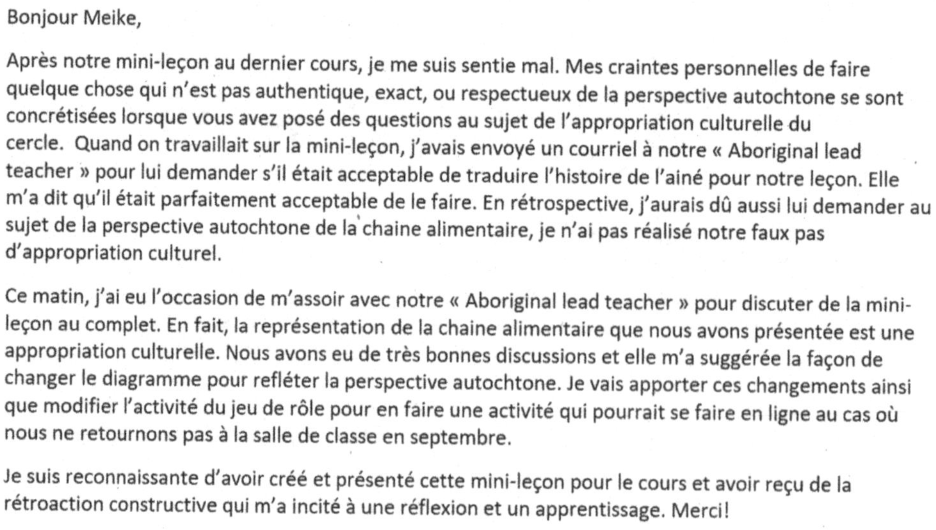

Bonjour Meike,

Après notre mini-leçon au dernier cours, je me suis sentie mal. Mes craintes personnelles de faire quelque chose qui n'est pas authentique, exact, ou respectueux de la perspective autochtone se sont concrétisées lorsque vous avez posé des questions au sujet de l'appropriation culturelle du cercle. Quand on travaillait sur la mini-leçon, j'avais envoyé un courriel à notre « Aboriginal lead teacher » pour lui demander s'il était acceptable de traduire l'histoire de l'ainé pour notre leçon. Elle m'a dit qu'il était parfaitement acceptable de le faire. En rétrospective, j'aurais dû aussi lui demander au sujet de la perspective autochtone de la chaine alimentaire, je n'ai pas réalisé notre faux pas d'appropriation culturel.

Ce matin, j'ai eu l'occasion de m'assoir avec notre « Aboriginal lead teacher » pour discuter de la mini-leçon au complet. En fait, la représentation de la chaine alimentaire que nous avons présentée est une appropriation culturelle. Nous avons eu de très bonnes discussions et elle m'a suggérée la façon de changer le diagramme pour refléter la perspective autochtone. Je vais apporter ces changements ainsi que modifier l'activité du jeu de rôle pour en faire une activité qui pourrait se faire en ligne au cas où nous ne retournons pas à la salle de classe en septembre.

Je suis reconnaissante d'avoir créé et présenté cette mini-leçon pour le cours et avoir reçu de la rétroaction constructive qui m'a incité à une réflexion et un apprentissage. Merci!

Figure 6. Email from on of the teachers who presented the mini-lesson, which recounts her reaction to the cultural appropriation incident and her two consultations with the district's Aboriginal lead teacher (reproduced with permission of the email author).

2019), being open to the tensions that arise in tentatively embracing decolonizing approaches as non-Indigenous teachers.

Concluding thoughts

During a recent conference I attended, keynote speaker Suhanthie Motha (2020) asked us to consider why we had entered the field of applied linguistics, and what we think we are contributing to the world through our work in this field. Over the past three decades as language educator, whether teaching French, German, or teacher candidates, I have tended to position the expertise I bring to this work as always situated, as a first language German speaker from Northern Germany, as an additional language speaker of various French varieties, as someone who can share plenty of 'ESL' stories with teacher candidates learning to navigate multilingual classrooms. This position leaves me open to learn from the situated expertise of my students, one of the reasons I see the courses I teach as ongoing conversations of learning. In this sense, the course described above offers a space that allows us to interrogate our ongoing participation in settler colonialism and the racialization of minoritized people, their languages, actions, desires, and knowledges; a space that lets us understand language as always political and inextricably connected to identity, culture, and knowledge and where we see intercultural understanding not only in terms of cultural but also epistemological difference, as developing out of the power-laden interactions in the classroom. More than anything, the four moments above point to the need for 'a space of listening' (LeBaron 2002) deep, responsible, ethical listening. First and foremost, then, decolonizing higher education requires of us to continue asking (drawing an Regan 2010, 190): How do we learn to listen differently, taking on our responsibility to decolonize ourselves, making space for the history and experience of others?

Acknowledgements

I would like to thank the students who have taken this course, who have contributed in such meaningful and enriching ways to the discussions and many moments of intercultural learning. I thank them for the thoughtfulness, enthusiasm, courage, vulnerability, and the immense knowledge that each one has been so willing to share.

Disclosure statement

No potential conflict of interest was reported by the author(s).

References

Wuhan: The rise of a city | 武汉大城崛起. 2016, February 24. [YouTube]. https://www.youtube.com/watch?v=hsseRWoi_44&feature=youtu.be

Ahenakew, Cash. 2016. "Grafting Indigenous Ways of Knowing Onto non-Indigenous Ways of Being: The (Underestimated) Challenges of a Decolonial Imagination." *International Review of Qualitative Research* 9 (3): 323–340.

Aman, Robert. 2018. *Decolonising Intercultural Education: Colonial Differences, the Geopolitics of Knowledge, and Inter-Epistemic Dialogue.* New York: Routledge.

Arao, Brian, and Kristi Clemens. 2013. "From Safe Spaces to Brave Spaces." In *The Art of Effective Facilitation: Reflections from Social Justice Educators*, edited by Lisa M. Landreman, 135–150. Sterling: Stylus Publishing, LLC.

Borchert, Wolfgang. 1949/2007. Das Gesamtwerk. Hamburg: Rowohlt Verlag GmbH.

British Columbia Ministry of Education. 2021. "Indigenous Education Resources." BC's Curriculum. Accessed January 4, 2021. https://curriculum.gov.bc.ca/curriculum/indigenous-education-resources.

Byram, Michael. 1997. *Teaching and Assessing Intercultural Communicative Competence.* Bristol: Multilingual Matters.

Byrd Clark, Julie, Eve Haque, and Sylvie Lamoureux. 2012. "The Role of Language in Processes of Internationalization in Two Diverse Contexts in Ontario: Considering Multiple Voices from Within and Outside." *Comparative and International Education* 41 (3 (Article 5)): 1–15.

Deardorff, Darla K. 2009. "Implementing Intercultural Competence Assessment." In *The SAGE Handbook of Intercultural Competence*, edited by Darla K. Deardorff, 477–491. North York: SAGE Publications.

Dion, Susan D. 2007. "Disrupting Molded Images: Identities, Responsibilities and Relationships—Teachers and Indigenous Subject Material." *Teaching Education* 18 (4): 329–342. doi:10.1080/10476210701687625.

Dion, Susan D. 2019. "'We Made our Own Little Spot in the Corner of the Library': Teaching and Learning from the Voices of Indigenous Students Surviving, Resisting and Transforming Schools." Paper presented at the Two-Day International Symposium: Supporting Teachers to Work With Culturally, Linguistically, and Racially Diverse Students, Families, and Communities, Vancouver, BC, May 30–31.

First Nations Education Steering Committee (FNESC) and First Nations Schools Association (FNSA). 2016. Authentic First Peoples Resources K-9. Author. http://www.fnesc.ca/wp/wp-content/uploads/2015/06/PUBLICATION-	61502-updated-FNESC-Authentic-Resources-Guide-October-2016.pdf.

Gaudry, Adam, and Danielle E. Lorenz. 2018. "Decolonization for the Masses? Grappling with Indigenous Content Requirements in the Changing Canadian Post-Secondary Environment." In *Indigenous and Decolonizing Studies in Education: Mapping the Long View*, edited by Linda Tuhiwai Smith, Eve Tuck, and K. Wayne, 159–174. New York: Routledge.

Haig-Brown, Celia. 2009. "Decolonizing Diaspora: Whose Traditional Land are We on?" *Cultural and Pedagogical Inquiry* 1 (2): 4–21. https://doi.org/10.18733/C3H59V.

Hare, Jan, and Sarah F. Davidson. 2016. "Learning from Indigenous Knowledge in Education." In *Visions of the Heart: Issues Involving Aboriginal Peoples in Canada*, edited by Olive P. Dickason, and David A. Long, 241–262. Toronto: Oxford University Press Canada.

Hart, Michael A. 2010. "Indigenous Worldviews, Knowledge, and Research: The Development of an Indigenous Research Paradigm." *Journal of Indigenous Social Development* 1 (1A): 1–16. https://136.159.200.199/index.php/jisd/article/view/63043.

Kramsch, Claire. 2011. "The Symbolic Dimensions of the Intercultural." *Language Teaching*, 44 (3): 354–367. https://doi.org/10.1017/S0261444810000431

LeBaron, Michele. 2002. *Bridging Troubled Waters: Conflict Resolution from the Heart.* San Francisco: Jossey-Bass.

Liddicoat, Anthony J. and Angela Scarino. 2013. *Intercultural Language Teaching and Learning.* West Sussex: Wiley-Blackwell.

Lopez, Ann. 2016. "A Conversation with Dr. Ann Spence Lopez." Talk presented at the Teacher Education Talks, University of British Columbia, May 27.

Motha, Suhanthie. 2020. "Is an Antiracist and Decolonizing Applied Linguistics Possible?" *Annual Review of Applied Linguistics* 40: 128–133. https://doi.org/10.1017/S0267190520000100.

Pevec, Illéne. 2002. *Ethnobotany: Patterns in Relationships.* Vancouver: Evergreen & Grandview/?uuqinak'uuh Elementary School. https://www.evergreen.ca/downloads/pdfs/Patterns-Relationships-Ethnobotany.pdf

Regan, Paulette. 2010. *Unsettling the Settler Within: Indian Residential Schools, Truth Telling, and Reconciliation in Canada.* Vancouver: UBC Press.

Styres, Sandra, Celia Haig-Brown, and Melissa Blimkie. 2013. "Towards a Pedagogy of Land: The Urban Context." *Canadian Journal of Education*, 36 (2): 34–67.

Tien, Celine. 2020. "I'm Chinese. That Doesn't Mean I Have Coronavirus." *The New York Times*, March 7.

Truth and Reconciliation Commission of Canada. 2015. *Honouring the Truth, Reconciling for the Future: Summary of the Final Report of the Truth and Reconciliation Commission of Canada.* Winnipeg: National Centre for Truth and Reconciliation. https://ehprnh2mwo3.exactdn.com/wp-content/uploads/2021/01/Executive_Summary_English_Web.pdf.

Wernicke, Meike. 2019. "La mise en place d'une culture professionnelle dans la formation initiale et continue à l'enseignement du français en Colombie-Britannique." Paper presented at the Symposium sur la francophonie en Colombie-Britannique, Simon Fraser University, October 4th.

Index

Note: Figures are indicated by *italics*. Tables are indicated by **bold**. Endnotes are indicated by the page number followed by 'n' and the endnote number e.g., 20n1 refers to endnote 1 on page 20.

Abdullah, Saifuddin 84
Aboriginal Knowledge 9, 177, 187
'abyssal knowledge' 107
academic capitalism 70
academic elitism 89–90, 94
Adefarakan, T. 242n1
Adomako Ampofo, A. 233n2
aesthetic estrangement 90, 94
'affective counterpolitics' 73
affective economies 68, 74
Africa 37, 49n4
African-American 191
Afro-Latin American Studies 191; communities 192, 194, 199; pedagogical theory of *Calle* 196–8; populations 10, 192; spatial narratives 191; spirituality and creative expression 195–6; untold history of racial segregation in 194–5
Agathangelou, A. 73
Ahmed, Sara 18, 25, 27, 73, 231
Alexander, M. J. 68, 77
Algeria 224n3
'American Economics' Association 26
Anderson, B. 78
Andreotti, Vanessa de Oliveira 1, 12, 39, 52, 56, 64n7, 101, 103, 104, 105, 111, 176, 177
Ansley, L. 4
Anthropocene 13n1
anti-racism 34, 43
anti-racist university 16
Archer, Margaret 12, 13n3, 85, 92
Asante, Molefi Kete 84
Ashcroft, Bill 83
Asia 37, 38, 49n4
Attas, R. 242n1
Australia 38; curriculum reconciliation in 174; high education context 175–7; Jindaola programme 175–180; 'radical reform' approaches 176; soft reform approaches 176

banking 22
Bartlett, Cheryl 157–8, 168
Basedau, M. 233n2
Bassichis, M. D. 73

Battiste, Marie 39, 103, 111
Beckett, L. 10
Behari-Leak, K. 227
Bell Jr., D. A. 35, 37
Berlant, L. 78
Bhaskar, Roy 84
Biko, S. 84
'black African' 120
Black and Minority Ethnic (BME) students 37
Black communities 192, 194, 199
Black Consciousness 84
Black Lives Matters (BLM) 34
Black mirrors 29n1
Black, Asian and Minority Ethnic (BAME) 18
Black, Indigenous, and People of Color (BIPOC) 224n5
Blue, J. 9, 10
Bologna process 138
Borchert, Wolfgang 247
Bovell, D. 9, 10
Brazil 59, 138, 145
Briggs, R. C. 233n2
Bulhan, Hussein Abdilahi 91
Bullen, Jonathan 176

California 212, 224n13; water crisis 214
Calle (street) 9; pedagogical theory of 196–8
the Caribbean 49n4
Canada 245; data contributions from institutions **160**; decolonization 164; discussion 164–8; etuaptmumk 157–8; findings 159–160; inclusion 160–2; indigenization, spectrum of 158; indigenizing engineering education in 152, **161**; language education in 6; limitations 159; methodology 158–9; reconciliation 163; two-eyed seeing 157–8
Carley, K. 87
Carnell, Brent 92
Catalano, George D. 155
CEAB (Canadian Engineering Accreditation Board) 156
Charbonneau, Irène 5, 62

Chile 138, 224n3
China 38, 248
Cicek, J. S. 8, 9
Colombia 138, 145
colonial climate crisis 212
colonialism 69, 134, 135–6; and racial
capitalism 68
'coloniality' 1–2
Comaroff, J. 1
'concrete utopianism' 84
Connell, R. 1
Connolly, P. 4
Cornbleth, C. 3
Costa Rica 138
Coulthard, G. S. 72, 73
'counter-conduct' 71
Covid-19 pandemic 37, 59–60, 120; healthcare
laboratory room instructions for *249*;
impacts of 18
Cragun-Rehders, K. 10
'critical border thinking' 147
'critical discourse analysis' 87
'critical race theory' 37
critical realism 85
critical social theory 1
critical water studies 212; affective and relational
dimensions 220–2; anticolonial pedagogies
217, 222–3; class composition and dynamics
215–16; developing anticolonial dispositions
214–15; positionality and place in praxis 219;
research as pedagogy 213–14; situating our
collaboration 216–17
Cross, M. 119, 128
cruel optimism 78
cultural anthropology 68
cultural solipsism 5
curriculum decolonisation 16
curriculum reconciliation 175–6, 178
'The Cycle of Life' 249–251

Dache, A. 9, 10, 192, 195, 198
Das Brot 247
Davis, D. R. 238, 239
Dawson, Marcelle C. 137
decolonial; indigenization 158; pedagogy 53–4;
praxis and reflexivity 11; theory 1
'decolonial turn' 1
decolonialism 134, 135–6
'decoloniality' 1, 53, 198
decolonisation 129; belonging, support and
care 128; curriculum 126–7; language
struggles 125–6; material deprivation 128–9;
pedagogic interactions with lecturers 123–5;
uneven understanding of 121–3
'decolonise education' 36–7
'decolonised curriculum' 35
'decolonising work' 36, 40–1; grassroots/top-down
decolonisation 46–7; mainstreaming 42–3;
reluctant acceptance 44–5; staff and

student-led 43; strategic rejection 43–5; student
officer-initiated decolonising initiatives 41
decolonizing curriculum and pedagogy
(DCP) 236; past orientations 237–9; present
allocations of time 239–240; future self and
global subjectivity 240–1
Delahunty, J. 8, 9
Diab, M. 242n1
DiAngelo, R. 228
disciplinary knowledge 177
DMU (De Montfort University) 18;
decolonising 19–21
dominant culture 22
Donati, Pierpaolo 85, 96
Downey, Gary Lee 155
DuBois, W. E. B. 192–3
Dumm, Thomas 188
Dutta, U. 238, 242n1

ECTS (European Credits Transfer and
Accumulation System) 63n4
Ecuador 138, 143
Edwards, K. T. 6
England 48n1; higher education in 34;
decolonising claims of universities in 37–9
English, as global language 127
epistemicide 88, 94
Equalities and Human Rights Commission
(EHRC) 20
Ethiopia 59
etuaptmumk 157–8
Eurocentrism 18, 36, 48n2, 85, 88–9
European Union (EU) 64n11

Fa'avae, D. T. M. 6–7
Fellner, K. D. 239
Field, G. 83
Fine, M. 231
Finland 61; University Partnership in
International Development (UniPID) 52, 61–3;
colonization in 63–4n5
Flam, H. 85
Flavell, Helen 176
Fomunyan, K. G. 240
food chain *251*
Foucault, Michel 71, 180, 182, 185; concept
of heterotopia 175
fractured reflexivity 92
Franklin, V. P. 194
Freire, Paulo 11, 13, 84
French, K. B. 17
Funaki, Hine 110
Fung, Dilly 92

Gadotti, M. 11
Gandhian philosophy of education 59
Garba, T. 17
Gaudry, Adam 39, 154, 156, 158, 160, 167, 168
Gauthier, S. 8

Gebrial, D. 24
Geiger, A. 10
Girard College 201–2
Girard, Stephen 201, *202, 203*
global education development 51, *55*, 63n1; and decoloniality 55–8; methods 54–5; pluriverse, challenges and possibilities 59–61; problematising binaries within 58–9; reflections 55–8; research questions 53; theoretical framings 53–4
Global Education Monitoring Report (GEM Report) 64n10
Global Education Network Europe (GENE) 64n8
global financial crisis 38
Gokay, B. 4, 5
Goldsmiths Anti-Racist Action (GARA) 36
Gordon, Lewis 232
Grande, S. 74, 77
Green, C. 5

(H)ACER program 213–14, 224n5
Haig-Brown, Celia 246
Hall, R. 4, 8
Hartwig, Mervyn 84
hegemonic culture 22
heterotopia 175
Heynen, N. 69
higher education (HE); affective and pedagogical practice in 67; affirmative investment 68; decolonization 67; institutions 83, 236; modes of refusal 73–6; pedagogies of refusal 76–9
Hise, K. 10
Hispanic Association of Contractors and Enterprises (HACE) 205
Hook, Derek 231, 233n5
hooks, b. 22
Hountondji, P. 233n2
Hundle, A. K. 79

India 38, 59, 224n3
indigenization 158
Indigenous Knowledge 1, 176; into curriculum 8–11
indigenous peoples 70; in North America 152
Indigenous Strategy 9
Indigenous Traditional Knowledge (TK) 154
inequality 88–9, 94
'institutional racism' 91
Intellectual and Cultural Solipsism (ICS) 85, *93*; as model of causality 91; testing for 94–5; theorising 91–4
intercultural encountering 244
intercultural universities 138
'internal deliberation' 12

Jansen, J. 119
Jindaola programme 9, 175–180, *178*; counter-hegemonic space 183–5; disturbing

spatio-temporal arrangements 185–6; intersecting with spaces 187; regulated entry 180–2; space of deviation 182–3; transforming overtime 186
Johnson, A. 23
Joseph-Salisbury, R. 23

Kahn, P. 5
Keil, M. 6–7
Kennedy, J. 8, 9
Knight, J. 242n1
de Kock, T. 7
Koloto, N. K. 102
Kothari, Ashish 59, 64n12

la paperson 79
language 1, 2, 6, 6, 10, 28, 90, 125–6, 135, **140**, 145, 195, 240, 246–7, 252
Latin American universities 1, 3, 9, 18, 49n4, 133; colonialism and neo-colonialism 136–7; colonialism 134, 135–6; cultural criteria 146; cultural domination 133; curricula and pedagogies in 133; decolonialism 134, 135–6; ecological criteria 146; economic criteria 146; epistemological criteria 146; indigenous communities 145; 'intercultural universities' 134; political criteria 146; post colonialism 134, 135–6; relational criteria 146
Latinx communities 192, 194, 199
Latinx spatial narratives 191
Leenen-Young, M. 6–7, 7–8
Lehtomäki, E. 5
linguistic microaggressions 22
Loonat, S. 4
Lopez, Ann 248
Lorde, Audre 110
Lorenz, Danielle 39, 154, 156, 158, 160, 167, 168
Lucena, Juan 155
Luckett, Kathy 92
Luke, N. 69
Luutu, B. Mukasa 84

MacDonald, Liana 110
Mafi, B. 5
Maldonado-Torres, N. 1
Manchus, Cree Elder 250–1
Manganyi, N. C. 84
Mante, A. A. 8
Marshall, Albert 168
Marshall, Murdena 168
Matapo, J. 6–7
Matthews, S. 6, 8
Mattucci, S. 8
Mbembe, Achille Joseph 1, 3, 12, 13n1, 84
McCowan, Tristan 51, 53, 63n2
McGranahan, C. 68, 71, 72, 73, 74, 75
McKenzie, M. 214
Menon, S. 5, 7, 8
'meta-reflexivity' 12

Mexico 18, 138, 143
microaggressions 22
Mignolo, Walter D. 1, 36, 59
Miguest, D. 9, 10
'modernity' 201
Moon, Dreama 84, 91
Moore, Cecil B. 194, 202
Moosavi, L. 18, 227
Morocco 215, 224n3
Morreira, Shannon 56, 118, 127
Motala, S. 7, 119, 128
Motha, Suhanthie 252
MOVE Bombing Marker 196, 199–201
Moyle, C. 8, 9
Mühlhoff, R. 68

Naepi, S. 6–7
Najera, A. 10
Nakata, Martin 179
National Science Foundation (NSF) 224n3
Ndlovu-Gatsheni, S. J. 118
'neoliberal pragmatism' 45–6
New Zealand 7; universities 101, 104
Nyamnjoh, A. 118
Nygaard, Arnfinn 56, 64n8

de Oliveira Andreotti 201, 206
Olukoshi, A. 233n2
Osifeso, S. 9, 10
Otero, Solimar 195, 196

Pacific early career academics (PECA)
    7, 100; beyond-reform 109–11; decolonial
    pedagogies 103; method 103–4; pacific
    pedagogies 102–3; radical-reform 107–9;
    soft-reform 105–7; Talanoa framing 104–5
Particles for Justice 26
Patel, K. 4, 224n2
Percy, A. 8, 9
Peru 138, 145, 224n3
Pete, S. 237, 239
Philadelphia 191; community and schooling
    194–5; Afro-Latinx population of 197;
    El Centro De Oro 204–5, 204
'planetary entanglement' 3
'pluriverse' 10
Poku, V. 4, 5
Political Blackness 49n4
Portugal 133
post colonialism 134, 135–6
'practical reconciliation' 175
Puerto Rica 195

quality education 58
Quijano, Aníbal 36, 133, 135

Race Equality Charter (REC) 17
racial discrimination 49n4
racism 90–1, 94–5; and anti-racism 24
reconciliation indigenization 158

'reflexive imperative' 12
'reflexive practitioner' 11
Robinson, M. 8
Rodríguez, Y. 77
Russia 64n11
Rutazibwa, Olivia 56

Sabati, S. 10
Said, Edward 135
Sanchez, A. 17
Santos, B. de Sousa 13
Sayed, Y. 7
Schultz, T. D. 242n1
SciELO 138, 139, **141–3**
SCOPUS 138, 139, **140–1**
Scott, J. 71
self-entrepreneurship; neoliberal cultures of 21–3
Seniuk Cicek, Jillian 156
Shahjahan, R. A. 6
Shaik, A. 5
Shain, F. 4, 5
Sian, K. P. 242n1
Simpson, A. 71, 72, 73, 75
Smit, R. 119, 121
Smith, Avery 110
social and cultural solipsism 5
social realist theory 85
Sorentino, S. -M. 17
South Africa 134, 227; academic elitism 89–90;
    aesthetic estrangement 90; belonging, support
    and care, decolonising 128; curriculum,
    decolonising 126–7; decolonisation
    of curriculum in 116, 117–19;
    epistemicide 88; higher education pedagogy
    in 116, 121; inequality 88–9; language
    struggles 125–6; material deprivation,
    decolonising 128–9; methodology 120–1;
    #RhodesMustFall protests 227; presentation
    of findings 121–3; racism 90–1; research
    design 85–8; theorising ICS 91–5; university
    curricula 227–230; university 84; white scholars
    in 230–1
South Korea 38
Spain 133
Spanish colonial rule 224n13
Spira, T. L. 73
Spivak, G. 77, 83
Steele, A. 8
Stein, Sharon 12, 39, 68, 70, 78
Steyn, M. E. 84
strategic advancement 34
structures of dissipation 23–6
'substantive' (horizontal) reconciliation 175,
    179–180
Sustainable Development Goal (SDG) 56
Sweden 59, 64n11
'system hacking' 198

talanoa 7
Tanzania 224n3

Thaman, Konai Helu 103, 111
Thomas, L. 8, 9
Thomsen, P. S. 6–7
Transformations to Groundwater Sustainability (T2GS) 213–14
Truth and Reconciliation Commission (TRC) of Canada 153
Tuck, E. 17, 62, 77, 102, 214, 227, 231
Tucux, F. 9, 10
two-eyed seeing 157–8

UK 48n1; higher education sector 38
Ullom, E. 17
the United States 59, 224n3, 248
unproductive reflexivity 92
Unterhalter, Elaine 51, 52, 63n2

Valenzuela, Guzmán 3, 8, 9
Vice, Samantha 231
Vietnam 38
Vuorela, Ulla 56, 58, 61, 64n11

Walsh, C. E. 242n1
Warwick University 36
Water Justice 212, 213
Weathers, S. 233n2

Web of Science (WoS) 138, **140**
Wegimont, Liam 56, 64n8
Wernicke, M. 6
Western hegemony 89
Western science as universal knowledge 218
Wetherell, M. 72
'whiteness' concept 83–4
Whitham, B. 4
Wildcat strike 224n15
Wilder, C. 70
Williams, Clay K. 86
Winberg, C. 240
Wolf, P. 8
Wolfe, P. 69
'Wuhan-Virus' 248
Wynn, Donald 86

Yang, K. Wayne 17, 62, 77, 102
Yıldız, Ü. K. 4, 5
Yosso, Tara J. 192
Yunkaporta, Tyson 186

Zavala, Manuel 56, 64n6
Zembylas, M. 5
Zimbabwe 224n3

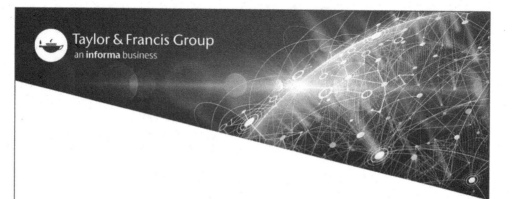